Elegant Glassware
of the
Depression Era

NINTH EDITION
IDENTIFICATION AND VALUE GUIDE

Gene Florence

Cambridge
Fostoria
Heisey
& Others

COLLECTOR BOOKS

A Division of Schroeder Publishing Co., Inc.

The current values in this book should be used only as a guide. They are not intended to set prices, which vary from one section of the country to another. Auction prices as well as dealer prices vary greatly and are affected by condition as well as demand. Neither the author nor the publisher assumes responsibility for any losses that might be incurred as a result of consulting this guide.

Searching For A Publisher?

We are always looking for knowledgeable people considered to be experts within their fields. If you feel that there is a real need for a book on your collectible subject and have a large comprehensive collection, contact Collector Books.

Front cover:
Lariat, flashed red, 7" fan vase, $40.00.
Golf Ball, ritz blue, irish coffee, $180.00.
Cleo, emerald green pitcher $225.00.

Back cover:
Cleo, emerald green, creamer, $55.00.
Cleo, emerald green, sugar, $55.00.

Cover design by Beth Summers
Book design by Beth Ray

COLLECTOR BOOKS
P.O. Box 3009
Paducah, Kentucky 42002-3009

www.collectorbooks.com

Gene Florence
P.O. Box 22186   P.O. Box 64
Lexington, KY 40522   Astutula, FL 34705

ABOUT THE AUTHOR

Gene M. Florence, Jr., a native Kentuckian, graduated from the University of Kentucky in 1967. He held a double major in mathematics and English that he immediately put to use in industry and subsequently, in teaching junior and senior high school. He taught one year at the Lincoln Institute for gifted, but disadvantaged, students — a wonderful teaching experience, but a 160 mile daily commute!

A collector since childhood, Mr. Florence progressed from baseball cards, comic books, coins, and bottles to glassware. His buying and selling glassware "hobby" began to override his nine-year teaching career. During a teaching hiatus in the summer of 1972, he wrote a book on Depression glassware that was well received by collectors in the field, persuading him to leave teaching in 1976 and pursue the antique glass business full time. This allowed time to travel to glass shows throughout the country, where he assiduously studied the prices of glass being sold... and of that remaining unsold. This change, also, permitted him to dedicate more time to research on glass, a time consuming process.

Books written by Mr. Florence include the following titles: *The Collector's Encyclopedia of Depression Glass, Stemware Identification, The Collector's Encyclopedia of Akro Agate, The Pocket Guide to Depression Glass, Kitchen Glassware of the Depression Years, Collectible Glassware from the 40s, 50s, and 60s..., Glass Candlesticks of the Depression Era, Standard Baseball Card Price Guide*, and six editions of *Very Rare Glassware of the Depression Years*. He has also written five volumes of *The Collector's Encyclopedia of Occupied Japan* and a book on Degenhart glassware for that museum. His most recent books are *Anchor Hocking's Fire-King and More* and two volumes of *Glassware Pattern Identification Guide*. Mr. Florence has now authored 70 books on collectibles.

PRICING

All prices in this book are retail for mint condition glassware. This book is intended only as a **guide** to prices. There continue to be regional price disparities that cannot be adequately dealt with herein.

You may expect dealers to pay approximately 30 to 60 percent less than the prices listed. My personal knowledge of prices comes from buying and selling glass for 32 years and from traveling to and selling at shows in various parts of the United States. Strangely, I am working even harder at markets and shows, today, to remain current with the ever fluctuating prices. You can find me on the Internet at *www.geneflorence.com*. I readily admit that I solicit price information from persons known to be authorities in certain wares in order to provide you with the latest, most accurate pricing information. However, final pricing judgments are always mine!

MEASUREMENTS AND TERMS

All measurements and terminology in this book are from factory catalogs and advertisements or actual measurements from the piece. It has been my experience that actual measurements vary slightly from those listed in most factory catalogs; so, do not get unduly concerned over slight variations. For example, Fostoria always measured plates to the nearest inch, but I have found that most Fostoria plates are never exact inches in measurement.

PREFACE

"Elegant" glassware, as defined in this book, refers mostly to the hand-worked, acid-etched glassware that was sold by better department and jewelry stores during the Depression era through the 1950s, differentiating it from the dime store and give-away glass that has become known as Depression glass.

The rise in collecting Elegant glassware has been incredible the past few years. Many dealers who would dare not stock that crystal glass a few years ago are buying as much or more Elegant than basic Depression glass, today. Glass shows used to display 15% to 20% Elegant glass; now, there is more than 50% at most shows. Many collectors who have completed sets of Depression glassware have now switched to acquiring sets of Elegant.

I hope you enjoy this book, and will feel my years of working to furnish you the best books possible on glassware were well spent.

ACKNOWLEDGMENTS

Photography sessions for this book were spread over a two-year period with one session lasting longer than a week. We never photograph for only one book anymore. We were working on six or seven this time. Recognition is due Dick and Pat Spencer for loaning their glass, borrowing other glassware to bring to our session, helping at the photography sessions, and lending their expertise on pricing patterns in this book. As I write this, Dick is retiring tomorrow; Pat may send him back to work shortly thereafter.

People behind the scenes make this book what it is. Some loaned glass, some gave their time; others used their abilities or furnished information. These amazing people have continued to be friends even after arduous hours of packing, unpacking, arranging, sorting, and repacking glass! Some traveled hundreds of miles to bring their valuable glass to share with you. Some spent hours cussing and discussing or listing their prices, often late at night after long show hours. Without these marvelous people, this book would not be a reality. Those remarkable people include Charles and Maxine Larson, Paul and Margaret Arras, Joe and Florence Solito, Kelly O'Kane, Dan Tucker, Lorrie Kitchen, Barbara Adt Namon, Jane White, Beth Ray, Terri Hunter, Zibby Walker, and numerous anonymous readers from throughout the U.S. and Canada who shared pictures and information about their collections and findings. Richard Walker, Charles R. Lynch, and Larry Lipsky (now deceased) did the photography for this book. Richard and Zibby trek from New York each October to see the South's fall leaves. One of their fringe benefits is working ten to twelve hour days for over a week helping us capture the wide range of patterns in this book. It really is a daunting task that is performed yearly.

Thanks, too, to Cathy's parents, Charles and Sibyl, who helped shelve, sort, list, and pack glass for photography and shows! Chad, my eldest son, took time from lateral drilling to help Cathy move, load, and unload boxes of glass; Marc, my youngest son, teaching in the world of computer technology, tries to see that my web page is available when you look for it at *www.geneflorence.com*.

Our middle age health idiosyncrasies are causing us to try to readjust our lives to a less frenetic pace. Cathy will no longer be setting up and selling glass at shows after this summer. The stress of this procedure is getting to her; so we will be reducing our inventory through my web site *www.geneflorence.com*. I will continue to sell books and teach seminars at shows, but I even plan to cut back on that. Thirty years of our lives have been involved in this business and we need some time to enjoy the benefits of all that work. I have only been fishing in my boat one time in four months. That's being way too busy!

Always working extended hours as chief editor, sounding board, research assistant, and proofreader, few could have taken my thoughts and worked them into coherent paragraphs as well as Cathy. This book has been completed via e-mail and long phone conversations since she has been relegated to the Kentucky computer while I am completing manuscripts here in Florida. The stress of deadlines on this book, the recently finished *Pocket Guide to Depression Glass* and the second volume of *Pattern Identification* are not conducive to achieving the peaceful atmosphere she really needs.

Regretfully, another thing I will be slowing is answering letters. In the past, I have asked that questions be limited to patterns in my books that I have researched. Very few do that, and the Internet and U.S. mail are just overpowering me! I will try to continue answering requests that follow the guidelines, when I get the time. I will no longer even try to identify every picture of glassware sent me. I definitely will **not** go through the stacks of photos sent asking, "What is it; what is it worth; and where can I sell it?" In that regard, I have specifically tried to show and identify much of what I have received letters regarding in my two new *Pattern Identification* books. You should look there first to find unknown glassware items. These *Pattern Identification* books should save you research time and writing letters. After you find a pattern, and if you want to learn more, you can then look for one of the books in the Bibliography for more information. The likelihood of your having too many known Depression era patterns not in one of these books will be slim. Most known patterns are covered there. You are getting years of learning in these two books.

I want to say thank you to readers whose generous responses to my books have made this career possible. Know, too, everyone, that many pieces have been added to lists over the years via your efforts, and collectors as a whole have benefited.

CONTENTS

CONTENTS BY COMPANY

Colors: crystal; some amber, blue, green, yellow, pink tinting to purple in late 1920s; white, red in 1980s; and being newly made in crystal for Lancaster Colony

Fostoria American, manufactured for over 70 years, is one of those long lived patterns that almost everyone recognizes! Many auction lists say Fostoria is being sold when they actually mean American pattern. Families used this for years, and about ten years ago, descendants began seriously searching for items to add to their hand-me-down sets. Today, an abundance of available American keeps most of the prices within the range of the average collector's pocketbook; but the harder to find pieces have almost priced themselves out of the realm of the general collector. Only the well financed can afford to pursue many of the rarely seen items.

Though Fostoria American was cherished by collectors for decades, it has begun to be ignored by many dealers because it is, presently, a slow selling pattern due to its continuing manufacture. Lancaster Colony, buyer of Fostoria, continues to make American pattern. There are still Fostoria outlets throughout the Midwest where this newly made American can be bought. Thus, the market for the older glassware has been depressed. None of the current American or look-alike American pieces are marked in any way. American pieces currently being remade or pieces that have been produced in recent years are marked with an asterisk (*) in the price listing. Even before the closing of the original Fostoria factory in 1986, Lancaster Colony marketed its "Whitehall" glassware line that is similar to American, and made by Indiana Glass at Dunkirk, Indiana. Often I have seen the red trimmed or plain "Whitehall" punch set being passed off as American. The punch cups to this set are footed and do not have the same clarity as American. An abundance of "Whitehall" is found in colors of pink, avocado green, and several shades of blue. The glassware section of your local discount store is a good place to peruse new colors and items being made. Numerous specialty catalogs insinuate this colored glassware to be Depression glass in an effort to enhance its value. "Whitehall's" pink colored ware is also commonly mistaken for Jeannette's Depression era Cube pattern judging by the letters I receive from novice collectors. There is no footed pitcher or tumbler in Cube.

There are significant price adjustments for American pieces found in England. Some of those pieces are selling for less than half of their former prices, if they sell at all. You will still find a few behind-the-times dealers pricing these items quite high; but if you shop around, you will find a better price! The Internet has evened the playing field on pricing internationally. European antique dealers have become observant of our glass collecting inclinations. Those previously hard-to-find Fostoria American pieces (from England) are now not as hard to find here — since so many have traveled back! Dealers who own wash bowl and pitcher sets, for example, have been gradually setting their monetary sights a little lower. Once any collectible glass item reaches prices in the four digit area, modest collectors often do without!

Reissued cookie jars continue to pose a problem for collectors! A majority of the new issues have wavy lines in the pattern itself and crooked knobs on the top. Old cookie jars do not. (A telling point that works 80% of the time is to try to turn the lid around while it rests inside the cookie jar. The new lids seem to hang up and stop somewhere along the inside making the whole cookie jar turn. The old jars will allow you to turn the lid completely around without catching on the sides!)

If you enjoy the classic look American pattern exhudes, then by all means buy it! You never go wrong collecting what you like!

	*Crystal
Appetizer, tray, 10½", w/6 inserts	295.00
Appetizer, insert, 3¼"	32.50
Ash tray, 2⅞", sq.	7.50
Ash tray, 3⅞", oval	9.00
Ash tray, 5", sq.	45.00
Ash tray, 5½", oval	20.00
Basket, w/reed handle, 7" x 9"	95.00
Basket, 10", new in 1988	40.00
Bell	425.00
Bottle, bitters, w/tube, 5¾", 4½ oz.	72.50
Bottle, condiment/ketchup w/stopper	145.00

	*Crystal
Bottle, cologne, w/stopper, 6 oz., 5¾"	72.50
Bottle, cologne, w/stopper, 7¼", 8 oz.	80.00
Bottle, cordial, w/stopper, 7¼", 9 oz.	90.00
Bottle, water, 44 oz., 9¼"	610.00
Bowl, banana split, 9" x 3½"	495.00
Bowl, finger, 4½" diam., smooth edge	40.00
Bowl, 3½", rose	20.00
Bowl, 3¾", almond, oval	18.00
Bowl, 4¼", jelly, 4¼" h.	15.00
* Bowl, 4½", 1 hdld.	10.00
Bowl, 4½", 1 hdld., sq.	11.00

*See note in second paragraph above.

	*Crystal			*Crystal
Bowl, 4½", jelly, w/cover, 6¾" h.	28.00		Bowl, 5½", lemon, w/cover	60.00
* Bowl, 4½", nappy	13.00		Bowl, 5½", preserve, 2 hdld., w/cover	100.00
Bowl, 4½", oval	15.00		Bowl, 6", bonbon, 3 ftd.	15.00
Bowl, 4¾", fruit, flared	15.00		* Bowl, 6", nappy	15.00
Bowl, 5", cream soup, 2 hdld.	45.00		Bowl, 6", olive, oblong	12.00
Bowl, 5", 1 hdld., tri-corner	12.00		Bowl, 6½", wedding, w/cover, sq., ped. ft., 8" h.	110.00
* Bowl, 5", nappy	10.00			
Bowl, 5", nappy, w/cover	30.00		Bowl, 6½", wedding, sq., ped. ft., 5¼" h.	75.00
Bowl, 5", rose	30.00		Bowl, 7", bonbon, 3 ftd.	12.50

	*Crystal
Bowl, 7", cupped, 4½" h.	55.00
* Bowl, 7", nappy	25.00
Bowl, 8", bonbon, 3 ftd.	17.50
Bowl, 8", deep	60.00
Bowl, 8", ftd.	90.00
Bowl, 8", ftd., 2 hdld., "trophy" cup	125.00
* Bowl, 8", nappy	25.00
* Bowl, 8", pickle, oblong	15.00
Bowl, 8½", 2 hdld.	50.00
* Bowl, 8½", boat	16.00
Bowl, 9", boat, 2 pt.	12.50
* Bowl, 9", oval veg.	30.00
Bowl, 9½", centerpiece	50.00
Bowl, 9½", 3 pt., 6" w.	37.50
Bowl, 10", celery, oblong	20.00
* Bowl, 10", deep	35.00
Bowl, 10", float	45.00
Bowl, 10", oval, float	32.50
Bowl, 10", oval, veg., 2 pt.	35.00
Bowl, 10½", fruit, 3 ftd.	40.00
Bowl, 11", centerpiece	45.00
Bowl, 11", centerpiece, tri-corner	45.00
Bowl, 11", relish/celery, 3 pt.	30.00
Bowl, 11½", float	65.00
Bowl, 11½", fruit, rolled edge, 2¾" h.	42.50
Bowl, 11½", oval, float	45.00
Bowl, 11½", rolled edge	50.00
Bowl, 11¾", oval, deep	42.50
Bowl, 12", boat	17.50
* Bowl, 12", fruit/sm. punch, ped. ft., (Tom & Jerry)	195.00
Bowl, 12", lily pond	65.00
Bowl, 12", relish "boat," 2 pt.	20.00
Bowl, 13", fruit, shallow	75.00
Bowl, 14", punch, w/high ft. base (2 gal.)	395.00
Bowl, 14", punch, w/low ft. base	350.00
Bowl, 15", centerpiece, "hat" shape	200.00
Bowl, 16", flat, fruit, ped. ft.	195.00
Bowl, 18", punch, w/low ft. base (3¾ gal.)	400.00
Box, pomade, 2" square	325.00
* Box, w/cover, puff, 3⅛" x 2¾"	225.00
Box, w/cover, 4½" x 4½"	225.00
Box, w/cover, handkerchief, 5⅝" x 4⅝"	295.00
Box, w/cover, hairpin, 3½" x 1¾"	325.00
Box, w/cover, jewel, 5¼" x 2¼"	375.00
Box, w/cover, jewel, 2 drawer, 4¼" x 3¼"	5,000.00
* Box, w/cover, glove, 9½" x 3½"	295.00
* Butter, w/cover, rnd. plate, 7¼"	125.00
* Butter, w/cover, ¼ lb.	25.00
Cake stand, (see salver)	
Candelabrum, 6½", 2-lite, bell base w/bobeche & prisms	145.00
Candle lamp, 8½", w/chimney, candle part, 3½"	135.00
Candlestick, twin, 4⅛" h., 8½" spread	60.00

	*Crystal
Candlestick, 2", chamber with finger-hold	47.50
* Candlestick, 3", rnd. ft.	15.00
Candlestick, 4⅜", 2-lite, rnd. ft.	40.00
Candlestick, 6", octagon ft.	25.00
Candlestick, 6½", 2-lite, bell base	125.00
Candlestick, 6¼", round ft.	195.00
* Candlestick, 7", sq. column	110.00
Candlestick, 7¼", "Eiffel" tower	145.00
Candy box, w/cover, 3 pt., triangular	90.00
Candy, w/cover, ped. ft.	37.50
Cheese (5¾" compote) & cracker (11½" plate)	65.00
Cigarette box, w/cover, 4¾"	40.00
Coaster, 3¾"	9.00
Comport, 4½", jelly	15.00
* Comport, 5", jelly, flared	15.00
* Comport, 6¾", jelly, w/cover	35.00
Comport, 8½", 4" high	45.00
Comport, 9½", 5¼" high	85.00
Comport, w/cover, 5"	25.00
* Cookie jar, w/cover, 8⅞" h.	295.00
Creamer, tea, 3 oz., 2⅜" (#2056½)	9.00
Creamer, individual, 4¾ oz.	9.00
Creamer, 9½ oz.	12.50
Crushed fruit, w/cover & spoon, 10"	2,000.00
Cup, flat	7.50
Cup, ftd., 7 oz.	8.00
Cup, punch, flared rim	11.00
Cup, punch, straight edge	10.00
Decanter, w/stopper, 24 oz., 9¼" h.	85.00
Dresser set: powder boxes w/covers & tray	475.00
Flower pot, w/perforated cover, 9½" diam.; 5½" h.	1,750.00
Goblet, #2056, 2½ oz., wine, hex ft., 4⅜" h.	12.00
Goblet, #2056, 4½ oz., oyster cocktail, 3½" h.	17.50
Goblet, #2056, 4½ oz., sherbet, flared, 4⅜" h.	9.00
Goblet, #2056, 4½ oz., fruit, hex ft., 4¾" h.	9.00
Goblet, #2056, 5 oz., low ft., sherbet, flared, 3¼" h.	9.00
Goblet, #2056, 6 oz., low ft., sundae, 3⅛" h.	9.00
Goblet, #2056, 7 oz., claret, 4⅞" h.	60.00
* Goblet, #2056, 9 oz., low ft., 4⅜" h.	11.00
Goblet, #2056, 10 oz., hex ft., water, 6⅞" h.	14.00
Goblet, #2056, 12 oz., low ft., tea, 5¾" h.	15.00
Goblet, #2056½, 4½ oz., sherbet, 4½" h.	10.00
Goblet, #2056½, 5 oz., low sherbet, 3½" h.	10.00

	*Crystal
Goblet, #5056, 1 oz., cordial, 3⅛", w/plain bowl	40.00
Goblet, #5056, 3½ oz., claret, 4⅝", w/plain bowl	18.00
Goblet, #5056, 3½ oz., cocktail, 4", w/plain bowl	15.00
Goblet, #5056, 4 oz., oyster cocktail, 3½", w/plain bowl	15.00
Goblet, #5056, 5½ oz., sherbet, 4⅛", w/plain bowl	12.00
Goblet, #5056, 10 oz., water, 6⅛", w/plain bowl	18.00
Hair receiver, 3" x 3"	395.00
Hat, 2⅛" (sm. ash tray)	16.00
Hat, 3" tall	27.50
Hat, 4" tall	65.00
Hat, western style	295.00
Hotel washbowl and pitcher	3,750.00
Hurricane lamp, 12" complete	195.00
Hurricane lamp base	55.00
Ice bucket, w/tongs	60.00
Ice cream saucer (2 styles)	55.00
Ice dish for 4 oz. crab or 5 oz. tomato liner	40.00
Ice dish insert	10.00
Ice tub, w/liner, 5⅝"	90.00
Ice tub, w/liner, 6½"	95.00
Jam pot, w/cover	65.00
Jar, pickle, w/pointed cover, 6" h.	325.00
Marmalade, w/cover & chrome spoon	50.00
* Mayonnaise, div.	17.50
Mayonnaise, w/ladle, ped. ft.	55.00
Mayonnaise, w/liner & ladle	35.00
Molasses can, 11 oz., 6¾" h., 1 hdld.	425.00
* Mug, 5½ oz., "Tom & Jerry," 3¼" h.	40.00
* Mug, 12 oz., beer, 4½" h.	70.00
Mustard, w/cover	35.00
Napkin ring	12.50
Oil, 5 oz.	35.00
Oil, 7 oz.	35.00
Picture frame	15.00
Pitcher, ½ gal. w/ice lip, 8¼", flat bottom	85.00
Pitcher, ½ gal., w/o ice lip	295.00
Pitcher, ½ gal., 8", ftd.	70.00
Pitcher, 1 pt., 5⅜", flat	27.50
Pitcher, 2 pt., 7¼", ftd.	65.00
Pitcher, 3 pt., 8", ftd.	70.00
Pitcher, 3 pt., w/ice lip, 6½", ftd., "fat"	60.00
* Pitcher, 1 qt., flat	30.00
Plate, cream soup liner	12.00
Plate, 6", bread & butter	12.00
Plate, 7", salad	10.00
Plate, 7½" x 4⅜", crescent salad	50.00
Plate, 8", sauce liner, oval	27.50

	*Crystal
Plate, 8½", salad	12.00
Plate, 9", sandwich (sm. center)	14.00
Plate, 9½", dinner	22.50
Plate, 10", cake, 2 hdld.	27.50
Plate, 10½", sandwich (sm. center)	20.00
Plate, 11½", sandwich (sm. center)	20.00
Plate, 12", cake, 3 ftd.	25.00
Plate, 13½", oval torte	50.00
Plate, 14", torte	75.00
Plate, 18", torte	135.00
Plate, 20", torte	195.00
Plate 24", torte	250.00
* Platter, 10½", oval	40.00
Platter, 12", oval	55.00
Ring holder	200.00
Salad set: 10" bowl, 14" torte, wood fork & spoon	135.00
Salt, individual	9.00
Salver, 10", sq., ped. ft. (cake stand)	185.00
Salver, 10", rnd., ped. ft. (cake stand)	130.00
* Salver, 11", rnd., ped. ft. (cake stand)	30.00
Sauce boat & liner	55.00
Saucer	3.00
Set: 2 jam pots w/tray	165.00
Set: decanter, 6 – 2 oz. whiskeys on 10½" tray	245.00
Set: toddler, w/baby tumbler & bowl	90.00
Set: youth, w/bowl, hdld. mug, 6" plate	90.00
Set: condiment, 2 oils, 2 shakers, mustard w/cover & spoon w/tray	350.00
Shaker, 3", ea.	10.00
* Shaker, 3½", ea.	7.00
Shaker, 3¼", ea.	10.00
Shakers w/tray, individual, 2"	22.00
Sherbet, handled, 3½" high, 4½ oz.	110.00
Shrimp bowl, 12¼"	395.00
Spooner, 3¾"	35.00
**Strawholder, 10", w/cover	255.00
Sugar, tea, 2¼" (#2056½)	13.00
Sugar, hdld., 3¼" h.	12.00
Sugar shaker	65.00
Sugar, w/o cover	10.00
Sugar, w/cover, no hdl., 6¼" (cover fits strawholder)	65.00
Sugar, w/cover, 2 hdld.	20.00
Syrup, 6½ oz., #2056½, Sani-cut server	80.00
Syrup, 6 oz., non pour screw top, 5¼" h.	225.00
Syrup, 10 oz., w/glass cover & 6" liner plate	235.00
Syrup, w/drip proof top	35.00
Toothpick	25.00
Tray, cloverleaf for condiment set	165.00
Tray, tid bit, w/question mark metal handle	40.00

** Bottom only

	*Crystal
Tray, 5" x 2½", rect.	80.00
Tray, 6" oval, hdld.	35.00
Tray, pin, oval, 5½" x 4½"	210.00
Tray, 6½" x 9" relish, 4 part	45.00
Tray, 9½", service, 2 hdld.	35.00
Tray, 10", muffin (2 upturned sides)	30.00
Tray, 10", square, 4 part	85.00
Tray, 10", square	165.00
Tray, 10½", cake, w/question mark metal hdl.	32.00
Tray, 10½" x 7½", rect.	70.00
Tray, 10½" x 5", oval hdld.	45.00
Tray, 10¾", square, 4 part	155.00
Tray, 12", sand. w/ctr. handle	35.00
Tray, 12", round	165.00
Tray, 13½", oval, ice cream	185.00
Tray for sugar & creamer, tab. hdld., 6¾"	12.00
Tumbler, hdld. iced tea	350.00
Tumbler, #2056, 2 oz., whiskey, 2½" h.	11.00
Tumbler, #2056, 3 oz., ftd. cone, cocktail, 2⅞" h.	14.00
Tumbler, #2056, 5 oz., ftd., juice, 4¾"	13.00
Tumbler, #2056, 6 oz., flat, old-fashioned, 3⅜" h.	15.00
Tumbler, #2056, 8 oz. flat, water, flared, 4⅛" h.	15.00
* Tumbler, #2056, 9 oz. ftd., water, 4⅞" h.	15.00
Tumbler, #2056, 12 oz., flat, tea, flared, 5¼" h.	17.00
Tumbler, #2056½, 5 oz., straight side, juice	13.00

	*Crystal
Tumbler, #2056½, 8 oz., straight side, water, 3⅞" h.	13.00
Tumbler, #2056½, 12 oz., straight side, tea, 5" h.	18.00
Tumbler, #5056, 5 oz., ftd., juice, 4⅛" w/plain bowl	12.00
Tumbler, #5056, 12 oz., ftd., tea, 5½" w/plain bowl	12.00
Urn, 6", sq., ped. ft	30.00
Urn, 7½", sq. ped. ft.	37.50
Vase, 4½", sweet pea	80.00
Vase, 6", bud, ftd.	18.00
* Vase, 6", bud, flared	18.00
Vase, 6", straight side	35.00
Vase, 6½", flared rim	15.00
Vase, 7", flared	80.00
* Vase, 8", straight side	40.00
* Vase, 8", flared	80.00
Vase, 8", porch, 5" diam.	450.00
Vase, 8½", bud, flared	25.00
Vase, 8½", bud, cupped	25.00
Vase, 9", w/sq. ped. ft.	45.00
Vase, 9½", flared	150.00
Vase, 10", cupped in top	225.00
Vase, 10", porch, 8" diam.	450.00
* Vase, 10", straight side	90.00
Vase, 10", swung	225.00
Vase, 10", flared	90.00
Vase, 12", straight side	195.00
Vase, 12", swung	250.00
Vase, 14", swung	250.00
Vase, 20", swung	395.00

Colors: amber, amethyst, crystal, crystal w/ebony stem, light and dark Emerald, Heatherbloom, Peach Blo, Topaz, Willow blue

Cambridge's Apple Blossom has undergone some serious price adjustments, particularly in the harder to find items and serving pieces. Yellow is the easiest Apple Blossom color to accumulate. Crystal Apple Blossom is not nearly as abundant. Other colors can be found with time and funds; however, availability of pink, green, and blue is quite limited in comparison to yellow or crystal. Very little dark Emerald Green, amethyst, or amber is found. A small set of those colors could be gathered, a piece here and a piece there.

Butter dishes are rarely seen in any colors other than yellow or crystal. Beverage items can still be obtained in most colors. Finding additional pieces to match those colors becomes a problem. Serving pieces, dinner plates, and unusual items are elusive in any color; buy them whenever you have the chance!

Apple Blossom is found on several Cambridge stemware lines, but the #3130 line is most often seen and collected.

	Crystal	Yellow Amber	Pink *Green
Ash tray, 6", heavy	50.00	125.00	150.00
Bowl, #3025, ftd., finger, w/plate	45.00	65.00	75.00
Bowl, #3130, finger, w/plate	40.00	60.00	70.00
Bowl, 3", indiv. nut, 4 ftd	55.00	75.00	80.00
Bowl, 5¼", 2 hdld., bonbon	25.00	40.00	45.00
Bowl, 5½", 2 hdld., bonbon	25.00	40.00	40.00
Bowl, 5½", fruit "saucer"	20.00	28.00	30.00
Bowl, 6", 2 hdld., "basket" (sides up)	30.00	48.00	50.00
Bowl, 6", cereal	35.00	50.00	55.00
Bowl, 9", pickle	30.00	55.00	60.00
Bowl, 10", 2 hdld.	55.00	95.00	110.00
Bowl, 10", baker	60.00	100.00	110.00
Bowl, 11", fruit, tab hdld.	65.00	110.00	125.00
Bowl, 11", low ftd.	60.00	100.00	120.00
Bowl, 12", relish, 4 pt.	45.00	70.00	75.00
Bowl, 12", 4 ftd.	60.00	100.00	110.00
Bowl, 12", flat	55.00	90.00	95.00
Bowl, 12", oval, 4 ftd.	55.00	75.00	80.00
Bowl, 12½", console	55.00	75.00	80.00
Bowl, 13"	55.00	90.00	100.00
Bowl, cream soup, w/liner plate	35.00	55.00	60.00
Butter w/cover, 5½"	145.00	295.00	410.00
Candelabrum, 3-lite, keyhole	35.00	50.00	65.00
Candlestick, 1-lite, keyhole	24.00	35.00	40.00
Candlestick, 2-lite, keyhole	30.00	45.00	50.00
Candy box w/cover, 4 ftd. "bowl"	85.00	125.00	165.00
Cheese (compote) & cracker (11½" plate)	45.00	75.00	100.00
Comport, 4", fruit cocktail	20.00	28.00	30.00
Comport, 7", tall	45.00	70.00	95.00
Creamer, ftd.	20.00	25.00	28.00
Creamer, tall ftd.	22.00	28.00	30.00
Cup	16.00	28.00	35.00
Cup, A.D.	50.00	65.00	90.00
Fruit/oyster cocktail, #3025, 4½ oz.	20.00	25.00	30.00
Mayonnaise, w/liner & ladle (4 ftd. bowl)	45.00	65.00	80.00
Pitcher, 50 oz., ftd., flattened sides	195.00	275.00	350.00
Pitcher, 64 oz., #3130	215.00	295.00	350.00
Pitcher, 64 oz., #3025	215.00	295.00	350.00
Pitcher, 67 oz., squeezed middle, loop hdld.	225.00	325.00	395.00
Pitcher, 76 oz.	125.00	315.00	395.00
Pitcher, 80 oz., ball	195.00	395.00	495.00
Pitcher w/cover, 76 oz., ftd., #3135	250.00	375.00	495.00
Plate, 6", bread/butter	8.00	10.00	12.00
Plate, 6", sq., 2 hdld.	10.00	20.00	22.00
Plate, 7½", tea	12.00	22.00	25.00

* Blue prices 25% to 30% more.

	Crystal	Yellow Amber	Pink *Green
Plate, 8½"	20.00	25.00	30.00
Plate, 9½", dinner	55.00	75.00	85.00
Plate, 10", grill	35.00	55.00	65.00
Plate, sandwich, 11½", tab hdld.	30.00	45.00	50.00
Plate, sandwich, 12½", 2 hdld.	32.00	50.00	60.00
Plate, sq., bread/butter	8.00	10.00	12.00
Plate, sq., dinner	55.00	75.00	85.00
Plate, sq., salad	12.00	22.00	25.00
Plate, sq., servce	30.00	45.00	50.00
Platter, 11½	55.00	95.00	120.00
Platter, 13½" rect., w/tab handle	60.00	100.00	150.00
Salt & pepper, pr.	50.00	95.00	125.00
Saucer	5.00	7.00	8.00
Saucer, A.D.	15.00	25.00	30.00
Stem, #1066, parfait	25.00	110.00	150.00
Stem, #3025, 7 oz., low fancy ft., sherbet	17.00	25.00	28.00
Stem, #3025, 7 oz., high sherbet	18.00	30.00	33.00
Stem, #3025, 10 oz.	24.00	35.00	45.00
Stem, #3130, 1 oz., cordial	65.00	110.00	175.00
Stem, #3130, 3 oz., cocktail	18.00	32.00	35.00
Stem, #3130, 6 oz., low sherbet	16.00	24.00	28.00
Stem, #3130, 6 oz., tall sherbet	18.00	30.00	33.00
Stem, #3130, 8 oz., water	22.00	30.00	45.00
Stem, #3135, 3 oz., cocktail	18.00	32.00	35.00
Stem, #3135, 6 oz., low sherbet	16.00	24.00	28.00
Stem, #3135, 6 oz., tall sherbet	18.00	30.00	33.00
Stem, #3135, 8 oz., water	22.00	30.00	33.00
Stem, #3400, 6 oz., ftd., sherbet	15.00	22.00	26.00
Stem, #3400, 9 oz., water	22.00	30.00	45.00
Sugar, ftd.	20.00	25.00	28.00
Sugar, tall ftd.	20.00	28.00	30.00
Tray, 7", hdld. relish	25.00	40.00	45.00
Tray, 11", ctr. hdld. sand.	35.00	50.00	60.00
Tumbler, #3025, 4 oz.	16.00	24.00	28.00
Tumbler, #3025, 10 oz.	20.00	30.00	35.00
Tumbler, #3025, 12 oz.	25.00	40.00	45.00
Tumbler, #3130, 5 oz., ftd.	16.00	28.00	33.00
Tumbler, #3130, 8 oz., ftd.	22.00	30.00	35.00
Tumbler, #3130, 10 oz., ftd.	25.00	35.00	40.00
Tumbler, #3130, 12 oz., ftd.	30.00	40.00	50.00
Tumbler, #3135, 5 oz., ftd.	16.00	30.00	35.00
Tumbler, #3135, 8 oz., ftd.	22.00	35.00	40.00
Tumbler, #3135, 10 oz., ftd.	25.00	35.00	45.00
Tumbler, #3135, 12 oz., ftd.	30.00	40.00	50.00
Tumbler, #3400, 2½ oz., ftd.	30.00	60.00	75.00
Tumbler, #3400, 9 oz., ftd.	22.00	30.00	35.00
Tumbler, #3400, 12 oz., ftd.	30.00	40.00	50.00
Tumbler, 12 oz., flat (2 styles) – 1 mid indent to match 67 oz. pitcher	25.00	50.00	60.00
Tumbler, 6"	25.00	45.00	50.00
Vase, 5"	65.00	95.00	125.00
Vase, 6", rippled sides	75.00	125.00	150.00
Vase, 8", 2 styles	85.00	135.00	175.00
Vase, 12", keyhole base w/neck indent	95.00	175.00	250.00

* Blue prices 25% to 30% more.
Note: See pages 228 – 229 for stem identification.

Colors: Amber, Amethyst, green, pink

We know "Balda" to be a Central Glass Works pattern that was designed by Joseph Balda who was better known for his Heisey designs. It is my understanding that this information was first uncovered by Barbara Adt Namon who presented it at a meeting attended by Ed Trindle who wrote an article on it for the Daze newspaper, thus informing the collecting community as a whole. As yet, no one has discovered if it had a "real" name at the factory, or was merely Etch #410; hence its designer's appellation thus far.

Stemware constitutes the most seen item as is the case with most Elegant glassware from this time. Amethyst (lilac) is the most often found color. There may be additional pieces or colors other than those I have listed. You are unlikely to find large batches of "Balda," but it does happen occasionally.

I have very little catalog information on this pattern which has caught the eye of some competitive collectors. I am hoping the added exposure "Balda" receives here will result in new discoveries. The information I have was furnished by fellow dealers. Whatever you can add will be helpful.

Central Glass pattern Morgan (page 129) is also found on the same stem line shown here in Amethyst. Morgan is etched on two additional stems, but I have only seen "Balda" etched on this one. Do, please, tell me what you find!

	Amethyst	Pink Green Amber		Amethyst	Pink Green Amber
Cup	25.00	20.00	Stem, claret	75.00	40.00
Decanter and stopper	495.00	295.00	Stem, cordial	65.00	40.00
Pitcher		695.00	Stem, water	45.00	25.00
Plate, 6"	12.50	10.00	Stem, wine	45.00	30.00
Plate, lunch	20.00	14.00	Tumbler, ftd. juice	25.00	15.00
Platter	65.00	45.00	Tumbler, ftd. tea	35.00	25.00
Saucer	5.00	4.00	Tumbler, ftd. water	30.00	20.00
Shaker, pr		100.00	Tumbler, ftd. whiskey	37.50	22.50
Stem, champagne/sherbet	25.00	20.00			

Colors: crystal, Azure blue, Topaz yellow, amber, green, pink, red, cobalt blue, black amethyst

Indiana has made a few pieces of Baroque in a color similar to Wisteria for Tiara. I have had reports of bowls, vases, and even a single candlestick. I have seen the bowl and vase, but not the candle. My Tiara catalog does not show the candle. These items are a purple/pink tint; do not pay a high price for Baroque pieces in this color. Baroque was never originally made in that color. This Indiana color does not change hues in natural or artificial light as does the original Fostoria Wisteria.

Triple candlesticks have been encountered in all the colors listed above, but matching console bowls have not yet been found in red, cobalt blue, or amethyst. Some pieces of Azure Baroque appear to be light green (bad batches of blue that were released anyway). That light green color is not as accepted as Azure. Actually, it is harder to sell since it is so difficult to find additional pieces of that hue. Only a few collectors pursue color variances; you probably could not find enough pieces of light green to complete a set.

Candlesticks are an item that many new collectors are seeking regardless of the pattern. I have a new book out addressing this collecting fancy. It's called *Glass Candlesticks of the Depression Era*. Baroque pattern enjoys several different varieties of candlesticks. You will find both 4" and 5½" single lite candles and a 4½" double candle. The 6", 3-lite (triple) candlesticks were previously discussed. It is the candelabra with prisms many collectors covet. These candelabra are elusive, and a torment to keep the older prism wires attached. Some collectors are substituting modern wires for the old, rusty ones. Once these are clamped on tightly, they rarely come off, even if moved.

Baroque cream soups and individual shakers are elusive in all colors, including crystal. They have always been expensive. Speaking of shakers, the regular size came with both metal and glass tops. Today, most collectors fancy glass lids. Glass lids were easily broken by over tightening them; and Fostoria changed to metal lids before Baroque was discontinued. Replacement lids were always metal. Metal tops are most often found on the Baroque mould, etched crystal patterns of Navarre, Chintz, and Meadow Rose.

Blue pitchers and punch bowls are not abundant. Straight tumblers are more difficult to find than footed ones, but are seemingly preferred to cone-shaped, footed pieces. Collectors just do not like the 30s era cone shape.

	Crystal	Blue	Yellow
Ash tray	7.50	16.00	14.00
Bowl, cream soup	35.00	75.00	75.00
Bowl, ftd., punch	400.00	1,250.00	
Bowl, 3¾", rose	25.00	95.00	65.00
Bowl, 4", hdld. (4 styles)	11.00	28.00	20.00
Bowl, 5", fruit	15.00	30.00	25.00
Bowl, 6", cereal	20.00	42.00	35.00
Bowl, 6", sq.	8.00	20.00	22.00
Bowl, 6½", 2 pt.	9.00	35.00	20.00
Bowl, 7", 3 ftd.	12.50	25.00	25.00
Bowl, 7½", jelly, w/cover	30.00	150.00	100.00
Bowl, 8", pickle	8.50	30.00	25.00
Bowl, 8½", hdld.	14.00	35.00	30.00
Bowl, 9½", veg., oval	25.00	65.00	50.00
Bowl, 10", hdld.	30.00	95.00	70.00
Bowl, 10½", hdld., 4 ftd.	17.50	75.00	37.50
Bowl, 10" x 7½"	25.00		
Bowl, 10", relish, 3 pt.	20.00	45.00	30.00
Bowl, 11", celery	18.00	45.00	25.00
Bowl, 11", rolled edge	20.00	75.00	60.00
* Bowl, 12", flared	21.50	40.00	32.50
Candelabrum, 8¼", 2-lite, 16 lustre	100.00	140.00	110.00
Candelabrum, 9½", 3-lite, 24 lustre	135.00	195.00	165.00
Candle, 7¾", 8 lustre	50.00	90.00	80.00
Candlestick, 4"	12.50	50.00	35.00
Candlestick, 4½", 2-lite	15.00	55.00	50.00

*Pink just discovered.

	Crystal	Blue	Yellow
Candlestick, 5½"	9.00	60.00	45.00
*Candlestick, 6", 3-lite	30.00	90.00	75.00
Candy, 3 part w/cover	50.00	125.00	85.00
Comport, 4¾"	15.00	38.00	30.00
Comport, 6½"	17.50	50.00	40.00
Creamer, 3¼", indiv.	9.00	30.00	25.00
Creamer, 3¾", ftd.	9.00	20.00	18.00
Cup	10.00	30.00	20.00
Cup, 6 oz., punch	15.00	30.00	
Ice bucket	55.00	125.00	80.00
Mayonnaise, 5½", w/liner	15.00	80.00	70.00
Mustard, w/cover	22.00	65.00	50.00
Oil, w/stopper, 5½"	85.00	400.00	225.00
Pitcher, 6½"	110.00	800.00	450.00
Pitcher, 7", ice lip	110.00	750.00	550.00
Plate, 6"	3.00	12.00	10.00
Plate, 7½"	5.00	16.00	10.00
Plate, 8½"	6.00	20.00	17.50
Plate, 9½"	15.00	65.00	47.50
Plate, 10", cake	30.00	35.00	30.00
Plate, 11", ctr. hdld., sand	25.00		
Plate, 14", torte	13.00	40.00	35.00
Platter, 12", oval	22.00	65.00	45.00
Salt & pepper, pr.	50.00	140.00	110.00
Salt & pepper, indiv., pr.	50.00	250.00	200.00
Sauce dish	30.00	70.00	40.00
Sauce dish div	25.00	60.00	35.00
Saucer	2.00	7.00	6.00
Sherbet, 3¾", 5 oz.	10.00	27.50	20.00
Stem, 6¾", 9 oz., water	15.00	33.00	22.50
Sugar, 3", indiv.	5.00	27.50	22.50
Sugar, 3½", ftd.	8.00	30.00	16.00
Sweetmeat, covered, 9"	75.00	200.00	150.00
Tray, 11", oval	15.00	47.50	37.50
Tray, 6¼" for indiv. cream/sugar	15.00	25.00	20.00
Tumbler, 3½", 6½ oz., old-fashioned	22.50	95.00	60.00
Tumbler, 3", 3½ oz., ftd., cocktail	10.00	20.00	15.00
Tumbler, 6", 12 oz., ftd., tea	20.00	40.00	30.00
Tumbler, 3¾", 5 oz., juice	12.00	42.00	30.00
Tumbler, 5½", 9 oz., ftd., water	12.00	30.00	25.00
Tumbler, 4¼", 9 oz., water	25.00	50.00	33.00
Tumbler, 5¾", 14 oz., tea	30.00	80.00	55.00
Vase, 6½"	45.00	135.00	110.00
Vase, 7"	40.00	165.00	120.00

* Red $150.00
  Green $120.00
  Black Amethyst $140.00
  Cobalt Blue $140.00
  Amber $75.00

Colors: amber, black, ice blue, crystal, green, pink, red, cobalt

Black Forest has been discovered by collectors on the Internet. There was a small collecting community of Black Forest admirers that kept the pricing of this very limited pattern under wraps. The Internet auctions have blown the previously "standard" prices out of the water. Black items and those with gold encrusting are particularly pricey the last two years. The throng of new collectors has caused a noticeable deficiency of pieces for those seeking it. Those black 10" gold encrusted dinner plates and perfumes reported last book are all in new collectors' hands.

This activity has also stimulated sales in Deerwood, a pattern often confused with Black Forest. Some pieces of etched Deerwood (made at the Tiffin plant of U. S. Glass) have been found on Paden City blanks which adds to the confusion. You can see a pink Deerwood candy on page 71 that is a typical, flat, divided blank of Paden City. Black Forest pattern depicts moose and trees, while deer and trees are on Deerwood.

I am regularly asked about those Black Forest etched, heavy goblets that were made in the 1970s in amber, amberina, dark green, blue, crystal, and ruby by L. G. Wright, a glass company dedicated to remaking glass from older moulds or from newly made moulds of older designs. These are selling in the $25.00 to $40.00 range with red and blue on the upper side of that price. These newer goblets have a heavy, predominant "Daisy and Button" cubed stem.

	Amber	*Black	Crystal	Green	Pink	Red
Batter jug			200.00			
Bowl, 4½", finger				40.00		
Bowl, 9¼", center hdld.				85.00	85.00	
Bowl, 11", console	75.00	110.00	50.00	85.00	85.00	
Bowl, 11", fruit		110.00		85.00	85.00	
Bowl, 13", console		175.00				
Bowl, 3 ftd.			75.00			
Cake plate, 2" pedestal	75.00	100.00		85.00	85.00	
Candlestick, mushroom style	35.00	75.00	30.00	55.00	55.00	
Candlestick double			60.00			
Candy dish, w/cover, several styles	135.00	225.00		195.00	195.00	
Creamer, 2 styles	50.00	60.00	30.00	50.00	50.00	
Comport, 4", low ftd.				65.00	65.00	
Comport, 5½", high ftd.		95.00		60.00	60.00	
Cup and saucer, 3 styles		125.00		100.00	100.00	150.00
Decanter, w/stopper, 8½", 28 oz., bulbous				295.00	295.00	
Decanter w/stopper, 8¾", 24 oz., straight			150.00	295.00	295.00	
Ice bucket		195.00		125.00	125.00	
Ice pail, 6", 3" high	110.00					
Ice tub, 2 styles (ice blue $195.00)	125.00	175.00		125.00	125.00	
Mayonnaise, with liner		125.00		90.00	90.00	
Night set: pitcher, 6½", 42 oz. & tumbler				550.00	550.00	
Pitcher, 8", 40 oz. (cobalt $1,250.00)						
Pitcher, 8", 62 oz.			225.00			
Pitcher, 9", 80 oz.					500.00	
Pitcher, 10½", 72 oz.				600.00	600.00	
Plate, 6½", bread/butter		35.00		25.00	25.00	
Plate, 8", luncheon		45.00		30.00	30.00	
Plate, 10", dinner		225.00				
Plate, 11", 2 hdld.		125.00		65.00	65.00	
Plate, 13¾", 2 hdld.				100.00	100.00	
Relish, 10½", 5 pt. covered				195.00	195.00	
Salt and pepper, pr.			125.00		175.00	
Server, center hdld.	50.00	40.00	35.00	50.00	35.00	
Shot glass, 2 oz., 2½"	40.00					
Stem, 2 oz., wine, 4¼"			17.50	50.00		
Stem, 6 oz., champagne, 4¾"			17.50		30.00	
Stem, 9 oz., water, 6"			22.50			
Sugar, 2 styles	50.00	60.00	30.00	50.00	50.00	
Tumbler, 3 oz., juice, flat or footed, 3½"			35.00	60.00	60.00	
Tumbler, 8 oz., old fashioned, 3⅞"				65.00	65.00	
Tumbler, 9 oz., ftd., 5½"	40.00					
Tumbler, 12 oz., tea, 5½"				75.00	75.00	
Vase, 6½" (cobalt $300.00)		150.00	100.00	125.00	125.00	
Vase, 10", 2 styles in black		200.00		150.00	150.00	
Whipped cream pail	95.00					

*Add 20% for gold decorated.

Colors: Pink, Pink & Green w/crystal, Green, all w/Optic

Bo Peep is credited by another author as being made by Monongah; but the shapes are very similar to those we so readily recognize as Tiffin. Cathy bought that green footed juice tumbler about twenty-five years ago and asked me to look for other pieces, which, frankly, I forgot. Mosser Glass Company in Cambridge, Ohio, put out their miniature Cameo Depression glass pattern called Jennifer in the middle 1980s, and I sold those in my shop. One day, when I was at the factory, the owner approached me with a picture of Bo Peep and asked if I knew where he could find a piece of that. I, then, remembered Cathy's purchase which I took to show him the next trip. They kept the piece for over two years, but were unable to miniaturize this delicate etching. Moulded patterns such as Cameo he said could be miniaturized, but those acid etchings were a whole different problem!

Several years later, I was in a shop where the dealer knew I looked for Bo Peep for Cathy. He asked me if I had seen that set in an antique mall down the road. I had never been to that mall, but made the out of the way trip. It was priced way more than I could pay; but I forced myself to buy the pitcher and vase pictured here since I had never seen them. The pitcher has an unetched lid as in Tiffin. I understand another dealer/collector ultimately bought the set after I turned it down; I have always found it difficult to wear both hats of collector and dealer. Right now, I am wishing for us all that I had floated a loan!

	Pink Green
Finger bowl, ftd.	75.00
Jug w/cover	595.00
Jug w/o cover	495.00
Plate, 7 ½", salad	25.00
Stem, cocktail	45.00
Stem, high sherbet	40.00
Stem, low sherbet	35.00
Stem, parfait	75.00

	Pink Green
Stem, water	65.00
Stem, wine	75.00
Tumbler, 5 oz., ftd. juice	25.00
Tumbler, 9 oz., ftd. water	30.00
Tumbler, 12 oz., ftd. iced tea	45.00
Tumbler, ftd. seltzer	35.00
Vase, 9", ruffled edge	295.00

Grape

BROCADE, Fostoria Glass Company, 1927 – 1931
Colors: Azure blue, crystal, Ebony, green, Orchid, Rose

Pictured above are examples of several Fostoria Brocades, illustrating how you can blend the different designs rather than buy only one. Designs are shown separately on page 25. Hopefully, the labeled small group shots will make identification easy. You should know that Oak Leaf pattern with iridescence is correctly referred to as Oak Wood and Paradise with iridescence is Victoria, Decoration #71. Please notify me of any unlisted pieces.

	crystal	#290 Oakleaf green/Rose	Ebony	#72 Oakwood Orchid/Azure	#289 Paradise green/Orchid	#73 Palm Leaf Rose/green	blue	#287 Grape green	Orchid
Bon bon, #2375	30.00	40.00		50.00		50.00		40.00	
Bowl, finger, #869	60.00	70.00		75.00					
Bowl, 4½", mint #2394	35.00	40.00							
Bowl, 7½", "D," cupped rose, #2339							85.00	60.00	95.00
Bowl, 10", scroll hdld, #2395	70.00	100.00	100.00			200.00			
Bowl, 10", 2 hdld, dessert, #2375	80.00	110.00		150.00		165.00			
Bowl, 10½", "A," 3 ftd., #2297					95.00		95.00	70.00	100.00
Bowl, 10½", "C," sm roll rim deep, #2297							95.00	70.00	100.00
Bowl, 10½", "C," pedestal ftd., #2315					95.00				
Bowl, 11", roll edge ctrpiece, #2329					100.00		155.00	135.00	165.00
Bowl, 11", ctrpiece, #2375				125.00		155.00			
Bowl, 11", cornucopia hdld, #2398	85.00	115.00							
Bowl, 12", 3 toe, flair rim, #2394	85.00	115.00		115.00		150.00			
Bowl, 12", console, #2375	85.00	115.00							
Bowl, 12" low, "saturn rings" #2362					85.00		115.00	90.00	120.00
Bowl, 12" oval	100.00	135.00							
Bowl, 12", hexagonal, 3 tab toe, #2342	80.00	130.00		155.00	100.00				
Bowl, 12", "A," 3 tab toe, #2297					115.00		125.00	110.00	120.00
Bowl, 12½", "E," flat, shallow, #2297							125.00	100.00	120.00
Bowl, 13", ctrpiece rnd., #2329					140.00		225.00	195.00	210.00

	crystal	#290 Oakleaf green/Rose	Ebony	#72 Oakwood Orchid/Azure	#289 Paradise green/Orchid	#73 Palm Leaf Rose/green	#287 Grape blue	#287 Grape green	Orchid
Bowl, ctrpiece oval, #2375½	125.00	145.00		295.00					
Bowl, 13" oval, roll edge w/grid frog, #2371					175.00		225.00	185.00	225.00
Bowl, #2415 Comb, candle hdld.	120.00	155.00	155.00	200.00		250.00			
Candlestick, 2" mushroom, #2372					25.00		35.00	30.00	35.00
Candlestick, 2", 3 toe, #2394	95.00	60.00				70.00			
Candlestick, 3" scroll, #2395	50.00	60.00	75.00						
Candlestick, 3", #2375	45.00	60.00		65.00		75.00			
Candlestick, 3", stack disc, #2362					40.00		35.00	30.00	35.00
Candlestick, 4", #2324					35.00		35.00	30.00	35.00
Candlestick, hex mushroom, #2375½	45.00	55.00		75.00					
Candlestick, trindle, #2383 ea.						145.00			
Candy box, cov., 3 pt., #2331	100.00	125.00	200.00	110.00			185.00	145.00	175.00
Candy, box, cone lid #2380	100.00	145.00			115.00				
Candy, cov., oval, #2395		135.00		200.00					
Cheese & cracker, #2368	65.00	90.00							
Cigarette & cov. (small), #2391	65.00	90.00	100.00	125.00					
Cigarette & cov. (large), #2391	75.00	100.00	110.00	125.00					
Comport, 6", #2400						125.00			
Comport, 7" tall twist stem, #2327					75.00		75.00	55.00	75.00
Comport, 8", short, ftd., #2350					65.00				
Comport, 8", pulled stem, #2400				115.00					
Comport, 11" stack disc stem ftd., #2362					100.00		125.00	100.00	120.00
Ice bucket, #2378	100.00	115.00		165.00		155.00	100.00	90.00	95.00
Ice bucket, w drainer, handle & tongs #2378					115.00		120.00	110.00	115.00
Jug, #5000	395.00	500.00		795.00	695.00				
Lemon, "bow" hdld, #2375	35.00	45.00		40.00	60.00	40.00		40.00	
Mayonnaise, #2315	55.00	70.00		165.00					
Plate, finger liner, #2283	15.00	20.00							
Plate, mayonnaise, #2332	20.00	30.00		35.00					
Plate, 6", #2283	15.00	20.00							
Plate, 7", #2283	20.00	25.00		30.00					
Plate, 8" sq., #2419						35.00			
Plate, 8", #2283	22.00	30.00		35.00					
Plate, 10 cake, #2375	65.00	90.00		125.00		155.00			
Plate, 12" salver, #2315	100.00	125.00		150.00					
Plate, 13" lettuce, #2315	60.00	90.00		100.00					
Stem, ¾ oz. cordial, #877	65.00			110.00					
Stem, 2¾ oz. wine, #877	35.00			85.00					
Stem, 3½ oz. cocktail, #877	25.00			55.00					
Stem, 4 oz. claret, #877	35.00			85.00					
Stem, 6 oz. hi sherbet, #877	35.00			55.00					
Stem, 6 oz. low sherbet, #877	30.00			45.00					
Stem, 10 oz. water, #877	40.00			65.00					
Sugar Pail, #2378	105.00	150.00		195.00		250.00			
Sweetmeat, hex 2 hdld bowl, #2375	35.00	45.00		40.00		60.00		40.00	
Tray, rnd, fleur de lis hdld., #2387							95.00	90.00	95.00
Tray, ctr, hdld., #2342	65.00	95.00		125.00	75.00	140.00	95.00	90.00	95.00
Tumbler, 2½ oz. ftd. whiskey, #877	30.00	75.00							
Tumbler, 4½ oz. ftd. oyster cocktail	45.00								
Tumbler, 5 oz. ftd. juice, #877	50.00								
Tumbler, 5½ oz. parfait, #877	40.00	65.00							
Tumbler, 9 oz. ftd., #877				50.00	60.00				
Tumbler, 12 oz. ftd. tea, #877				60.00	65.00				
Urn & cover, #2413		175.00		395.00		495.00			
Vase, 3", 4", #4103, bulbous	50.00	60.00	75.00		70.00		85.00	70.00	80.00
Vase, 5", 6", #4103, optic					75.00		105.00	90.00	100.00
Vase, 6", #4100, flat straight side optic					85.00		105.00	90.00	100.00
Vase, 6", #4105, scallop rim	65.00	85.00		120.00	85.00				

	#290 Oakleaf crystal	#290 Oakleaf green/Rose	Ebony	#72 Oakwood Orchid/Azure	#289 Paradise green/Orchid	#73 Palm Leaf Rose/green	#287 Grape blue	#287 Grape green	#287 Grape Orchid
Vase, 7", 9", ftd. urn, #2369	85.00	115.00					135.00	120.00	130.00
Vase, 8", cupped melon, #2408						245.00			
Vase, 8", #2292, ftd. flair flat, straight side	85.00	100.00	110.00						
Vase, 8", #4100					95.00		125.00	115.00	120.00
Vase, 8", #4105	85.00	95.00		250.00		250.00			
Vase, 8", melon, #2387	90.00	115.00		185.00					
Vase, 8½" fan, #2385	150.00	200.00		250.00		285.00			
Vase, 10½" ftd., #2421						295.00			
Vase, sm. or lg. window & cov., #2373	150.00	200.00	300.00	350.00		350.00			
Whip cream, scallop 2 hdld bowl #2375	35.00	50.00		55.00		40.00			
Whip cream pail, #2375	105.00							40.00	
Whip cream pail, #2378		255.00		275.00					

Oak Leaf

Palm Leaf

Paradise

BROCADE, McKee, 1930s
Colors: pink and green

McKee's Brocade only came in the one pattern unlike Fostoria's many. I have heard it referred to many times by collectors as "Poinsettia" though I have no official reference for that name. Give it a look!

	pink/green
Bowl, 12" flared edge	55.00
Bowl, center, hdld. nut	45.00
Bowl, 12", console, rolled edge	55.00
Candlestick, rolled edge, octagonal	25.00
Candy box/cover	75.00
Candy jar, ftd., w/cover	65.00
Cheese and cracker	55.00
Compote, 10", flared edge	65.00
Compote, cone shape, octagonal	65.00
Mayonnaise, 3 pc.	50.00
Salver, ftd. (cake stand)	45.00
Server, center hdld.	40.00

Colors: crystal, yellow; some pink

Beautiful bi-colored Cadena stemware is a collector's bane; and finding serving pieces is nearly impossible even if you are willing to pay the price for them! They are rarely available! Never pass a piece you discover. Someone wants it, even if you don't!

Pitchers were sold with or without a lid. Pitchers without lids were often curved in or "cupped" so much that a lid will not fit inside. Thus, buying a lid separately may be a bit chancy. Remember that the pitcher cover is plain.

	Crystal	Pink Yellow		Crystal	Pink Yellow
Bowl, cream soup	25.00	45.00	Plate, 7¾"	10.00	20.00
Bowl, finger, ftd.	25.00	45.00	Plate, 9¼"	40.00	65.00
Bowl, grapefruit, ftd.	50.00	95.00	Saucer	15.00	25.00
Bowl, 6", hdld.	20.00	30.00	Stem, 4¾", sherbet	18.00	25.00
Bowl, 10", pickle	30.00	40.00	Stem, 5¼", cocktail	22.00	30.00
Bowl, 12", console	35.00	60.00	Stem, 5¼", ¾ oz., cordial	65.00	125.00
Candlestick	30.00	55.00	Stem, 6", wine	35.00	65.00
Creamer	20.00	30.00	Stem, 6⁵⁄₁₆", 8 oz., parfait	35.00	65.00
Cup	45.00	100.00	Stem, 6½", champagne	25.00	32.00
Mayonnaise, ftd., w/liner	50.00	75.00	Stem, 7½", water	35.00	38.00
Oyster cocktail	20.00	30.00	Sugar	20.00	30.00
Pitcher, ftd.	225.00	295.00	Tumbler, 4¼", ftd., juice	22.00	30.00
Pitcher, ftd., w/cover	295.00	395.00	Tumbler, 5¼", ftd., water	25.00	33.00
Plate, 6"	8.00	12.00	Vase, 9"	95.00	135.00

Colors: crystal, crystal and Crown Tuscan with gold decoration

Unfortunately, Candlelight pieces are not found with the regularity of some other Cambridge patterns. On page 28 is a 1951 Candlelight brochure of the type usually given to people who were registering a pattern. We have opened it to show you the typical stems found in Candlelight. Hopefully, this will help you identify them. Terminology has changed over the years. For instance, today, when people ask a dealer if he has wine goblets for sale, he needs to find out if they really want water goblets. Traditionally, wine goblets held 2½ to 4 ounces; but, now, many people think of wine goblets as holding 8 or 9 ounces. Clarify this, or you could lose a sale or buy the wrong item for your customer. It has happened!

Candlelight was manufactured in two ways. The pattern was cut into some pieces, but was acid etched on others. The cut items are more scarce, but there are fewer collectors searching for cut pieces. To illustrate the difference, there are two icers and liners in the photograph, one etched, the other cut. The pattern is harder to see on the cut! Etching was accomplished by covering the glass except where the design was desired and then dipping the glass into acid.

Shakers, basic serving pieces, candlesticks, and cups and saucers are not easily found. Don't pass any of those items.

	Crystal		Crystal
Bonbon, 7", ftd., 2 hdld., #3900/130	40.00	Cocktail shaker, 36 oz., #P101	225.00
Bowl, 10", 4 toed, flared, #3900/54	75.00	Comport, 5", cheese, #3900/135	45.00
Bowl, 11", 2 hdld., #3900/34	90.00	Comport, 5⅜", blown, #3121	75.00
Bowl, 11", 4 ftd., fancy edge, #3400/48	100.00	Comport, 5½", #3900/136	70.00
Bowl, 11½", ftd., 2 hdld., #3900/28	85.00	Creamer, #3900/41	25.00
Bowl, 12", 4 ftd., flared, #3400/4	85.00	Creamer, indiv., #3900/40	25.00
Bowl, 12", 4 ftd., oblong, #3400/160	90.00	Cruet, 6 oz., w/stopper, #3900/100	150.00
Bowl, 12", 4 toed, flared, #3900/62	90.00	Cup, #3900/17	33.00
Bowl, 12", 4 toed, oval, hdld., #3900/65	110.00	Decanter, 28 oz., ftd., #1321	225.00
Butter dish, 5", #3400/52	295.00	Ice bucket, #3900/671	165.00
Candle, 5", #3900/67	60.00	Icer, 2 pc., cocktail, #968	120.00
Candle, 6", 2-lite, #3900/72	75.00	Lamp, hurricane, #1617	225.00
Candle, 6", 3-lite, #3900/74	95.00	Lamp, hurricane, keyhole, w/bobeche, #1603	275.00
Candlestick, 5", #646	65.00	Lamp, hurricane, w/bobeche, #1613	325.00
Candlestick, 6", 2-lite, #647	75.00	Mayonnaise, 3 pc., #3900/129	75.00
Candlestick, 6", 3-lite, #1338	95.00	Mayonnaise, div., 4 pc., #3900/111	85.00
Candy box and cover, 3-part, #3500/57	135.00	Mayonnaise, ftd., 2 pc., #3900/19	75.00
Candy w/lid, rnd. #3900/165	150.00	Nut cup, 3", 4 ftd., #3400/71	70.00

	Crystal
Oil, 6 oz., #3900/100	125.00
Pitcher, Doulton, #3400/141	395.00
Plate, 6½", #3900/20	14.00
Plate, 8", 2 hdld., #3900/131	30.00
Plate, 8", salad, #3900/22	22.00
Plate, 10½", dinner, #3900/24	85.00
Plate, 12", 4 toed, #3900/26	75.00
Plate, 13", torte, 4 toed, #3900/33	85.00
Plate, 13½", cake, 2 hdld., #3900/35	85.00
Plate, 13½", cracker, #3900/135	75.00
Plate, 14", rolled edge, #3900/166	85.00
Relish, 7", 2 hdld., #3900/123	45.00
Relish, 7", div., 2 hdld., #3900/124	50.00
Relish, 8", 3 part, #3400/91	65.00
Relish, 9", 3 pt., #3900/125	65.00
Relish, 12", 3 pt., #3900/126	75.00
Relish, 12", 5 pt., #3900/120	85.00
Salt & pepper, pr., #3900/1177	135.00
Saucer, #3900/17	7.00
Stem, 1 oz., cordial, #3776	85.00
Stem, 2 oz., sherry, #7966	85.00
Stem, 2½ oz., wine, #3111	75.00
Stem, 3 oz., cocktail, #3111	40.00
Stem, 3 oz., cocktail, #3776	40.00
Stem, 3½ oz., wine, #3776	65.00
Stem, 4 oz., cocktail, #7801	35.00

	Crystal
Stem, 4½ oz., claret, #3776	85.00
Stem, 4½ oz., oyster cocktail, #3111	40.00
Stem, 4½ oz., oyster cocktail, #3776	40.00
Stem, 7 oz., low sherbet, #3111	23.00
Stem, 7 oz., low sherbet, #3776	24.00
Stem, 7 oz., tall sherbet, #3111	30.00
Stem, 7 oz., tall sherbet, #3776	28.00
Stem, 9 oz., water, #3776	45.00
Stem, 10 oz., water, #3111	45.00
Sugar, #3900/41	25.00
Sugar, indiv., #3900/40	35.00
Tumbler, 5 oz., ftd., juice, #3111	30.00
Tumbler, 5 oz., juice, #3776	30.00
Tumbler, 12 oz., ftd., iced tea, #3111	40.00
Tumbler, 12 oz., iced tea, #3776	40.00
Tumbler, 13 oz., #3900/115	45.00
Vase, 5", ftd., bud, #6004	95.00
Vase, 5", globe, #1309	85.00
Vase, 6", ftd., #6004	100.00
Vase, 8", ftd., #6004	120.00
Vase, 9", ftd., keyhole, #1237	125.00
Vase, 10", bud, #274	95.00
Vase, 11", ftd., pedestal, #1299	175.00
Vase, 11", ftd., #278	125.00
Vase, 12", ftd., keyhole, #1238	150.00
Vase, 13", ftd, #279	165.00

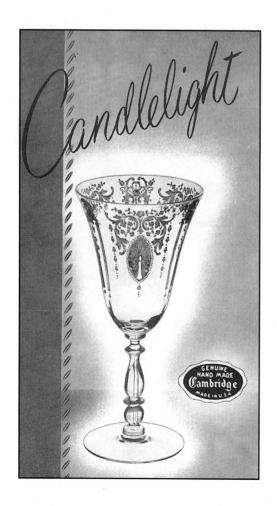

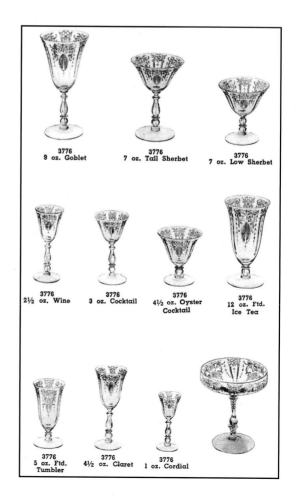

Colors: crystal, blue, pink, yellow, black, red, cobalt blue, green, caramel slag

Candlewick stemware and tumbler classification is a primary concern of new collectors until they learn all the different lines. In the bottom photo on page 31 are two different stem lines on which ruby and cobalt Candlewick is found. The round stems and tumblers are 3800 line while the flared rim style is 3400. If your red or cobalt stemware has some other shape, then it is not Candlewick and might even be Bryce. Stemware line 400/190 comes with a hollow stem. These are not pictured this time, but should be self explanatory. The tumblers designated 400/19 have flat bases with knobs around that base as opposed to 400/18 that has a domed foot. The 400/... was Imperial's factory listing for each piece. If you can find a copy of my first *Elegant Glassware of the Depression Era* book, there is a 15 page reprint of Imperial's Catalog B showing Candlewick listings as given by the factory.

Viennese blue Candlewick (shown below) continues to sell, but those higher priced red and black items have presently leveled. Even the Internet sales are not bustling for those colors. Prices of colored Candlewick used to increase swiftly; now, those prices have stalled, the result of a too rapid price rise and color reproductions made by Dalzell Viking before their demise last year. Just this morning, I saw a set of three square bowls in Jadite at the Webster flea market here in Florida. I am not sure what else has been made (or in what colors); be aware that reproductions abound in all sorts of colors. It will take some time to accumulate a listing for these newly made items. Please send me any information you have on such pieces.

Ruby and black fancy bowls sell in the ball park of $225.00 – 250.00 with the Viennese blue pieces bringing 50 to 60 percent of that. Ruby stems continue to be found in the 3400 and 3800 lines with most of these selling in the $65.00 to $100.00 range. However, cordials are selling in Ruby and Ritz blue (cobalt) from $125.00 to $175.00. Other Ritz blue stems are fetching $100.00 to $125.00. All of these colored pieces of Candlewick, except black, were made before 1940.

Be sure to notice the hanging lamp on page 30. It was interesting watching the photographers figure how to support it for a photo. It was heftier than it looked.

	Crystal
Ash tray, eagle, 6½", 1776/1	55.00
Ash tray, heart, 4½", 400/172	10.00
Ash tray, heart, 5½", 400/173	12.00
Ash tray, heart, 6½", 400/174	15.00
Ash tray, indiv., 400/64.	8.00
Ash tray, oblong, 4½", 400/134/1	6.00
Ash tray, round, 2¾", 400/19	9.00
Ash tray, round, 4", 400/33	11.00
Ash tray, round, 5", 400/133	8.00
Ash tray, square, 3¼", 400/651	40.00
Ash tray, square, 4½", 400/652	40.00
Ash tray, square, 5¾", 400/653	50.00
Ash tray, 6", matchbook holder center, 400/60	150.00
Ash tray set, 3 pc. rnd. nest. (crys. or colors), 400/550	35.00
Ash tray set, 3 pc. sq. nesting, 400/650	130.00
Ash tray set, 4 pc. bridge (cig. hold at side), 400/118	45.00
Basket, 5", beaded hdld., 400/273	255.00
Basket, 6½", hdld., 400/40/0	35.00
Basket, 11", hdld., 400/73/0	275.00
Bell, 4", 400/179	65.00
Bell, 5", 400/108	75.00
Bottle, bitters, w/tube, 4 oz., 400/117	65.00
Bowl, bouillon, 2 hdld., 400/126	50.00
Bowl, #3400, finger, ftd.	35.00
Bowl, #3800, finger	35.00
Bowl, 4½", nappy, 3 ftd., 400/206	80.00
Bowl, 4¾", round, 2 hdld., 400/42B	12.50
Bowl, 5", cream soup, 400/50	45.00
Bowl, 5", fruit, 400/1F	12.00
Bowl, 5", heart w/hand., 400/49H	22.00
Bowl, 5", square, 400/231	100.00

	Crystal
Bowl, 5½", heart, 400/53H	22.00
Bowl, 5½", jelly, w/cover, 400/59	75.00
Bowl, 5½", sauce, deep, 400/243	40.00
Bowl, 6", baked apple, rolled edge, 400/53X	30.00
Bowl, 6", cottage cheese, 400/85	25.00
Bowl, 6", fruit, 400/3F	12.00
Bowl, 6", heart w/hand., 400/51H	30.00
Bowl, 6", mint w/hand., 400/51F	23.00
Bowl, 6", round, div., 2 hdld., 400/52	25.00
Bowl, 6", 2 hdld., 400/52B	15.00
Bowl, 6", 3 ftd., 400/183	60.00
Bowl, 6", sq., 400/232	135.00
Bowl, 6½", relish, 2 pt., 400/84	25.00
Bowl, 6½", 2 hdld., 400/181	30.00
Bowl, 7", round, 400/5F	25.00
Bowl, 7", round, 2 hdld., 400/62B	17.50
Bowl, 7", relish, sq., div., 400/234	165.00
Bowl, 7", ivy, high, bead ft., 400/188	225.00
Bowl, 7", lily, 4 ft., 400/74J	75.00
Bowl, 7", relish, 400/60	25.00
Bowl, 7", sq., 400/233	165.00
Bowl, 7¼", rose, ftd. w/crimp edge, 400/132C	495.00
Bowl, 7½", pickle/celery, 400/57	27.50
Bowl, 7½", lily, bead rim, ftd., 400/75N	295.00
Bowl, 7½", belled (console base), 400/127B	85.00
Bowl, 8", round, 400/7F	37.50
Bowl, 8", relish, 2 pt., 400/268	20.00
Bowl, 8", cov. veg., 400/65/1	325.00
Bowl, 8½", rnd., 400/69B	35.00
Bowl, 8½", nappy, 4 ftd., 400/74B	75.00
Bowl, 8½", 3 ftd., 400/182	135.00
Bowl, 8½", 2 hdld., 400/72B	22.00
Bowl, 8½", pickle/celery, 400/58	20.00
Bowl, 8½", relish, 4 pt., 400/55	22.00
Bowl, 9", round, 400/10F	50.00
Bowl, 9", crimp, ftd., 400/67C	165.00
Bowl, 9", sq., fancy crimp edge, 4 ft., 400/74SC	85.00
Bowl, 9", heart, 400/49H	135.00
Bowl, 9", heart w/hand., 400/73H	175.00
Bowl, 10", 400/13F	45.00
Bowl, 10", banana, 400/103E	1,500.00
Bowl, 10", 3 toed, 400/205	165.00
Bowl, 10", belled (punch base), 400/128B	75.00
Bowl, 10", cupped edge, 400/75F	45.00
Bowl, 10", deep, 2 hdld., 400/113A	145.00
Bowl, 10", divided, deep, 2 hdld., 400/114A	165.00
Bowl, 10", fruit, bead stem (like compote), 400/103F	225.00
Bowl, 10", relish, oval, 2 hdld., 400/217	40.00
Bowl, 10", relish, 3 pt., 3 ft., 400/208	110.00
Bowl, 10", 3 pt., w/cover, 400/216	495.00
Bowl, 10½", belled, 400/63B	60.00
Bowl, 10½", butter/jam, 3 pt., 400/262	195.00
Bowl, 10½", salad, 400/75B	40.00

	Crystal
Bowl, 10½", relish, 3 section, 400/256	30.00
Bowl, 11", celery boat, oval, 400/46	65.00
Bowl, 11", centerpiece, flared, 400/13B	55.00
Bowl, 11", float, inward rim, ftd., 400/75F	40.00
Bowl, 11", oval, 400/124A	275.00
Bowl, 11", oval w/partition, 400/125A	325.00
Bowl, 12", round, 400/92B	45.00
Bowl, 12", belled, 400/106B	100.00
Bowl, 12", float, 400/92F	40.00
Bowl, 12", hdld., 400/113B	165.00
Bowl, 12", shallow, 400/17F	47.50
Bowl, 12", relish, oblong, 4 sect., 400/215	135.00
Bowl, 13", centerpiece, mushroom, 400/92L	60.00
Bowl, 13", float, 1½" deep, 400/101	65.00
Bowl, 13½", relish, 5 pt., 400/209	82.50
Bowl, 14", belled, 400/104B	90.00
Bowl, 14", oval, flared, 400/131B	250.00
Butter and jam set, 5 piece, 400/204	395.00
Butter, w/ cover, rnd., 5½", 400/144	35.00
Butter, w/ cover, no beads, California, 400/276	150.00
Butter, w/ bead top, ¼ lb., 400/161	30.00
Cake stand, 10", low foot, 400/67D	60.00
Cake stand, 11", high foot, 400/103D	75.00
Calendar, 1947, desk	235.00
Candleholder, 3 way, beaded base, 400/115	125.00
Candleholder, 2-lite, 400/100	24.00
Candleholder, flat, 3½", 400/280	50.00
Candleholder, 3½", rolled edge, 400/79R	14.00
Candleholder, 3½", w/fingerhold, 400/81	60.00
Candleholder, flower, 4", 2 bead stem, 400/66F	60.00
Candleholder, flower, 4½", 2 bead stem, 400/66C	65.00
Candleholder, 4½", 3 toed, 400/207	85.00
Candleholder, 3-lite on cir. bead. ctr., 400/147	40.00
Candleholder, 5", hdld./bowled up base, 400/90	65.00
Candleholder, 5", heart shape, 400/40HC	85.00
Candleholder, 5½", 3 bead stems, 400/224	100.00
Candleholder, flower, 5" (epergne inset), 400/40CV	195.00
Candleholder, 5", flower, 400/40C	35.00
Candleholder, 6½", tall, 3 bead stems, 400/175	110.00
Candleholder, flower, 6", round, 400/40F	25.00
Candleholder, urn, 6", holders on cir. ctr. bead, 400/129R	150.00
Candleholder, flower, 6½", square, 400/40S	50.00
Candleholder, mushroom, 400/86	35.00
Candleholder, flower, 9", centerpiece, 400/196FC	195.00
Candy box, round, 5½", 400/59	45.00
Candy box, sq., 6½", rnd. lid, 400/245	245.00
Candy box, w/ cover, 7", 400/259	165.00
Candy box, w/ cover, 7" partitioned, 400/110	95.00
Candy box, w/ cover, round, 7", 3 sect., 400/158	195.00
Candy box, w/ cover, beaded, ft., 400/140	395.00
Cigarette box w/cover, 400/134	35.00
Cigarette holder, 3", bead ft., 400/44	35.00
Cigarette set: 6 pc. (cigarette box & 4 rect. ash trays), 400/134/6	67.50

	Crystal
Clock, 4", round	295.00
Coaster, 4", 400/78	8.00
Coaster, w/spoon rest, 400/226	16.00
Cocktail, seafood w/bead ft., 400/190	60.00
Cocktail set: 2 pc., plate w/indent; cocktail, 400/97	40.00
Compote, 4½", 400/63B	40.00
Compote, 5", 3 bead stems, 400/220	85.00
Compote, 5½", 4 bead stem, 400/45	30.00
Compote, 5½, low, plain stem, 400/66B	22.00
Compote, 5½", 2 bead stem, 400/66B	22.00
Compote, 8", bead stem, 400/48F	90.00
Compote, 10", ftd. fruit, crimped, 40/103C	195.00
Compote, ft. oval, 400/137	1,250.00
Condiment set: 4 pc. (2 squat bead ft. shakers, marmalade), 400/1786	75.00
Console sets: 3 pc. (14" oval bowl, two 3-lite candles), 400/1531B	325.00
3 pc. (mushroom bowl, w/mushroom candles), 400/8692L	115.00
Creamer, domed foot, 400/18	135.00
Creamer, 6 oz., bead handle, 400/30	8.00
Creamer, indiv. bridge, 400/122	7.50
Creamer, plain ft., 400/31	9.00
Creamer, flat, bead handle, 400/126	32.50
Cup, after dinner, 400/77	17.50
Cup, coffee, 400/37	7.50
Cup, punch, 400/211	7.50
Cup, tea, 400/35	8.00
Decanter, w/stopper, 15 oz. cordial, 400/82/2	325.00
Decanter, w/stopper, 18 oz., 400/18	425.00
Decanter, w/stopper, 26 oz., 400/163	325.00
Deviled egg server, 12", ctr. hdld., 400/154	125.00
Egg cup, bead. ft., 400/19	47.50
Fork & spoon, set, 400/75	38.00

CANDLEWICK

	Crystal
Hurricane lamp, 2 pc. candle base, 400/79	135.00
Hurricane lamp, 2 pc., hdld. candle base, 400/76	195.00
Hurricane lamp, 3 pc. flared & crimped edge globe, 400/152	195.00
Ice tub, 5½" deep, 8" diam., 400/63	110.00
Ice tub, 7", 2 hdld., 400/168	225.00
Icer, 2 pc., seafood/fruit cocktail, 400/53/3	95.00
Icer, 2 pc., seafood/fruit cocktail #3800 line, one bead stem	70.00
Jam set, 5 pc., oval tray w/2 marmalade jars w/ladles, 400/1589	115.00
Jar tower, 3 sect., 400/655	395.00
Knife, butter, 4000	350.00
Ladle, marmalade, 3 bead stem, 400/130	12.00
Ladle, mayonnaise, 6¼", 400/135	12.00
Marmalade set, 3 pc., beaded ft. w/cover & spoon, 400/1989	40.00
Marmalade set, 3 pc. tall jar, domed bead ft., lid, spoon, 400/8918	75.00
Marmalade set, 4 pc., liner saucer, jar, lid, spoon, 400/89	45.00
Mayonnaise set, 2 pc. scoop side bowl, spoon, 400/23	40.00
Mayonnaise set, 3 pc. hdld. tray/hdld. bowl/ladle, 400/52/3	50.00
Mayonnaise set, 3 pc. plate, heart bowl, spoon, 400/49	35.00
Mayonnaise set, 3 pc. scoop side bowl, spoon, tray, 400/496	45.00

	Crystal
Mayonnaise 4 pc., plate, divided bowl, 2 ladles, 400/84	45.00
Mirror, 4½", rnd., standing	135.00
Mustard jar, w/spoon, 400/156	33.00
Oil, 4 oz., bead base, 400/164	55.00
Oil, 6 oz., bead base, 400/166	65.00
Oil, 4 oz., bulbous bottom, 400/274	45.00
Oil, 4 oz., hdld., bulbous bottom, 400/278	75.00
Oil, 6 oz., hdld., bulbous bottom, 400/279	90.00
Oil, 6 oz., bulbous bottom, 400/275	60.00
Oil, w/stopper, etched "Oil," 400/121	65.00
Oil, w/stopper, etched "Vinegar," 400/121	65.00
Party set, 2 pc., oval plate w/indent for cup, 400/98	27.50
Pitcher, 14 oz., short rnd., 400/330	195.00
Pitcher, 16 oz., low ft., 400/19	225.00
Pitcher, 16 oz., no ft., 400/16	175.00
Pitcher, 20 oz., plain, 400/416	40.00
Pitcher, 40 oz., juice/cocktail, 400/19	195.00
Pitcher, 40 oz., manhattan, 400/18	235.00
Pitcher, 40 oz., plain, 400/419	40.00
Pitcher, 64 oz., plain, 400/424	50.00
Pitcher, 80 oz., plain, 400/424	55.00
Pitcher, 80 oz., 400/24	150.00
Pitcher, 80 oz., beaded ft., 400/18	235.00
Plate, 4½", 400/34	6.00
Plate, 5½", 2 hdld., 400/42D	11.00
Plate, 6", bread/butter, 400/1D	8.00
Plate, 6", canape w/off ctr. indent, 400/36	15.00

33

	Crystal
Plate, 6¾", 2 hdld. crimped, 400/52C	25.00
Plate, 7", salad, 400/3D	8.00
Plate, 7½", 2 hdld., 400/52D	13.00
Plate, 7½", triangular, 400/266	95.00
Plate, 8", oval, 400/169	25.00
Plate, 8", salad, 400/5D	9.00
Plate, 8", w/indent, 400/50	12.00
Plate, 8¼", crescent salad, 400/120	55.00
Plate, 8½", 2 hdld., crimped, 400/62C	22.00
Plate, 8½", 2 hdld., 400/62D	13.00
Plate, 8½", salad, 400/5D	12.00
Plate, 8½", 2 hdld. (sides upturned), 400/62E	28.00
Plate, 9", luncheon, 400/7D	13.50
Plate, 9", oval, salad, 400/38	40.00
Plate, 9", w/indent, oval, 400/98	20.00
Plate, 10", 2 hdld., sides upturned, 400/72E	25.00
Plate, 10", 2 hdld. crimped, 400/72C	33.00
Plate, 10", 2 hdld., 400/72D	27.50
Plate, 10½", dinner, 400/10D	40.00
Plate, 12", 2 hdld., 400/145D	27.50
Plate, 12", 2 hdld. crimp., 400/145C	32.50
Plate, 12", service, 400/13D	33.00
Plate, 12½", cupped edge, torte, 400/75V	27.50
Plate, 12½", oval, 400/124	85.00
Plate, 13½", cupped edge, serving, 400/92V	43.00
Plate, 14" birthday cake (holes for 72 candles), 400/160	525.00

	Crystal
Plate, 14", 2 hdld., sides upturned, 400/113E	40.00
Plate, 14", 2 hdld., torte, 400/113D	40.00
Plate, 14", service, 400/92D	40.00
Plate, 14", torte, 400/17D	45.00
Plate, 17", cupped edge, 400/20V	95.00
Plate, 17", torte, 400/20D	95.00
Platter, 13", 400/124D	110.00
Platter, 16", 400/131D	225.00
Punch ladle, 400/91	30.00
Punch set, family, 8 demi cups, ladle, lid, 400/139/77	695.00
Punch set, 15 pc. bowl on base, 12 cups, ladle, 400/20	255.00
Relish & dressing set, 4 pc. (10½" 4 pt. relish w/marmalade), 400/1112	95.00
Salad set, 4 pc. (buffet; lg. rnd. tray, div. bowl, 2 spoons), 400/17	125.00
Salad set, 4 pc. (rnd. plate, flared bowl, fork, spoon), 400/75B	95.00
Salt & pepper pr., bead ft., straight side, chrome top, 400/247	16.00
Salt & pepper pr., bead ft., bulbous, chrome top, 400/96	15.00
Salt & pepper pr., bulbous w/bead stem, plastic top, 400/116	85.00
Salt & pepper, pr., indiv., 400/109	11.00
Salt & pepper, pr., ftd. bead base, 400/190	47.50

	Crystal
Salt dip, 2", 400/61	10.00
Salt dip, 2¼", 400/19	10.00
Salt spoon, 3, 400/616	11.00
Salt spoon, w/ribbed bowl, 4000	11.00
Sauce boat, 400/169	115.00
Sauce boat liner, 400/169	45.00
Saucer, after dinner, 400/77AD	6.00
Saucer, tea or coffee, 400/35 or 400/37	2.50
Set: 2 pc. hdld. cracker w/cheese compote, 400/88	45.00
Set: 2 pc. rnd. cracker plate w/indent; cheese compote, 400/145	50.00
Snack jar w/cover, bead ft., 400/139/1	550.00
Stem, 1 oz., cordial, 400/190	70.00
Stem, 4 oz., cocktail, 400/190	18.00
Stem, 5 oz., tall sherbet, 400/190	15.00
Stem, 5 oz., wine, 400/190	22.50
Stem, 6 oz., sherbet, 400/190	14.00
Stem, 10 oz., water 400/190	20.00
Stem, #3400, 1 oz., cordial	40.00
Stem, #3400, 4 oz., cocktail	18.00
Stem, #3400, 4 oz., oyster cocktail	15.00
Stem, #3400, 4 oz., wine	26.00
Stem, #3400, 5 oz., claret	58.00
Stem, #3400, 5 oz., low sherbet	11.00
Stem, #3400, 6 oz., parfait	58.00
Stem, #3400, 6 oz., sherbet/saucer champagne	18.00
Stem, #3400, 9 oz., goblet, water	20.00
Stem, #3800, low sherbet	25.00
Stem, #3800, brandy	35.00
Stem, #3800, 1 oz., cordial	45.00
Stem, #3800, 4 oz., cocktail	25.00
Stem, #3800, 4 oz., wine	27.50
Stem, #3800, 6 oz., champagne/sherbet	25.00
Stem, #3800, 9 oz., water goblet	35.00
Stem, #3800, claret	75.00
Stem, #4000, 1¼ oz., cordial	33.00
Stem, #4000, cocktail	22.00
Stem, #4000, 5 oz., wine	28.00
Stem, #4000, 6 oz., tall sherbet	22.00
Stem, #4000, 11 oz., goblet	32.00
Stem, #4000, 12 oz., tea	25.00
Strawberry set, 2 pc. (7" plate/sugar dip bowl), 400/83	50.00
Sugar, domed foot, 400/18	135.00
Sugar, 6 oz., bead hdld., 400/30	7.00
Sugar, flat, bead handle, 400/126	40.00
Sugar, indiv. bridge, 400/122	6.00
Sugar, plain ft., 400/31	6.50
Tete-a-tete 3 pc. brandy, a.d. cup, 6½" oval tray, 400/111	75.00
Tid bit server, 2 tier, cupped, 400/2701	50.00
Tid bit set, 3 pc., 400/18TB	225.00
Toast, w/cover, set, 7¾", 400/123	325.00
Tray, 5½", hdld., upturned handles, 400/42E	20.00
Tray, 5½", lemon, ctr. hdld., 400/221	35.00

	Crystal
Tray, 5¼" x 9¼", condiment, 400/148	45.00
Tray, 6½", 400/29	15.00
Tray, 6", wafer, handle bent to ctr. of dish, 400/51T	22.00
Tray, 10½", ctr. hdld. fruit, 400/68F	125.00
Tray, 11½", ctr. hdld. party, 400/68D	33.00
Tray, 13½", 2 hdld. celery, oval, 400/105	33.00
Tray, 13", relish, 5 sections, 400/102	75.00
Tray, 14", hdld., 400/113E	45.00
Tumbler, 3½ oz., cocktail, 400/18	45.00
Tumbler, 5 oz., juice, 400/18	45.00
Tumbler, 6 oz., sherbet, 400/18	45.00
Tumbler, 7 oz., old-fashioned, 400/18	45.00
Tumbler, 7 oz., parfait, 400/18	55.00
Tumbler, 9 oz., water, 400/18	45.00
Tumbler, 12 oz., tea, 400/18	50.00
Tumbler, 3 oz., ftd., cocktail, 400/19	16.00
Tumbler, 3 oz., ftd., wine, 400/19	22.00
Tumbler, 5 oz., low sherbet, 400/19	15.00
Tumbler, 5 oz., juice, 400/19	10.00
Tumbler, 7 oz., old-fashioned, 400/19	38.00
Tumbler, 10 oz., 400/19	12.00
Tumbler, 12 oz., 400/19	25.00
Tumbler, 14 oz., 400/19, tea	25.00
Tumbler, #3400, 5 oz., ft., juice	17.50
Tumbler, #3400, 9 oz., ftd.	16.00
Tumbler, #3400, 10 oz., ftd.	15.00
Tumbler, #3400, 12 oz., ftd.	17.00
Tumbler, #3800, 5 oz., juice	26.00
Tumbler, #3800, 9 oz.	26.00
Tumbler, #3800, 12 oz.	33.00
Vase, 4", bead ft., sm. neck, ball, 400/25	50.00
Vase, 5¾", bead ft., bud, 400/107	60.00
Vase, 5¾", bead ft., mini bud, 400/107	65.00
Vase, 6", flat, crimped edge, 400/287C	32.00
Vase, 6", ftd., flared rim, 400/138B	125.00
Vase, 6" diam., 400/198	300.00
Vase, 6", fan, 400/287 F	30.00
Vase, 7", ftd., bud, 400/186	250.00
Vase, 7", ftd., bud, 400/187	215.00
Vase, 7", ivy bowl, 400/74J	135.00
Vase, 7", rolled rim w/bead hdld., 400/87 R	40.00
Vase, 7", rose bowl, 400/142 K	225.00
Vase, 7¼", ftd., rose bowl, crimped top, 400/132C	495.00
Vase, 7½", ftd., rose bowl, 400/132	425.00
Vase, 8", fan, w/bead hdld., 400/87F	35.00
Vase, 8", flat, crimped edge, 400/143C	70.00
Vase, 8", fluted rim w/bead hdlds., 400/87C	27.50
Vase, 8½", bead ft., bud, 400/28C	85.00
Vase, 8½", bead ft., flared rim, 400/21	225.00
Vase, 8½", bead ft., inward rim, 400/27	225.00
Vase, 8½", hdld. (pitcher shape), 400/227	495.00
Vase, 10", bead ft., straight side, 400/22	195.00
Vase, 10", ftd., 400/193	185.00

Color: crystal, Sapphire blue, Cape Cod blue, Chartreuse, Ruby, Cranberry pink, Jasmine yellow

Canterbury, or line No. 115, was the mould blank used for several of Duncan's etched patterns. First Love is the most recognized etching on Canterbury. In order to have space for the 22 new patterns in this book I have removed most of the copies of original catalog pages that were included in previous editions. If you are a new collector and wish to see Canterbury as listed by Duncan, you will have to track down my earlier editions. I will warn you that older editions have become collectible themselves and sell at a premium price.

Canterbury is moderately priced when compared to patterns made by Cambridge, Heisey, or Fostoria. The pieces are a bit on the heavy side which bothers some collectors, but that has also meant greater survival over the years. This was a durable ware; but count on usage scratches on the flat pieces. Thin and delicate glassware does break and chip more easily than Canterbury.

That yellow-green colored Canterbury was christened Chartreuse which was also a Tiffin color name. Many of the items found in this color are Tiffin pieces manufactured from Duncan's moulds. I have now gathered several items that have the original Tiffin sticker on them that I will show in the future. Prices for this color run about 10% to 20% higher than crystal. I have not found enough Canterbury in other colors to get a feel for those prices. Opalescent items seem to be priced three to four times those for the crystal.

Duncan's light blue was called Sapphire and the opalescent blue was dubbed Cape Cod blue. The red was Ruby. Although not illustrated, you may find opalescent pieces of Canterbury in pink, called Cranberry, or yellow, called Jasmine. I keep running into Ruby pieces that are priced either very high or rather low. There does not seem to be any consensus. Time will determine whether this color is rare.

In Florida, I have noticed that Canterbury pieces are often cloudy or stained. I assume that condition results from the hard water from wells here. Be aware of this problem when buying early in the morning by flashlight when dew is on the glass! If you know of additional pieces not listed or wish to relate prices on colored wares, just drop me a postcard! The 64 ounce water pitcher and candlesticks seem to be the items that sell the fastest should you find them.

	Crystal
Ash tray, 3"	6.00
Ash tray, 3", club	8.00
Ash tray, 4½", club	10.00
Ash tray, 5"	12.00
Ash tray, 5½", club	15.00
Basket, 3" x 3" x 3¼", oval, hdld.	20.00
Basket, 3" x 4", crimped, hdld.	27.50
Basket, 3½", crimped, hdld	35.00
Basket, 3½", oval, hdld	25.00
Basket, 4½" x 4¾" x 4¾", oval, hdld	40.00
Basket, 4½" x 5" x 5", crimped, hdld.	45.00
Basket, 9¼" x 10" x 7¼"	55.00
Basket, 10" x 4¼" x 7", oval, hdld.	70.00
Basket, 10" x 4½" x 8", oval, hdld.	75.00
Basket, 11½", oval, hdld.	75.00
Bowl, 4¼" x 2", finger	9.00
Bowl, 5" x 3¼", 2 part, salad dressing	12.50
Bowl, 5" x 3¼", salad dressing	12.50
Bowl, 5½" x 1¾", one hdld., heart	9.00
Bowl, 5½" x 1¾", one hdld., square	9.00
Bowl, 5½" x 1¾", one hdld., star	10.00
Bowl, 5½" x 1¾", one hdld., fruit	7.00
Bowl, 5½" x 1¾", one hdld., round	7.00
Bowl, 5", fruit nappy	8.00
Bowl, 6" x 2", 2 hdld., round	10.00
Bowl, 6" x 2", 2 hdld., sweetmeat, star	15.00
Bowl, 6" x 3¼", 2 part, salad dressing	14.00
Bowl, 6" x 3¼", salad dressing	14.00
Bowl, 6" x 5¼" x 2¼", oval olive	10.00
Bowl, 7½" x 2¼", crimped	15.00
Bowl, 7½" x 2¼", gardenia	15.00
Bowl, 8" x 2¾", crimped	20.00
Bowl, 8" x 2½", flared	17.50
Bowl, 8½" x 4"	22.00
Bowl, 9" x 2", gardenia	25.00
Bowl, 9" x 4¼", crimped	27.50
Bowl, 9" x 6" x 3", oval	30.00
Bowl, 10" x 5", salad	30.00

	Crystal
Bowl, 10" x 8½" x 5", oval	27.50
Bowl, 10¾" x 4¾"	27.50
Bowl, 10½" x 5", crimped	30.00
Bowl, 11½" x 8¼", oval	30.00
Bowl, 12" x 2¾", gardenia	30.00
Bowl, 12" x 3½", flared	30.00
Bowl, 12" x 3¾", crimped	32.50
Bowl, 13" x 8½" x 3¼", oval, flared	35.00
Bowl, 13" x 10" x 5", crimped, oval	40.00
Bowl, 15" x 2¾", shallow salad	42.00
Candle, 3", low	12.50
Candle, 3½"	12.50
Candlestick, 6", 3-lite	30.00
Candlestick, 6"	25.00
Candlestick, 7", w/U prisms	75.00
Candy and cover, 8" x 3½", 3 hdld., 3 part	35.00
Candy, 6½", w/5" lid	32.50
Celery and relish, 10½" x 6¾" x 1¼", 2 hdld., 2 part	30.00
Celery and relish, 10½" x 6¾" x 1¼", 2 hdld., 3 part	32.50
Celery, 9" x 4" x 1¼", 2 hdld.	20.00
Cheese stand, 5½" x 3½" high	10.00
Cigarette box w/cover, 3½" x 4½"	18.00
Cigarette jar w/cover, 4"	20.00
Comport, high, 6" x 5½" high	20.00
Comport, low, 6" x 4½" high	18.00
Creamer, 2¾", 3 oz., individual	9.00
Creamer, 3¾", 7 oz.	7.50
Cup	10.00
Decanter w/stopper, 12", 32 oz.	65.00
Ice bucket or vase, 7"	40.00
Ice bucket or vase, 6"	40.00
Lamp, hurricane, w/prisms, 15"	90.00
Marmalade, 4½" x 2¾", crimped	12.00
Mayonnaise, 5" x 3¼"	15.00
Mayonnaise, 5½" x 3¼", crimped	17.50
Mayonnaise, 6" x 3¼"	17.50

	Crystal
Pitcher, 9¼", 32 oz., hdld., martini	85.00
Pitcher, 9¼", 32 oz., martini	75.00
Pitcher, 64 oz.	250.00
Plate, 6½", one hdld., fruit	6.00
Plate, 6", finger bowl liner	6.00
Plate, 7½"	9.00
Plate, 7½", 2 hdld., mayonnaise	9.00
Plate, 8½"	10.00
Plate, 11¼", dinner	27.50
Plate, 11", 2 hdld. w/ring, cracker	20.00
Plate, 11", 2 hdld., sandwich	22.00
Plate, 13½", cake, hdld.	35.00
Plate, 14", cake	25.00
Relish, 6" x 2", 2 hdld., 2 part, round	12.00
Relish, 6" x 2", 2 hdld., 2 part, star	12.00
Relish, 7" x 5¼" x 2¼", 2 hdld., 2 part, oval	15.00
Relish, 8" x 1¾", 3 hdld., 3 part	17.50
Relish, 9" x 1½", 3 hdld., 3 part	20.00
Rose bowl, 5"	20.00
Rose bowl, 6"	22.50
Salt and pepper	22.50
Sandwich tray, 12" x 5¼", center handle	40.00
Saucer	3.00
Sherbet, crimped, 4½", 2¾" high	10.00
Sherbet, crimped, 5½", 2¾" high	12.00
Stem, 3¾", 6 oz., ice cream	6.00
Stem, 4", 4½ oz., oyster cocktail	12.50
Stem, 4¼", 1 oz., cordial, #5115	28.00
Stem, 4¼", 3½ oz., cocktail	10.00
Stem, 4½", 6 oz., saucer champagne	9.00
Stem, 5", 4 oz., claret or wine	20.00
Stem, 5¼", 3 oz., cocktail, #5115	14.00
Stem, 5½", 5 oz., saucer champagne, #5115	12.00
Stem, 6", 3½ oz., wine, #5115	27.50
Stem, 6", 9 oz., water	14.00
Stem, 6¾", 5 oz., claret, #5115	27.00
Stem, 7¼", 10 oz., water, #5115	17.50
Sugar, 2½", 3 oz., individual	8.00
Sugar, 3", 7 oz.	7.50

	Crystal
Top hat, 3"	18.00
Tray, 9", individual cr/sug	10.00
Tray, 9" x 4" x 1¼", 2 part, pickle and olive	17.50
Tumbler, 2½", 5 oz., ftd., ice cream, #5115	10.00
Tumbler, 3¼", 4 oz., ftd., oyster cocktail, #5115	15.00
Tumbler, 3¾", 5 oz., flat, juice	8.00
Tumbler, 4¼", 5 oz., ftd., juice	7.50
Tumbler, 4¼", 5 oz., ftd., juice, #5115	10.00
Tumbler, 4½", 9 oz., flat, table, straight	12.00
Tumbler, 4½", 10 oz., ftd., water, #5115	12.50
Tumbler, 5½", 9 oz., ftd., luncheon goblet	12.50
Tumbler, 5¾", 12 oz., ftd., ice tea, #5115	14.00
Tumbler, 6¼", 13 oz., flat, ice tea	18.00
Tumbler, 6¼", 13 oz., ftd., ice tea	18.00
Urn, 4½" x 4½"	15.00
Vase, 3", crimped violet	15.00
Vase, 3½", clover leaf	15.00
Vase, 3½", crimped	15.00
Vase, 3½", crimped violet	15.00
Vase, 3½", oval	15.00
Vase, 4", clover leaf	17.50
Vase, 4", crimped	17.50
Vase, 4", flared rim	17.50
Vase, 4", oval	17.50
Vase, 4½" x 4¾"	15.00
Vase, 4½", clover leaf	20.00
Vase, 4½", crimped violet	17.50
Vase, 4½", oval	17.50
Vase, 5" x 5", crimped	17.50
Vase, 5", clover leaf	25.00
Vase, 5", crimped	17.50
Vase, 5½", crimped	20.00
Vase, 5½", flower arranger	27.50
Vase, 6½", clover leaf	35.00
Vase, 7", crimped	32.00
Vase, 7", flower arranger	40.00
Vase, 8½" x 6"	60.00
Vase, 12", flared	85.00

Colors: amber, Antique blue, Azalea, black, crystal, Evergreen, milk glass, Ritz blue, Ruby, Verde

Although colored Cape Cod has caught the eye of some collectors, crystal is most collected. Colored items were mostly made in the late 1960s and 1970s. You can see the colors of Cape Cod pictured in the eighth edition of this book.

One of the most difficult problems facing new collectors is identifying all the many stems and tumblers; I will try to point these out for you. In Row 2, I have placed the 1602 juice (third from left) next to the 1602 parfait so you can see the shape differences in these often confused items. The first item is a 1602 tea. In the bottom row are two flat tumblers: an old-fashioned, 7 ounce, and a double old-fashioned, 14 ounce. On the right of those is a 1602 cordial and to its left, in order are a 1602 water, 1602 claret, and 1602 wine. The sixth item in Row 1 is a 160 wine. Note the differences in the stems of the 160 and 1602 items to determine which you have. The 160 and 1602 are Imperial designations for these stemware lines.

The spouted "Aladdin" style mayonnaise with liner is shown next to the 18 ounce gravy in Row 3. You can also find that mayonnaise blank with a candle insert making a very hard to find candleholder. That hurricane shade in the top row is harder to get than the Cape Cod base it fits. Those thin shades had a tendency to shatter easily. You can still buy most of the basic pieces of Cape Cod reasonably, but for how long is anybody's guess. Better buy it now if you like it!

	Crystal
Ash tray, 4", 160/134/1	14.00
Ash tray, 5½", 160/150	17.50
Basket, 9", handled, crimped, 160/221/0	225.00
Basket, 11" tall, handled, 160/40	135.00
Bottle, bitters, 4 oz., 160/235	60.00
Bottle, cologne, w/stopper, 1601	60.00
Bottle, condiment, 6 oz., 160/224	65.00
Bottle, cordial, 18 oz., 160/256	115.00
Bottle, decanter, 26 oz., 160/244	115.00
Bottle, ketchup, 14 oz., 160/237	250.00
Bowl, 3", handled mint, 160/183	20.00
Bowl, 3", jelly, 160/33	12.00
Bowl, 4", finger, 1602	12.00
Bowl, 4½", finger, 1604½A	12.00
Bowl, 4½", handled spider, 160/180	22.50
Bowl, 4½", dessert, tab handled, 160/197	23.00
Bowl, 5", dessert, heart shape, 160/49H	22.00
Bowl, 5", flower, 1605N	25.00
Bowl, 5½", fruit, 160/23B	10.00
Bowl, 5½", handled spider, 160/181	25.00
Bowl, 5½", tab handled, soup, 160/198	18.00
Bowl, 6", fruit, 160/3F	10.00
Bowl, 6", baked apple, 160/53X	9.00
Bowl, 6", handled, round mint, 160/51F	22.00
Bowl, 6", handled heart, 160/40H	20.00
Bowl, 6", handled mint, 160/51H	22.00
Bowl, 6", handled tray, 160/51T	20.00
Bowl, 6½", handled portioned spider, 160/187	27.50
Bowl, 6½", handled spider, 160/182	32.50
Bowl, 6½", tab handled, 160/199	25.00
Bowl, 7", nappy, 160/5F	22.00
Bowl, 7½", 160/7F	22.00
Bowl, 7½", 2-handled, 160/62B	27.50
Bowl, 8¾", 160/10F	27.50
Bowl, 9", footed fruit, 160/67F	62.50
Bowl, 9½", 2 handled, 160/145B	37.50
Bowl, 9½", crimped, 160/221C	75.00
Bowl, 9½", float, 160/221F	65.00
Bowl, 10", footed, 160/137B	75.00
Bowl, 10", oval, 160/221	75.00
Bowl, 11", flanged edge, 1608X	150.00
Bowl, 11", oval, 160/124	70.00
Bowl, 11", oval divided, 160/125	80.00
Bowl, 11", round, 1608A	65.00
Bowl, 11", salad, 1608D	40.00
Bowl, 11¼", oval, 1602	75.00
Bowl, 12", 160/75B	40.00

	Crystal
Bowl, 12", oval, 160/131B	75.00
Bowl, 12", oval crimped, 160/131C	110.00
Bowl, 12", punch, 160/20B	65.00
Bowl, 13", console, 160/75L	42.50
Bowl, 15", console, 1601/0L	75.00
Butter, 5", w/cover, handled, 160/144	30.00
Butter, w/cover, ¼ lb., 160/161	45.00
Cake plate, 10", 4 toed, 160/220	100.00
Cake stand, 10½", footed, 160/67D	50.00
Cake stand, 11", 160/103D	85.00
Candleholder, twin, 160/100	70.00
Candleholder, 3", single, 160/170	17.50
Candleholder, 4", 160/81	25.00
Candleholder, 4", Aladdin style, 160/90	150.00
Candleholder, 4½", saucer, 160/175	25.00
Candleholder, 5", 160/80	20.00
Candleholder, 5", flower, 160/45B	60.00
Candleholder, 5½", flower, 160/45N	110.00
Candleholder, 6", centerpiece, 160/48BC	95.00
Candy, w/cover, 160/110	85.00
Carafe, wine, 26 oz., 160/185	195.00
Celery, 8", 160/105	30.00
Celery, 10½", 160/189	55.00
Cigarette box, 4½", 160/134	45.00
Cigarette holder, ftd., 1602	12.50
Cigarette holder, Tom & Jerry mug, 160/200	32.50
Cigarette lighter, 1602	30.00
Coaster, w/spoon rest, 160/76	10.00
Coaster, 3", square, 160/85	12.50
Coaster, 4", round, 160/78	12.50
Coaster, 4½", flat, 160/1R	9.00
Comport, 5¼", 160F	27.50
Comport, 5¾", 160X	30.00
Comport, 6", 160/45	25.00
Comport, 6", w/cover, ftd., 160/140	75.00
Comport, 7", 160/48B	35.00
Comport, 11¼", oval, 1602, 6½" tall	195.00
Creamer, 160/190	30.00
Creamer, 160/30	8.00
Creamer, ftd., 160/31	15.00
Cruet, w/stopper, 4 oz., 160/119	25.00
Cruet, w/stopper, 5 oz., 160/70	30.00
Cruet, w/stopper, 6 oz., 160/241	40.00
Cup, tea, 160/35	7.00
Cup, coffee, 160/37	7.00
Cup, bouillon, 160/250	30.00
Decanter, bourbon, 160/260	80.00

	Crystal
Decanter, rye, 160/260	80.00
Decanter w/stopper, 30 oz., 160/163	65.00
Decanter w/stopper, 24 oz., 160/212	75.00
Egg cup, 160/225	32.50
Epergne, 2 pc., plain center, 160/196	250.00
Fork, 160/701	12.00
Gravy bowl, 18 oz., 160/202	85.00
Horseradish, 5 oz. jar, 160/226	95.00
Ice bucket, 6½", 160/63	195.00
Icer, 3 pc., bowl, 2 inserts, 160/53/3	60.00
Jar, 12 oz., hdld. peanut w/lid, 160/210	75.00
Jar, 10", "Pokal," 160/133	80.00
Jar, 11", "Pokal," 160/128	85.00
Jar, 15", "Pokal," 160/132	135.00
Jar, candy w/lid, wicker hand., 5" h., 160/194	85.00
Jar, cookie, w/lid, wicker hand., 6½" h., 160/195	110.00
Jar, peanut butter w/lid, wicker hand., 4" h., 160/193	85.00
Ladle, marmalade, 160/130	10.00
Ladle, mayonnaise, 160/165	10.00
Ladle, punch	25.00
Lamp, hurricane, 2 pc., 5" base, 160/79	95.00
Lamp, hurricane, 2 pc., bowl-like base, 1604	135.00
Marmalade, 3 pc. set, 160/89/3	32.50
Marmalade, 4 pc. set, 160/89	40.00
Mayonnaise, 3 pc. set, 160/52H	37.50
Mayonnaise, 3 pc., 160/23	27.50
Mayonnaise, 12 oz., hdld., spouted, 160/205	50.00
Mug, 12 oz., handled, 160/188	50.00
Mustard, w/cover & spoon, 160/156	22.50
Nut dish, 3", hdld., 160/183	35.00
Nut dish, 4", hdld., 160/184	35.00
Pepper mill, 160/236	30.00
Pitcher, milk, 1 pt., 160/240	45.00
Pitcher, ice lipped, 40 oz., 160/19	85.00
Pitcher, martini, blown, 40 oz., 160/178	195.00
Pitcher, ice lipped, 2 qt. 160/239	95.00
Pitcher, 2 qt., 160/24	100.00
Pitcher, blown, 5 pt., 160/176	195.00
Plate, 4½" butter, 160/34	8.00
Plate, 6", cupped (liner for 160/208 salad dressing), 160/209	30.00
Plate, 6½", bread & butter, 160/1D	7.00
Plate, 7", 160/3D	8.00
Plate, 7", cupped (liner for 160/205 Mayo), 160/206	40.00
Plate, 8", center handled tray, 160/149D	40.00
Plate, 8", crescent salad, 160/12	50.00
Plate, 8" cupped (liner for gravy), 160/203	45.00
Plate, 8", salad, 160/5D	9.00
Plate, 8½", 2 handled, 160/62D	30.00
Plate, 9", 160/7D	20.00
Plate, 9½", 2 hdld., 160/62D	40.00
Plate, 10", dinner, 160/10D	37.50
Plate, 11½", 2 handled, 160/145D	40.00
Plate, 12½" bread, 160/222	70.00
Plate, 13", birthday, 72 candle holes, 160/72	365.00
Plate, 13", cupped torte, 1608V	35.00
Plate, 13", torte, 1608F	40.00
Plate, 14", cupped, 160/75V	50.00
Plate, 14", flat, 160/75D	50.00
Plate, 16", cupped, 160/20V	80.00
Plate, 17", 2 styles, 160/10D or 20D	95.00
Platter, 13½", oval, 160/124D	65.00

	Crystal
Puff Box, w/cover, 1601	50.00
Relish, 8", hdld., 2 part, 160/223	37.50
Relish, 9½", 4 pt., 160/56	35.00
Relish, 9½", oval, 3 part, 160/55	25.00
Relish, 11", 5 part, 160/102	55.00
Relish, 11¼", 3 part, oval, 1602	75.00
Salad dressing, 6 oz., hdld., spouted, 160/208	60.00
Salad set, 14" plate, 12" bowl, fork & spoon, 160/75	95.00
Salt & pepper, individual, 160/251	15.00
Salt & pepper, pr., ftd., 160/116	20.00
Salt & pepper, pr., ftd., stemmed, 160/243	40.00
Salt & pepper, pr., 160/96	15.00
Salt & pepper, pr. square, 160/109	25.00
Salt dip, 160/61	15.00
Salt spoon, 1600	8.00
Saucer, tea, 160/35	2.00
Saucer, coffee, 160/37	2.00
Server, 12", ftd. or turned over, 160/93	85.00
Spoon, 160/701	12.00
Stem, 1½ oz., cordial, 1602	10.00
Stem, 3 oz., wine, 1602	8.00
Stem, 3½ oz., cocktail, 1602	8.00
Stem, 5 oz., claret, 1602	12.00
Stem, 6 oz., low sundae, 1602	5.00
Stem, 6 oz., parfait, 1602	11.00
Stem, 6 oz., sherbet, 1600	15.00
Stem, 6 oz., tall sherbet, 1602	11.00
Stem, 9 oz., water, 1602	9.50
Stem, 10 oz., water, 1600	20.00
Stem, 11 oz., dinner goblet, 1602	10.00
Stem, 14 oz., goblet, magnum, 160	40.00
Stem, oyster cocktail, 1602	10.00
Sugar, 160/190	30.00
Sugar, 160/30	7.00
Sugar, ftd., 160/31	15.00
Toast, w/cover, 160/123	165.00
Tom & Jerry footed punch bowl, 160/200	350.00
Tray, square covered sugar & creamer, 160/25/26	150.00
Tray, 7", for creamer/sugar, 160/29	15.00
Tray, 11", pastry, center handle, 160/68D	70.00
Tumbler, 2½ oz., whiskey, 160	12.50
Tumbler, 6 oz., ftd., juice, 1602	8.00
Tumbler, 6 oz., juice, 1600	8.00
Tumbler, 7 oz., old-fashioned, 160	12.50
Tumbler, 10 oz., ftd., water, 1602	10.00
Tumbler, 10 oz., water, 160	10.00
Tumbler, 12 oz., ftd., ice tea, 1602	12.00
Tumbler, 12 oz., ftd., tea, 160	19.00
Tumbler, 12 oz., ice tea, 160	12.50
Tumbler, 14 oz., double old-fashioned, 160	30.00
Tumbler, 16 oz., 160	35.00
Vase, 6¼", ftd., 160/22	35.00
Vase, 6½", ftd., 160/110B	70.00
Vase, 7½", ftd., 160/22	40.00
Vase, 8", fan, 160/87F	225.00
Vase, 8½", flip, 160/143	50.00
Vase, 8½", ftd., 160/28	42.50
Vase, 10", cylinder, 160/192	80.00
Vase, 10½", hdld., urn, 160/186	195.00
Vase, 11", flip, 1603	175.00
Vase, 11½", ftd., 160/21	70.00

Colors: crystal, Moonlight Blue, amber, amethyst, La Rosa, Emerald green dark, Pistachio Ritz blue, milk glass

Caprice can be collected in a variety of colors that are shown on the next page. Only white and cobalt are missing from the illustration. Pistachio is that light green in the top row. Only luncheon sets, vases, bowls, and candles can be amassed in any color besides crystal, Moonlight Blue, and La Rosa (pink).

Moonlight Blue is the most sought color, but there are plenty of devotees for crystal and pink. Pink is the most difficult color to find; yet, a few are trying to put large sets together. Finding pink is difficult, but not as expensive as buying blue pieces. Let me qualify that by saying if you found a large number of pieces of pink at one time, it would be expensive; but you probably will only spot a piece or two at a time. Prices for infrequently seen colors of Caprice follow those of blue. There are few collectors searching for amber or amethyst, and those particular colored pieces are priced closer to crystal.

Scarce Caprice items are becoming the norm in recent years. Clarets, moulded, straight side, nine and twelve ounce tumblers, and footed whiskeys are rarely seen at any price. Many new collectors have never seen them let alone had the opportunity to buy them. Blue bitters bottles and covered cracker jars are buried deep in long-time collections. Many major collections have a Doulton pitcher. The small supply of those has drastically diminished; and the price shocks all but the opulent.

Alpine Caprice items are being collected by many beginners. Alpine pieces have satinized panels or bases and are found on both crystal and blue items. For a while they were avoided, but collecting tastes change as more people come into our collecting society. It is now possible to attain this finish with equipment from a craft shop. The satinized decoration on newly embellished pieces is not as smoothly done as it was originally — but it can be done! Crystal Caprice candle reflectors and punch bowls are seldom found; but there is serious money waiting for those that do. Should you desire, you can put a fairly large set of crystal together for a reasonable figure when compared to other patterns of this quality.

Be aware that the non-designed centers on all flat pieces had a tendency to be marred with use. Do not pay mint condition prices for items found that way. Check these closely. You may at some future time wish to sell your collection.

	Crystal	Blue Pink
Ash tray, 2¾", 3 ftd., shell, #213	8.00	15.00
* Ash tray, 3", #214	6.00	12.00
* Ash tray, 4", #215	8.00	16.00
* Ash tray, 5", #216	10.00	25.00
Bonbon, 6", oval, ftd., #155	20.00	42.00
Bonbon, 6", sq., 2 hdld., #154	15.00	40.00
Bonbon, 6", sq., ftd., #133	20.00	50.00
Bottle, 7 oz., bitters, #186	225.00	595.00
Bowl, 2", 4 ftd., almond #95	25.00	65.00
* Bowl, 5", 2 hdld., jelly, #151	15.00	35.00
Bowl, 5", fruit, #18	30.00	75.00
Bowl, 5", fruit, crimped, #19	30.00	90.00
Bowl, 8", 4 ftd., #49	40.00	115.00
Bowl, 8", sq., 4 ftd., #50	50.00	125.00
* Bowl, 8", 3 pt., relish, #124	20.00	45.00
Bowl, 9½", crimped, 4 ftd., #52	40.00	115.00
Bowl, 9", pickle, #102	25.00	60.00
Bowl, 10", salad, 4 ftd., #57	40.00	125.00
Bowl, 10", sq., 4 ftd., #58	35.00	115.00
Bowl, 10½", belled, 4 ftd., #54	35.00	75.00
Bowl, 10½", crimped, 4 ftd., #53	40.00	110.00
Bowl, 11", crimped, 4 ftd., #60	35.00	115.00
* Bowl, 11", 2 hdld., oval, 4 ftd., #65	40.00	115.00
Bowl, 11½", shallow, 4 ftd., #81	35.00	100.00
* Bowl, 12", 4 pt. relish, oval, #126	90.00	250.00
* Bowl, 12", relish, 3 pt., rect., #125	50.00	150.00
Bowl, 12½", belled, 4 ftd., #62	35.00	90.00
Bowl, 12½", crimped, 4 ftd., #61	35.00	100.00
Bowl, 13", cupped, salad, #80	75.00	195.00
Bowl, 13", crimped, 4 ftd., #66	40.00	125.00
Bowl, 13½", 4 ftd., shallow cupped #82	40.00	110.00
Bowl, 15", salad, shallow, #84	55.00	175.00
Bridge set:		
* Cloverleaf, 6½", #173	32.00	115.00
* Club, 6½", #170	32.00	115.00
Diamond, 6½", #171	32.00	115.00
* Heart, 6½", #169	38.00	130.00
* Spade, 6½", #172	32.00	115.00

	Crystal	Blue Pink
* Butterdish, ¼ lb., #52	235.00	
Cake plate, 13", ftd., #36	150.00	395.00
Candle reflector, #73	350.00	
Candlestick, 2½", ea., #67	15.00	32.50
Candlestick, 2-lite, keyhole, 5", #647	20.00	65.00
Candlestick, 3-lite, #74	40.00	125.00
Candlestick, 3-lite, keyhole, #638	25.00	75.00
Candlestick, 3-lite, #1338	35.00	75.00
Candlestick, 5-lite, #1577	165.00	
Candlestick, 5", ea., keyhole, #646	20.00	35.00
Candlestick, 6", 2-lite, ea., #72	40.00	95.00
Candlestick, 7", ea., w/prism, #70	25.00	75.00
Candlestick, 7½", dbl., ea., #69	195.00	650.00
Candy, 6", 3 ftd., w/cover, #165	42.50	120.00
Candy, 6", w/cover (divided), #168	55.00	150.00
Celery & relish, 8½", 3 pt., #124	20.00	45.00
Cigarette box, w/cover, 3½" x 2¼", #207	20.00	50.00
Cigarette box, w/cover, 4½" x 3½", #208	25.00	75.00
Cigarette holder, 2" x 2¼", triangular, #205	20.00	72.50
Cigarette holder, 3" x 3", triangular, #204	22.00	55.00
Coaster, 3½", #13	15.00	35.00
Comport, 6", low ftd., #130	22.00	50.00
Comport, 7", low ftd., #130	24.00	50.00
Comport, 7", tall, #136	40.00	100.00
Cracker jar & cover, #202	400.00	1,500.00
* Creamer, large, #41	13.00	30.00
* Creamer, medium, #38	11.00	22.00
* Creamer, ind., #40	12.00	27.50
Cup, #17	14.00	35.00
Decanter, w/stopper, 35 oz., #187	195.00	495.00
Finger bowl & liner, #16	40.00	110.00
Finger bowl and liner, blown, #300	45.00	125.00
Ice bucket, #201	60.00	185.00
Marmalade, w/cover, 6 oz., #89	75.00	225.00
* Mayonnaise, 6½", 3 pc. set, #129	42.00	115.00
* Mayonnaise, 8", 3 pc. set, #106	55.00	135.00
Mustard, w/cover, 2 oz., #87	60.00	175.00

*Moulds owned by Summit Art Glass; many pieces have been renamed.   42

CAPRICE

	Crystal	Blue Pink
Nut Dish, 2½", #93	22.00	55.00
Nut Dish, 2½", divided, #94	25.00	60.00
* Oil, 3 oz., w/stopper, #101	30.00	85.00
* Oil, 5 oz., w/stopper, #100	70.00	250.00
Pitcher, 32 oz., ball shape, #179	135.00	350.00
Pitcher, 80 oz., ball shape, #183	110.00	335.00
Pitcher, 90 oz., tall Doulton style, #178	750.00	3,995.00
Plate, 5½", bread & butter, #20	12.00	27.50
Plate, 6½", bread & butter, #21	11.00	24.00
Plate, 6½", hdld., lemon, #152	11.00	25.00
Plate, 7½", salad, #23	15.00	27.50
Plate, 8½", luncheon, #22	14.00	32.50
* Plate, 9½", dinner, #24	45.00	155.00
Plate, 11", cabaret, 4 ftd., #32	30.00	70.00
Plate, 11½", cabaret, #26	30.00	70.00
Plate, 14", cabaret, 4 ftd., #33	35.00	85.00
Plate, 14", 4 ftd., #28	35.00	85.00
Plate, 16", #30	40.00	125.00
Punch bowl, ftd., #498	2,750.00	
* Salad dressing, 3 pc., ftd. & hdld., 2 spoons, #112	195.00	525.00
Salt & pepper, pr., ball, #91	40.00	115.00
* Salt & pepper, pr., flat, #96	28.00	100.00
Salt & pepper, indiv., ball, pr., #90	45.00	155.00
Salt & pepper, indiv., flat, pr., #92	40.00	135.00
Salver, 13", 2 pc. (cake atop pedestal), #31	165.00	600.00
Saucer, #17	2.50	5.50
Stem, #300, blown, 1 oz., cordial	50.00	150.00
Stem, #300, blown, 2½ oz., wine	27.50	62.50
Stem, #300, blown, 3 oz., cocktail	22.00	45.00
Stem, #300, blown, 4½ oz., claret	80.00	265.00
Stem, #300, blown, 4½ oz., low oyster cocktail	20.00	50.00
Stem, #300, blown, 5 oz., parfait	95.00	225.00
Stem, #300, blown, 6 oz., low sherbet	11.00	18.00
Stem, #300, blown, 6 oz., tall sherbet	12.00	33.00
Stem, #300, blown, 9 oz., water	18.00	38.00
Stem, #301, blown, 1 oz., cordial	40.00	
Stem, #301, blown, 2½ oz., wine	27.50	
Stem, #301, blown, 3 oz., cocktail	20.00	
Stem, #301, blown, 4½ oz., claret	50.00	
Stem, #301, blown, 6 oz., sherbet	13.00	
Stem, #301, blown, 9 oz., water	17.50	
* Stem, 3 oz., wine, #6	40.00	140.00
* Stem, 3½ oz., cocktail, #3	25.00	60.00
* Stem, 4½ oz., claret, #5	80.00	265.00
Stem, 4½ oz., fruit cocktail, #7	37.50	110.00
Stem, 5 oz., low sherbet, #4	25.00	85.00
* Stem, 7 oz., tall sherbet, #2	17.50	36.00
Stem, 10 oz., water, #1	27.50	47.50
* Sugar, large, #41	12.50	25.00
* Sugar, medium, #38	10.00	22.50
* Sugar, indiv., #40	12.00	25.00
* Tray, for sugar & creamer, #37	17.50	40.00
Tray, 9" oval, #42	22.00	50.00
* Tumbler, 2 oz., flat, #188	22.00	65.00
Tumbler, 3 oz., ftd., #12	27.50	75.00
Tumbler, 5 oz., ftd., #11	20.00	50.00
Tumbler, 5 oz., flat, #180	22.00	50.00
Tumbler, #300, 2½ oz., whiskey	45.00	225.00
Tumbler, #300, 5 oz., ftd., juice	18.00	37.50
Tumbler, #300, 10 oz., ftd. water	20.00	40.00
Tumbler, #300, 12 oz., ftd. tea	20.00	40.00

	Crystal	Blue Pink
Tumbler, #301, blown, 4½ oz., low oyster cocktail	17.50	
Tumbler, #301, blown, 5 oz., juice	15.00	
Tumbler, #301, blown, 12 oz., tea	20.00	
* Tumbler, 9 oz., straight side, #14	40.00	125.00
* Tumbler, 10 oz., ftd., #10	20.00	40.00
Tumbler, 12 oz., flat, #184	53.00	53.00
Tumbler, 12 oz., ftd., #9	22.50	47.50
* Tumbler, 12 oz., straight side, #15	37.50	95.00
Tumbler, #310, 5 oz., flat, juice	25.00	75.00
Tumbler, #310, 7 oz., flat, old-fashioned	35.00	145.00
Tumbler, #310, 10 oz., flat, table	25.00	65.00
Tumbler, #310, 11 oz., flat, tall, 4¹³⁄₁₆"	25.00	80.00
Tumbler, #310, 12 oz., flat, tea	30.00	135.00
Vase, 3½", #249	70.00	195.00
Vase, 4", blown, #251, blown	70.00	195.00
Vase, 4¼", #241, ball	45.00	115.00
Vase, 4½", #237, ball	175.00	175.00
Vase, 4½", #252, blown	55.00	160.00
Vase, 4½", #337, crimped top	55.00	110.00
Vase, 4½", #344, crimped top	85.00	185.00
Vase, 4½", #244	60.00	150.00
Vase, 5", ivy bowl, #232	60.00	225.00
Vase, 5½", #245	65.00	165.00
Vase, 5½", #345, crimped top	65.00	210.00
Vase, 6", #242, ftd.	35.00	140.00
Vase, 6", blown, #254	185.00	395.00
Vase, 6", #342, crimped top	95.00	200.00
Vase, 6", #235, ftd., rose bowl	75.00	150.00
Vase, 6½", #238, ball	65.00	165.00
Vase, 6½", #338, crimped top	100.00	250.00
Vase, 7½", #246	65.00	195.00
Vase, 7½", #346, crimped top	115.00	295.00
Vase, 8", #236, ftd., rose bowl	100.00	225.00
Vase, 8½", #243	110.00	225.00
Vase, 8½", #239, ball	95.00	210.00
Vase, 8½", #339, crimped top	85.00	225.00
Vase, 8½", #343, crimped top	140.00	350.00
Vase, 9¼" #240, ball	140.00	310.00
Vase, 9½" #340, crimped top	175.00	425.00

Colors: blue, crystal, amber, red

Collectors searching for basic Caribbean dinnerware items (dinner plates, cups, and saucers) are not finding quantities enough to keep them happy. Other items are elusive enough, but when basic items are not being found, new collectors tend to avoid starting the pattern. I see fewer pieces of crystal on the market than I did a few years ago. Of course, dealers have a tendency to avoid stocking patterns that few collectors seek; and that is a double whammy for crystal Caribbean. The punch bowl, pitchers, and some of the stemware, particularly cordials, will all dent your pocketbook — if you can even find them to buy.

A combination of blue and crystal makes a stunning array. Only in the last few years have collectors started mixing color, a trend that has come about from necessity as much as anything. However, it's producing some wonderfully aesthetic settings!

Notice the amber piece here and on page 46. Amber Caribbean is rarely seen except for the cigarette jar and ash trays. That powder jar and candle are unusual. I have been unable to garner a mate for the one shown. A three-footed blue candle would be a find!

That crystal punch set with the colored handled punch cup and ladle sells for about $75.00 more than the plain crystal set priced in the listings. Red and cobalt blue handled pieces appear to be more alluring than amber! Many collectors mix the colored punch cups so that they have four of each handle with their set. This is yet another version of blending colors.

	Crystal	Blue
Ash tray, 6", 4 indent	15.00	32.50
Bowl, 3¾" x 5", folded side, hdld.	16.00	35.00
Bowl, 4½", finger	16.00	32.00
Bowl, 5", fruit nappy (takes liner), hdld.	12.00	25.00
Bowl, 5" x 7", folded side, hdld.	16.00	37.50
Bowl, 6½", soup (takes liner)	16.00	37.50
Bowl, 7", hdld.	25.00	45.00
Bowl, 7¼", ftd., hdld., grapefruit	20.00	45.00
Bowl, 8½"	27.50	70.00
Bowl, 9", salad	30.00	75.00
Bowl, 9¼", veg., flared edge	30.00	65.00
Bowl, 9¼", veg., hdld.	30.00	75.00
Bowl, 9½", epergne, flared edge	37.50	95.00
Bowl, 10", 6¼ qt., punch	90.00	475.00
Bowl, 10", 6¼ qt. punch, flared top (catalog lists as salad)	90.00	425.00
Bowl, 10¾", oval, flower, hdld.	35.00	80.00
Bowl, 12", console, flared edge	40.00	90.00
Candelabrum, 4¾", 2-lite	40.00	90.00
Candlestick, 7¼", 1-lite, w/bl. prisms	65.00	185.00
Candy dish w/cover, 4" x 7"	40.00	95.00
Cheese/cracker crumbs, 3½" h., plate 11", hdld.	40.00	85.00
Cigarette holder (stack ash tray top)	35.00	80.00
Cocktail shaker, 9", 33 oz.	90.00	225.00
Creamer	14.00	25.00
Cruet	45.00	95.00
Cup, tea	15.00	60.00
Cup, punch	8.00	22.50
Epergne, 4 pt., flower (12" bowl; 9½" bowl; 7¾" vase; 14" plate)	225.00	450.00
Ice bucket, 6½", hdld.	75.00	195.00
Ladle, punch	35.00	100.00
Mayonnaise, w/liner, 5¾", 2 pt., 2 spoons, hdld.	42.50	100.00
Mayonnaise, w/liner, 5¾", hdld., 1 spoon	35.00	80.00
Mustard, 4", w/slotted cover	35.00	65.00
Pitcher, 4¼", 9 oz., syrup	65.00	165.00
Pitcher, 4¾" 16 oz., milk	95.00	275.00
Pitcher, w/ice lip, 9", 72 oz., water	225.00	650.00
Plate, 6", hdld., fruit nappy liner	4.00	12.00

	Crystal	Blue
Plate 6¼", bread/butter	5.00	12.00
Plate, 7¼", rolled edge, soup liner	5.00	12.50
Plate, 7½", salad	10.00	20.00
Plate, 8", hdld., mayonnaise liner	6.00	14.00
Plate, 8½", luncheon	15.00	35.00
Plate, 10½", dinner	65.00	150.00
Plate, 11", hdld., cheese/cracker liner	20.00	42.50
Plate, 12", salad liner, rolled edge	22.00	55.00
Plate, 14"	25.00	75.00
Plate, 16", torte	35.00	110.00
Plate, 18", punch underliner	40.00	110.00
Relish, 6", round, 2 pt.	12.00	25.00
Relish, 9½", 4 pt., oblong	30.00	65.00
Relish, 9½", oblong	27.50	60.00
Relish, 12¾", 5 pt., rnd.	40.00	95.00
Relish, 12¾", 7 pt., rnd.	40.00	95.00
Salt dip, 2½"	11.00	25.00
Salt & pepper, 3", metal tops	32.00	95.00
Salt & pepper, 5", metal tops	37.50	125.00
Saucer	4.00	8.00
Server, 5¾", ctr. hdld.	13.00	45.00
Server, 6½", ctr. hdld.	22.00	50.00
Stem, 3", 1 oz., cordial	75.00	265.00
Stem, 3½", 3½ oz., ftd., ball stem, wine	20.00	40.00
Stem, 3⅝", 2½ oz., wine (egg cup shape)	22.50	35.00
Stem, 4", 6 oz., ftd., ball stem, champagne	14.00	27.50
Stem, 4¼", ftd., sherbet	8.00	17.50
Stem, 4¾", 3 oz., ftd., ball stem, wine	22.00	55.00
Stem, 5¾", 8 oz., ftd., ball stem	18.00	42.50
Sugar	11.00	22.00
Syrup, metal cutoff top	90.00	225.00
Tray, 6¼", hand., mint, div.	14.00	30.00
Tray, 12¾", rnd.	25.00	50.00
Tumbler, 2¼", 2 oz., shot glass	25.00	60.00
Tumbler, 3½", 5 oz., flat	20.00	45.00
Tumbler, 5¼", 11½ oz., flat	20.00	45.00
Tumbler, 5½", 8½ oz., ftd.	22.00	50.00
Tumbler, 6½", 11 oz., ftd., ice tea	27.50	60.00
Vase, 5¾", ftd., ruffled edge	22.00	55.00
Vase, 7¼", ftd., flared edge, ball	27.50	60.00
Vase, 7½", ftd., flared edge, bulbous	32.50	70.00
Vase, 7¾", flared edge, epergne	40.00	125.00
Vase, 8", ftd., straight side	40.00	85.00
Vase, 9", ftd., ruffled top	50.00	225.00
Vase, 10", ftd.	55.00	145.00

Colors: crystal, Ebony (gold encrusted)

I have included a couple of pages from a pamphlet showing Chantilly stems at the bottom of page 49. Cambridge's Chantilly is most often collected on stemware line #3625. The right side shows stem line #3625. It is nearly impossible to put numbers by each piece in the actual photographs we do, but maybe this will help in identification for those having trouble distinguishing stems or line numbers.

There is a more expansive inventory for Cambridge pieces under Rose Point in this book. Many Chantilly pieces are still unlisted here as I am only trying to expose you to the pattern itself. When pricing missing Chantilly items by using the Rose Point list, do remember that Rose Point items are presently a minimum of 30% to 50% higher due to collector demand!

	Crystal
Bowl, 7", bonbon, 2 hdld., ftd.	25.00
Bowl, 7", relish/pickle, 2 pt.	30.00
Bowl, 7", relish/pickle	32.00
Bowl, 9", celery/relish, 3 pt.	35.00
Bowl, 10", 4 ftd., flared	50.00
Bowl, 11", tab hdld.	45.00
Bowl, 11½", tab hdld. ftd.	50.00
Bowl, 12", celery/relish, 3 pt.	50.00
Bowl, 12", 4 ftd., flared	45.00
Bowl, 12", 4 ftd., oval	50.00
Bowl, 12", celery/relish, 5 pt.	55.00
Butter, w/cover, round	145.00
Butter, ¼ lb.	250.00
Candlestick, 5"	28.00
Candlestick, 6", 2-lite, "keyhole"	40.00
Candlestick, 6", 3-lite	50.00
Candy box, w/cover, ftd.	165.00
Candy box, w/cover, rnd.	85.00
Cocktail icer, 2 pc.	65.00
Comport, 5½"	35.00
Comport, 5⅜", blown	40.00
Creamer	18.00
Creamer, indiv., #3900, scalloped edge	15.00
Cup	17.50
Decanter, ftd.	195.00
Decanter, ball	225.00
Hat, small	210.00
Hat, large	295.00
Hurricane lamp, candlestick base	130.00
Hurricane lamp, keyhole base w/prisms	195.00
Ice bucket, w/chrome handle	75.00
Marmalade & cover	60.00
Mayonnaise (sherbet type bowl w/ladle)	25.00
Mayonnaise, div. w/liner & 2 ladles	65.00
Mayonnaise, w/liner & ladle	50.00
Mustard & cover	65.00
Oil, 6 oz., hdld., w/stopper	95.00
Pitcher, ball	195.00
Pitcher, Doulton	395.00
Pitcher, upright	225.00
Plate, crescent, salad	150.00
Plate, 6½", bread/butter	8.00
Plate, 8", salad	12.50
Plate, 8", tab hdld., ftd., bonbon	20.00
Plate, 10½", dinner	60.00
Plate, 12", 4 ftd., service	40.00
Plate, 13", 4 ftd.	45.00
Plate, 13½", tab hdld., cake	45.00
Plate, 14", torte	45.00
Salad dressing bottle	150.00
Salt & pepper, pr., flat	30.00
Salt & pepper, footed	35.00
Salt & pepper, handled	35.00
Saucer	4.00

	Crystal
Stem, #3600, 1 oz., cordial	60.00
Stem, #3600, 2½ oz., cocktail	26.00
Stem, #3600, 2½ oz., wine	35.00
Stem, #3600, 4½ oz., claret	45.00
Stem, #3600, 4½ oz., low oyster cocktail	18.00
Stem, #3600, 7 oz., tall sherbet	20.00
Stem, #3600, 7 oz., low sherbet	18.00
Stem, #3600, 10 oz., water	28.00
Stem, #3625, 1 oz., cordial	60.00
Stem, #3625, 3 oz., cocktail	30.00
Stem, #3625, 4½ oz., claret	45.00
Stem, #3625, 4½ oz., low oyster cocktail	20.00
Stem, #3625, 7 oz., low sherbet	18.00
Stem, #3625, 7 oz., tall sherbet	20.00
Stem, #3625, 10 oz., water	28.00
Stem, #3775, 1 oz., cordial	60.00
Stem, #3775, 2½ oz., wine	35.00
Stem, #3775, 3 oz., cocktail	28.00
Stem, #3775, 4½ oz., claret	45.00
Stem, #3775, 4½ oz., oyster cocktail	18.00
Stem, #3775, 6 oz., low sherbet	18.00
Stem, #3775, 6 oz., tall sherbet	20.00
Stem, #3779, 1 oz., cordial	75.00
Stem, #3779, 2½ oz., wine	35.00
Stem, #3779, 3 oz., cocktail	28.00
Stem, #3779, 4½ oz., claret	45.00
Stem, #3779, 4½ oz., low oyster cocktail	18.00
Stem, #3779, 6 oz., tall sherbet	20.00
Stem, #3779, 6 oz., low sherbet	18.00
Stem, #3779, 9 oz., water	28.00
Sugar	18.00
Sugar, indiv., #3900, scalloped edge	15.00
Syrup	175.00
Tumbler, #3600, 5 oz., ftd., juice	18.00
Tumbler, #3600, 12 oz., ftd., tea	25.00
Tumbler, #3625, 5 oz., ftd., juice	18.00
Tumbler, #3625, 10 oz., ftd., water	20.00
Tumbler, #3625, 12 oz., ftd., tea	26.00
Tumbler, #3775, 5 oz., ftd., juice	18.00
Tumbler, #3775, 10 oz., ftd., water	20.00
Tumbler, #3775, 12 oz., ftd., tea	24.00
Tumbler, #3779, 5 oz., ftd., juice	20.00
Tumbler, #3779, 12 oz., ftd., tea	25.00
Tumbler, 13 oz.	26.00
Vase, 5", globe	55.00
Vase, 6", high ftd., flower	50.00
Vase, 8", high ftd., flower	55.00
Vase, 9", keyhole base	60.00
Vase, 10", bud	55.00
Vase, 11", ftd., flower	95.00
Vase, 11", ped. ftd., flower	100.00
Vase, 12", keyhole base	95.00
Vase, 13", ftd., flower	150.00

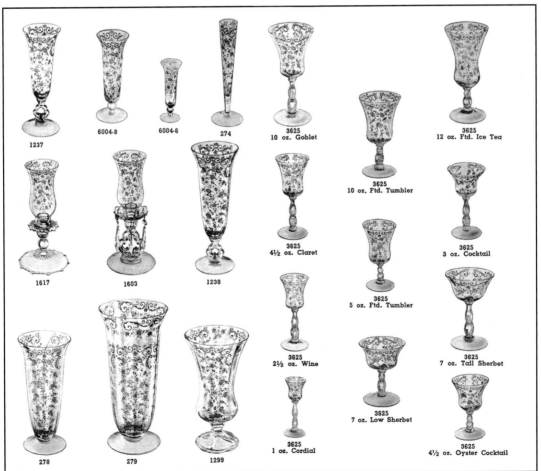

1237

6004-8

6004-6

274

3625
10 oz. Goblet

3625
12 oz. Ftd. Ice Tea

3625
10 oz. Ftd. Tumbler

1617

1603

1238

3625
4½ oz. Claret

3625
3 oz. Cocktail

3625
5 oz. Ftd. Tumbler

278

279

1299

3625
2½ oz. Wine

3625
7 oz. Tall Sherbet

3625
7 oz. Low Sherbet

3625
1 oz. Cordial

3625
4½ oz. Oyster Cocktail

Colors: Crystal, Flamingo, Moongleam, Hawthorne, Marigold

Flamingo Charter Oak pieces are showing up occasionally, but I rarely see other colors. Stemware seems to turn up in small batches. Prices have remained steady over the last few years. That usually means there has been an adequate supply for the demand. Price hikes often signal there is not enough being found to supply all the collectors who want it.

One problem for collectors now is that more people recognize this as a Heisey pattern, possibly because of its inclusion in my book, and mistakes in pricing are not as easily found! Many pieces are unmarked, however, and bargains can still be uncovered. Those acorns are the hallmark of this pattern. Plantation with its pineapple stems and Charter Oak with acorn stems are hard to miss.

Unfortunately, I did not find that clever "Acorn" #130, one lite candleholder to photograph for my *Glass Candlesticks of the Depression Era* book! However, I did find one for the *Pattern Identification II* book. The base is an oak leaf with stem curled up and an acorn for the candle cup! Strictly speaking, this is not considered to be Charter Oak pattern per se; but a number of Charter Oak collectors try to obtain these to go with their sets. Heisey designed a number of candles to "blend" (their words) with numerous patterns. This candle was made in the same time frame of Charter Oak and mostly in the same colors!

I have only exhibited Flamingo (pink) over the years since that is what I have been able to borrow, but there are several other colors of Charter Oak that can be collected. I am fond of the Moongleam. It's worth a trip to a Heisey show to see these patterns displayed.

Yeoman cups and saucers are often used with this set since there were no cups and saucers made. A Yeoman set is pictured here, but not priced in the Charter Oak listing. I mention that since several readers have wanted to know why I did not price the cup and saucer in my listings. These are priced under Yeoman.

	Crystal	Flamingo	Moongleam	Hawthorne	Marigold
Bowl, 11", floral, #116 (oak leaf)	30.00	45.00	47.50	75.00	
Bowl, finger, #3362	10.00	17.50	20.00		
Candleholder, 1-lite, #130, "Acorn"	100.00	125.00	135.00		
Candlestick, 3", #116 (oak leaf)	25.00	35.00	45.00	125.00	
Candlestick, 5", 3-lite, #129, "Tricorn"		90.00	110.00	140.00	150.00
Comport, 6", low ft., #3362	45.00	55.00	60.00	80.00	100.00
Comport, 7", ftd., #3362	50.00	65.00	70.00	160.00	175.00
Lamp, #4262 (blown comport/water filled to magnify design & stabilize lamp)	400.00	700.00	850.00		

	Crystal	Flamingo	Moongleam	Hawthorne	Marigold
Pitcher, flat, #3362		160.00	180.00		
Plate, 6", salad, #1246 (Acorn & Leaves)	5.00	10.00	12.50	20.00	
Plate, 7", luncheon/salad, #1246 (Acorn & Leaves)	8.00	12.00	17.50	22.50	
Plate, 8", luncheon, #1246 (Acorn & Leaves)	10.00	15.00	20.00	25.00	
Plate, 10½", dinner, #1246 (Acorn & Leaves)	30.00	45.00	55.00	70.00	
Stem, 3 oz., cocktail, #3362	10.00	25.00	25.00	45.00	40.00
Stem, 3½ oz., low ft., oyster cocktail, #3362	8.00	20.00	20.00	40.00	35.00
Stem, 4½ oz., parfait, #3362	15.00	25.00	35.00	60.00	50.00
Stem, 6 oz., saucer champagne, #3362	10.00	15.00	20.00	50.00	40.00
Stem, 6 oz., sherbet, low ft. #3362	10.00	15.00	22.00	50.00	40.00
Stem, 8 oz., goblet, high ft., #3362	20.00	35.00	35.00	95.00	60.00
Stem, 8 oz., luncheon goblet, low ft., #3362	20.00	40.00	40.00	95.00	60.00
Tumbler, 10 oz., flat, #3362	10.00	20.00	25.00	35.00	30.00
Tumbler, 12 oz., flat, #3362	12.50	20.00	25.00	40.00	35.00

Colors: crystal

Cherokee Rose stemware line #17399 is the tear drop style, while the #17403 stem is represented by the cordial in the front row below. Should you find a Cherokee Rose cup or saucer, please let me know.

	Crystal
Bowl, 5", finger.	30.00
Bowl, 6", fruit or nut	28.00
Bowl, 7", salad	45.00
Bowl, 10", deep salad	75.00
Bowl, 10½", celery, oblong	50.00
Bowl, 12", crimped	60.00
Bowl, 12½", centerpiece, flared	65.00
Bowl, 13", centerpiece	75.00
Cake plate, 12½", center hdld.	50.00
Candlesticks, pr., double branch	110.00
Comport, 6"	50.00
Creamer	22.00
Icer	110.00
Mayonnaise, liner and ladle	65.00
Pitcher	395.00
Plate, 6", sherbet	8.00
Plate, 8", luncheon	15.00
Plate, 13½", turned-up edge, lily	45.00
Plate, 14", sandwich	45.00
Relish, 6½", 3 pt.	30.00
Relish, 12½", 3 pt.	55.00
Shaker, pr.	75.00

	Crystal
Stem, 1 oz., cordial	55.00
Stem, 2 oz., sherry	35.00
Stem, 3½ oz., cocktail	20.00
Stem, 3½ oz., wine	35.00
Stem, 4 oz., claret	50.00
Stem, 4½ oz., parfait	50.00
Stem, 5½ oz., sherbet/champagne	20.00
Stem, 9 oz., water	25.00
Sugar	22.00
Table bell	75.00
Tumbler, 4½ oz., oyster cocktail	24.00
Tumbler, 5 oz., ftd., juice	24.00
Tumbler, 8 oz., ftd., water	25.00
Tumbler, 10½ oz., ftd., ice tea	38.00
Vase, 6", bud	25.00
Vase, 8", bud	35.00
Vase, 8½", tear drop	85.00
Vase, 9¼", tub	95.00
Vase, 10", bud	45.00
Vase, 11", bud	50.00
Vase, 11", urn	110.00
Vase, 12", flared	135.00

Colors: crystal, Sahara yellow, Moongleam green, Flamingo pink, and Alexandrite orchid

Heisey Chintz is found in two forms. Pieces pictured below are Chintz. Pieces with encircled flowers are pictured at the bottom of page 54 and are dubbed "formal" Chintz. These patterns are similar and mix well together. Were you to set a table mixing the patterns, I doubt that anyone would realize that there were differences. I have never seen any tumblers or stemware in "formal" Chintz. At this stage of the game, I doubt that they were made. I like the detailed design of "formal" Chintz better than the Chintz itself, but that is only a personal choice. I would mix them; but for clarity, I show them separate.

Chintz salt and pepper shakers have been reported by several long-time collectors. Some items slip by my listings until someone writes. If you have pieces that are not in any pattern's listing, please let me know!

Sahara is the color most collected, but a few search for crystal. Alexandrite Chintz is quite rare and very striking when displayed in quantity. There is so little of that color that putting a set together would be an extreme challenge. However, someone might still run into a large set as happened a few years ago.

Do not confuse this pattern with Fostoria's or Tiffin's Chintz; and recognize that you must also specify the company name when you ask for a pattern named Chintz. It was a popular designation that was used by many glass companies for their wares.

	Crystal	Sahara
Bowl, cream soup	18.00	35.00
Bowl, finger, #4107	10.00	20.00
Bowl, 5½", ftd., preserve, hdld.	15.00	30.00
Bowl, 6", ftd., mint	20.00	32.00
Bowl, 6", ftd., 2 hdld., jelly	17.00	35.00
Bowl, 7", triplex relish	20.00	40.00
Bowl, 7½", Nasturtium	20.00	40.00
Bowl, 8½", ftd., 2 hdld., floral	35.00	70.00
Bowl, 11", dolphin ft., floral	45.00	110.00
Bowl, 13", 2 pt., pickle & olive	15.00	35.00
Comport, 7", oval	40.00	85.00
Creamer, 3 dolphin ft.	20.00	45.00
Creamer, individual	12.00	30.00
Cup	15.00	25.00
Grapefruit, ftd., #3389, Duquesne	30.00	60.00
Ice bucket, ftd.	85.00	135.00
Mayonnaise, 5½", dolphin ft.	35.00	65.00

	Crystal	Sahara
Oil, 4 oz.	60.00	135.00
Pitcher, 3 pint, dolphin ft.	200.00	300.00
Plate, 6", square, bread	6.00	15.00
Plate, 7", square, salad	8.00	18.00
Plate, 8", square, luncheon	10.00	22.00
Plate, 10½", square, dinner	40.00	85.00
Plate, 12", two hdld.	25.00	47.50
Plate, 13", hors d' oeuvre, two hdld.	30.00	65.00
Platter, 14", oval	35.00	85.00
Salt and pepper, pr.	40.00	85.00
Saucer	3.00	5.00
Stem, #3389, Duquesne, 1 oz., cordial	115.00	250.00
Stem, #3389, 2½ oz., wine	25.00	50.00
Stem, #3389, 3 oz., cocktail	17.50	35.00
Stem, #3389, 4 oz., claret	25.00	50.00
Stem, #3389, 4 oz., oyster cocktail	12.50	25.00
Stem, #3389, 5 oz., parfait	17.50	35.00
Stem, #3389, 5 oz., saucer champagne	12.50	25.00
Stem, #3389, 5 oz., sherbet	10.00	17.50
Stem, #3389, 9 oz., water	17.50	35.00
Sugar, 3 dolphin ft.	20.00	45.00
Sugar, individual	12.00	30.00
Tray, 10", celery	15.00	30.00
Tray, 12", sq., ctr. hdld., sandwich	35.00	65.00
Tray, 13", celery	18.00	45.00
Tumbler, #3389, 5 oz., ftd., juice	12.00	22.00
Tumbler, #3389, 8 oz., soda	13.00	24.00
Tumbler, #3389, 10 oz., ftd., water	14.00	27.50
Tumbler, #3389, 12 oz., iced tea	16.00	33.00
Vase, 9", dolphin ft.	95.00	185.00

Colors: crystal, pink

One of the things that keep authors busy is documenting patterns for which there are incomplete catalog listings. Classic has newly discovered pieces added for each book. I have been unable to find a saucer for my lone cup shown at the bottom of this page, but I am sure one will turn up eventually. I prefer the pink, but only stemmed beverage items are surfacing in that color. Tiffin pitchers (one pictured in pink) came with and without a lid. The one here has the top curved in so it will not take a lid. Remember, the Tiffin pitcher lids have no pattern etched on them.

Note the crystal pitcher at the bottom of the next page which is a different style, but holds approximately 60 ounces. I have priced both styles in the same listing. As with all glass dinner plates with no pattern in the center, you need to check for marring and scratching from use. Of course, finding any dinner plate seventy or eighty years after its manufacture is a problem. I, personally, have found few serving pieces save for that two-handled bowl. As one lady in her nineties explained to me recently, "Everybody bought stems to go with their china. No one wanted to drink coffee or serve on glass back then!" Some research done for the *Pattern Identification II* book verified that statement by calling attention to the fact that Fostoria mounted a big campaign to convince people that glass was just as elegant to serve from as china!

Pink Classic stems are found on the #17024 line that is also found with Tiffin's Flanders pattern. Crystal stemmed items seem to surface on the #14185 line. There are some size discrepancies within these two stemware lines. We have measured both colors and noted the incongruities in these price listings.

	Crystal	Pink
Bowl, 2 hdld., 8" x 9¼"	125.00	
Comport, 6" wide, 3¼" tall	70.00	
Creamer, flat	35.00	75.00
Creamer,. ftd.	35.00	
Cup	60.00	
Finger bowl, ftd.	20.00	40.00
Mayonnaise, ftd.	65.00	

	Crystal	Pink
Pitcher, 61 oz.	275.00	495.00
Pitcher, 61 oz., w/cover	350.00	595.00
Plate, 6⅜", champagne liner	10.00	
Plate, 8"	12.50	20.00
Plate, 10", dinner	100.00	
Saucer	10.00	
Sherbet, 3⅛", 6½ oz., short	17.50	35.00
Stem, 3⅞", 1 oz., cordial	55.00	
Stem, 4¹⁵⁄₁₆", 3 oz., wine	32.50	55.00
Stem, 4⅞", 3¾ oz., cocktail	40.00	
Stem, 4⅞", 4 oz., cocktail	27.50	
Stem, 6½", 5 oz., parfait	35.00	65.00
Stem, 6", 7½ oz., saucer champagne	22.50	40.00
Stem, 7¼", 9 oz., water	30.00	55.00
Sugar, flat	35.00	75.00
Sugar, ftd.	35.00	
Tumbler, 3½", 5 oz., ftd., juice	17.50	
Tumbler, 4½", 8½ oz., ftd., water	20.00	45.00
Tumbler, 4⅛", 10½ oz., flat, water	25.00	
Tumbler, 5⁹⁄₁₆", 14 oz., ftd., tea	30.00	
Tumbler, 6", 13 oz., ftd., iced tea		55.00
Tumbler, 6¹⁄₁₆", 14 oz., ftd., iced tea	30.00	
Tumbler, 6¼", 6½ oz., ftd., Pilsner	32.50	
Vase, bud, 6½"	27.50	
Vase, bud, 10½"	42.50	

Colors: amber, Willow blue, crystal, Ebony, Emerald green light, Gold Krystol, Peach Blo

Cleo prices for both Peach Blo (pink) and Willow blue items continue to surge. Recently, some collectors of blue have broken up their sets and made a tidy profit. Green Cleo has seen little activity of late. It appears to be sitting in dealer inventories; why is a mystery; but it would only take a few collectors to change that. Maybe those green pieces chosen for the cover will light a spark! Cleo can be collected in large sets of pink or green, but not all pieces were made in the other colors.

I have a knack for spotting rare pieces in Cleo but they always seem to be amber rather than colors that excite collectors. Be sure to note the blue gravy and liner on the bottom of the next page. A grateful collector in Michigan is giving it a new home.

A pink Cleo grill plate is pictured on the bottom of page 59. Grill plates are rather uncommon in all Elegant patterns unlike the ubiquitous ones in Depression glass patterns. Cambridge and Fostoria made a few grill plates.

The normally found icer in Cleo is shown below in green. Note the crystal one on the bottom of page 59 that looks more like a Fostoria grapefruit.

	Blue	Pink Green Yellow Amber		Blue	Pink Green Yellow Amber
Almond, 2½", individual	110.00	75.00	Bowl, 6½", 2 hdld., bonbon,		
Basket, 7", 2 hdld. (upturned			Decagon	35.00	22.00
sides), Decagon	45.00	25.00	Bowl, 6½", cranberry	65.00	40.00
Basket, 11", 2 hdld. (upturned			Bowl, 7½", tab hdld., soup	55.00	35.00
sides), Decagon	75.00	45.00	Bowl, 8", miniature console		165.00
Bouillon cup, w/saucer, 2 hdld.,			Bowl, 8½"	75.00	40.00
Decagon	95.00	55.00	Bowl, 8½" 2 hdld., Decagon	85.00	40.00
Bowl, 2 pt., relish	40.00	22.00	Bowl, 9", covered vegetable		225.00
Bowl, 5½", fruit	40.00	25.00	Bowl, 9½", oval veg., Decagon	145.00	60.00
Bowl, 5½" 2 hdld., bonbon,			Bowl, 9", pickle, Decagon	60.00	45.00
Decagon	40.00	20.00	Bowl, 10", 2 hdld., Decagon	75.00	50.00
Bowl, 6", 4 ft., comport	60.00	35.00	Bowl, 11", oval	125.00	75.00
Bowl, 6", cereal, Decagon	60.00	35.00	Bowl, 11½", oval	125.00	75.00

CLEO

	Blue	Pink Green Yellow Amber
Bowl, 12", console	140.00	60.00
Bowl, 15½", oval, Decagon		225.00
Bowl, cream soup w/saucer, 2 hdld., Decagon	85.00	45.00
Bowl, finger w/liner, #3077	75.00	45.00
Bowl, finger w/liner, #3115	75.00	45.00
Candlestick, 1-lite, 2 styles	40.00	30.00
Candlestick, 2-lite	110.00	65.00
Candlestick, 3-lite	150.00	85.00
Candy box w/lid		185.00
Candy & cover, tall		195.00
Comport, 7", tall, #3115	110.00	75.00
Creamer, Decagon	35.00	25.00
Creamer, ewer style, 6"	195.00	150.00
Creamer, ftd.	40.00	22.00
Cup, Decagon	30.00	15.00
Decanter, w/stopper		295.00
Gravy boat, w/liner plate, Decagon	450.00	300.00
Ice pail	200.00	95.00
Ice tub	175.00	125.00
Mayonnaise, w/liner and ladle, Decagon	145.00	90.00
Mayonnaise, ftd.	75.00	45.00
Oil, 6 oz., w/stopper, Decagon		145.00
Pitcher, 3½ pt., #38		225.00
Pitcher, w/cover, 22 oz.		250.00
Pitcher, w/cover, 60 oz., #804		395.00
Pitcher, w/cover, 62 oz., #955		395.00
Pitcher, w/cover, 63 oz., #3077	895.00	425.00
Pitcher, w/cover, 68 oz., #937		395.00
Plate, 7"	28.00	18.00
Plate, 7", 2 hdld., Decagon	30.00	20.00
Plate, 8½", luncheon, Decagon	40.00	20.00
Plate, 9½", dinner, Decagon	110.00	75.00
Plate, 9½", grill		100.00
Plate, 11", 2 hdld., Decagon	120.00	40.00

	Blue	Pink Green Yellow Amber
Platter, 12"	195.00	125.00
Platter, 15"	325.00	225.00
Platter, w/cover, oval (toast)		400.00
Platter, asparagus, indented, w/sauce & spoon		395.00
Salt dip, 1½"	145.00	95.00
Saucer, Decagon	8.00	5.00
Server, 12", ctr. hand.	65.00	45.00
Stem, #3077, 1 oz., cordial	225.00	195.00
Stem, #3077, 2½ oz., cocktail	55.00	35.00
Stem, #3077, 3½ oz., wine	95.00	70.00
Stem, #3077, 6 oz., low sherbet	35.00	20.00
Stem, #3077, 6 oz., tall sherbet	45.00	25.00
Stem, #3115, 9 oz.		30.00
Stem, #3115, 3½ oz., cocktail		25.00
Stem, #3115, 6 oz., fruit		16.00
Stem, #3115, 6 oz., low sherbet		16.00
Stem, #3115, 6 oz., tall sherbet		18.00
Stem, #3115, 9 oz., water		27.50
Sugar cube tray		185.00
Sugar, Decagon	35.00	25.00
Sugar, ftd.	40.00	22.00
Sugar sifter, ftd., 6¾"	750.00	325.00
Syrup pitcher, drip cut		195.00
Syrup pitcher, glass lid		250.00
Toast & cover, round		425.00
Tobacco humidor		500.00
Tray, 12", handled serving		155.00
Tray, 12", oval service Decagon	225.00	145.00
Tray, creamer & sugar, oval		50.00
Tumbler, #3077, 2½ oz., ftd.	125.00	65.00
Tumbler, #3077, 5 oz., ftd.	60.00	20.00
Tumbler, #3077, 8 oz., ftd.	60.00	25.00
Tumbler, #3077, 10 oz., ftd.	65.00	27.50
Tumbler, #3022, 12 oz., ftd.	95.00	35.00
Tumbler, #3115, 2½ oz., ftd.		55.00
Tumbler, #3115, 5 oz., ftd.		25.00
Tumbler, #3115, 8 oz., ftd.		25.00
Tumbler, #3115, 10 oz., ftd.		37.50
Tumbler, #3115, 12 oz., ftd.		35.00
Tumbler, 12 oz., flat		65.00
Vase, 5½"		95.00
Vase, 9½"		155.00
Vase, 11"		195.00
Wafer tray		250.00

Colors: crystal; some yellow, blue, green, white, amber, red in 1980s as Maypole

Fostoria's Colony developed from an earlier Fostoria pattern called Queen Ann. A few Colony pieces were made as late as 1983. Colored pieces were christened Maypole in the 1980s by the company. The candlesticks and oval bowl pictured on page 62 were issued under that name. Red vases, candlesticks, and bowls being found were produced by Viking for Fostoria in the early 1980s. Dalzell Viking made red for Lancaster Colony who now owns the Fostoria name. Dalzell Viking went out of business in 1999.

The thin, plain bowl with a Colony patterned foot (sold to go with this pattern) was called Colonial Dame. You might even find these stems with colored bases.

Colony prices have been rather steady with few price adjustments since the last book. Some pieces you may have trouble locating include finger bowls, cream soups, and cigarette boxes. The supply of pitchers is adequate for now. All the flat pieces with plain centers need to be checked closely for wear, but that is always true for any pattern.

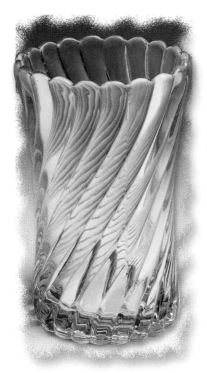

	Crystal
Ash tray, 2⅞", sq.	8.00
Ash tray, 3", round	7.00
Ash tray, 3½", sq.	12.00
Ash tray, 4½", round	14.00
Ash tray, 6", round	17.50
Bowl, 2¾" ftd., almond	15.00
Bowl, 4½", rnd.	7.00
Bowl, 4¾", finger	55.00
Bowl, 4¾", hdld.	8.00
Bowl, 5", bonbon	9.00
Bowl, 5", cream soup	50.00
Bowl, 5", hdld.	11.00
Bowl, 5½", sq.	15.00
Bowl, 5¾", high ft.	16.00
Bowl, 5", rnd.	12.00
Bowl, 6", rose	25.00
Bowl, 7", bonbon, 3 ftd.	12.00
Bowl, 7", olive, oblong	12.00
Bowl, 7¾", salad	22.50
Bowl, 8", cupped	35.00
Bowl, 8", hdld.	35.00
Bowl, 9", rolled console	35.00
Bowl, 9½", pickle	16.00
Bowl, 9¾", salad	37.50
Bowl, 10", fruit	35.00

	Crystal
Bowl, 10½", low ft.	75.00
Bowl, 10½", high ft.	95.00
Bowl, 10½", oval	44.00
Bowl, 10½", oval, 2 part	35.00
Bowl, 11", oval, ftd.	40.00
Bowl, 11", flared	40.00
Bowl, 11½", celery	30.00
Bowl, 13", console	35.00
Bowl, 13¼", punch, ftd.	375.00
Bowl, 14", fruit	45.00
Butter dish, ¼ lb.	40.00
Candlestick, 3½"	15.00
Candlestick, 6½", double	30.00
Candlestick, 7"	30.00
Candlestick, 7½", w/8 prisms	75.00
Candlestick, 9"	30.00
Candlestick, 9¾", w/prisms	85.00
Candlestick, 14½", w/10 prisms	175.00
Candy, w/cover, 6½"	45.00
Candy, w/cover, ftd., ½ lb.	75.00
Cheese & cracker	50.00
Cigarette box	45.00
Comport, 4"	15.00
Comport, cover, 6½"	45.00
Creamer, 3¼", indiv.	12.50
Creamer, 3¾"	8.00
Cup, 6 oz., ftd.	7.50
Cup, punch	12.50
Ice bucket	75.00
Ice bucket, plain edge	165.00

	Crystal		Crystal
Lamp, electric	175.00	Salt & pepper, pr., 3⅝"	28.00
Mayonnaise, 3 pc.	35.00	Saucer	2.00
Oil w/stopper, 4½ oz.	37.50	Stem, 3⅜", 4 oz., oyster cocktail	12.00
Pitcher, 16 oz., milk	70.00	Stem, 3⅝", 5 oz., sherbet	11.00
Pitcher, 48 oz., ice lip	210.00	Stem, 4", 3½ oz., cocktail	12.00
Pitcher, 2 qt., ice lip	115.00	Stem, 4¼", 3¼ oz., wine	25.00
Plate, ctr. hdld., sandwich	30.00	Stem, 5¼", 9 oz., goblet	17.00
Plate, 6", bread & butter	7.00	Sugar, 2¾", indiv.	12.50
Plate, 6½", lemon, hdld.	12.00	Sugar, 3½"	8.00
Plate, 7", salad	10.00	Tray for indiv. sugar/cream	12.00
Plate, 8", luncheon	12.00	Tumbler, 3⅝", 5 oz., juice	22.00
Plate, 9", dinner	25.00	Tumbler, 3⅞", 9 oz., water	16.00
Plate, 10", hdld., cake	22.00	Tumbler, 4⅞", 12 oz., tea	30.00
Plate, 12", ftd., salver	65.00	Tumbler, 4½", 5 oz., ftd.	18.00
Plate, 13", torte	30.00	Tumbler, 5¾", 12 oz., ftd.	22.00
Plate, 15", torte	65.00	Vase, 6", bud, flared	15.00
Plate, 18", torte	110.00	Vase, 7", cupped	40.00
Platter, 12"	50.00	Vase, 7½", flared	65.00
Relish, 10½", hdld., 3 part	25.00	Vase, 9", cornucopia	70.00
Salt, 2½" indiv.	15.00	Vase, 12", straight	195.00

Colors: crystal, Zircon/Limelight, Sahara, and rare in amber

Crystolite is one of the most acknowledged Heisey patterns since most pieces are marked with the well-known H inside a diamond. That easily found mark means you will seldom find a bargain piece of Crystolite in today's market.

The listing points out the hard to find items by their prices. Non-scratched dinner plates, 5" comport, 6" basket, rye bottle, cocktail shaker, and pressed tumblers have always been difficult to locate. Many collectors find that the punch set is a practical piece to use and display. You might need to workout before picking it up filled. That 20" punch liner is harder to find than the punch bowl!

	Crystal
Ash tray, 3½", square	6.00
Ash tray, 4½", square	10.00
Ash tray, 5", w/book match holder	45.00
Ash tray (coaster), 4", rnd.	8.00
Basket, 6", hdld.	550.00
Bonbon, 7", shell	22.00
Bonbon, 7½", 2 hdld.	15.00
Bottle, 1 qt., rye, #107 stopper	300.00
Bottle, 4 oz., bitters, w/short tube	175.00
Bottle, 4 oz., cologne, w/#108 stopper	75.00
w/drip stop	150.00
Bottle, syrup, w/drip & cut top	135.00
Bowl, 7½ quart, punch	120.00
Bowl, 2", indiv. swan nut (or ash tray)	20.00
Bowl, 3", indiv. nut, hdld.	20.00
Bowl, 4½", dessert (or nappy)	20.00
Bowl, 5", preserve	20.00
Bowl, 5", 1000 island dressing, ruffled top	30.00
Bowl, 5½", dessert	14.00
Bowl, 6", oval jelly, 4 ft.	22.00
Bowl, 6", preserve, 2 hdld.	20.00
Bowl, 7", shell praline	35.00
Bowl, 8", dessert (sauce)	30.00
Bowl, 8", 2 pt. conserve, hdld.	55.00
Bowl, 9", leaf pickle	30.00

	Crystal
Bowl, 10", salad, rnd.	50.00
Bowl, 11", w/attached mayonnaise (chip 'n dip)	225.00
Bowl, 12", gardenia, shallow	65.00
Bowl, 13", oval floral, deep	60.00
Candle block, 1-lite, sq.	20.00
Candle block, 1-lite, swirl	20.00
Candlestick, 1-lite, ftd.	25.00
Candlestick, 1-lite, w/#4233, 5", vase	35.00
Candlestick, 2-lite	35.00
Candlestick, 2-lite, bobeche & 10 "D" prisms	65.00
Candlestick sans vase, 3-lite	45.00
Candlestick, w/#4233, 5", vase, 3-lite	55.00
Candy, 5½", shell and cover	55.00
Candy box, w/cover, 7", 3 part	70.00
Candy box, w/cover, 7"	60.00
Cheese, 5½", ftd.	27.00
Cigarette box, w/cover, 4"	35.00
Cigarette box, w/cover, 4½"	40.00
Cigarette holder, ftd.	35.00
Cigarette holder, oval	25.00
Cigarette holder, rnd.	25.00
Cigarette lighter	30.00
Coaster, 4"	12.00
Cocktail shaker, 1 qt. w/#1 strainer; #86 stopper	325.00
Comport, 5", ftd., deep, #5003, blown rare	300.00

CRYSTOLITE

	Crystal
Creamer, indiv.	20.00
Creamer, reg.	30.00
Creamer, round	40.00
Cup	22.00
Cup, punch or custard	9.00
Hurricane block, 1-lite, sq.	40.00
Hurricane block, w/#4061, 10" plain globe, 1-lite, sq.	100.00
Ice tub, w/silver plate handle	120.00
Jar, covered cherry	110.00
Jam jar, w/cover	70.00
Ladle, glass, punch	35.00
Ladle, plastic	10.00
Mayonnaise, 5½", shell, 3 ft.	35.00
Mayonnaise, 6", oval, hdld.	40.00
Mayonnaise ladle	12.00
Mustard & cover	55.00
Oil bottle, 3 oz.	45.00
Oil bottle, w/stopper, 2 oz.	35.00
Oval creamer, sugar, w/tray, set	70.00
Pitcher, ½ gallon, ice, blown	140.00
Pitcher, 2 quart swan, ice lip	700.00
Plate, 7", salad	15.00
Plate, 7", shell	32.00
Plate, 7", underliner for 1000 island dressing bowl	20.00
Plate, 7½", coupe	40.00
Plate, 8", oval, mayonnaise liner	20.00
Plate, 8½", salad	20.00
Plate, 10½", dinner	100.00
Plate, 11", ftd., cake salver	350.00
Plate, 11", torte	40.00
Plate, 12", sand.	45.00
Plate, 13", shell torte	100.00

	Crystal
Plate, 14", sand.	55.00
Plate, 14", torte	50.00
Plate, 20", buffet or punch liner	125.00
Puff box, w/cover, 4¾"	75.00
Salad dressing set, 3 pc.	38.00
Salt & pepper, pr.	45.00
Saucer	6.00
Stem, 1 oz., cordial, wide optic, blown, #5003	130.00
Stem, 3½ oz., cocktail, w.o., blown, #5003	28.00
Stem, 3½ oz., claret, w.o., blown, #5003	38.00
Stem, 3½ oz., oyster cocktail, w.o. blown, #5003	28.00
Stem, 6 oz., sherbet/saucer champagne, #5003	18.00
Stem, 10 oz., water, #1503, pressed	500.00
Stem, 10 oz., w.o., blown, #5003	35.00
Sugar, indiv.	20.00
Sugar, reg.	30.00
Sugar, round	40.00
Syrup pitcher, drip cut	135.00
Tray, 5½", oval, liner indiv. creamer/sugar set	40.00
Tray, 9", 4 pt., leaf relish	40.00
Tray, 10", 5 pt., rnd. relish	45.00
Tray, 12", 3 pt., relish, oval	35.00
Tray, 12", rect., celery	38.00
Tray, 12", rect., celery/olive	35.00
Tumbler, 5 oz., ftd., juice, w.o., blown, #5003	38.00
Tumbler, 8 oz., pressed, #5003	60.00
Tumbler, 10 oz., pressed	70.00
Tumbler, 10 oz., iced tea, w.o., blown, #5003	40.00
Tumbler, 12 oz., ftd., iced tea, w.o., blown, #5003	38.00
Urn, 7", flower	75.00
Vase, 3", short stem	45.00
Vase, 6", ftd.	35.00
Vase, 12"	225.00

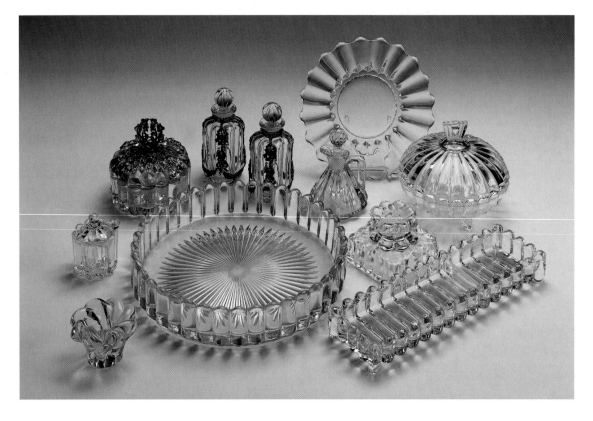

Colors: crystal, crystal w/gold encrusting

Daffodil is a later Cambridge pattern that is beginning to be noticed by new collectors who have difficulty starting with more expensive glassware such as Rose Point. It is being introduced here, but I will be transferring it to my *Collectible Glassware from the 40s, 50s, and 60s* book. I bought only enough to photograph. Do notice the two styles of mayonnaise dishes shown.

	Crystal
Basket, 6", 2 hdld. low ft. #55	35.00
Bonbon, #1181	30.00
Bonbon, 5¼", 2 hdld., #3400/1180	35.00
Bowl, 11" oval, tuck hdld. #384	75.00
Bowl, 12" belled #430	85.00
Candle, 2 lite, arch #3900/72	65.00
Candlestick, 3½" #628	50.00
Candy Box & cover, cut hexagon knob #306	135.00
Celery, 11" #248	65.00
Comport, 5½" Ftd. #533	45.00
Comport, 6½", 2 hdld. low ftd. #54	55.00
Comport, 6" tall, pulled stem #532	65.00
Creamer #254	25.00
Creamer, indiv. #253	30.00
Cup #11770	25.00
Jug, #3400/140	225.00
Jug, 76 oz #3400/141	250.00
Mayonnaise, 3 pc. ftd. w ladle & liner plate #533	95.00
Mayonnaise, ftd. w/ladle and plate	95.00
Oil, 6 oz. #293	112.50
Plate, #1174	30.00
Plate, 6", 2 hdld. bonbon #3400/1181	22.50
Plate, 8½" Salad	18.00
Plate, 8" sq. #1176	20.00
Plate, 8", 2 hdld. low ft. #56	30.00
Plate, 11½" cake #1495	75.00
Plate, 13½" Cabaret #166	95.00
Relish, 10", 3 pt. #214	65.00
Salad dressing set, twin, 4 pc w ladles & liner #1491	110.00

	Crystal
Salt & pepper, squat, pr. #360	65.00
Saucer #1170	5.00
Stem, brandy, ¾ oz. #1937	75.00
Stem, claret, 4½ oz. #3779	65.00
Stem, claret, 4½ oz., #1937	65.00
Stem, cocktail, 3½ oz., #1937	35.00
Stem, cocktail, 3 oz. #3779	35.00
Stem, cordial, 1 oz. #3779	85.00
Stem, cordial, 1 oz., #1937	85.00
Stem, oyster cocktail, 5 oz., #1937	20.00
Stem, oyster cocktail, 4½ oz. #3779	20.00
Stem, sherbet, 6 oz. low, #1937	18.00
Stem, sherbet, 6 oz. low, #3779	18.00
Stem, sherbet, 6 oz. tall, #1937	22.00
Stem, sherbet, 6 oz. tall, #3779	22.00
Stem, sherry, 2 oz., #1937	65.00
Stem, water, 9 oz. low, #3779	30.00
Stem, water, 9 oz. tall, #3779	35.00
Stem, water, 11 oz., #1937	45.00
Stem, wine, 2½ oz. #3779	55.00
Stem, wine, 3 oz., #1937	55.00
Sugar #254	25.00
Sugar, indiv. #253	30.00
Tumbler, ftd., 5 oz., #1937	22.00
Tumbler, ftd., 5 oz. #3779	22.00
Tumbler, ftd., 10 oz., #1937	27.50
Tumbler, ftd., 12 oz. iced tea #3779	35.00
Tumbler, ftd., 12 oz., #1937	35.00
Vase, 8" ftd. #6004	95.00
Vase, 11" ftd. #278	125.00

and Glass Co., 1926 – 1940s

Colors: crystal, French crystal, frosted crystal, green and frosted green, pink and frosted pink, Ruby flashed, white and assorted ceramic colors

Dancing Nymph is now known to be the Consolidated name for this pattern which has been referred to as "Dance of the Nudes" for the 30 years I have known it. Established names are nearly impossible to just toss away in the collecting world; but the correct name has been reintroduced all these years later. When the expensive Ruba Rombic was listed in this book eight years ago, bargains in that pattern became rare. The introduction of Dancing Nymph has not been quite so dramatic since glassware depicting nudes has always been noticed and collected! People may not have known its name, but it caught their attention. Dancing Nymph prices are, in fact, more sensible when contrasted with most other Consolidated patterns.

This multi-dimensional pattern is one of a few 3-D patterns that exist in this collecting field and was influenced in its concept by the graceful curves of the Art Nouveau movement as well as European wares of the time. We sought the pattern for years trying to find enough to display. Now, you can hardly visit a show without some being there.

You will note that the green has a bluish cast to it as illustrated in the photograph. French Crystal is clear nudes with etched background like the plate in row 3. The other colors are self-explanatory except for the unusual ceramic colors. Ceramic colors were obtained by covering the bottom of a crystal plate with color, wiping the nude designs clear, and firing the plate. The Honey (yellow) plate in row 3 is an example. (Older glassware often involved several hand processes that would be prohibitive to perform today!) These ceramic colors are highly desirable and costly! Other colors with this process are Sepia (brown), white, dark blue, light blue, pinkish lavender, and light green. You could find an ice blue plate with frosted background, but ice blue is a rare color.

Dancing Nymph was introduced in 1926 and made until Consolidated closed in 1932. In 1936 the plant was restarted and a cupped up saucer and sherbet plates were added to this production. You can see the cupped saucer in Row 2 and the cupped sherbet plates in Row 3. These sherbet plates are like a shallow bowl and were often referred to as "ice cream" plates in other patterns of the time. The flatter version is shown in Row 1 with sherbets atop. Sherbet plates are harder to find than salad plates and should actually sell for more if scarcity were the only determining factor. Ironically, Fire-King collectors are often willing to pay three to four times the price of salad plates for 6" plates in some patterns. Yet, collectors of really Elegant glass have been slow to accept the idea that smaller plates might be worth more. Salad plates usually came with basic sets, but sherbet plates were often special order items.

Candlesticks in Dancing Nymph are rare. Notice the two different ones in the bottom row. I have been told the crystal items were never sold, but were supposed to be frosted. I have seen enough crystal to wonder about that. However, one story I heard was that the crystal came out of the factory when it closed for good in the 1940s. It was supposed to be frosted, but had not received the treatment before the plant went out of business.

Additionally, the 16" palace bowl and (18") plate are very rarely found. Be on the lookout for them.

	Crystal	Frosted Crystal French Crystal	*Frosted Pink or Green	Ceramic Colors
Bowl, 4½"	35.00	65.00	85.00	110.00
Bowl, 8"	75.00	125.00	200.00	275.00
Bowl, 16", palace	600.00	1250.00		1600.00
Candle, pr.	395.00	600.00		750.00
Cup	35.00	55.00	85.00	110.00
Plate, 6", cupped			75.00	
Plate, 6", sherbet	25.00	45.00	75.00	100.00
Plate, 8", salad	35.00	65.00		125.00
Plate, 10"	65.00	95.00	140.00	195.00
Platter, 18", palace	600.00	1000.00		1250.00
Saucer, coupe			35.00	
Saucer, flat	15.00	20.00	35.00	40.00
Sherbet	35.00	65.00	85.00	
Tumbler, 3½", cocktail	35.00	65.00		
Tumbler, 5½", goblet	45.00	75.00	125.00	175.00
Vase, 5½", crimped	75.00	135.00		165.00
Vase, 5½", fan	75.00	135.00		165.00

*Subtract 10% to 15% for unfrosted.

DECAGON, Cambridge Glass Company, 1930s – 1940s

Colors: Emerald green, Peach-Blo, Carmen, Royal blue, Amber, Moonlight blue, Ebony

Decagon is the name for the ten-sided mould blank on which many of Cambridge's etchings were produced. This blank is over-looked whenever Cleo, Rosalie, and Imperial Hunt Scene patterns are etched on it. Collectors naturally see the pattern itself rather than the Decagon blank! Yet, there are some ardent collectors of this plain, unadorned Decagon "pattern." Amber Decagon has admir-ers, but not as many as for the Moonlight blue.

Moonlight blue Decagon can be found at reasonable prices when compared with Cleo or Imperial Hunt Scene etch. You will find that Peach-Blo (pink), Emerald (green), and amber are more plentiful, but Moonlight blue is the color of choice. Pattern availability is only one important consideration in collecting! Color also plays a primary role; and blue wins out more often than not.

The off-center snack plate (shown in Row 3), with cup atop and shakers (top row) are the pieces most difficult to find of all those pictured. Flat soups, cordials, and pitchers are not easily spotted. I still need one blue relish insert to finish that tray pictured in case you should have one. One reader sent a similar one last year; but, alas, it was only similar.

	Pastel Colors	Blue
Basket, 7", 2 hdld. (upturned sides)	15.00	30.00
Bowl, bouillon, w/liner	15.00	35.00
Bowl, cream soup, w/liner	22.00	35.00
Bowl, 2½", indiv., almond	30.00	50.00
Bowl, 3¾", flat rim, cranberry	20.00	32.00
Bowl, 3½" belled, cranberry	20.00	32.00
Bowl, 5½", 2 hdld., bonbon	12.00	22.00
Bowl, 5½", belled, fruit	10.00	20.00
Bowl, 5¾", flat rim, fruit	10.00	20.00
Bowl, 6", belled, cereal	20.00	30.00
Bowl, 6", flat rim, cereal	22.00	40.00
Bowl, 6", ftd., almond	30.00	50.00
Bowl, 6¼", 2 hdld., bonbon	12.00	22.00
Bowl, 8½", flat rim, soup "plate"	25.00	50.00
Bowl, 9", rnd., veg.	30.00	55.00
Bowl, 9", 2 pt., relish	30.00	40.00
Bowl, 9½", oval, veg.	35.00	50.00
Bowl, 10", berry	35.00	50.00
Bowl, 10½", oval, veg.	35.00	50.00
Bowl, 11", rnd. veg.	40.00	48.00
Bowl, 11", 2 pt., relish	38.00	40.00
Comport, 5¾"	20.00	35.00
Comport, 6½", low ft.	20.00	35.00
Comport, 7", tall	25.00	48.00
Creamer, ftd.	10.00	20.00
Creamer, scalloped edge	9.00	18.00
Creamer, lightning bolt handles	10.00	15.00
Creamer, tall, lg. ft.	10.00	22.00
Cup	6.00	11.00
French dressing bottle, "Oil/Vinegar"	90.00	150.00
Gravy boat, w/2 hdld. liner (like spouted cream soup)	100.00	125.00
Ice bucket	45.00	75.00
Ice tub	45.00	65.00
Mayonnaise, 2 hdld., w/2 hdld. liner and ladle	27.00	45.00

	Pastel Colors	Blue
Mayonnaise, w/liner & ladle	25.00	65.00
Oil, 6 oz., tall, w/hdld. & stopper	70.00	175.00
Plate, 6¼", bread/butter	5.00	10.00
Plate, 7", 2 hdld.	9.00	15.00
Plate, 7½"	8.00	12.00
Plate, 8½", salad	15.00	25.00
Plate, 9½", dinner	50.00	70.00
Plate, 10", grill	35.00	50.00
Plate, 10", service	35.00	50.00
Plate, 12½", service	30.00	60.00
Relish, 6 inserts	100.00	165.00
Salt dip, 1½", ftd.	25.00	40.00
Sauce boat & plate	100.00	125.00
Saucer	3.00	4.00
Server, center hdld.	30.00	45.00
Stem, 1 oz., cordial	45.00	70.00
Stem, 3½ oz., cocktail	15.00	24.00
Stem, 6 oz., low sherbet	12.00	18.00
Stem, 6 oz., high sherbet	15.00	25.00
Stem, 9 oz., water	20.00	35.00
Sugar, lightning bolt handles	10.00	15.00
Sugar, ftd.	9.00	20.00
Sugar, scalloped edge	9.00	20.00
Sugar, tall, lg. ft.	20.00	35.00
Tray, 8", 2 hdld., flat pickle	25.00	40.00
Tray, 9", pickle	25.00	40.00
Tray, 11", oval, service	30.00	50.00
Tray, 11", celery	30.00	50.00
Tray, 12", center handled	30.00	45.00
Tray, 12", oval, service	25.00	45.00
Tray, 13", 2 hdld., service	35.00	50.00
Tray, 15", oval, service	45.00	75.00
Tumbler, 2½ oz., ftd.	20.00	25.00
Tumbler, 5 oz., ftd.	15.00	20.00
Tumbler, 8 oz., ftd.	18.00	25.00
Tumbler, 10 oz., ftd.	20.00	30.00
Tumbler, 12 oz., ftd.	25.00	38.00

Colors: light amber, green, pink, black, crystal

Look on page 21 for the Black Forest pattern shot if you tend to confuse these two patterns. **Deer** and trees are the theme of "Deerwood," whereas Black Forest portrays **moose** and trees. Moose have much longer (horse like) noses!

Gold decorated, black "Deerwood" is being bought by people who are not necessarily collectors of "Deerwood," but who just like its looks. Internet auctions have also discovered "Deerwood" but not to the extent of Black Forest. These occurrences have caused some price adjustments! "Deerwood," itself, is not commonly found, but gold decorated pieces, which really make the pattern stand out, are extremely hard to come by. See the sugar in the pattern shot. Large sets can only be garnered in green and pink. You will have to settle for an occasional piece or two in the other colors.

That flat, three-part, pink candy in the bottom photo is a Paden City mould and not U.S. Glass. This makes a researcher's job more "entertaining" than needed! A U.S. Glass etching on a Paden City candy! We are uncovering more and more instances of "shared" wares between companies, for whatever reasons. There is some catalog documentation for "Deerwood," but not nearly enough. That is why new pieces keep turning up even 30 years into serious collecting. It makes you wonder if some other company did some etchings of "Deerwood." The mould definitely was produced at Tiffin, but perhaps etching contracts were sublet to someone else whom we have not yet found.

There is no mayonnaise per se listed although several readers have reported that they own one. This piece was cataloged as a whipped cream rather than a mayonnaise. Terminology of the old glass companies often differs from today's notions. I do not believe either mayonnaise or whipped cream would have kept very well in those days of ice boxes! Perhaps that is why they displayed these "treats" in such elegant fashion!

	*Black	Amber	Green	Pink
Bowl, 10", footed	165.00			
Bowl, 10", straight edge				75.00
Bowl, 12", console			85.00	80.00
Cake plate, low pedestal			75.00	75.00
Candlestick, 2½"	75.00		40.00	
Candlestick, 4"				60.00
Candy dish, w/cover, 3 part, flat				135.00
Candy jar, w/cover, ftd. cone			150.00	150.00
Celery, 12"			75.00	
Cheese and cracker			115.00	115.00
Comport, 10", low, ftd., flared	150.00			75.00
Creamer, 2 styles	70.00		45.00	45.00
Cup				80.00
Plate, 5½"			15.00	15.00
Plate, 7½", salad				25.00
Plate, 9½", dinner				95.00
Plate, 10¼", 2 hdld.	145.00			
Saucer				20.00
Server, center hdld.			55.00	55.00
Stem, 2 oz., wine, 4½"				60.00
Stem, 6 oz., sherbet, 4¾"			30.00	
Stem, 6 oz., cocktail, 5"			40.00	
Stem, 9 oz., water, 7"	135.00		65.00	65.00
Sugar, 2 styles	70.00		45.00	45.00
Tumbler, 9 oz.			37.50	37.50
Tumbler, 12 oz., tea, 5½"		55.00		
Vase, 7", sweet pea, rolled edge			125.00	125.00
Vase, 10", ruffled top			145.00	145.00
Vase, 12", 2 handles	195.00			
Whipped cream pail, w/ladle			75.00	75.00

*Add 20% for gold decorated.

Colors: crystal; some pink, yellow, blue, Heatherbloom, Emerald green, amber, Crown Tuscan

Cambridge's Diane pattern can be found in various colors; but only crystal can be collected in a large setting. You might be able to acquire a luncheon set in color, but after that only an occasional bowl, candle, or tumbler will be seen. Evidently the price of colored handmade glass may have contributed to its scarcity; in any case, colored Diane is scarce.

Crystal is presently pictured; you will have to search earlier books for Diane in color. As with other Cambridge patterns in this book, you will have to look at Rose Point listings for pricing unlisted Diane items. Diane will run 30% to 40% less than comparable items listed in Rose Point. The bitters bottle and round ball shaker are difficult to find, but not impossible. That ball shaker has a square, screw-on glass base that is often damaged. I wonder if written instructions were given for filling these shakers. Holding them upside down to fill would cause the salt or pepper to run out the holes; and we know there is nothing "common" about common sense.

The "barrel" shot glass pictured on the right, next to the cruet, was found with round decanters; and the one in the center, with a sham bottom, came with the footed decanters. A cigarette holder sits between the ball shaker and the small sugar on the left. Cigarette items are being gathered by some as a disappearing collectible.

You have choices for stemware collecting in Diane; pick whichever you like. Each line looks excellent with the set.

	Crystal
Basket, 6", 2 hdld., ftd.	30.00
Bottle, bitters	165.00
Bowl, #3106, finger, w/liner	40.00
Bowl, #3122	25.00
Bowl, #3400, cream soup, w/liner	35.00
Bowl, 3", indiv. nut, 4 ftd.	60.00
Bowl, 5", berry	30.00
Bowl, 5¼", 2 hdld., bonbon	25.00
Bowl, 6", 2 hdld., ftd., bonbon	25.00
Bowl, 6", 2 pt., relish	25.00
Bowl, 6", cereal	35.00
Bowl, 6½", 3 pt. relish	35.00
Bowl, 7", 2 hdld., ftd., bonbon	38.00
Bowl, 7", 2 pt., relish	35.00
Bowl, 7", relish or pickle	35.00
Bowl, 9", 3 pt., celery or relish	40.00
Bowl, 9½", pickle (like corn)	40.00
Bowl, 10", 4 ft., flared	60.00
Bowl, 10", baker	60.00
Bowl, 11", 2 hdld.	65.00
Bowl, 11", 4 ftd.	65.00
Bowl, 11½", tab hdld., ftd.	62.00
Bowl, 12", 3 pt., celery & relish	55.00
Bowl, 12", 4 ft.	70.00
Bowl, 12", 4 ft., flared	75.00
Bowl, 12", 4 ft., oval	75.00
Bowl, 12", 4 ft., oval, w/"ears" hdld.	75.00
Bowl, 12", 5 pt., celery & relish	65.00
Butter, rnd.	165.00
Cabinet flask	295.00
Candelabrum, 2-lite, keyhole	33.00
Candelabrum, 3-lite, keyhole	40.00
Candlestick, 1-lite, keyhole	30.00
Candlestick, 5"	20.00
Candlestick, 6", 2-lite, "fleur-de-lis"	35.00
Candlestick, 6", 3-lite	40.00
Candy box, w/cover, rnd.	95.00
Cigarette urn	50.00
Cocktail shaker, glass top	195.00
Cocktail shaker, metal top	135.00
Cocktail icer, 2 pc.	85.00

	Crystal
Comport, 5½"	35.00
Comport, 5⅜", blown	45.00
Creamer	20.00
Creamer, indiv., #3500 (pie crust edge)	20.00
Creamer, indiv., #3900, scalloped edge	20.00
Creamer, scroll handle, #3400	20.00
Cup	20.00
Decanter, ball	235.00
Decanter, lg. ftd.	195.00
Decanter, short ft., cordial	250.00
Hurricane lamp, candlestick base	175.00
Hurricane lamp, keyhole base w/prisms	235.00
Ice bucket, w/chrome hand	75.00
Mayonnaise, div., w/liner & ladles	65.00
Mayonnaise (sherbet type w/ladle)	55.00
Mayonnaise, w/liner, ladle	50.00
Oil, 6 oz., w/stopper	135.00
Pitcher, ball	195.00
Pitcher, Doulton	335.00
Pitcher, martini	750.00
Pitcher, upright	225.00
Plate, 6", 2 hdld., plate.	15.00
Plate, 6", sq., bread/butter	10.00
Plate, 6½", bread/butter	8.00
Plate, 8", 2 hdld., ftd., bonbon	18.00
Plate, 8", salad	14.00
Plate, 8½"	20.00
Plate, 10½", dinner	70.00
Plate, 12", 4 ft., service	45.00
Plate, 13", 4 ft., torte	50.00
Plate, 13½", 2 hdld.	45.00
Plate, 14", torte	75.00
Platter, 13½"	70.00
Salt & pepper, ftd., w/glass tops, pr.	40.00
Salt & pepper, pr., flat	40.00
Saucer	6.00
Stem, #1066, 1 oz., cordial	65.00
Stem, #1066, 3 oz., cocktail	25.00
Stem, #1066, 3 oz., wine	35.00
Stem, #1066, 3½ oz., tall cocktail	28.00
Stem, #1066, 4½ oz., claret	60.00

	Crystal
Stem, #1066, 5 oz., oyster/cocktail	20.00
Stem, #1066, 7 oz., low sherbet	18.00
Stem, #1066, 7 oz., tall sherbet	20.00
Stem, #1066, 11 oz., water	32.00
Stem, #3122, 1 oz., cordial	65.00
Stem, #3122, 2½ oz., wine	35.00
Stem, #3122, 3 oz., cocktail	20.00
Stem, #3122, 4½ oz., claret	60.00
Stem, #3122, 4½ oz., oyster/cocktail	20.00
Stem, #3122, 7 oz., low sherbet	18.00
Stem, #3122, 7 oz., tall sherbet	20.00
Stem, #3122, 9 oz., water goblet	30.00
Sugar, indiv., #3500 (pie crust edge)	20.00
Sugar, indiv., #3900, scalloped edge	20.00
Sugar, scroll handle, #3400	20.00
Tumbler, 2½ oz., sham bottom	50.00
Tumbler, 5 oz., ft., juice	40.00
Tumbler, 5 oz., sham bottom	45.00
Tumbler, 7 oz., old-fashioned, w/sham bottom	55.00
Tumbler, 8 oz., ft.	30.00
Tumbler, 10 oz., sham bottom	35.00
Tumbler, 12 oz., sham bottom	40.00
Tumbler, 13 oz.	35.00
Tumbler, 14 oz., sham bottom	45.00

	Crystal
Tumbler, #1066, 3 oz.	28.00
Tumbler, #1066, 5 oz., juice	20.00
Tumbler, #1066, 9 oz., water	22.00
Tumbler, #1066, 12 oz., tea	28.00
Tumbler, #3106, 3 oz., ftd.	26.00
Tumbler, #3106, 5 oz., ftd., juice	22.00
Tumbler, #3106, 9 oz., ftd., water	20.00
Tumbler, #3106, 12 oz., ftd., tea	26.00
Tumbler, #3122, 2½ oz.	33.00
Tumbler, #3122, 5 oz., juice	20.00
Tumbler, #3122, 9 oz., water	25.00
Tumbler, #3122, 12 oz., tea	30.00
Tumbler, #3135, 2½ oz., ftd., bar	40.00
Tumbler, #3135, 10 oz., ftd., tumbler	22.00
Tumbler, #3135, 12 oz., ftd., tea	33.00
Vase, 5", globe	55.00
Vase, 6", high ft., flower	55.00
Vase, 8", high ft., flower	65.00
Vase, 9", keyhole base	75.00
Vase, 10", bud	60.00
Vase, 11", flower	95.00
Vase, 11", ped. ft., flower	100.00
Vase, 12", keyhole base	95.00
Vase, 13", flower	150.00

Note: See pages 228 – 229 for stem identification.

ELAINE, Cambridge Glass Company, 1934 – 1950s

Colors: crystal

Elaine is frequently confused with Chantilly, and not only by new collectors. A seasoned dealer admitted to such confusion! Be sure to look at our outlined design at the top of the page. The Elaine design has a thin and angled scroll like the top of the capital letter "E" (for Elaine) as you write it in script. Elaine is most often found on Cambridge's #3500 Gadroon line that has the ornate "pie crust" edge shown in the photographs. You will find accessory pieces not listed here since I have used as much listing space as I have. Many pieces listed under Rose Point etch are found etched Elaine. Bear in mind that prices for Elaine will be 30% to 40% lower than those for Rose Point.

	Crystal
Basket, 6", 2 hdld. (upturned sides)	22.00
Bowl, #3104, finger, w/liner	40.00
Bowl, 3", indiv. nut, 4 ftd.	60.00
Bowl, 5¼", 2 hdld., bonbon	20.00
Bowl, 6", 2 hdld., ftd., bonbon	25.00
Bowl, 6", 2 pt., relish	25.00
Bowl, 6½", 3 pt., relish	25.00
Bowl, 7", 2 pt., pickle or relish	30.00
Bowl, 7", ftd., tab hdld., bonbon	35.00
Bowl, 7", pickle or relish	35.00
Bowl, 9", 3 pt., celery & relish	40.00
Bowl, 9½", pickle (like corn dish)	45.00
Bowl, 10", 4 ftd., flared	65.00
Bowl, 11", tab hdld.	75.00
Bowl, 11½", ftd., tab hdld.	85.00
Bowl, 12", 3 pt., celery & relish	55.00
Bowl, 12", 4 ftd., flared	75.00
Bowl, 12", 4 ftd., oval, "ear" hdld.	75.00
Bowl, 12", 5 pt. celery & relish	65.00
Candlestick, 5"	28.00
Candlestick, 6", 2-lite	45.00
Candlestick, 6", 3-lite	55.00
Candy box, w/cover, rnd.	100.00
Cocktail icer, 2 pc.	85.00
Comport, 5½"	35.00
Comport, 5⅜", #3500 stem	45.00
Comport, 5⅜", blown	50.00
Creamer (several styles)	20.00
Creamer, indiv.	20.00
Cup	20.00
Decanter, lg., ftd.	210.00
Hat, 9"	395.00
Hurricane lamp, candlestick base	175.00
Hurricane lamp, keyhole ft., w/prisms	235.00
Ice bucket, w/chrome handle	95.00
Mayonnaise (cupped sherbet w/ladle)	50.00
Mayonnaise (div. bowl, liner, 2 ladles)	60.00
Mayonnaise, w/liner & ladle	55.00
Oil, 6 oz., hdld., w/stopper	125.00
Pitcher, ball, 80 oz.	295.00
Pitcher, Doulton	335.00
Pitcher, upright	225.00
Plate, 6", 2 hdld.	15.00
Plate, 6½", bread/butter	12.00
Plate, 8", 2 hdld., ftd.	22.00
Plate, 8", salad	22.00
Plate, 8", tab hdld., bonbon	25.00
Plate, 10½", dinner	70.00
Plate, 11½" 2 hdld., ringed "Tally Ho" sand.	60.00
Plate, 12", 4 ftd., service	45.00
Plate, 13", 4 ftd., torte	50.00
Plate, 13½", tab hdld., cake	75.00
Plate, 14", torte	65.00
Salt & pepper, flat, pr.	40.00

	Crystal
Salt & pepper, ftd., pr	40.00
Salt & pepper, hdld., pr	45.00
Saucer	5.00
Stem, #1402, 1 oz., cordial	65.00
Stem, #1402, 3 oz., wine	35.00
Stem, #1402, 3½ oz., cocktail	25.00
Stem, #1402, 5 oz., claret	45.00
Stem, #1402, low sherbet	18.00
Stem, #1402, tall sherbet	20.00
Stem, #1402, goblet	28.00
Stem, #3104 (very tall stems), ¾ oz., brandy	195.00
Stem, #3104, 1 oz., cordial	195.00
Stem, #3104, 1 oz., pousse-cafe	195.00
Stem, #3104, 2 oz., sherry	195.00
Stem, #3104, 2½ oz., creme de menthe	150.00
Stem, #3104, 3 oz., wine	150.00
Stem, #3104, 3½ oz., cocktail	100.00
Stem, #3104, 4½ oz., claret	150.00
Stem, #3104, 5 oz., roemer	150.00
Stem, #3104, 5 oz., tall hock	150.00
Stem, #3104, 7 oz., tall sherbet	125.00
Stem, #3104, 9 oz., goblet	150.00
Stem, #3121, 1 oz., cordial	65.00
Stem, #3121, 3 oz., cocktail	26.00
Stem, #3121, 3½ oz., wine	40.00
Stem, #3121, 4½ oz., claret	50.00
Stem, #3121, 4½ oz., oyster cocktail	24.00
Stem, #3121, 5 oz., parfait, low stem	40.00
Stem, #3121, 6 oz., low sherbet	18.00
Stem, #3121, 6 oz., tall sherbet	20.00
Stem, #3121, 10 oz., water	28.00
Stem, #3500, 1 oz., cordial	65.00
Stem, #3500, 2½ oz., wine	40.00
Stem, #3500, 3 oz., cocktail	30.00
Stem, #3500, 4½ oz., claret	50.00
Stem, #3500, 4½ oz., oyster cocktail	23.00
Stem, #3500, 5 oz., parfait, low stem	40.00
Stem, #3500, 7 oz., low sherbet	20.00
Stem, #3500, 7 oz., tall sherbet	22.00
Stem, #3500, 10 oz., water	30.00
Sugar (several styles)	20.00
Sugar, indiv.	20.00
Tumbler, #1402, 9 oz., ftd., water	20.00
Tumbler, #1402, 12 oz., tea	35.00
Tumbler, #1402, 12 oz., tall ftd., tea	35.00
Tumbler, #3121, 5 oz., ftd., juice	25.00
Tumbler, #3121, 10 oz., ftd., water	38.00
Tumbler, #3121, 12 oz., ftd., tea	33.00
Tumbler, #3500, 5 oz., ftd., juice	25.00
Tumbler, #3500, 10 oz., ftd., water	28.00
Tumbler, #3500, 12 oz., ftd., tea	35.00
Vase, 6", ftd.	75.00
Vase, 8", ftd.	95.00
Vase, 9", keyhole, ftd.	145.00

Colors: Flamingo pink, Sahara yellow, Moongleam green, cobalt, and Alexandrite; some Tangerine

Empress is shown in Sahara on page 77 and Alexandrite on page 79. Crystal listings will now be found under the pattern Queen Ann. When the colors were made, this pattern was called Empress; but later on, when crystal was produced, the pattern name was changed to Queen Ann. One of the things most requested by readers is identification of pieces pictured. The shelf shot of Alexandrite on page 79 gives an opportunity for this, so I hope it helps.

Row 1: 7", 3-part relish, shaker, cup and saucer, shaker, 7" round plate
Row 2: 6" mint, nut dish, 6" square plate, sugar, creamer
Row 3: Mayonnaise w/ladle, 10" celery tray, 11" floral bowl
Row 4: 8" square plate, ash tray, 7" candlestick (#135), 9" vase

	Flamingo	Sahara	Moongleam	Cobalt	Alexandrite
Ash tray.	175.00	185.00	375.00	300.00	225.00
Bonbon, 6"	20.00	25.00	30.00		
Bowl, cream soup	30.00	30.00	50.00		110.00
Bowl, cream soup, w/sq. liner	40.00	40.00	55.00		175.00
Bowl, frappe, w/center	45.00	60.00	75.00		
Bowl, nut, dolphin ftd., indiv.	30.00	32.00	45.00		170.00
Bowl, 4½", nappy	25.00	30.00	35.00		
Bowl, 5", preserve, 2 hdld.	20.00	25.00	30.00		
Bowl, 6", ftd., jelly, 2 hdld.	20.00	25.00	30.00		
Bowl, 6", dolphin ftd., mint	35.00	40.00	45.00		230.00
Bowl, 6", grapefruit, sq. top, grnd. bottom	12.50	20.00	25.00		
Bowl, 6½", oval, lemon, w/cover	65.00	80.00	110.00		
Bowl, 7", 3 pt., relish, triplex	40.00	45.00	50.00		300.00
Bowl, 7", 3 pt., relish, ctr. hand.	45.00	50.00	75.00		
Bowl, 7½", dolphin ftd., nappy	65.00	65.00	80.00	300.00	350.00
Bowl, 7½", dolphin ftd., nasturtium	130.00	130.00	150.00	350.00	425.00
Bowl, 8", nappy	35.00	37.00	45.00		

	Flamingo	Sahara	Moongleam	Cobalt	Alexandrite
Bowl, 8½", ftd., floral, 2 hdld	45.00	50.00	70.00		
Bowl, 9", floral, rolled edge	40.00	42.00	50.00		
Bowl, 9", floral, flared	70.00	75.00	90.00		
Bowl, 10", 2 hdld., oval dessert	50.00	60.00	70.00		
Bowl, 10", lion head, floral	550.00	550.00	700.00		
Bowl, 10", oval, veg.	50.00	55.00	75.00		
Bowl, 10", square, salad, 2 hdld.	55.00	60.00	80.00		
Bowl, 10", triplex, relish	50.00	55.00	65.00		
Bowl, 11", dolphin ftd., floral	65.00	75.00	100.00	400.00	500.00
Bowl, 13", pickle/olive, 2 pt.	35.00	45.00	50.00		
Bowl, 15", dolphin ftd., punch	900.00	900.00	1,100.00		
Candlestick, low, 4 ftd., w/2 hdld.	100.00	100.00	170.00		
Candlestick, 6", dolphin ftd.	170.00	100.00	155.00	260.00	265.00
Candy, w/cover, 6", dolphin ftd.	150.00	150.00	200.00	450.00	
Comport, 6", ftd.	110.00	70.00	100.00		
Comport, 6", square	70.00	75.00	85.00		
Comport, 7", oval	70.00	75.00	80.00		
Compotier, 6", dolphin ftd.	260.00	225.00	275.00		
Creamer, dolphin ftd.	50.00	40.00	45.00		250.00
Creamer, indiv.	45.00	45.00	50.00		210.00
Cup	30.00	30.00	35.00		115.00
Cup, after dinner	60.00	60.00	70.00		
Cup, bouillon, 2 hdld.	35.00	35.00	45.00		
Cup, 4 oz., custard or punch	30.00	35.00	45.00		
Cup, #1401½, has rim as demi-cup	28.00	32.00	40.00		
Grapefruit, w/square liner	30.00	30.00	35.00		
Ice tub, w/metal handles	100.00	150.00	165.00		
Jug, 3 pint, ftd.	200.00	210.00	250.00		

	Flamingo	Sahara	Moongleam	Cobalt	Alexandrite
Jug, flat			175.00		
Marmalade, w/cover, dolphin ftd.	200.00	170.00	225.00		
Mayonnaise, 5½", ftd. with ladle	85.00	90.00	100.00		400.00
Mustard, w/cover	85.00	80.00	95.00		
Oil bottle, 4 oz.	125.00	125.00	135.00		
Plate, bouillon liner	12.00	15.00	17.50		25.00
Plate, 4½"	10.00	15.00	20.00		
Plate, 6"	11.00	14.00	16.00		40.00
Plate, 6", square	10.00	13.00	15.00		40.00
Plate, 7"	12.00	15.00	17.00		50.00
Plate, 7", square	12.00	15.00	17.00	60.00	65.00
Plate, 8", square	18.00	22.00	35.00	70.00	75.00
Plate, 8"	16.00	20.00	24.00	70.00	75.00
Plate, 9"	25.00	35.00	40.00		
Plate, 10½"	100.00	100.00	140.00		335.00
Plate, 10½", square	100.00	100.00	140.00		335.00
Plate, 12"	45.00	55.00	65.00		
Plate, 12", muffin, sides upturned	55.00	80.00	90.00		
Plate, 12", sandwich, 2 hdld.	35.00	45.00	60.00		180.00
Plate, 13", hors d'oeuvre, 2 hdld.	50.00	60.00	70.00		
Plate, 13", square, 2 hdld.	40.00	45.00	55.00		
Platter, 14"	40.00	45.00	80.00		
Salt & pepper, pr.	100.00	110.00	135.00		450.00
Saucer, square	10.00	10.00	15.00		25.00
Saucer, after dinner	10.00	10.00	15.00		
Saucer, rnd.	10.00	10.00	15.00		25.00
Stem, 2½ oz., oyster cocktail	20.00	25.00	30.00		
Stem, 4 oz., saucer champagne	35.00	40.00	60.00		
Stem, 4 oz., sherbet	22.00	28.00	35.00		
Stem, 9 oz., Empress stemware, unusual	55.00	65.00	75.00		
Sugar, indiv.	45.00	45.00	50.00		210.00
Sugar, dolphin ftd., 3 hdld.	50.00	40.00	45.00		250.00
Tray, condiment & liner for indiv. sugar/creamer	40.00	35.00	50.00		
Tray, 10", 3 pt., relish	50.00	55.00	65.00		
Tray, 10", 7 pt., hors d'oeuvre	160.00	150.00	200.00		
Tray, 10", celery	25.00	35.00	40.00		150.00
Tray, 12", ctr. hdld., sand.	48.00	57.00	65.00		
Tray, 12", sq. ctr. hdld., sand.	52.00	60.00	67.50		
Tray, 13", celery	30.00	40.00	45.00		
Tray, 16", 4 pt., buffet relish	75.00	75.00	86.00		160.00
Tumbler, 8 oz., dolphin ftd., unusual	150.00	170.00	160.00		
Tumbler, 8 oz., grnd. bottom	60.00	50.00	70.00		
Tumbler, 12 oz., tea, grnd. bottom	70.00	65.00	75.00		
Vase, 8", flared	140.00	150.00	190.00		
Vase, 9", dolphin ftd.	200.00	200.00	220.00		850.00

Colors: Blue, Azure blue, Orchid, amber, Rose, green, Topaz; some Ruby, Ebony, and Wisteria

Fostoria utilized Fairfax (the name of this mould blank #2375) for several of their most popular etchings, particularly June, Versailles, and Trojan. Pictured on page 81 are Orchid and green. The Orchid is a dark lavender color that is sometimes confused with Wisteria. Wisteria changes color depending upon the light source (natural or florescent), but Orchid does not. See Hermitage on page 104 for an example of Wisteria. The stems and tumblers pictured in Orchid have the Spartan pattern needle etch on them. You can also find unetched Orchid stems. The Spartan was available and fit my purpose without buying additional pieces to photograph. The Orchid and Azure blue are the colors most sought in Fairfax. I just this morning found an Azure sauce boat and liner at a Florida antique fair.

Luckily, Fairfax collectors have a choice of two stemware lines which does not happen in some collectible patterns. In the Fostoria stems and shapes shown on page 82 are the #5298 stem and tumbler line even though the pieces shown are etched June and Versailles. The other stem line, #5299, is commonly found in yellow with Trojan etch. Collectors call this stem "waterfall." Some collectors mix stem lines; but tumblers are more difficult to mix because they have distinctly different shapes. The #5299 tumblers (oyster cocktail on page 82) are more flared at the top than the #5298 (all other tumblers on page 82).

I have shown the array of Fostoria's stemware on page 82 so that all shapes can be seen. The claret and high sherbets are major concerns. Each is 6" high. The claret is shaped like the wine. I recently had to show that difference to someone who told me he had some blue June clarets that turned out to be crystal high sherbets, a few hundred dollars difference! The parfait is also taller than the juice, although shaped similarly.

	Rose, Blue, Orchid	Amber	Green, Topaz
Ash tray, 2½"	15.00	8.00	11.00
Ash tray, 4"	17.50	10.00	12.50
Ash tray, 5½"	20.00	13.00	17.50
Baker, 9", oval	45.00	16.00	30.00
Baker, 10½", oval	50.00	20.00	30.00
Bonbon	12.50	9.00	10.00
Bottle, salad dressing	210.00	75.00	110.00
Bouillon, ftd.	15.00	8.00	10.00
Bowl, 9", lemon, 2 hdld.	20.00	10.00	13.00
Bowl, sweetmeat	22.00	12.00	16.00
Bowl, 5", fruit	20.00	8.00	10.00
Bowl, 6", cereal	30.00	10.00	15.00
Bowl, 6⅞", 3 ftd.	25.00	15.00	20.00
Bowl, 7", soup	60.00	30.00	40.00
Bowl, 8", rnd., nappy	45.00	20.00	30.00
Bowl, lg., hdld., dessert	45.00	20.00	30.00
Bowl, 12"	50.00	25.00	35.00
Bowl, 12", centerpiece	50.00	25.00	35.00
Bowl, 13", oval, centerpiece	50.00	25.00	35.00
Bowl, 15", centerpiece	55.00	30.00	40.00
Butter dish, w/cover	135.00	80.00	110.00
Candlestick, flattened top	25.00	12.00	15.00
Candlestick, 3"	25.00	12.00	18.00
Candy w/cover, flat, 3 pt.	75.00	45.00	55.00
Candy w/cover, ftd.	85.00	50.00	65.00
Celery, 11½"	30.00	15.00	18.00
Cheese & cracker set (2 styles)	45.00	20.00	25.00
Cigarette box	32.00	20.00	25.00
Comport, 5"	35.00	15.00	25.00
Comport, 7"	40.00	15.00	25.00
Cream soup, ftd.	23.00	10.00	15.00
Creamer, flat		10.00	14.00
Creamer, ftd.	15.00	7.00	10.00
Creamer, tea	25.00	8.00	12.00
Cup, after dinner	30.00	12.00	18.00
Cup, flat		4.00	6.00
Cup, ftd.	14.00	6.00	7.00
Flower holder, oval, window box	125.00	75.00	60.00
Grapefruit	35.00	18.00	25.00
Grapefruit liner	30.00	12.00	20.00
Ice bucket	65.00	30.00	40.00
Ice bowl	25.00	15.00	20.00
Ice bowl liner	20.00	15.00	* 15.00
Mayonnaise	25.00	12.00	15.00
Mayonnaise ladle	35.00	20.00	25.00
Mayonnaise liner, 7"	10.00	5.00	6.00

	Rose, Blue, Orchid	Amber	Green, Topaz
Nut cup, blown	35.00	22.00	25.00
Oil, ftd.	175.00	85.00	110.00
Pickle, 8½"	25.00	8.00	12.00
Pitcher, #5000	300.00	130.00	175.00
Plate, canape	20.00	10.00	10.00
Plate, whipped cream	11.00	8.00	9.00
Plate, 6", bread/butter	8.00	3.00	4.00
Plate, 7½", salad	10.00	4.00	5.00
Plate, 7½", cream soup or mayonnaise liner	10.00	5.00	6.00
Plate, 8¾", salad	14.00	7.00	8.00
Plate, 9½", luncheon	17.00	7.00	10.00
Plate, 10¼", dinner	45.00	20.00	32.00
Plate, 10¼", grill	40.00	18.00	22.00
Plate, 10", cake	22.00	13.00	15.00
Plate, 12", bread, oval	45.00	25.00	27.50
Plate, 13", chop	30.00	15.00	20.00
Platter, 10½", oval	38.00	20.00	30.00
Platter, 12", oval	42.00	22.00	35.00
Platter, 15", oval	85.00	30.00	50.00
Relish, 3 part, 8½"	30.00	10.00	15.00
Relish, 11½"	22.00	11.00	13.00
Sauce boat	50.00	20.00	30.00
Sauce boat liner	20.00	10.00	15.00
Saucer, after dinner	8.00	4.00	5.00
Saucer	4.00	2.50	3.00
Shaker, ftd., pr	70.00	30.00	45.00
Shaker, indiv., ftd., pr.		20.00	25.00
Stem, 4", ¾ oz., cordial	70.00	25.00	40.00
Stem, 4¼", 6 oz., low sherbet	18.00	9.00	11.00
Stem, 5¼", 3 oz., cocktail	24.00	12.00	18.00
Stem, 5½", 3 oz., wine	35.00	18.00	25.00
Stem, 6", 4 oz., claret	45.00	25.00	35.00
Stem, 6", 6 oz., high sherbet	22.00	10.00	15.00
Stem, 8¼", 10 oz., water	32.00	16.00	22.00
Sugar, flat		10.00	12.00
Sugar, ftd.	15.00	6.00	8.00
Sugar cover	35.00	20.00	25.00
Sugar pail	70.00	30.00	45.00
Sugar, tea	25.00	8.00	12.00
Tray, 11", ctr. hdld.	25.00	14.00	18.00
Tumbler, 2½ oz., ftd.	32.00	12.00	18.00
Tumbler, 4½", 5 oz., ftd.	18.00	10.00	11.00
Tumbler, 5¼", 9 oz., ftd.	22.00	12.00	13.00
Tumbler, 6", 12 oz., ftd.	28.00	13.50	18.00
Vase, 8" (2 styles)	95.00	40.00	60.00
Whipped cream pail	45.00	25.00	30.00

*Green $20.00

FOSTORIA STEMS AND SHAPES

Top Row: Left to Right
1. Water, 10 oz., 8¼"
2. Claret, 4 oz., 6"
3. Wine, 3 oz., 5½"
4. Cordial, ¾ oz., 4"
5. Sherbet, low, 6 oz., 4¼"
6. Cocktail, 3 oz., 5¼"
7. Sherbet, high, 6 oz., 6"

Bottom Row: Left to Right
1. Grapefruit and liner
2. Ice tea tumbler, 12 oz., 6"
3. Water tumbler, 9 oz., 5¼"
4. Parfait, 6 oz., 5¼"
5. Juice tumbler, 5 oz., 4½"
6. Oyster cocktail, 5½ oz.
7. Bar tumbler, 2½ oz.

Color: crystal

First Love is the most recognized Duncan & Miller etching! Several mould lines were employed for this large pattern. Among those are #30 (Pall Mall), #111 (Terrace), #115 (Canterbury), #117 (Three Feathers), #126 (Venetian), and #5111½ (Terrace blown stemware). Canterbury can be found on pages 36 to 39 and Terrace can be seen on pages 200 and 201. You will have to check earlier editions of this book for catalog pages showing details of those other lines. Most pieces of First Love will be found on lines #111 or #115.

I received numerous letters from collectors who thought the darker background highlighted the pattern much better; we have stuck to that format again even though the blue tends to show through the glass more than I'd like it to do.

	Crystal
Ash tray, 3½" sq., #111	17.50
Ash tray, 3½" x 2½", #30	16.50
Ash tray, 5" x 3", #12, club	37.50
Ash tray, 5" x 3¼", #30	24.00
Ash tray, 6½" x 4¼", #30	35.00
Basket, 9¼" x 10" x 7¼", #115	175.00
Basket, 10" x 4¼" x 7", oval hdld., #115	195.00
Bottle, oil w/stopper, 8", #5200	60.00
Bowl, 3" x 5", rose, #115	40.00
Bowl, 4" x 1½", finger, #30	32.00
Bowl, 4¼", finger, #5111½	35.00
Bowl, 6" x 2½", oval, olive, #115	25.00
Bowl, 6¾" x 4¼", ftd., flared rim, #111	30.00
Bowl, 7½" x 3", 3 pt., ftd., #117	35.00
Bowl, 8" sq. x 2½", hdld., #111	60.00
Bowl, 8½" x 4", #115	37.50
Bowl, 9" x 4½", ftd., #111	42.00
Bowl, 9½" x 2½", hdld., #111	45.00
Bowl, 10" x 3¾", ftd., flared rim, #111	55.00
Bowl, 10" x 4½", #115	45.00
Bowl, 10½" x 5", crimped, #115	44.00
Bowl, 10½" x 7" x 7", #126	62.00
Bowl, 10¾" x 4¾", #115	42.50
Bowl, 11" x 1¾", #30	55.00
Bowl, 11" x 3¼", flared rim, #111	62.50
Bowl, 11" x 5¼", flared rim, #6	70.00
Bowl, 11½" x 8¼", oval, #115	45.00
Bowl, 12" x 3½", #6	70.00
Bowl, 12" x 3¼", flared, #115	60.00
Bowl, 12" x 4" x 7½", oval, #117	65.00
Bowl, 12½", flat, ftd., #126	75.00
Bowl, 13" x 3¼" x 8¾", oval, flared, #115	55.00
Bowl, 13" x 7" x 9¼", #126	67.50
Bowl, 13" x 7", #117	62.50
Bowl, 14" x 7½" x 6", oval, #126	65.00
Box, candy w/lid, 4¾" x 6¼"	60.00
Butter or cheese, 7" sq. x 1¼", #111	130.00
Candelabra, 2-lite, #41	35.00
Candelabrum, 6", 2-lite w/prisms, #30	60.00
Candle, 3", 1-lite, #111	25.00
Candle, 3", low, #115	25.00
Candle, 3½", #115	25.00
Candle, 4", cornucopia, #117	25.00
Candle, 4", low, #111	25.00
Candle, 5¼", 2-lite, globe, #30	35.00
Candle, 6", 2-lite, #30	35.00
Candy box, 6" x 3½", 3 hdld., 3 pt., w/lid, #115	85.00
Candy box, 6" x 3½", 3 pt., w/lid, crown finial, #106	90.00

	Crystal
Candy jar, 5" x 7¼", w/lid, ftd., #25	85.00
Candy, 6½", w/5" lid, #115	75.00
Carafe, w/stopper, water, #5200	195.00
Cheese stand, 3" x 5¼", #111	25.00
Cheese stand, 5¾" x 3½", #115	25.00
Cigarette box w/lid, 4" x 4¼"	32.00
Cigarette box w/lid, 4½" x 3½", #30	35.00
Cigarette box w/lid, 4¾" x 3¾"	35.00
Cocktail shaker, 14 oz., #5200	135.00
Cocktail shaker, 16 oz., #5200	135.00
Cocktail shaker, 32 oz., #5200	175.00
Comport w/lid, 8¾" x 5½", #111	135.00
Comport, 3½"x 4¾"W, #111	30.00
Comport, 5" x 5½", flared rim, #115	32.00
Comport, 5¼" x 6¾", flat top, #115	32.00
Comport, 6" x 4¾", low #115	37.50
Creamer, 2½", individual, #115	18.00
Creamer, 3", 10 oz., #111	18.00
Creamer, 3¾", 7 oz., #115	15.00
Creamer, sugar w/butter pat lid, breakfast set, #28	75.00
Cruet, #25	90.00
Cruet, #30	90.00
Cup, #115	18.00
Decanter w/stopper, 16 oz., #5200	150.00
Decanter w/stopper, 32 oz., #30	175.00
Decanter w/stopper, 32 oz., #5200	175.00
Hat, 4½", #30	395.00
Hat, 5½" x 8½" x 6¼", #30	350.00
Honey dish, 5" x 3", #91	30.00
Ice bucket, 6", #30	110.00
Lamp, hurricane, w/prisms, 15", #115	175.00
Lamp shade only, #115	125.00
Lid for candy urn, #111	35.00
Mayonnaise, 4¾" x 4½", div. w/7½" underplate	35.00
Mayonnaise, 5¼" x 3", div. w/6½" plate, #115	35.00
Mayonnaise, 5½" x 2½", ftd., hdld., #111	35.00
Mayonnaise, 5½" x 2¾", #115	35.00
Mayonnaise, 5½" x 3½", crimped, #11	32.00
Mayonnaise, 5¾" x 3", w/dish hdld. tray, #111	35.00
Mayonnaise, w/7" tray hdld. #111	35.00
Mustard w/lid & underplate	57.50
Nappy, 5" x 1", w/bottom star, #25	20.00
Nappy, 5" x 1¾", one hdld., #115	18.00
Nappy, 5½" x 2", div., hdld., #111	18.00
Nappy, 5½" x 2", one hdld., heart, #115	28.00
Nappy, 6" x 1¾", hdld., #111	22.00

	Crystal
Perfume tray, 8" x 5", #5200	25.00
Perfume, 5", #5200	85.00
Pitcher, #5200	175.00
Pitcher, 9", 80 oz., ice lip, #5202	195.00
Plate, 6", #111	12.00
Plate, 6", #115	12.00
Plate, 6", hdld., lemon, #111	14.00
Plate, 6", sq., #111	14.00
Plate, 7", #111	17.50
Plate, 7½", #111	18.00
Plate, 7½", #115	18.00
Plate, 7½", mayonnaise liner, hdld. #115	15.00
Plate, 7½", sq., #111	19.00
Plate, 7½", 2 hdld., #115	19.00
Plate, 8½", #30	20.00
Plate, 8½", #111	20.00
Plate, 8½", #115	20.00
Plate, 11", #111	47.50
Plate, 11", 2 hdld., sandwich, #115	30.00
Plate, 11", hdld., #111	40.00
Plate, 11", hdld., cracker w/ring, #115	40.00
Plate, 11", hdld., cracker w/ring, #111	40.00
Plate, 11", hdld., sandwich, #111	40.00
Plate, 11¼", dinner, #115	55.00
Plate, 12", egg, #30	135.00
Plate, 12", torte, rolled edge, #111	40.00
Plate, 13", torte, flat edge, #111	50.00
Plate, 13", torte, rolled edge, #111	60.00
Plate, 13¼", torte, #111	60.00
Plate, 13½", cake, hdld., #115	50.00
Plate, 14", #115	50.00
Plate, 14", cake, #115	50.00
Plate, 14½", cake, lg. base, #30	55.00
Plate, 14½", cake, sm. base, #30	55.00
Relish, 6" x 1¾", hdld., 2 pt., #111	20.00
Relish, 6" x 1¾", hdld., 2 pt., #115	20.00
Relish, 8" x 4½", pickle, 2 pt., #115	25.00
Relish, 8", 3 pt., hdld., #115	25.00
Relish, 9" x 1½", 2 pt. pickle, #115	25.00
Relish, 9" x 1½", 3 hdld, 3 pt., #115	32.50
Relish, 9" x 1½", 3 hdld., flared, #115	32.50
Relish, 10", 5 pt. tray, #30	65.00
Relish, 10½" x 1½", hdld., 5 pt., #111	85.00
Relish, 10½" x 1¼", 2 hdld. 3 pt., #115	60.00
Relish, 10½" x 7", #115	37.50
Relish, 11¾", tray, #115	45.00
Relish, 12", 4 pt., hdld., #111	40.00
Relish, 12", 5 pt., hdld., #111	55.00
Salt and pepper pr., #30	30.00
Salt and pepper pr., #115	40.00
Sandwich tray, 12" x 5¼", ctr. handle, #115	80.00
Saucer, #115	8.50
Stem, 3¾", 1 oz., cordial, #5111½	65.00
Stem, 3¾", 4½ oz., oyster cocktail, #5111½	22.50
Stem, 4", 5 oz., ice cream, #5111½	14.00
Stem, 4¼", 3 oz., cocktail, #115	22.50

	Crystal
Stem, 4½", 3½ oz., cocktail, #5111½	22.50
Stem, 5", 5 oz., saucer champagne, #5111½	18.00
Stem, 5¼", 3 oz., wine, #5111½	32.50
Stem, 5¼", 5 oz., ftd. juice, #5111½	24.00
Stem, 5¾", 10 oz., low luncheon goblet, #5111½	17.50
Stem, 6", 4½ oz., claret, #5111½	50.00
Stem, 6½", 12 oz., ftd. ice tea, #5111½	35.00
Stem, 6¾", 14 oz., ftd. ice tea, #5111½	35.00
Stem, cordial, #111	20.00
Sugar, 2½", individual, #115	15.00
Sugar, 3", 7 oz., #115	14.00
Sugar, 3", 10 oz., #111	15.00
Tray, 8" x 2", hdld. celery, #111	17.50
Tray, 8" x 4¾", individual sug/cr., #115	17.50
Tray, 8¾", celery, #91	30.00
Tray, 11", celery, #91	40.00
Tumbler, 2", 1½ oz., whiskey, #5200	65.00
Tumbler, 2½" x 3⅜", sham, Teardrop, ftd.	60.00
Tumbler, 3", sham, #5200	32.50
Tumbler, 4¾", 10 oz., sham, #5200	37.50
Tumbler, 5½", 12 oz., sham, #5200	37.50
Tumbler, 6", 14 oz., sham, #5200	37.50
Tumbler, 8 oz., flat, #115	30.00
Urn, 4½" x 4½", #111	27.50
Urn, 4½" x 4½", #115	27.50
Urn, 4¾", rnd ft.	27.50
Urn, 5", #525	37.50
Urn, 5½", ring hdld, sq. ft.	65.00
Urn, 5½", sq. ft.	37.50
Urn, 6½", sq. hdld.	70.00
Urn, 7", #529	37.50
Vase, 4", flared rim, #115	25.00
Vase, 4½" x 4¾", #115	30.00
Vase, 5" x 5", crimped, #115	35.00
Vase, 6", #507	55.00
Vase, 8" x 4¾", cornucopia, #117	65.00
Vase, 8", ftd., #506	90.00
Vase, 8", ftd., #507	90.00
Vase, 8½" x 2¾", #505	110.00
Vase, 8½" x 6", #115	90.00
Vase, 9" x 4½", #505	95.00
Vase, 9", #509	90.00
Vase, 9", bud, #506	80.00
Vase, 9½" x 3½", #506	125.00
Vase, 10" x 4¾", #5200	90.00
Vase, 10", #507	95.00
Vase, 10", ftd., #111	115.00
Vase, 10", ftd., #505	115.00
Vase, 10", ftd., #506	115.00
Vase, 10½" x 12 x 9½", #126	155.00
Vase, 10½", #126	175.00
Vase, 11" x 5¼", #505	145.00
Vase, 11½ x 4½", #506	140.00
Vase, 12", flared #115	145.00
Vase, 12", ftd., #506	145.00
Vase, 12", ftd., #507	155.00

Colors: crystal, pink, yellow

Tiffin's Flanders is continually mistaken for Cambridge's Gloria by collectors, particularly in yellow and crystal. Refer to Gloria to see that curved stem floral design.

Flanders popularity seems to have increased recently. Internet activity has been rather heavy when pieces of this pattern have been offered for sale. An entire new wave of collectors has discovered these patterns via the Internet. This is bound to impact prices on these already scarce wares! True, initially it may make more available to buy; but I do not expect those supplies to be long lived. If you want a pattern, do not dawdle about getting it.

Flanders stems are prevalently found on Tiffin's #17024 blank. Frequently these have a crystal foot and stem with tops of crystal, pink, or yellow. Color blending that is seen infrequently includes green foot with pink stems, and pink tumblers as well as pitchers with crystal handle and foot. One green Flanders vase was found a couple of years ago and is pictured in *Very Rare Glassware of the Depression Years, Fifth Series.*

Round plates are Tiffin's line #8800 and each size plate has a different number. Scalloped plates are line #5831. I see more of the round plates than I do the scalloped ones. As with most Tiffin pitchers of this time, you can find Flanders with and without a cover. Keep in mind that the pitcher top is plain with no pattern etched on it.

Shakers are being found in crystal occasionally, but only a few pink shakers have been seen. I have had a few reports of yellow, but I have never seen one. New listings are continuing to grow! Thanks are due readers and dealers for postcards and pictures sent with this information!

Lamps are found only in crystal; pink or yellow ones have never turned up. That cylindrical shade is sometimes found over a candlestick and designated as a Chinese hurricane lamp.

The bouillon cup was placed next to the sugar for comparison. I recently had a report of a cream soup; so, be on the lookout for that.

	Crystal	Pink	Yellow
Ash tray, 2¼x3¾"			
w/cigarette rest	55.00		
Bowl, 2 hdld., bouillon	50.00	135.00	85.00
Bowl, finger, w/liner	35.00	95.00	60.00
Bowl, 2 hdld., bonbon	25.00	65.00	45.00
Bowl, 11", ftd., console	45.00	110.00	65.00
Bowl, 12", flanged rim,			
console	45.00	125.00	70.00
Candlestick, 2 styles	40.00	75.00	50.00
Candy jar, w/cover, flat	135.00	350.00	250.00
Candy jar, w/cover, ftd.	100.00	250.00	185.00
Celery, 11"	30.00	75.00	50.00
Cheese & cracker	55.00	130.00	100.00
Comport, 3½"	30.00	70.00	60.00
Comport, 6"	65.00	175.00	95.00
Creamer, flat	45.00	135.00	90.00
Creamer, ftd.	40.00	120.00	70.00
Cup, 2 styles	50.00	100.00	65.00
Decanter	195.00	350.00	275.00
Electric lamp	325.00		
Grapefruit, w/liner	60.00	150.00	100.00

	Crystal	Pink	Yellow
Hurricane lamp, Chinese			
style	255.00		
Mayonnaise, w/liner	35.00	100.00	80.00
Nut cup, ftd., blown	40.00	80.00	60.00
Oil bottle & stopper	150.00	350.00	250.00
Parfait, 5⅝", hdld.	70.00	180.00	125.00
Pitcher & cover	250.00	395.00	295.00
Plate, 6"	5.00	15.00	12.00
Plate, 8"	10.00	20.00	15.50
Plate, 10¼", dinner	50.00	95.00	75.00
Relish, 3 pt.	35.00	90.00	80.00
Salt & pepper, pr.	175.00	395.00	275.00
Sandwich server,			
center hdld.		165.00	
Saucer	8.00	15.00	10.00
Stem, 4½", oyster cocktail	15.00	40.00	25.00
Stem, 4½", sherbet	10.00	28.00	17.50
Stem, 4¾", cocktail	15.00	40.00	30.00
Stem, 5", cordial	60.00	110.00	85.00
Stem, 5⅝", parfait	40.00	110.00	80.00
Stem, 6⅛", wine	30.00	75.00	45.00
Stem, 6¼", saucer			
champagne	15.00	35.00	20.00
Stem, claret	40.00	150.00	95.00
Stem, 8¼", water	15.00	50.00	35.00
Sugar, flat	45.00	135.00	90.00
Sugar, ftd.	40.00	120.00	70.00
Tumbler, 2¾", 2½ oz., ftd.	45.00	90.00	60.00
Tumbler, 4¾", 9 oz., ftd.,			
water	15.00	40.00	25.00
Tumbler, 4¾", 10 oz., ftd.	20.00	45.00	30.00
Tumbler, 5⅞", 12 oz., ftd.,			
tea	30.00	65.00	40.00
Vase, bud	35.00	90.00	70.00
Vase, ftd.	100.00	250.00	175.00
Vase, Dahlia style	150.00	275.00	200.00
Vase, fan	100.00	250.00	150.00

Colors: crystal w/green, Twilight, Twilight w/crystal, pink, crystal w/amber

Fontaine is a Tiffin pattern that would attract more collectors were they ever given the chance to see much of it. The purple color in the photograph is Tiffin's earlier Twilight color that does not change colors when exposed to different light sources. Tiffin's later Twilight changes from pink to purple depending upon fluorescent or natural light. See page 238 for this later color with the same name.

The birds at the fountain are readily recognized, once you are familiar with this pattern. As with all Tiffin patterns, cup and saucers are rarely found. I bought the set pictured about ten years ago, before I even considered this pattern for the book. I knew cups and saucers were hard to find. I have not found cup and saucers in any other colors.

I found only the one cordial pictured while I was seeking those. Water goblets seem to be more plentiful than sherbets, but that may be true only in the areas I shop. I, personally, favor the crystal tops with colored stems over the monotone colored pieces. However, I just bought a beautiful all pink water goblet last week to use for the next photograph.

I remember a dealer exhibiting a covered Fontaine pitcher in Wisteria at the Houston Depression glass show about six or seven years ago. He had a very high price on it for that time. Several dealers looked at his price and laughed (several out loud), telling him that he would never sell it. That night a lady walked into his booth and saw that extraordinary Fontaine pitcher. She told her husband that she wanted it. He looked at the price, swallowed real hard and pulled out a stack of hundred dollar bills. It would, perhaps, still be difficult to sell one for that price; but the right person came in and wanted it; so it sold at the price asked. Who knows? That may turn out to be a bargain down the collecting road!

	amber green pink	Twilight
Bowl, 13" centerpiece, #8153	75.00	175.00
Candlestick, low, #9758	35.00	75.00
Creamer, ftd., #4	35.00	65.00
Cup, #8869	55.00	100.00
Finger bowl, #022	35.00	65.00
Grape fruit, #251 & footed liner, #881	65.00	125.00
Jug & cover, #194	395.00	1195.00
Plate, 6" #8814	12.50	20.00
Plate, 8", #8833	20.00	35.00
Plate, 10", #8818	65.00	125.00
Plate, 10", cake w/ctr. hdld., #345	65.00	125.00

	amber green pink	Twilight
Saucer, #8869	12.50	25.00
Stem, cafe parfait, #033	65.00	135.00
Stem, claret, #033	60.00	115.00
Stem, cocktail, #033	35.00	55.00
Stem, saucer champagne, #033	30.00	55.00
Stem, sundae, #033	25.00	45.00
Stem, water, #033	45.00	95.00
Stem, wine, 2½ oz., #033	55.00	110.00
Sugar, ftd., #4	35.00	65.00
Tumbler, 9 oz. table, #032	35.00	65.00
Vase, 8" ftd., #2	95.00	195.00
Vase, 9¼", bowed top, #7	125.00	225.00

Colors: crystal and crystal w/wisteria base

Fostoria's Fuchsia is a new pattern for this book. Be sure to look at Tiffin's Fuchsia pattern so that you do not confuse these. This Fuchsia is mostly etched on Fostoria's Lafayette mould blank #2244 which can be found on page 118. Stemware line #6044 was also used for Fuchsia.

Notice that champagne with the Wisteria stem. Most of those were sold to go with Lafayette Wisteria tableware that was unetched. I have run into several sets that had this Wisteria stem, but they all had plain Wisteria cups, saucers, plates, and creamers and sugars.

The center surface areas of flat pieces are easily scratched from use or from stacking. I have seen some recently that were cloudy looking from all the marks. These will not sell for much, if at all. Collectors do put a premium on mint condition, but few value damaged merchandise. I have been told a few people around the country are trying their hand at buffing out the scratches from these plates; but I understand it's expensive and not always successful.

	Crystal	Wisteria
Bon bon, #2470	33.00	
Bowl, 10", #2395	95.00	
Bowl, 10½", #2470½	70.00	
Bowl 11½" "B," #2440	75.00	
Bowl, 12" #2470	90.00	165.00
Candlestick, 3", #2375	35.00	
Candlestick, 5", #2395½	55.00	
Candlestick, 5½", #2470½	75.00	
Candlestick, 5½", #2470	75.00	195.00
Comport, 6" low, #2470	40.00	70.00
Comport, 6" tall, #2470	75.00	135.00
Creamer, ftd., #2440	35.00	
Cup, #2440	20.00	
Finger bowl, #869	35.00	
Lemon dish, #2470	32.00	
Oyster cocktail, 4½ oz., #6004	17.50	35.00
Plate, 10" cake	65.00	
Plate, 6" bread & butter, #2440	10.00	
Plate, 7" salad, #2440	15.00	
Plate, 8" luncheon, #2440	22.00	
Plate, 9" dinner, #2440	67.50	

	Crystal	Wisteria
Saucer, #2440	7.50	
Stem, ¾ oz. cordial, #6004	65.00	150.00
Stem, 2½ oz. wine, #6004	35.00	55.00
Stem, 3 oz. cocktail, #6004	25.00	45.00
Stem, 4 oz. claret, #6004	45.00	75.00
Stem, 5 oz. low sherbet, #6004	22.50	35.00
Stem, 5½ oz. 6" parfait, #6004	37.50	67.50
Stem, 5½ oz., 5⅜" saucer champagne, #6004	27.50	47.50
Stem, 9 oz. water, #6004	35.00	55.00
Sugar, ftd., #2440	35.00	
Sweetmeat, #2470	38.00	
Tumbler, 2 oz., #833	25.00	
Tumbler, 2½ oz. ftd. whiskey, #6004	35.00	55.00
Tumbler, 5 oz., #833	22.50	
Tumbler, 5 oz. ftd. juice, #6004	20.00	40.00
Tumbler, 8 oz., #833	22.00	
Tumbler, 9 oz. ftd., #6004	18.00	37.50
Tumbler, 12 oz., #833	30.00	
Tumbler, 12 oz. ftd., #6004	32.00	57.50

Colors: crystal

Please note the Tiffin Pearl Edge Fuchsia creamer and sugar shown to the right. I'm showing them for style comparison to Fostoria's Fuchsia on page 89 and to alert collectors regarding these same named patterns.

New pieces continue to be unearthed. Fuchsia has always attracted collectors; and because of this, dealers are searching every nook and cranny, explaining why so many new pieces are being found! I now have four different collectors who are buying Fuchsia patterns regardless of the glass manufacturer.

Only the bell, and the plate behind the creamer and sugar (top photo on page 91) are considered hard to find. The bowl style of mayonnaise in the center of that picture is often found without the plate. It is not a berry bowl as several readers have thought they had.

The bottom photo shows a rarely seen bitters bottle and, on the left, the icer and liner. A Chinese hurricane lamp can be seen here. That cylinder cover can also be used on an electric lamp pictured under Flanders. On the right are the rarely seen cup and saucer in addition to two styles of finger bowls, footed and flat. In between the finger bowls is a footed mayonnaise. There are three styles of double candlesticks shown in the two photos with the pointed knob type being the most difficult to find!

Fuchsia has three known stemware lines; #15083 is the most often found though you cannot prove it by my photos that omitted all but one, a #17457. Sorry!

	Crystal
Ash tray, 2¼" x 3¾" w/cigarette rest	35.00
Bell, 5", #15083	75.00
Bitters bottle	395.00
Bowl, 4", finger, ftd., #041	60.00
Bowl, 4½" finger, w/#8814 liner	75.00
Bowl, 5³⁄₁₆", 2 hdld., #5831	35.00
Bowl, 6¼", cream soup, ftd., #5831	50.00
Bowl, 7¼", salad, #5902	40.00
Bowl, 8⅜", 2 hdld., #5831	55.00
Bowl, 9¾", deep salad	75.00
Bowl, 10", salad	65.00
Bowl, 10½", console, fan shaped sides, #319	70.00
Bowl, 11⅞", console, flared, #5902	80.00
Bowl, 12", flanged rim, console, #5831	60.00
Bowl, 12⅝", console, flared, #5902	90.00
Bowl, 13", crimped, #5902	80.00
Candlestick, 2-lite, w/pointed center, #5831	80.00
Candlestick, 2-lite, tapered center, #15306	80.00
Candlestick, 5", 2-lite, ball center	80.00
Candlestick, 5⅝", 2-lite, w/fan center, #5902	80.00
Candlestick, single, #348	40.00
Celery, 10", oval, #5831	35.00
Celery, 10½", rectangular, #5902	37.50
Cigarette box, w/lid, 4" x 2¾", #9305	120.00
Cocktail shaker, 8", w/metal top	250.00
Comport, 6¼", #5831	30.00
Comport, 6½", w/beaded stem, #15082	35.00
Creamer, 2⅞", individual, #5831	45.00
Creamer, 3⅜", flat w/beaded handle, #5902	27.50
Creamer, 4½", ftd., #5831	22.50
Creamer, pearl edge	45.00
Cup, #5831	80.00
Electric lamp	300.00
Hurricane, 12", Chinese style	250.00
Icer, with insert	155.00
Mayonnaise, flat, w/6¼" liner, #5902 w/ladle	50.00
Mayonnaise, ftd., w/ladle, #5831	50.00
Nut dish, 6¼"	40.00
Pickle, 7⅜", #5831	40.00
Pitcher & cover, #194	395.00
Pitcher, flat	395.00
Plate, 6¼", bread and butter, #5902	8.00
Plate, 6¼", sherbet, #8814	10.00
Plate, 6⅜", 2 hdld., #5831	12.50
Plate, 7", marmalade, 3-ftd., #310½	27.50
Plate, 7⅞", clam soup or mayo liner, #5831	12.50
Plate, 7⅞", salad, #8814	15.00
Plate, 7½", salad, #5831	15.00
Plate, 8¼", luncheon, #5902	17.50
Plate, 8⅛", luncheon, #8833	22.50

	Crystal
Plate, 8⅜", bonbon, pearl edge	27.50
Plate, 9½", dinner, #5902	65.00
Plate, 10½", 2 hdld., cake, #5831	55.00
Plate, 10½", muffin tray, pearl edge	55.00
Plate, 13", lily rolled and crimped edge	65.00
Plate, 14¼", sandwich, #8833	55.00
Relish, 6⅜", 3 pt., #5902	25.00
Relish, 9¼", square, 3 pt.	40.00
Relish, 10½" x 12½", hdld., 3 pt., #5902	60.00
Relish, 10½" x 12½", hdld., 5 pt.	70.00
Salt and pepper, pr., #2	125.00
Saucer, #5831	15.00
Stem, 4¹⁄₁₆", cordial, #15083	32.50
Stem, 4⅛", sherbet, #15083	12.00
Stem, 4¼", cocktail, #15083	18.00
Stem, 4⅝", 3½ oz., cocktail, #17453	37.50
Stem, 4⅞", saucer champagne, hollow stem	95.00
Stem, 5¹⁄₁₆", wine, #15083	30.00
Stem, 5¼", claret, #15083	37.50
Stem, 5⅜", cocktail, "S" stem, #17457	50.00
Stem, 5⅜", cordial, "S" stem, #17457	125.00
Stem, 5⅜", 7 oz., saucer champagne, #17453	30.00
Stem, 5⅜", saucer champagne, #15083	15.00
Stem, 5⅜", saucer champagne, "S" stem, #17457	45.00
Stem, 5¹⁵⁄₁₆", parfait, #15083	40.00
Stem, 6¼", low water, #15083	25.00
Stem, 7⅜", 9 oz., water, #17453	40.00
Stem, 7½", water, high, #15083	25.00
Stem, 7⅝", water, "S" stem, #17457	65.00
Sugar, 2⅞", individual, #5831	40.00
Sugar, 3⅜", flat, w/beaded handle, #5902	27.50
Sugar, 4½", ftd., #5831	22.50
Sugar, pearl edge	45.00
Tray, sugar/creamer	55.00
Tray, 9½", 2 hdld. for cream/sugar	45.00
Tumbler, 2⁷⁄₁₆", 2 oz., bar, flat, #506	65.00
Tumbler, 3⁵⁄₁₆", oyster cocktail, #14196	14.00
Tumbler, 3⅜", old-fashioned, flat, #580	50.00
Tumbler, 4¹³⁄₁₆" flat, juice	30.00
Tumbler, 4⁵⁄₁₆", 5 oz., ftd., juice, #15083	18.00
Tumbler, 5⅛", water, flat, #517	27.50
Tumbler, 5⁵⁄₁₆", 9 oz., ftd., water, #15083	15.00
Tumbler, 6⁵⁄₁₆", 12 oz., ftd., tea, #15083	30.00
Vase, 6½", bud, #14185	30.00
Vase, 8¹³⁄₁₆", flared, crimped	90.00
Vase, 8¼", bud, #14185	35.00
Vase, 10½", bud, #14185	45.00
Vase, 10¾", bulbous bottom, #5872	195.00
Vase, 10⅞", beaded stem, #15082	75.00
Vase, 11¾", urn, 2 hdld., trophy.	105.00
Whipped cream, 3-ftd., #310	40.00

Colors: black, blue, crystal, yellow

Gazebo and another pattern, Utopia, are two very similar Paden City designs. The designs on Utopia are larger and fuller than those on Gazebo. Utopia may have been converted from Gazebo for use on larger items. Yes, we are speculating as no one knows why the glass companies did some of the things they did. Thirty years ago, I believed all of the retired workers' recollections; time has proved many of those stories false, or at least exaggerated.

The finite availability of Paden City patterns creates major problems for collectors today. There is just enough to whet your appetite. Until I listed this pattern a couple of books back, you could find most pieces in the $45.00 range due to size more than anything else. Most people selling Gazebo had no idea about the pattern. It looked old and elegant and was never priced inexpensively.

Several different Paden City mould lines were used for this etching. All measurements are taken from actual pieces. We have not yet found a punch bowl to go with our punch cups. We have found a flat, heart shaped candy dish. There are crystal ones and blue bottoms with crystal tops being found. If you find one with a blue top, please let me know.

Another blue cheese dish has been found, but I have not spotted one in crystal yet. That cheese has also been spotted in Ruby, but without an etching. All pieces may not be found in color! Blue seems only to be found on the beaded edge pieces. The yellow and black vases are the only pieces I have spotted in those colors. If you have other pieces, please let me know!

	Crystal	Blue
Bowl, 9", fan handles	45.00	
Bowl, 9", bead handles	45.00	75.00
Bowl, 13", flat edge	55.00	
Bowl, 14", low flat	55.00	
Candlestick, 5¼"	45.00	
Candlestick, double, 2 styles	60.00	
Candy Dish w/lid "heart"	100.00	
Candy w/lid, 10¼", small	75.00	110.00
Candy w/lid, 11", large	90.00	
Cheese dish and cover	100.00	195.00
Cocktail shaker, w/glass stopper	125.00	
Creamer	22.50	

	Crystal	Blue
Mayonnaise liner	15.00	225.00
Mayonnaise, bead handles	25.00	
Plate, 10¾"	45.00	
Plate, 12½", bead handles	55.00	85.00
Plate, 13", fan handles	50.00	
Plate, 16", beaded edge		95.00
Relish, 9¾", three part	35.00	60.00
Server, 10", swan handle	50.00	
Server, 11", center handle	40.00	75.00
Sugar	22.50	
Tumbler, ftd. juice	22.00	
Vase, 10¼"	75.00	195.00*

*Black or yellow

Colors: crystal, yellow, Peach-Blo, green, Emerald green (light and dark), amber, blue, Heatherbloom, Ebony with white gold

Cambridge's Gloria is regularly confused with Tiffin's Flanders. Look closely at these two similar patterns and notice that the flower on Gloria bends the stem. They are easily identified once you place them side by side.

Gloria can be collected in large sets of yellow or crystal if you so desire; but any other color will frustrate you. Yellow Gloria is more obtainable than is crystal; so if you like that color, buy it. A luncheon set in blue and Peach-Blo (pink) is found occasionally, but larger sets may not be possible to assemble. For some inexplicable reason I have always been drawn to the dark Emerald green, but I have only owned a dozen or so pieces in that color as it is rarely found. Gold encrusted items bring 20% to 25% more than those without gold. However, pieces with worn gold are difficult to sell now. That may change with all the decorators touting the "distressed" look.

Amber footed, yellow stem Gloria turns up once in a while, but there is a Lilliputian's amount of this color combination available. Gloria might make an ideal candidate for blending of colors, since there are so many from which to choose.

I am amazed at the amount of Elegant glass that is being found in the West! When I travel out there, I see some glassware that I never see in the East. Distribution of patterns was unmistakably geographical, and the best way to discover this is to visit different areas of the country!

As with other Cambridge patterns in this book, not all Gloria pieces are listed. A more complete listing of Cambridge etched pieces is found under Rose Point. Be sure to note prices for Gloria will run 30% to 40% less than the prices listed there.

	Crystal	Green Pink Yellow
Basket, 6", 2 hdld. (sides up)	30.00	45.00
Bowl, 3", indiv. nut, 4 ftd.	65.00	85.00
Bowl, 3½", cranberry	35.00	65.00
Bowl, 5", ftd., crimped edge, bonbon	30.00	50.00
Bowl, 5", sq., fruit, "saucer"	20.00	35.00
Bowl, 5½", bonbon, 2 hdld.	25.00	38.00
Bowl, 5½", bonbon, ftd.	25.00	35.00
Bowl, 5½", flattened, ftd., bonbon	25.00	35.00
Bowl, 5½", fruit, "saucer"	22.00	35.00
Bowl, 6", rnd., cereal	35.00	50.00
Bowl, 6", sq., cereal	35.00	50.00
Bowl, 8", 2 pt., 2 hdld., relish	35.00	45.00
Bowl, 8", 3 pt., 3 hdld., relish	38.00	50.00
Bowl, 8¾", 2 hdld., figure, "8" pickle	30.00	50.00
Bowl, 8¾", 2 pt., 2 hdld., figure "8" relish	30.00	50.00
Bowl, 9", salad, tab hdld.	50.00	100.00
Bowl, 9½", 2 hdld., veg.	75.00	120.00
Bowl, 10", oblong, tab hdld., "baker"	65.00	100.00
Bowl, 10", 2 hdld.	55.00	90.00
Bowl, 11", 2 hdld., fruit	60.00	95.00
Bowl, 12", 4 ftd., console	60.00	95.00
Bowl, 12", 4 ftd., flared rim	60.00	95.00
Bowl, 12", 4 ftd., oval	65.00	100.00
Bowl, 12", 5 pt., celery & relish	60.00	90.00
Bowl, 13", flared rim	65.00	100.00

	Crystal	Green Pink Yellow
Bowl, cream soup, w/rnd. liner	40.00	65.00
Bowl, cream soup, w/sq. saucer	40.00	65.00
Bowl, finger, flared edge, w/rnd. plate	35.00	65.00
Bowl, finger, ftd.	35.00	60.00
Bowl, finger, w/rnd. plate	40.00	65.00
Butter, w/cover, 2 hdld.	150.00	350.00
Candlestick, 6", ea.	45.00	75.00
Candy box, w/cover, 4 ftd., w/tab hdld.	145.00	225.00
Cheese compote w/11½" cracker plate, tab hdld.	60.00	95.00
Cocktail shaker, grnd. stopper, spout (like pitcher)	145.00	250.00
Comport, 4", fruit cocktail	18.00	33.00
Comport, 5", 4 ftd.	25.00	75.00
Comport, 6", 4 ftd.	30.00	80.00
Comport, 7", low	40.00	100.00
Comport, 7", tall	45.00	125.00
Comport, 9½", tall, 2 hdld., ftd. bowl	80.00	195.00
Creamer, ftd.	20.00	30.00
Creamer, tall, ftd.	20.00	35.00
Cup, rnd. or sq.	20.00	33.00
Cup, 4 ftd., sq.	50.00	100.00
Cup, after dinner (demitasse), rnd. or sq.	75.00	125.00
Fruit cocktail, 6 oz., ftd. (3 styles)	15.00	25.00
Ice pail, metal handle w/tongs	75.00	150.00

	Crystal	Green Pink Yellow
Icer, w/insert	65.00	110.00
Mayonnaise, w/liner & ladle		
(4 ftd. bowl)	45.00	95.00
Oil, w/stopper, tall, ftd., hdld.	110.00	250.00
Oyster cocktail, #3035, 4½ oz.	20.00	30.00
Oyster cocktail, 4½ oz., low stem	20.00	30.00
Pitcher, 67 oz., middle indent	225.00	395.00
Pitcher, 80 oz., ball	295.00	495.00
Pitcher, w/cover, 64 oz.	295.00	595.00
Plate, 6", 2 hdld.	15.00	20.00
Plate, 6", bread/butter	12.00	15.00
Plate, 7½", tea	14.00	18.00
Plate, 8½"	16.00	25.00
Plate, 9½", dinner	65.00	100.00
Plate, 10", tab hdld., salad	45.00	65.00
Plate, 11", 2 hdld.	50.00	70.00
Plate, 11", sq., ftd. cake	100.00	265.00
Plate, 11½", tab hdld., sandwich	60.00	80.00
Plate, 14", chop or salad	65.00	100.00
Plate, sq., bread/butter	12.00	15.00
Plate, sq., dinner	70.00	110.00
Plate, sq., salad	14.00	20.00
Plate, sq., service	45.00	80.00
Platter, 11½"	75.00	150.00
Salt & pepper, pr., short	45.00	125.00

	Crystal	Green Pink Yellow
Salt & pepper, pr., w/glass top, tall	70.00	150.00
Salt & pepper, ftd., metal tops	60.00	150.00
Saucer, rnd.	4.00	6.00
Saucer, rnd. after dinner	12.00	20.00
Saucer, sq., after dinner (demitasse)	15.00	25.00
Saucer, sq.	4.00	6.00
Stem, #3035, 2½ oz., wine	30.00	60.00
Stem, #3035, 3 oz., cocktail	20.00	35.00
Stem, #3035, 3½ oz., cocktail	20.00	35.00
Stem, #3035, 4½ oz., claret	45.00	85.00
Stem, #3035, 6 oz., low sherbet	18.00	26.00
Stem, #3035, 6 oz., tall sherbet	22.00	30.00
Stem, #3035, 9 oz., water	28.00	50.00
Stem, #3035, 3½ oz., cocktail	20.00	35.00
Stem, #3115, 9 oz., goblet	28.00	50.00
Stem, #3120, 1 oz., cordial	70.00	155.00
Stem, #3120, 4½ oz., claret	45.00	85.00
Stem, #3120, 6 oz., low sherbet	18.00	26.00
Stem, #3120, 6 oz., tall sherbet	20.00	30.00
Stem, #3120, 9 oz., water	28.00	50.00
Stem, #3130, 2½ oz., wine	30.00	62.50
Stem, #3130, 6 oz., low sherbet	18.00	26.00
Stem, #3130, 6 oz., tall sherbet	20.00	30.00
Stem, #3130, 8 oz., water	28.00	50.00
Stem, #3135, 1 oz., cordial	75.00	155.00

	Crystal	Green Pink Yellow			Crystal	Green Pink Yellow
Stem, #3135, 6 oz., low sherbet	18.00	26.00		Tumbler, #3120, 5 oz., ftd.	20.00	30.00
Stem, #3135, 6 oz., tall sherbet	20.00	30.00		Tumbler, #3120, 10 oz., ftd.	22.00	40.00
Stem, #3135, 8 oz., water	28.00	50.00		Tumbler, #3120, 12 oz., ftd.	30.00	50.00
Sugar, ftd.	20.00	30.00		Tumbler, #3130, 5 oz., ftd.	18.00	30.00
Sugar, tall, ftd.	25.00	35.00		Tumbler, #3130, 10 oz., ftd.	20.00	40.00
Sugar shaker, w/glass top	195.00	395.00		Tumbler, #3130, 12 oz., ftd.	25.00	50.00
Syrup, tall, ftd.	95.00	195.00		Tumbler, #3135, 5 oz., juice	18.00	30.00
Tray, 11", ctr. hdld., sandwich	35.00	65.00		Tumbler, #3135, 10 oz., water	20.00	40.00
Tray, 2 pt., ctr. hdld., relish	30.00	50.00		Tumbler, #3135, 12 oz., tea	25.00	50.00
Tray, 4 pt., ctr. hdld., relish	35.00	65.00		Tumbler, 12 oz., flat (2 styles), one		
Tray, 9", pickle, tab hdld.	35.00	70.00		indent side to match 67 oz. pitcher	25.00	45.00
Tumbler, #3035, 5 oz., high ftd.	20.00	30.00		Vase, 9", oval, 4 indent	115.00	215.00
Tumbler, #3035, 10 oz., high ftd.	22.00	40.00		Vase, 10", keyhole base	85.00	160.00
Tumbler, #3035, 12 oz., high ftd.	30.00	50.00		Vase, 10", squarish top	115.00	215.00
Tumbler, #3115, 5 oz., ftd., juice	20.00	30.00		Vase, 11"	100.00	175.00
Tumbler, #3115, 8 oz., ftd.	22.00	40.00		Vase, 11", neck indent	135.00	200.00
Tumbler, #3115, 10 oz., ftd.	25.00	45.00		Vase, 12", keyhole base, flared rim	165.00	250.00
Tumbler, #3115, 12 oz., ftd.	30.00	50.00		Vase, 12", squarish top	185.00	275.00
Tumbler, #3120, 2½ oz., ftd. (used				Vase, 14", keyhole base, flared rim	175.00	250.00
w/cocktail shaker)	30.00	65.00				

Note: See pages 228 – 229 for stem identification.

Colors: crystal, Spanish red, Ritz blue, Stiegel green, 14K Topaz, Anna Rose, Old Amethyst, India Black, Venetian (shamrock) green, Azure blue, Aquamarine, Peach, Caramel, Meadow green, Copen blue, Smoke, Light amethyst, Mission gold, Milk

Morgantown's Golf Ball is the most recognized design of this company. Cambridge's #1066 is similar to Golf Ball and novices sometimes mistake that for Morgantown. I bought the Ritz blue (cobalt) 6" torch candle (middle of the vases on Row 3, page 98) as well as the 4" Jacobi candle (Row 1, #4) at a show in Ohio last fall. Both were labeled hard to find Cambridge. Morgantown's Golf ball has crosshatched bumps equally distributed throughout the stem; Cambridge stems have alternating lines of dimples between rows of crosshatching. See my *Stemware Identification* book for further clarification. The Spanish red item between the two Jacobi candles was a damaged candle that someone "cut down" to make it usable. I found it intriguing.

A major problem for everyone is color identification. Page 99 the top row shows Anna Rose, Smoke, Azure blue, Light amethyst, and Peach. Unfortunately the Peach has picked up the spotlight and appears somewhat yellow. Row 2 illustrates Topaz Mist, 14K Topaz, Copen blue, and Meadow green. Row 3 includes crystal, Spanish red, Smoke, Meadow green, and Azure blue. On page 98 additional colors shown are India Black, Old Amethyst (dark), Stiegel green (blue/green), and Milk.

In general, all pieces of Golf Ball are hard to find except for stems, most vases, and candles. The Dupont (inverted two tier) candle is not easily found. You may have noticed the Irish coffee at the right. A sugar with two handles, and a creamer with spout, come in this style. Some square footed stems can be found.

The Harlequin pastel colors, often found in sets of eight, include Amethyst, Copen blue, Gloria blue, Peach, Smoke, Topaz Mist, Shamrock green, and iridized yellow. Other Harlequin sets include Coral and Pink Champagne.

Row 3 on page 98 shows ivy balls with and without a rim. They are 4" in diameter but stand a little under 6" without rim and a little over 7" with one. The one with the ruffled top is the most difficult to find. The Spanish red piece in the bottom row is the urn.

To be consistent in terminology for collectors, in the listings I have used name designations found in Gallagher's *Handbook of Old Morgantown Glass*.

Steigel Green
Spanish Red
*Ritz Blue other colors

	Steigel Green Spanish Red *Ritz Blue	other colors
Amherst water lamp, super rare	1000.00+	
Bell	100.00	60.00
Candle, pr., 4⅝" Dupont, (inverted 2 tier)	350.00	250.00
Candle, pr., 6" torch	300.00	225.00
Candlestick, pr., 4" Jacobi (top flat rim)	175.00	135.00
Candy, flat w/golf ball knob cover, 6"x 5½" (Alexandra)	1000.00	750.00
Creamer	175.00	
Compote 10" diam., 7½" high w/14 crimp rim (Truman)	475.00	375.00
Compote w/cover, 6" diam. (Celeste)	750.00	550.00
Compote, 6" diam. (Celeste)	450.00	300.00
Irish coffee, 5¼", 6 oz.	165.00	130.00
Pilsner, 9⅛", 11 oz.	175.00	135.00
Schooner, 8½", 32 oz.	295.00	195.00
Stem, brandy snifter, 6½", 21 oz.	155.00	125.00
Stem, cafe parfait, 6¼", 4 oz.	85.00	55.00
Stem, champagne, 5", 5½ oz.	35.00	25.00
Stem, claret, 5¼", 4½ oz.	75.00	45.00
Stem, cocktail, 4⅛", 3½ oz.	25.00	18.00
Stem, cordial, 3½", 1½ oz.	50.00	40.00

	Steigel Green Spanish Red *Ritz Blue	other colors
Stem, oyster cocktail, 4⅜", 4½ oz., cupped	35.00	25.00
Stem, oyster cocktail, 4¼", 4 oz., flared	40.00	30.00
Stem, sherbet/sundae, 4⅛", 5½ oz.	25.00	18.00
Stem, sherry, 4⅝", 2½ oz.	55.00	40.00
Stem, water, 6¾", 9 oz.	50.00	35.00
Stem, wine, 4¾", 3 oz.	45.00	30.00
Sugar	175.00	
Tumbler, 4⅜", ftd. wine	25.00	17.00
Tumbler, 5", 5 oz. ftd. juice	28.00	19.00
Tumbler, 6⅛", 9 oz. ftd. water	32.00	22.00
Tumbler, 6¾", 12 oz. ftd. tea	40.00	30.00
Urn, 6½" high.	95.00	65.00
Vase, 4" Ivy ball, ruff	125.00	90.00
Vase, 4" Ivy ball w/rim (Kimball)	65.00	55.00
Vase, 4" Ivy ball, no rim (Kennon)	60.00	50.00
Vase, 6½" "brandy" w/short standing rm. (Stephanie)	95.00	75.00
Vase, 8" high, Charlotte w/crimped rim	225.00	150.00
Vase, 8" high, flair rim flute (Charlotte)	250.00	195.00
Vase, 10½" #78 Lancaster (cupped w/tiny stand up rim)	300.00	235.00
Vase, 11", #79 Montague (flair rim)	350.00	275.00

*Add 10% for Ritz Blue

Colors: crystal; Flamingo pink punch bowl and cups only

Greek Key is an older Heisey pattern that is easily recognized by collectors. Other companies made similar patterns but most Heisey pieces are marked. Stemware is difficult to find.

	Crystal		Crystal
Bowl, finger	40.00	Cup, punch, Flamingo	45.00
Bowl, jelly, w/cover, 2 hdld., ftd	145.00	Coaster	20.00
Bowl, indiv., ftd., almond	45.00	Egg cup, 5 oz.	80.00
Bowl, 4", nappy	25.00	Hair receiver	170.00
Bowl, 4", shallow, low ft., jelly	40.00	Ice tub, lg., tab hdld.	150.00
Bowl, 4½", nappy	25.00	Ice tub, sm., tab hdld.	130.00
Bowl, 4½", scalloped, nappy	25.00	Ice tub, w/cover, hotel	220.00
Bowl, 4½", shallow, low ft., jelly	40.00	Ice tub, w/cover, 5", individual, w/5" plate	200.00
Bowl, 5", ftd., almond	40.00	Jar, 1 qt., crushed fruit, w/cover	400.00
Bowl, 5", ftd., almond, w/cover	110.00	Jar, 2 qt., crushed fruit, w/cover	400.00
Bowl, 5", hdld., jelly	95.00	Jar, lg. cover, horseradish	140.00
Bowl, 5", low ft., jelly, w/cover	110.00	Jar, sm. cover, horseradish	130.00
Bowl, 5", nappy	30.00	Jar, tall celery	140.00
Bowl, 5½", nappy	40.00	Jar, w/knob cover, pickle	160.00
Bowl, 5½", shallow nappy, ftd.	65.00	Pitcher, 1 pint (jug)	130.00
Bowl, 6", nappy	30.00	Pitcher, 1 quart (jug)	210.00
Bowl, 6", shallow nappy	30.00	Pitcher, 3 pint (jug)	250.00
Bowl, 6½", nappy	35.00	Pitcher, ½ gal. (tankard)	240.00
Bowl, 7", low ft., straight side	90.00	Oil bottle, 2 oz., squat, w/#8 stopper	100.00
Bowl, 7", nappy	80.00	Oil bottle, 2 oz., w/#6 stopper	110.00
Bowl, 8", low ft., straight side	70.00	Oil bottle, 4 oz., squat, w/#8 stopper	100.00
Bowl, 8", nappy	70.00	Oil bottle, 4 oz., w/#6 stopper	100.00
Bowl, 8", scalloped nappy	65.00	Oil bottle, 6 oz., w/#6 stopper	100.00
Bowl, 8", shallow, low ft.	75.00	Oil bottle, 6 oz., squat, w/#8 stopper	100.00
Bowl, 8½", shallow nappy	75.00	Plate, 4½"	20.00
Bowl, 9", flat, banana split	45.00	Plate, 5"	25.00
Bowl, 9", ftd., banana split	55.00	Plate, 5½"	25.00
Bowl, 9", low ft., straight side	65.00	Plate, 6"	35.00
Bowl, 9", nappy	70.00	Plate, 6½"	35.00
Bowl, 9", shallow, low ft.	70.00	Plate, 7"	50.00
Bowl, 9½", shallow nappy	70.00	Plate, 8"	70.00
Bowl, 10", shallow, low ft.	85.00	Plate, 9"	90.00
Bowl, 11", shallow nappy	70.00	Plate, 10"	110.00
Bowl, 12", orange bowl	500.00	Plate, 16", orange bowl liner	180.00
Bowl, 12", punch, ftd.	300.00	Puff box, #1, w/cover	175.00
Flamingo	750.00	Puff box, #3, w/cover	175.00
Bowl, 12", orange, flared rim	450.00	Salt & pepper, pr.	125.00
Bowl, 14½", orange, flared rim	500.00	Sherbet, 4½ oz., ftd., straight rim	30.00
Bowl, 15", punch, ftd.	400.00	Sherbet, 4½ oz., ftd., flared rim	30.00
Bowl, 18", punch, shallow	400.00	Sherbet, 4½ oz., high ft., shallow	30.00
Butter, indiv. (plate)	35.00	Sherbet, 4½ oz., ftd., shallow	30.00
Butter/jelly, 2 hdld., w/cover	200.00	Sherbet, 4½ oz., ftd., cupped rim	30.00
Candy, w/cover, ½ lb.	140.00	Sherbet, 6 oz., low ft.	35.00
Candy, w/cover, 1 lb.	170.00	Spooner, lg.	110.00
Candy, w/cover, 2 lb.	210.00	Spooner, 4½" (or straw jar)	110.00
Cheese & cracker set, 10"	150.00	Stem, ¾ oz., cordial	250.00
Compote, 5"	90.00	Stem, 2 oz., wine	110.00
Compote, 5", w/cover	130.00	Stem, 2 oz., sherry	200.00
Creamer	50.00	Stem, 3 oz., cocktail	50.00
Creamer, oval, hotel	55.00	Stem, 3½ oz., burgundy	125.00
Creamer, rnd., hotel	50.00	Stem, 4½ oz., saucer champagne	60.00
Cup, 4½ oz., punch	20.00	Stem, 4½ oz., claret	170.00

	Crystal
Stem, 7 oz.	95.00
Stem, 9 oz.	125.00
Stem, 9 oz., low ft.	110.00
Straw jar, w/cover	375.00
Sugar	50.00
Sugar, oval, hotel	55.00
Sugar, rnd., hotel	50.00
Sugar & creamer, oval, individual	140.00
Tray, 9", oval celery	50.00
Tray, 12", oval celery	60.00
Tray, 12½", French roll	140.00
Tray, 13", oblong	260.00
Tray, 15", oblong	300.00
Tumbler, 2½ oz. (or toothpick)	450.00

	Crystal
Tumbler, 5 oz., flared rim	50.00
Tumbler, 5 oz., straight side	50.00
Tumbler, 5½ oz., water	50.00
Tumbler, 7 oz., flared rim	60.00
Tumbler, 7 oz., straight side	60.00
Tumbler, 8 oz., w/straight, flared, cupped, shallow	60.00
Tumbler, 10 oz., flared rim	90.00
Tumbler, 10 oz., straight wide	90.00
Tumbler, 12 oz., flared rim	100.00
Tumbler, 12 oz., straight side	100.00
Tumbler, 13 oz., straight side	100.00
Tumbler, 13 oz., flared rim	100.00
Water bottle	220.00

Colors: pink, crystal, crystal w/green trim, crystal w/gold, green; w/optic

Central's No. 401 etch was given the name "Harding" when President and Mrs. Harding selected a set of this "Dragon" design made up of over 300 pieces; it was etched with gold. Thereafter, Central advertised it as glass "for America's first families." There are few pieces available, today, but well worth your search. We have bought all the "Harding" pictured over the last five years.

	*All colors
Bowl, 12", console, octagon	85.00
Bowl, finger, #800	35.00
Bowl, soup, flat	60.00
Candlestick, octagon collar	45.00
Candlestick, rnd collar	40.00
Comport, 4½", short stem	30.00
Comport, 6", short stem	35.00
Comport, 6", 10 oz., tall stem	40.00
Creamer, ftd.	30.00
Cup, handled custard	20.00
Decanter, qt. w/cut stop	300.00
Ice tub, 2 hdld.	395.00
Jug, tall, flat bottom	395.00
Plate, 5" sherbet	12.00
Plate, 6" finger bowl liner	15.00
Plate, dinner	65.00
Plate, lunch	25.00

	*All colors
Shaker, ftd. indiv.	40.00
Stem style, indiv. almond	20.00
Stem, 5½ oz. sherbet	20.00
Stem, 6 oz. saucer champagne, #780	25.00
Stem, 9 oz. water #780	27.50
Stem, cordial	60.00
Stem, oyster cocktail	20.00
Stem, wine	28.00
Sugar, ftd.	30.00
Tumbler, 5 oz	18.00
Tumbler, 8 oz.	20.00
Tumbler, 10 oz., #530	20.00
Tumbler, 12 oz.	20.00
Tumbler, ftd., hdld. tea	45.00

* 25% less for crystal

Colors: Amber, Azure (blue), crystal, Ebony, green, Topaz, Wisteria

Hermitage is a Fostoria pattern that has few admirers at the present time; however, a few collectors are beginning to notice the Wisteria color. Other Fostoria patterns found in Wisteria are being priced out of sight. The Hermitage prices are reasonable; so if you like this color, now is the time to start buying it.

My listings are from a Fostoria catalog that had January 1, 1933, entered on the front page in pencil. Not all pieces were made in all colors according to this catalog. If there is no price listed, it means that no piece is supposed to have been made. If you have such an item, please let me know!

	Crystal	Amber/Green/Topaz	Azure	Wisteria
Ash tray holder, #2449	5.00	8.00	12.00	
*Ash tray, #2449	3.00	5.00	8.00	
Bottle, 3 oz., oil, #2449	20.00	40.00		
Bottle, 27 oz., bar w/stopper, #2449	45.00			
Bowl, 4½", finger, #2449½	4.00	6.00	10.00	20.00
Bowl, 5", fruit, #2449½	5.00	8.00	15.00	
Bowl, 6", cereal, #2449½	6.00	10.00	20.00	
Bowl, 6½", salad, #2449½	6.00	9.00	20.00	
Bowl, 7", soup, #2449½	8.00	12.00	22.00	35.00
Bowl, 7½", salad, #2449½	8.00	12.00	30.00	
Bowl, 8", deep, ped., ft., #2449	17.50	35.00	60.00	
Bowl, 10", ftd., #2449	20.00	35.00		115.00
Bowl, grapefruit, w/crystal liner, #2449	20.00	40.00		
Candle, 6", #2449	12.50	22.00	35.00	
Coaster, 5⅝", #2449	5.00	7.50	11.00	
Comport, 6", #2449	12.00	17.50	27.50	40.00
Creamer, ftd., #2449	4.00	6.00	10.00	30.00
Cup, ftd., #2449	6.00	10.00	15.00	22.00
Decanter, 28 oz., w/stopper, #2449	40.00	110.00	150.00	
Fruit cocktail, 2⅜", 5 oz., ftd., #2449	5.00	7.50	12.00	
Ice tub, 6", #2449	17.50	35.00	50.00	175.00
Icer, #2449	10.00	18.00	30.00	95.00
Mayonnaise, 5⅝" w/7" plate, #2449	20.00	35.00		
Mug, 9 oz., ftd., #2449	12.50			

	Crystal	Amber/Green/Topaz	Azure	Wisteria
Mug, 12 oz., ftd., #2449	15.00			
Mustard w/cover & spoon, #2449	17.50	35.00		
Pitcher, pint, #2449	22.50	40.00	60.00	
Pitcher, 3 pint, #2449	75.00	90.00	150.00	650.00
Plate, 6", #2449½	3.00	5.00	8.00	
Plate, 7", ice dish liner	4.00	6.00	10.00	
Plate, 7", #2449½	4.00	6.00	10.00	
Plate, 7⅜", crescent salad, #2449	10.00	17.50	35.00	70.00
Plate, 8", #2449½	6.00	10.00	15.00	25.00
Plate, 9", #2449½	12.50	20.00	30.00	
Plate, 12", sandwich, #2449		12.50	20.00	
Relish, 6", 2 pt., #2449	6.00	10.00	15.00	25.00
Relish, 7¼", 3 pt., #2449	8.00	11.00	17.50	50.00
Relish, 8", pickle, #2449	8.00	11.00	17.50	
Relish, 11", celery, #2449	10.00	15.00	25.00	50.00
Salt & pepper, 3⅜", #2449	25.00	50.00	75.00	
Salt, indiv., #2449	4.00	6.00	10.00	
Saucer, #2449	2.00	3.50	5.00	8.00
Sherbet, 3", 7 oz., low, ftd., #2449	6.00	8.00	12.50	15.00
Stem, 3¼", 5½ oz., high sherbet, #2449	8.00	11.00	17.50	25.00
Stem, 4⅝", 4 oz., claret, #2449	10.00	15.00		
Stem, 5¼", 9 oz., water goblet, #2449	10.00	15.00	25.00	40.00
Sugar, ftd., #2449	4.00	6.00	10.00	30.00
Tray, 6½", condiment, #2449	6.00	12.00	20.00	30.00
Tumbler, 2½", 2 oz., #2449½	8.00	10.00	20.00	40.00
Tumbler, 2½", 2 oz., ftd., #2449	5.00	10.00		
Tumbler, 3", 4 oz., cocktail, ftd., #2449	5.00	7.50	14.00	22.00
Tumbler, 3¼", 6 oz. old-fashioned, #2449½	6.00	10.00	18.00	28.00
Tumbler, 3⅞", 5 oz., #2449½	5.00	8.00	12.00	20.00
Tumbler, 4", 5 oz., ftd., #2449	5.00	8.00	12.00	20.00
Tumbler, 4⅛", 9 oz., ftd., #2449	6.00	10.00	15.00	25.00
Tumbler, 4¾", 9 oz., #2449½	6.00	10.00	15.00	30.00
Tumbler, 5¼", 12 oz., ftd., iced tea, #2449	10.00	16.00	28.00	
Tumbler, 5⅞", 13 oz., #2449½	10.00	16.00	28.00	
Vase, 6", ftd.	22.00	32.50		

* Ebony – $15.00

Colors: amber, black, crystal, Emerald green, Peach Blo, Willow blue

Imperial Hunt Scene certainly flaunts its pattern when the design is gold encrusted as shown by some of the Emerald green pieces below. Gold decoration adds 10% to 20% to the price listed. Be wary of worn gold; it is not very desirable! Rising prices on this pattern have been influenced by the Internet. Collectors seem to "fall" for glassware that depicts animals in some array. Cups, saucers, creamers, sugars, and shakers have always been scarce, but now more collectors are searching for them. Sets can be put together in pink (Peach Blo) and Emerald green as you can see from our pictures.

Stems are abundant in most sizes except for cordials and clarets. Abundant in comparison to serving pieces rather than abundant in comparison to other patterns. You will find bi-colored Hunt Scene stemware. Pink bowl with a green stem is the typical form.

Black and Emerald green (dark) with gold decorations sell 25% to 50% higher than prices listed if you should find any.

	Crystal	Colors
Bowl, 6", cereal	20.00	40.00
Bowl, 8"	40.00	90.00
Bowl, 8½", 3 pt.	45.00	95.00
Candlestick, 2-lite, keyhole	35.00	55.00
Candlestick, 3-lite, keyhole	45.00	95.00
Comport, 5½", #3085		60.00
Creamer, flat	15.00	50.00
Creamer, ftd.	20.00	50.00
Cup	50.00	65.00
Decanter		295.00
Finger bowl, w/plate, #3085		65.00
Humidor, tobacco		495.00
Ice bucket	65.00	110.00
Ice tub	55.00	95.00
Mayonnaise, w/liner	40.00	85.00
Pitcher, w/cover, 63 oz., #3085		395.00
Pitcher, w/cover, 76 oz., #711	165.00	375.00
Plate, 8"	15.00	25.00
Salt & pepper, pr.	65.00	175.00
Saucer	10.00	15.00
Stem, 1 oz., cordial, #1402	85.00	
Stem, 2½ oz., wine, #1402	65.00	

	Crystal	Colors
Stem, 3 oz., cocktail, #1402	50.00	
Stem, 6 oz., tomato, #1402	45.00	
Stem, 6½ oz., sherbet, #1402	40.00	
Stem, 7½ oz., sherbet, #1402	45.00	
Stem, 10 oz., water, #1402	50.00	
Stem, 14 oz., #1402	55.00	
Stem, 18 oz., #1402	65.00	
Stem, 1 oz., cordial, #3085		195.00
Stem, 2½ oz., cocktail, #3085		50.00
Stem, 2½ oz., wine, #3085		55.00
Stem, 4½ oz., claret, #3085		67.50
Stem, 5½ oz., parfait, #3085		75.00
Stem, 6 oz., low sherbet, #3085		22.50
Stem, 6 oz., high sherbet, #3085		35.00
Stem, 9 oz., water, #3085		55.00
Sugar, flat w/ lid	50.00	125.00
Sugar, ftd.	20.00	50.00
Tumbler, 2½ oz., 2⅞", flat, #1402	25.00	
Tumbler, 5 oz., flat, #1402	20.00	
Tumbler, 7 oz., flat, #1402	20.00	
Tumbler, 10 oz., flat, #1402	23.00	
Tumbler, 10 oz., flat, tall, #1402	25.00	
Tumbler, 15 oz., flat, #1402	35.00	
Tumbler, 2½ oz., ftd., #3085		55.00
Tumbler, 5 oz., 3⅞", ftd., #3085		35.00
Tumbler, 8 oz., ftd., #3085		35.00
Tumbler, 10 oz., ftd., #3085		35.00

Colors: crystal, Flamingo pink, Sahara yellow, Moongleam green, cobalt, and Alexandrite

I wish to repeat that if you find any colored piece of Ipswich, other than those listed, it was made at Imperial and not Heisey. It may be marked Heisey, but it was manufactured at Imperial from purchased Heisey moulds and, as such, is pretty much ignored at this point by true Heisey collectors. Mostly, I get letters on (Alexandrite) candy jars that are actually Imperial's Heather (purple) color. Imperial is now out of business; their wares may well lure future collectors.

Moongleam is the color of preference with collectors of Ipswich.

	Crystal	Pink	Sahara	Green	Cobalt	Alexandrite
Bowl, finger, w/underplate	40.00	90.00	80.00	120.00		
Bowl, 11", ftd., floral	80.00		300.00		400.00	
Candlestick, 6", 1-lite	150.00	275.00	200.00	300.00	400.00	
Candlestick centerpiece, ftd., vase, "A" prisms, complete	160.00	300.00	350.00	450.00	500.00	
Candy jar, ¼ lb., w/cover	175.00					
Candy jar, ½ lb., w/cover	175.00	325.00	300.00	400.00		
Cocktail shaker, 1 quart, strainer, #86 stopper	225.00	600.00	700.00	800.00		
Creamer	35.00	70.00	90.00	125.00		
Stem, 4 oz., oyster cocktail, ftd	25.00	60.00	50.00	70.00		
Stem, 5 oz., saucer champagne (knob in stem)	25.00	60.00	50.00	70.00		
Stem, 10 oz., goblet (knob in stem)	35.00	85.00	70.00	90.00		750.00
Stem, 12 oz., schoppen, flat bottom	100.00					
Pitcher, ½ gal.	350.00	600.00	550.00	750.00		
Oil bottle, 2 oz., ftd., #86 stopper	125.00	285.00	275.00	300.00		
Plate, 7", square	30.00	60.00	50.00	70.00		
Plate, 8", square	35.00	65.00	55.00	75.00		
Sherbet, 4 oz., ftd. (knob in stem)	15.00	35.00	30.00	45.00		
Sugar	35.00	70.00	90.00	125.00		
Tumbler, 5 oz., ftd. (soda)	30.00	45.00	40.00	85.00		
Tumbler, 8 oz., ftd. (soda)	30.00	45.00	40.00	85.00		
Tumbler, 10 oz., cupped rim, flat bottom	70.00	110.00	100.00	140.00		
Tumbler, 10 oz., straight rim, flat bottom	70.00	110.00	100.00	140.00		
Tumbler, 12 oz., ftd. (soda)	40.00	80.00	70.00	95.00		

Colors: crystal, Cobalt, Ruby, Light Blue, Emerald, Amethyst

Janice was one of the more recent additions to this book, and now there are many new collectors for it. In the last edition I report-ed that Dalzell Viking was making or had recently made both candlesticks pictured on the end of Row 2. These were made in crystal, cobalt blue, and red that I can confirm. Dalzell Viking has now gone out of business, but they made a bunch of Janice candles! The light blue was not made, but be wary of other colors. The only significant difference is that the newer ones are slightly heavier and not as fire polished as the old. The reissued ones have an oily feel as does much newer glass.

There is a separate line of swan handled items in the Janice pattern that I have not listed here. I have seen few of these items for sale, but they are usually reasonable in price. I guess those fragile swan ends may scare collectors. I can vouch that they are difficult pack and carry to shows. If you are an advanced collector of Janice, let me know what additional pieces you have found and feel free to pass along any pricing ideas you may have.

One of the blue candy jars in the bottom row has an etched pattern. I have only seen this etching on light blue and crystal. Baskets, pitchers, and footed ice buckets seem to be most collectors' aspirations for their collections.

Red Janice is found less often than blue, but there are more collectors soliciting blue at the present time. That has a tendency to balance the pricing for those colors. Demand will make up for scarcity without exception.

	Crystal	Blue Red		Crystal	Blue Red
Basket, 6½", 9" high	75.00	145.00	Ice tub, 6", ftd.	100.00	250.00
Basket, 11"	75.00	195.00	Jam jar w/cover, 6"	20.00	45.00
Basket, 12", oval, 10" high	85.00	225.00	Mayonnaise liner, 7", 2 hdld.	9.00	14.00
Bonbon, 5½", 2 hdld., 4½" high	18.00	30.00	Mayonnaise plate, 6"	7.50	12.50
Bonbon, 6", 2 hdld., 4" high	20.00	33.00	Mayonnaise, 6", 2 hdld.	18.00	30.00
Bonbon, 7", 2 hdld., 4¾" high	25.00	40.00	Mayonnaise, round	15.00	27.50
Bowl, 5½", flower, w/eight crimps	22.00	35.00	Oil, 5 oz., w/stopper	40.00	100.00
Bowl, 6", 2 hdld., crimped	20.00	33.00	Pitcher, 15 oz., berry cream	40.00	125.00
Bowl, 9½", cupped	35.00	65.00	Plate, 7", 2 hdld.	9.00	14.00
Bowl, 9½", flared	35.00	65.00	Plate, 8½", salad	10.00	17.50
Bowl, 9", 2 hdld.	37.50	75.00	Plate, 11", cheese	22.50	40.00
Bowl, 10"	37.50	75.00	Plate, 11", ftd., rolled edge	27.50	50.00
Bowl, 10½", cupped, 3 toed	45.00	75.00	Plate, 12", 2 hdld.	30.00	55.00
Bowl, 10½", flared, 3 toed	45.00	85.00	Plate, 13"	30.00	60.00
Bowl, 11", oval	40.00	75.00	Plate, 13", 2 hdld.	32.50	65.00
Bowl, 11", cupped, ftd.	45.00	85.00	Plate, 14", ftd., rolled edge	40.00	85.00
Bowl, 11", flared	40.00	65.00	Plate, 15"	40.00	
Bowl, 12", flared	42.50	90.00	Plate, 15", rolled edge torte	50.00	
Bowl, 12", fruit, ruffled top	50.00	100.00	Platter, 13", oval	35.00	85.00
Bowl, 12", oval	42.50	70.00	Relish, 6", 2 part, 2 hdld.	15.00	37.50
Bowl, 12", salad, scalloped top	50.00	85.00	Salt and pepper, pr.	40.00	85.00
Bowl, 12", six crimps	52.50	115.00	Saucer	2.00	4.50
Bowl, 13", flared	50.00	90.00	Sherbet	12.00	26.00
Canape set: tray w/ftd. juice	30.00		Sugar, 6 oz.	12.00	20.00
Candelbra, 5", 2-lt., 5" wide	40.00		Sugar, individual, flat	10.00	22.00
Candlestick, 5½", 1-lt., 5" wide	35.00	50.00	Sugar, individual, ftd.	12.50	25.00
Candlestick, 6", 1-lt., 4½" wide	37.50	60.00	Sugar, tall	15.00	40.00
Candy box w/cover, 5½"	55.00	150.00	Syrup, w/dripcut top	65.00	
Celery, 11"	20.00	45.00	Tray, oval, 2 hdld., ind. sug/cr	12.00	20.00
Comport, cracker for cheese plate	14.00	25.00	Tray, oval, 2 hdld., cr/sug	15.00	25.00
Condiment set: tray and 2 cov. jars	55.00	125.00	Tumbler	14.00	30.00
Creamer, 6 oz.	12.00	20.00	Vase, 4", ivy, 3½" high	22.00	50.00
Creamer, individual, flat	12.00	20.00	Vase, 4", ivy, 4½" high, w/base peg	25.00	60.00
Creamer, individual, ftd.	12.50	22.50	Vase, 7", ftd.	35.00	75.00
Creamer, tall	15.00	40.00	Vase, 8", ball, 7½" high	45.00	110.00
Cup	8.00	23.00	Vase, 8", cupped, 3 toed	50.00	125.00
Guest set: bottle w/tumbler	85.00		Vase, 8", flared, 3 toed	50.00	125.00
Ice pail, 10", hdld.	75.00	195.00	Vase, 9", ball	55.00	135.00

Color: crystal w/amber trim, wide optic

Julia is a Tiffin pattern that is just being discovered by collectors. I was told by a long-time collector that it was originally produced for about five years. Notice that the plates are totally amber while stems and other pieces are crystal with amber trim. Unfortunately, the design does not display as well on those amber flat pieces. When set flat, the design practically disappears. However, it really zings against the crystal! It was the fashion in the early thirties to make bi-colored glass. This is an excellent example of that practice. You can probably gather this pattern without much immediate competition, but I would not count on that lasting too long. There are just a few Tiffin patterns that can be collected in amber; so, if you like Tiffin styling and design, as a growing number of collectors are deciding they do, this would be an ideal pattern to pursue. Too, there is a growing cadre of collectors whose main interest is bi-colored glass!

I recently saw a Julia pitcher that was highly priced. I asked the dealer about it and was told it was rare Heisey. The pitcher has an amber handle and foot. The cover to the pitcher is also amber, slightly domed with a pointed knob, wide optic panels, and no etching. That "Heisey" pitcher had no cover, and when I asked if there were a lid, I was informed that Heisey pitchers never had lids! Nice comeback, and I guess, basically true were it Heisey.

	Amber			Amber
Bowl, finger	20.00		Stem, cocktail	25.00
Candy jar and cover, ftd.	125.00		Stem, cordial	45.00
Creamer	30.00		Stem, saucer champagne	22.00
Jug and cover, ftd.	295.00		Stem, sundae	18.00
Plate, 8" luncheon	20.00		Stem, water	30.00
Plate, dessert	12.00		Stem, wine	40.00
Plate, salad	14.00		Sugar	30.00
Stem, cafe parfait	35.00		Tumbler, ftd. seltzer	20.00
Stem, claret	45.00		Tumbler, ftd. table	22.00

Colors: crystal, Azure blue, Topaz yellow, Rose pink

June wins the title of most coveted etched Fostoria pattern. Azure and Rose have continued to rise in price. Prices for crystal and Topaz have remained fairly stable. Recently, I have seen indications of renewed collector interest in Topaz. If you have been putting off buying it, better start gathering now before prices catch up to blue or pink.

Shakers came with both glass and metal tops. Collectors prefer the glass ones first used. In later years, only metal tops were made; all replacement tops were metal.

If you will refer to Versailles (page 212), I have listed all the Fostoria line numbers for each piece. Since these are essentially the same listings as June, you can use the ware number listings from Versailles should you need them. Be sure to see the stemware illustrations on page 82. You would not want to pay for a claret and receive a high sherbet.

	Crystal	Rose Blue	Topaz
Ash tray	25.00	55.00	40.00
Bottle, salad dressing, #2083 or #2375	295.00	995.00	395.00
Bowl, baker, 9", oval	50.00	150.00	85.00
Bowl, baker, 10", oval	40.00	135.00	75.00
Bowl, bonbon	12.50	30.00	23.00
Bowl, bouillon, ftd.	18.00	50.00	27.00
Bowl, finger, w/liner	35.00	75.00	50.00
Bowl, mint, 3 ftd., 4½"	15.00	45.00	30.00
Bowl, 6", nappy, 3 ftd., jelly	15.00	45.00	25.00
Bowl, 6½", cereal	25.00	95.00	45.00
Bowl, 7", soup	65.00	195.00	175.00
Bowl, lg., dessert, hdld.	35.00	150.00	95.00
Bowl, 10"	35.00	135.00	85.00
Bowl, 10", Grecian	50.00	135.00	80.00
Bowl, 11", centerpiece	35.00	110.00	75.00
Bowl, 12", centerpiece, three types	55.00	125.00	75.00

	Crystal	Rose Blue	Topaz
Bowl, 13", oval centerpiece, w/flower frog	90.00	275.00	150.00
Candlestick, 2"	14.00	33.00	22.00
Candlestick, 3"	20.00	40.00	30.00
Candlestick, 3", Grecian	20.00	55.00	30.00
Candlestick, 5", Grecian	30.00	75.00	45.00
Candy, w/cover, 3 pt.		350.00	
Candy, w/cover, ½ lb., ¼ lb.			225.00
Celery, 11½"	35.00	110.00	65.00
Cheese & cracker set, #2368 or #2375	50.00	135.00	95.00
Comport, 5", #2400	30.00	75.00	50.00
Comport, 6", #5298 or #5299	30.00	95.00	55.00
Comport, 7", #2375	35.00	125.00	70.00
Comport, 8", #2400	50.00	165.00	80.00
Cream soup, ftd.	22.00	50.00	35.00
Creamer, ftd.	15.00	30.00	20.00

	Crystal	Rose Blue	Topaz
Creamer, tea	30.00	80.00	50.00
Cup, after dinner	25.00	100.00	50.00
Cup, ftd.	15.00	33.00	25.00
Decanter	425.00	2,000.00	645.00
Goblet, claret, 6", 4 oz.	50.00	165.00	90.00
Goblet, cocktail, 5¼", 3 oz.	24.00	48.00	35.00
Goblet, cordial, 4", ¾ oz.	60.00	155.00	85.00
Goblet, water, 8¼", 10 oz.	33.00	60.00	45.00
Goblet, wine, 5½", 3 oz.	25.00	110.00	50.00
Grapefruit	40.00	110.00	75.00
Grapefruit liner	35.00	90.00	50.00
Ice bucket	85.00	165.00	100.00
Ice dish	35.00	75.00	45.00
Ice dish liner (tomato, crab, fruit)	8.00	22.00	12.00
Mayonnaise, w/liner	30.00	85.00	50.00
Oil, ftd.	250.00	750.00	350.00
Oyster cocktail, 5½ oz.	20.00	40.00	28.00
Parfait, 5¼"	40.00	125.00	75.00
Pitcher	275.00	695.00	395.00
Plate, canape	20.00	50.00	30.00
Plate, lemon	16.00	30.00	25.00
Plate, 6", bread/butter	7.00	15.00	9.00
Plate, 6", finger bowl liner	4.50	15.00	10.00
Plate, 7½", salad	10.00	18.00	13.00
Plate, 7½, cream soup	7.00	20.00	15.00
Plate, 8¾", luncheon	6.00	25.00	18.00
Plate, 9½", sm. dinner	15.00	50.00	30.00
Plate, 10", grill	40.00	125.00	75.00
Plate, 10", cake, hdld (no indent)	35.00	75.00	45.00
Plate, 10", cheese with indent, hdld.	35.00	75.00	45.00
Plate, 10¼", dinner	40.00	125.00	75.00
Plate, 13", chop	25.00	90.00	65.00
Plate, 14", torte		135.00	75.00
Platter, 12"	40.00	135.00	85.00
Platter, 15"	75.00	250.00	135.00
Relish, 8½", 3 part	25.00		40.00
Sauce boat	40.00	295.00	125.00
Sauce boat liner	15.00	90.00	45.00
Saucer, after dinner	6.00	20.00	10.00
Saucer	4.00	8.00	5.00
Shaker, ftd., pr	60.00	225.00	130.00
Sherbet, high, 6", 6 oz.	20.00	40.00	27.50
Sherbet, low, 4¼", 6 oz.	18.00	33.00	25.00
Sugar, ftd., straight or scalloped top	15.00	30.00	22.00
Sugar cover	55.00	250.00	150.00
Sugar pail	70.00	250.00	150.00
Sugar, tea	25.00	80.00	45.00
Sweetmeat	25.00	40.00	25.00
Tray, service and lemon		350.00	300.00
Tray, 11", ctr. hdld.	25.00	50.00	40.00
Tumbler, 2½ oz., ftd.	20.00	100.00	65.00
Tumbler, 5 oz., 4½", ftd.	15.00	50.00	30.00
Tumbler, 9 oz., 5¼", ftd.	18.00	45.00	25.00
Tumbler, 12 oz., 6", ftd.	25.00	70.00	40.00
Vase, 8", 2 styles	80.00	325.00	225.00
Vase, 8½", fan, ftd.	90.00	275.00	175.00
Whipped cream bowl	10.00	22.00	16.00
Whipped cream pail	85.00	225.00	150.00

Note: See stemware identification on page 82.

Colors: crystal

June Night stemware is available. Evidently, Tiffin pushed this competitor of Cambridge's Rose Point for customers to use with their china. I see hundreds of stems for every bowl or candle. More of this pattern is being displayed at shows. I've noticed that similar pieces of Cherokee Rose have created an identity problem with many novices and part-time dealers. There is a **flower** encircled on June Night and an **urn** on Cherokee Rose. Shapes are important, but it is the **design** that makes the pattern! Since both of these patterns are on the same Tiffin mould blank, you have to be sure which one you have before you label it.

Shakers and the pitcher seem to be the most difficult ingredients of a set to acquire. The small bowl in the right hand corner is a mayonnaise without a liner. The finger bowl is thin and has a smooth rim.

June Night can be found on several different stemware lines, but the one most often encountered is Tiffin's #17392 that is shown in the photograph. You will also find line numbers #17378 (prism stem with pearl edge top), #17441 (quadrangle flowing to hexagonal cut), and #17471. The latter line has a bow tie stem, but I have never personally seen June Night on it. I need one for photography.

Gold-trimmed June Night stemware was called Cherry Laurel (photo at right). Name changing within same patterns is another glass company ploy. Any different treatment done to a pattern often resulted in a separate name. In the case of gold trim, often they would just add "golden" to the pattern name. Remember that gold trim did not and still does not hold up well with frequent use. Never put gold-trimmed items in the dishwasher especially if you use any soap with lemon in it. Lemon will remove gold trim!

	Crystal		Crystal
Bowl, 5", finger.	20.00	Shaker, pr.	185.00
Bowl, 6", fruit or nut	25.00	Stem, 1 oz., cordial	45.00
Bowl, 7", salad	35.00	Stem, 2 oz., sherry	35.00
Bowl, 10", deep salad	65.00	Stem, 3½ oz., cocktail	18.00
Bowl, 12", crimped	65.00	Stem, 3½ oz., wine	27.50
Bowl, 12½" centerpiece, flared	65.00	Stem, 4 oz., claret	37.50
Bowl, 13", centerpiece	75.00	Stem, 4½ oz., parfait	38.00
Candlesticks, pr., double branch	95.00	Stem, 5½ oz., sherbet/champagne	16.00
Celery, 10½", oblong	40.00	Stem, 9 oz., water	22.00
Creamer	17.50	Sugar	17.50
Mayonnaise, liner and ladle	45.00	Table bell	85.00
Pitcher	295.00	Tumbler, 4½ oz., oyster cocktail	18.00
Plate, 6", sherbet	6.00	Tumbler, 5 oz., ftd., juice	16.00
Plate, 8", luncheon	10.00	Tumbler, 8 oz., ftd., water	17.50
Plate, 13½", turned-up edge, lily	45.00	Tumbler, 10½ oz., ftd., ice tea	22.50
Plate, 14", sandwich	45.00	Vase, 6", bud	22.00
Relish, 6½", 3 pt.	35.00	Vase, 8", bud	35.00
Relish, 12½", 3 pt.	65.00	Vase, 10", bud	45.00

JUNGLE ASSORTMENT, Tiffin Glass Company, Decoration #14 Parrot, c. 1922 – 34

Colors: Green, pink and crystal satin; various flashed colors

Jungle Assortment is a fun Tiffin pattern that only a few collectors have paid much attention to over the years. Cathy started buying pieces and displaying them in Florida until she "got enough to photograph for a book." I pretty much ignored that comment, at first; but over the years, I kept running into reasonably priced pieces, so we accumulated quite a variety. I prefer the flashed colors to the satinized, but both treatments have had difficulty over the years in keeping those parrots from flying off their perches. There is another pitcher and tumbler set sitting at a local flea market here, but only one tumbler looks unused. Most of the parrots are missing on the other pieces, so no one will buy the set. This is one pattern where you might like to pick up some slightly worn pieces until mint condition ones appear. You do not find this every day!

All of the items pictured in the smaller photo here were bought in the few months leading up to our photo session last October. I was excited to find the red night cap set the day we left for photography. Shopping at 5 a.m. with a flashlight can be rewarding when hunting for new items for the books!

We have found three styles of candles, and I wonder how many colors were produced in each type. You will certainly find additional items not listed; let me know what you discover.

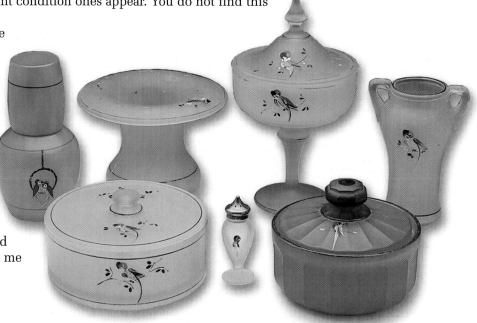

Basket, 6", #151	85.00		Jug and cover, 2 quart, #127	195.00
Bon bon & cover, 5½" high ft., #330	60.00		Marmalade & cover, 2 hdld., #330	45.00
Bon bon and cover, 5", low ft., #330	55.00		Night cap set, #6712	85.00
Bowl, centerpiece, #320	50.00		Puff box and cover, hexagonal	85.00
Candle, hdld., #330	35.00		Shaker, ftd. #6205	30.00
Candle, hdld. tall, octagonal base	37.50		Smoking set, 3 pc., #188	35.00
Candle, low, #10	25.00		Tumbler, 12 oz., #444	30.00
Candy and cover, ftd., #15179	55.00		Vase, 6", 2 hdld., #151	40.00
Candy box & cover, flat, #329	55.00		Vase, 7" ftd., flair from base, #330	65.00
Candy jar and cover, ftd., cone, #330	65.00		Vase, 7" ftd., flair rim, #151	65.00
Cologne bottle, #5722	125.00		Vase, 7" sweet pea, #151	65.00
Decanter & stopper	125.00		Vase, wall #320	65.00

Colors: Topaz yellow, Azure blue, some green

Kashmir was not as widely distributed as other Fostoria patterns, so collecting it will take longer. Blue Kashmir would be the Fostoria pattern to collect if you like that color. Other Azure Fostoria etched patterns have thousands of collectors searching for them; but few collectors pay attention to Kashmir.

Kashmir is found mostly in the Midwest; you can see from my pictures how well green Kashmir has avoided me; and I have been looking for it! Supposedly there are some 6", 7", and 8" plates to be had along with the two styles of cups and saucers!

What little Kashmir is found does not immediately disappear as do some of the other Fostoria patterns. The right collector has to come along; and since there are so few Kashmir admirers, it frequently takes a while to sell!

I would seriously suggest you look at this pattern. While everyone else is advancing the price on June and Versailles, you might gather a beautiful Kashmir set. I run across settings of yellow for sale. You could complete a set of yellow Kashmir more economically than any other etched, yellow Fostoria pattern.

The stemware and tumbler line is #5099 which is the same line on which Trojan is found. This is the "cascading waterfall" stem.

Both styles of after dinner cups are shown in the picture of blue. The square #2419 saucer set is more difficult to find than the round; but I have only found that in green, though it was made in Azure and Topaz.

	Yellow, Green	Blue
Ash tray	25.00	30.00
Bowl, cream soup	22.00	30.00
Bowl, finger	15.00	40.00
Bowl, 5", fruit	13.00	25.00
Bowl, 6", cereal	30.00	35.00
Bowl, 7", soup	35.00	95.00
Bowl, 8½", pickle	20.00	30.00
Bowl, 9", baker	37.50	85.00
Bowl, 10", 2 hdld	40.00	65.00
Bowl, 12", centerpiece	40.00	50.00
Candlestick, 2"	15.00	17.50
Candlestick, 3"	20.00	25.00
Candlestick, 5"	22.50	27.50
Candlestick, 9½"	40.00	60.00
Candy, w/cover	85.00	150.00
Cheese and cracker set	65.00	85.00
Comport, 6"	35.00	45.00
Creamer, ftd.	17.50	20.00
Cup	15.00	20.00
Cup, after dinner, flat	40.00	
Cup, after dinner, ftd.	40.00	55.00
Grapefruit	50.00	
Grapefruit liner	40.00	
Ice bucket	65.00	90.00
Oil, ftd.	295.00	495.00
Pitcher, ftd.	325.00	425.00
Plate, 6", bread & butter	5.00	6.00
Plate, 7", salad, rnd.	6.00	7.00
Plate, 7", salad, sq.	6.00	7.00
Plate, 8", salad	8.00	10.00
Plate, 9" luncheon	9.00	15.00

	Yellow, Green	Blue
Plate, 10", dinner	45.00	70.00
Plate, 10", grill	35.00	55.00
Plate, cake, 10"	35.00	
Salt & pepper, pr.	120.00	175.00
Sandwich, center hdld.	35.00	40.00
Sauce boat, w/liner	125.00	165.00
Saucer, rnd.	5.00	10.00
Saucer, after dinner, sq.	8.00	
Saucer, after dinner, rnd.	8.00	15.00
Stem, ¾ oz., cordial	85.00	115.00
Stem, 2½ oz., ftd.	30.00	45.00
Stem, 2 oz., ftd., whiskey	30.00	50.00
Stem, 2½ oz., wine	32.00	60.00
Stem, 3 oz., cocktail	22.00	25.00
Stem, 3½ oz., ftd., cocktail	22.00	25.00
Stem, 4 oz., claret	35.00	55.00
Stem, 4½ oz., oyster cocktail	16.00	18.00
Stem, 5½ oz., parfait	30.00	40.00
Stem, 5 oz., ftd., juice	15.00	25.00
Stem, 5 oz., low sherbet	13.00	20.00
Stem, 6 oz., high sherbet	17.50	30.00
Stem, 9 oz., water	20.00	35.00
Sugar, ftd.	15.00	20.00
Sugar lid	50.00	85.00
Tumbler, 10 oz., ftd., water	22.00	35.00
Tumbler, 11 oz.	22.50	
Tumbler, 12 oz., ftd.	25.00	35.00
Tumbler, 13 oz., ftd., tea	25.00	
Tumbler, 16 oz., ftd., tea	35.00	
Vase, 8"	90.00	145.00

Note: See stemware identification on page 82.

Colors: crystal, Topaz/Gold Tint (every piece of pattern); at least 12 pieces of Regal Blue, Empire Green, Burgundy; 6 pieces of Ruby & Silver Mist; some amber, green, wisteria, and rose

Crystal Lafayette is the mould line used for many of Fostoria's etchings, with Navarre being the most recognized. Colored pieces of Lafayette are collected for themselves. By far, the most sought color is Wisteria, but yellow can also be gathered into a large set. Right after our photo session, I found some Regal blue (cobalt) which is limited in availability. You might blend some of the colors with crystal in order to achieve a larger set.

	crystal/amber	rose/green/topaz	Wisteria	Regal blue	Burgundy	Empire Green
Almond, indiv.	15.00	20.00	20.00			
Bon bon, 5", 2 hdld.	18.00	22.50	40.00	35.00	30.00	33.00
Bowl, 4½" sweetmeat	18.00	22.50	40.00	35.00	35.00	33.00
Bowl, cream soup	22.50	35.00	85.00			
Bowl, 5" fruit		22.50	32.50			
Bowl, 6" cereal	20.00	25.00	45.00			
Bowl, 6½" olive	18.00	25.00	50.00			
Bowl, 6½" 2-pt relish	22.50	30.00	55.00	55.00	45.00	45.00
Ruby 50.00; Silver Mist 25.00						
Bowl, 6½" oval sauce	25.00	35.00	125.00	55.00	50.00	45.00
Ruby 65.00; Silver Mist 27.50						
Bowl, 7", "D" cupped	30.00	40.00	135.00			
Bowl, 7½" 3-pt relish	25.00	35.00	110.00	55.00	45.00	45.00
Ruby 55.00; Silver Mist 30.00						
Bowl, 8" nappy	30.00	40.00	85.00			
Bowl, 8½" pickle	18.00	27.50	55.00			
Bowl, 10" oval baker	35.00		45.00	75.00		
Bowl, 10" "B," flair	35.00	40.00				
Bowl, 12" salad, flair	38.00	45.00	155.00			
Cake, 10½" oval, 2 hdld.	40.00	45.00		60.00	60.00	60.00
Celery, 11½"	30.00	35.00	135.00			
Creamer, 4½", ftd.	15.00	25.00	55.00	40.00	40.00	40.00
Cup	15.00	18.00	22.50	35.00	35.00	35.00
Cup, demi	17.50	45.00	75.00			
Tray, 5", 2-hdld. lemon	17.50	22.50	40.00	35.00	30.00	33.00
Tray, 8½" oval, 2-hdld.	22.50	30.00	155.00	55.00	45.00	45.00
Ruby 55.00; Silver Mist 25.00						
Mayonnaise, 6½", 2 pt.	24.00	30.00	135.00	55.00	55.00	55.00
Ruby 55.00; Silver Mist 30.00						
Plate, 6"	8.00	12.00	14.00			
Plate, 7"	8.00	12.00	20.00			
Plate, 8"	10.00	15.00	22.50			
Plate, 9"	22.50	27.50	50.00			
Plate, 10"	35.00	45.00	95.00			
Plate, 13" torte	40.00	50.00	125.00	115.00	95.00	110.00
Ruby 110.00; Silver Mist 40.00						
Platter, 12"	40.00	52.50	115.00			
Platter, 15"	50.00	65.00				
Saucer	4.00	6.00	5.00	8.00	8.00	6.00
Saucer, demi	8.00	15.00	20.00			
Sugar, 3⅝" ftd.	15.00	25.00	50.00	40.00	40.00	40.00
Vase, 7" rim ft., flair	45.00	60.00				

Colors: crystal; rare in black and amber

Lariat prices have remained rather steady; but the rarer pieces still sell well since there are so many collectors looking for seldom found items. Common Lariat pieces are still available; you can ascertain the scarce pieces by their prices in my listing. The cutting most often seen on Lariat is Moonglo. Many non-Lariat collectors adore this cut; strangely, few Lariat collectors try to rope it! We have tried

to stimulate your interest with the multitude of pieces shown. Enjoy! The ads that I have previously shown are becoming collectible themselves. Watch for them in women's magazines of the 1940s and 1950s.

	Crystal
Ash tray, 4"	15.00
Basket, 7½", bonbon	100.00
Basket, 8½", ftd.	165.00
Basket, 10", ftd.	195.00
Bowl, 2 hdld., cream soup	50.00
Bowl, 7 quart, punch	130.00
Bowl, 4", nut, individual	32.00
Bowl, 7", 2 pt., mayo	24.00
Bowl, 7", nappy	20.00
Bowl, 8", flat, nougat	24.00
Bowl, 9½", camellia	28.00
Bowl, 10", hdld., celery	35.00
Bowl, 10½", 2 hdld., salad	38.00
Bowl, 10½", salad	40.00
Bowl, 11", 2 hdld., oblong, relish	30.00
Bowl, 12", floral or fruit	40.00
Bowl, 13", celery	50.00
Bowl, 13", gardenia	35.00
Bowl, 13", oval, floral	35.00
Candlestick, 1-lite, individual	30.00
Candlestick, 2-lite	40.00
Candlestick, 3-lite	45.00
Candy box, w/cover, caramel	75.00
Candy, w/cover, 7"	90.00
Candy, w/cover, 8", w/horsehead finial (rare)	1,500.00
Cheese, 5", ftd., w/cover	50.00
Cheese dish, w/cover, 8"	60.00
Cigarette box	55.00
Coaster, 4"	12.00
Cologne	95.00
Compote, 10", w/cover	100.00
Creamer	20.00

	Crystal
Creamer & sugar, w/tray, indiv.	45.00
Cup	20.00
Cup, punch	8.00
Ice tub	75.00
Jar, w/cover, 12", urn	175.00
Lamp & globe, 7", black-out	120.00
Lamp & globe, 8", candle, handled	95.00
Mayonnaise, 5" bowl, 7" plate w/ladle set	60.00
Oil bottle, 4 oz., hdld., w/#133 stopper	180.00
Oil bottle, 6 oz., oval	75.00
Plate, 6", finger bowl liner	8.00
Plate, 7", salad	14.00
Plate, 8", salad	22.00
Plate, 10½", dinner	125.00
Plate, 11", cookie	35.00
Plate, 12", demi-torte, rolled edge	40.00
Plate, 13", deviled egg, round	290.00
Plate, 14", 2 hdld., sandwich	50.00
Plate, 15", deviled egg, oval	220.00
Plate, 21", buffet	70.00
Platter, 15", oval	60.00
Salt & pepper, pr.	200.00
Saucer	5.00
Stem, 1 oz., cordial, double loop	250.00
Stem, 1 oz., cordial blown, single loop	150.00
Stem, 2½ oz., wine, blown	25.00
Stem, 3½ oz., cocktail, pressed	20.00
Stem, 3½ oz., cocktail, blown	20.00
Stem, 3½ oz., wine, pressed	24.00
Stem, 4 oz., claret, blown	28.00
Stem, 4¼ oz., oyster cocktail or fruit	18.00
Stem, 4½ oz., oyster cocktail, blown	18.00
Stem, 5½ oz., sherbet/saucer champagne, blown	17.00
Stem, 6 oz., low sherbet	10.00
Stem, 6 oz., sherbet/saucer champagne, pressed	17.00
Stem, 9 oz., pressed	22.00
Stem, 10 oz., blown	22.00
Sugar	20.00
Tray, rnd., center hdld., w/ball finial	165.00
Tray for sugar & creamer, 8", 2 hdld.	24.00
Tumbler, 5 oz., ftd., juice	22.00
Tumbler, 5 oz., ftd., juice, blown	22.00
Tumbler, 12 oz., ftd., ice tea	28.00
Tumbler, 12 oz., ftd., ice tea, blown	28.00
Vase, 7", ftd., fan	30.00
Vase, swung	135.00

Color: crystal

One of the questions I have been asked more often than any other is "Where can I find more of this beautiful pattern?" Duncan's Lily of the Valley is a pattern that even non-collectors appreciate. I first found out about this pattern from seeing a cordial when I started collecting stems about 25 years ago. I had to be told that it was Lily of the Valley, but bought it for my cordial collection without hesitation because of its beauty! Stemware has the Lily of the Valley cut into the stem itself, but the bowls atop of the stem are encountered with or without the cutting. The cutting on the bowl "makes" this pattern for me. Duncan's designation for this stem was D-4 and the cut variety was DC-4. Prices below are for cut (DC-4) bowl items; deduct about a third (or more) for plain bowl stems. Once you see this pattern, you will understand why collectors want the cut version!

As with First Love, Canterbury #115 and Pall Mall #30 blanks were used for this cutting. The mayonnaise pictured is #30 and the bowl and plate are #115. I have not seen a cup or saucer in this cut. Have you?

	Crystal
Ash tray, 3"	18.00
Ash tray, 6"	25.00
Bowl, 12"	55.00
Candy, w/lid	85.00
Cheese and cracker	75.00
Creamer	25.00
Mayonnaise	30.00
Mayonnaise ladle	8.00
Mayonnaise liner	15.00

	Crystal
Plate, 8"	20.00
Plate, 9"	45.00
Stem, cocktail	22.00
Stem, cordial	80.00
Stem, high sherbet	22.00
Stem, water goblet	40.00
Stem, wine	42.00
Sugar	25.00

Colors: black, crystal, green, pink

I have tried not to arbitrarily name pattern lines in my books, since that practice has added to confusion for collectors over the years. An author makes up his name for a pattern, another calls it something else and when the actual name is unearthed, it is difficult for everyone to convert. That being said, I have dubbed this New Martinsville "coat of arms style" etch "Lions." I almost called it "Lions Rampant"; but not being a heraldry expert, I was not quite sure they were in the correct attitude to be so labeled. I will be more than happy to convert to the original name if one can be determined later. I can already tell you, hunting "Lions" will be a challenge.

Most "Loins" etch is found on New Martinsville's Line #34 as pictured in color below. The only crystal items shown are on Line #37 known as "Moondrops" to collectors. I have not seen this etch on colored pieces of Line #37 or crystal pieces of Line #34, but it would not be surprising if those appear.

You can assemble a luncheon set in color, but adding serving pieces may be another matter. Note the pink candy with missing lid. I buy whatever I can find when I am adding new patterns to a book. I hope that a reader has a spare lid that he did not know about.

I am positive that additional pieces not in the list are available; so let me know what else you have or see.

	crystal	pink/green	black
Candleholder, #37	25.00		
Candy w/lid		55.00	85.00
Center handle server		45.00	
Creamer, #34		22.50	30.00
Creamer, #37	15.00		
Cup		25.00	35.00

	crystal	pink/green	black
Plate, 8"		20.00	30.00
Plate, 12"		30.00	40.00
Saucer		7.50	10.00
Sugar, #34		22.50	30.00
Sugar, #37	15.00		

Color: Dawn

Fair warning to collectors of this pattern: I will be removing it from this book and putting it in *Collectible Glassware from the 40s, 50s, and 60s* where it rightfully belongs. This Heisey pattern is named Lodestar in the Dawn color only. Crystal pieces in the same design are called Satellite and the prices decrease dramatically! Each piece has the star-like shape for its base. Dawn is expensive as you can see by the prices listed below. These are realistic selling prices, not hoped for or asking prices!

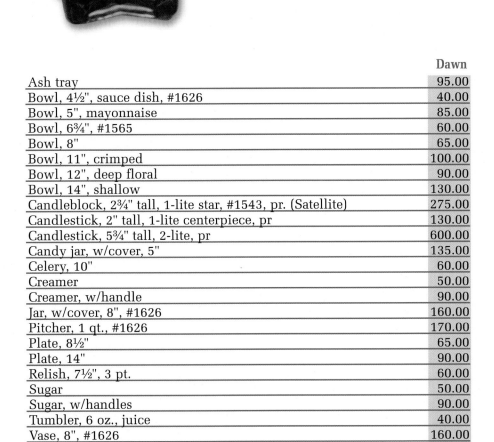

	Dawn
Ash tray	95.00
Bowl, 4½", sauce dish, #1626	40.00
Bowl, 5", mayonnaise	85.00
Bowl, 6¾", #1565	60.00
Bowl, 8"	65.00
Bowl, 11", crimped	100.00
Bowl, 12", deep floral	90.00
Bowl, 14", shallow	130.00
Candleblock, 2¾" tall, 1-lite star, #1543, pr. (Satellite)	275.00
Candlestick, 2" tall, 1-lite centerpiece, pr	130.00
Candlestick, 5¾" tall, 2-lite, pr	600.00
Candy jar, w/cover, 5"	135.00
Celery, 10"	60.00
Creamer	50.00
Creamer, w/handle	90.00
Jar, w/cover, 8", #1626	160.00
Pitcher, 1 qt., #1626	170.00
Plate, 8½"	65.00
Plate, 14"	90.00
Relish, 7½", 3 pt.	60.00
Sugar	50.00
Sugar, w/handles	90.00
Tumbler, 6 oz., juice	40.00
Vase, 8", #1626	160.00
Vase, 8", crimped, #1626	180.00

Colors: amethyst w/gold, crystal, Emerald green

    Cambridge's Marjorie was renamed Fuchsia in the 1930s; do not confuse it with Tiffin's or Fostoria's Fuchsia. The #7606 stems were advertised in the 1927 Sears calalog.

	Crystal
Comport, #4011	45.00
Comport, 5", #4004	35.00
Comport, 5" jelly (sherbet), #2090	35.00
Cream, flat, curved in side, #1917/10	50.00
Cream, flat, straight side, #1917/18	50.00
Decanter, 28 oz. cut stop #17	175.00
Decanter, 28 oz. #7606	175.00
Finger bowl, #7606	40.00
Grapefruit w/liner inside, #7606	85.00
Jug, 30 oz., #104	165.00
Jug w cover, 30 oz., #106	225.00
Jug, 3 pint, #93	155.00
Jug, 3½ pint, #108 short, flair bottom	195.00
Jug, 3½ pint, rim bottom, bulbous, #111	195.00
Jug, 54 oz. flat bottom, #51	225.00
Jug w cover, 66 oz., #106	250.00
Jug, 4 pint, tall, flat bottom, #110	235.00
Jug, guest room 38 oz w/tumbler fitting inside, #103	235.00
Marmelade & cover, #145	75.00
Nappie, 4", #4111	20.00
Nappie, 4" ftd., #5000	22.50
Nappie, 8", #4111	60.00
Nappie, 8" ftd., #5000	65.00
Night bottle, 20 oz. w/tumbler, #4002	235.00
Oil w/hex cone cut stop, #32	125.00
Plate, 7", finger bowl liner or salad, #7606	15.00
Plate, finger bowl liner, #7606	15.00

	Crystal
Stem, ⅞ oz. cordial, #7606	110.00
Stem, 1 oz. cordial, #3750	110.00
Stem, 2½ oz. wine, #7606	65.00
Stem, 2 oz. creme de menthe, #7606	95.00
Stem, 3 oz. cocktail, #7606	25.00
Stem, 3 oz. wine, #3750	35.00
Stem, 3½ oz. cocktail, #3750	25.00
Stem, 4½ oz claret, #3750	55.00
Stem, 4½ oz. claret, #7606	55.00
Stem, 5½oz. cafe parfait, #7606	45.00
Stem, 6 oz, low sherbet, #3750	15.00
Stem, 6 oz. low fruit/sherbet, #7606	15.00
Stem, 6 oz. high sherbet, #3750	18.00
Stem, 6 oz. high sherbet, #7606	18.00
Stem, 10 oz. water, #3750	22.00
Stem, 10 oz. water, #7606	22.00
Sugar, flat, curved in side, #1917/10	50.00
Sugar, flat, straight side, #1917/18	50.00
Syrup & cover, 8 oz., #106	125.00
Tumbler, #8851	20.00
Tumbler, 1½ oz. whiskey, #7606	22.50
Tumbler, 5 oz., #8858	15.00
Tumbler, 5 oz., #7606	15.00
Tumbler, 5 oz. ftd., #3750	18.00
Tumbler, 8 oz., #7606	20.00
Tumbler, 9 oz., #8858	20.00
Tumbler, 10 oz. ftd. & hdld., #7606	35.00
Tumbler, 10 oz. hnd. & ftd., #8023	25.00
Tumbler, 10 oz. table, #7606	25.00
Tumbler, 10 oz., ftd., #3750	25.00
Tumbler, 12 oz., #8858	22.00
Tumbler, 12 oz. ftd., #3750	25.00
Tumbler, 12 oz. tea, #7606	22.00
Tumbler, 12 oz., hdld., #8858	25.00

Glass Co, 1926 – 1944

Colors: crystal and some blue

New Martinsville's Meadow Wreath is normally found etched on Radiance Line #42, but there are exceptions. The #4457 Teardrop two-light candle stick in the center of the picture is Janice, a contemporary of Radiance. The light blue Meadow Wreath etch sometimes irritates Radiance collectors searching for that color. I see more Meadow Wreath etched candles than I do ones without the etch. If a collector were willing to mix the Meadow Wreath with unetched wares, a wider range of pieces would be open to him.

There is a multitude of bowls and serving pieces available, but basic luncheon items are lacking except for sugars and creamers. Use these serving items to complement some of those patterns where serving items are almost nonexistent. Blending color is already a trend; so blending patterns does not seem such a long stretch in this day of ever more expensive and hard to find glassware.

	Crystal
Bowl, 7", 2 pt. relish, #4223/26	18.00
Bowl, 8", 3 pt. relish, #4228/26	30.00
Bowl, 10" comport, #4218/26	35.00
Bowl, 10" crimped, #4220/26	40.00
Bowl, 10" oval celery, #42/26	35.00
Bowl, 10" flat, flared	35.00
Bowl, 11" crimped, ftd. #4266/26	40.00
Bowl, 11" ftd., flared, #4265/26	40.00
Bowl, 12" crimped, flat, #4212	45.00
Bowl, 12" flat, flared, deep, #42/26	47.50
Bowl, 12", flat, flared, #4213/26	47.50
Bowl, 13" crimped, flat	50.00
Bowl, 5 qt. punch, #4221/26	125.00
Candle, 2 light, rnd. ft.	40.00

	Crystal
Candy box (3 pt.) & cover, #42/26	65.00
Cheese & cracker, 11", #42/26	45.00
Creamer, ftd., tab hdld., #42/26	15.00
Cup, 4 oz. punch, tab hdld.	9.00
Ladle, punch, #4226	55.00
Mayonnaise set, liner & ladle, #42/26	45.00
Plate, 11"	35.00
Plate, 14", #42/26	45.00
Salver, 12" ftd., #42/26	40.00
Sugar, ftd., tab hdld., #42/26	15.00
Tray, oval for sugar & creamer, #42/26	15.00
Vase, 10" crimped, #4232/26	55.00
Vase, 10" flared, #42/26	50.00

MINUET, Etching #1530 on QUEEN ANN Blank, #1509; TOUJOURS Blank, #1511;
SYMPHONE Blank, #5010, et al.; A.H. Heisey & Co., 1939 – 1950s

Colors: crystal

The production of Minuet began in 1939 making it a borderline case for moving it into *Collectible Glassware from the 40s, 50s, and 60s*. This decision will be determined by how many new patterns I can fit into the allotted pages of the books. There are 22 new patterns in this book and I will have to find some space for new patterns next time.

Minuet is one Heisey pattern where stable prices have prevailed. There have been a few price adjustments, namely for dinner plates. By the way, dinner plates are listed as service plates in Heisey catalogs. That was often the case in Cambridge catalogs, also.

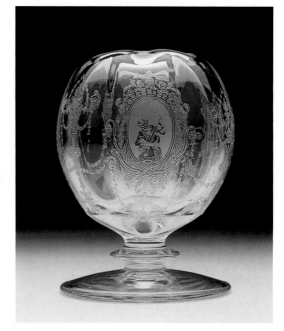

Minuet stemware is copious, but most tumblers are evasive. As with many other stemware lines, Minuet was purchased to go with china settings. Serving pieces were rarely bought as china was used for serving. Only the three-part relish and the three-footed bowl seem to be found with regularity. You will meet impassioned competition looking to buy this pattern.

	Crystal
Bell, dinner, #3408	75.00
Bowl, finger, #3309	50.00
Bowl, 6", ftd., dolphin, mint	45.00
Bowl, 6", ftd., 2 hdld., jelly	30.00
Bowl, 6½", salad dressings	35.00
Bowl, 7", salad dressings	40.00
Bowl, 7", triplex, relish	60.00
Bowl, 7½", sauce, ftd.	70.00
Bowl, 9½", 3 pt., "5 o'clock," relish	70.00
Bowl, 10", salad, #1511 Toujours	65.00
Bowl, 11", 3 pt., "5 o'clock," relish	80.00
Bowl, 11", ftd., dolphin, floral	120.00
Bowl, 12", oval, floral, #1511 Toujours	65.00
Bowl, 12", oval, #1514	65.00
Bowl, 13", floral, #1511 Toujours	60.00
Bowl, 13", pickle & olive	45.00
Bowl, 13½", shallow salad	75.00
Candelabrum, 1-lite, w/prisms	110.00
Candelabrum, 2-lite, bobeche & prisms	175.00
Candlestick, 1-lite, #112	35.00
Candlestick, 2-lite, #1511 Toujours	150.00
Candlestick, 3-lite, #142 Cascade	90.00
Candlestick, 5", 2-lite, #134 Trident	60.00

	Crystal
Centerpiece vase & prisms, #1511 Toujours	200.00
Cocktail icer, w/liner, #3304 Uinversal	125.00
Comport, 5½", #5010	40.00
Comport, 7½", #1511 Toujours	60.00
Creamer, #1511 Toujours	60.00
Creamer, dolphin ft.	42.50
Creamer, indiv., #1509 Queen Ann	37.50
Creamer, indiv., #1511 Toujours	70.00
Cup	30.00
Ice bucket, dolphin ft.	160.00
Marmalade, w/cover, #1511 Toujours (apple shape)	175.00
Mayonnaise, 5½", dolphin ft.	50.00
Mayonnaise, ftd., #1511 Toujours	75.00
Pitcher, 73 oz., #4164	450.00
Plate, 7", mayonnaise liner	10.00
Plate, 7", salad	18.00
Plate, 7", salad, #1511 Toujours	15.00
Plate, 8", luncheon	30.00
Plate, 8", luncheon, #1511 Toujours	25.00
Plate, 10½", service	190.00
Plate, 12", rnd., 2 hdld., sandwich	150.00

	Crystal
Plate, 13", floral, salver, #1511 Toujours	60.00
Plate, 14", torte, #1511 Toujours	60.00
Plate, 15", sand., #1511 Toujours	65.00
Plate, 16", snack rack, w/#1477 center	80.00
Salt & pepper, pr. (#10)	75.00
Saucer	10.00
Stem, #5010, Symphone, 1 oz., cordial	135.00
Stem, #5010, 2½ oz., wine	50.00
Stem, #5010, 3½ oz., cocktail	35.00
Stem, #5010, 4 oz., claret	40.00
Stem, #5010, 4½ oz., oyster cocktail	25.00
Stem, #5010, 6 oz., saucer champagne	25.00
Stem, #5010, 6 oz., sherbet	25.00
Stem, #5010, 9 oz., water	35.00
Sugar, indiv., #1511 Toujours	70.00
Sugar, indiv., #1509 Queen Ann	37.50
Sugar dolphin ft., #1509 Queen Ann	40.00

	Crystal
Sugar, #1511 Toujours	60.00
Tray, 12", celery, #1511 Toujours	50.00
Tray, 15", social hour	90.00
Tray for indiv. sugar & creamer	30.00
Tumbler, #5010, 5 oz., fruit juice	34.00
Tumbler, #5010, 9 oz., low ftd., water	35.00
Tumbler, #5010, 12 oz., tea	60.00
Tumbler, #2351, 12 oz., tea	60.00
Vase, 5", #5013	50.00
Vase, 5½", ftd., #1511 Toujours	95.00
Vase, 6", urn, #5012	75.00
Vase, 7½", urn, #5012	90.00
Vase, 8", #4196	95.00
Vase, 9", urn, #5012	110.00
Vase, 10", #4192	110.00
Vase, 10", #4192, Saturn optic	115.00

Colors: amber, amethyst, black, blue, crystal, green, pink, lilac, crystal stems w/color bowls

Morgan was designed in 1920 by Joseph Balda, who was better known for his Heisey designs. The pattern allegedly was adopted for use in the governor's mansion by a West Virginia governing family named Morgan. Thus, the very masculine pattern name attached to a swinging, fairy design.

This pattern has attracted a multitude of followers. Cathy found it intriguing about ten years ago and began buying what she could find. Since few knew what it was, very little turned up at shows or markets. With so many new collectors searching for this sparsely distributed pattern, it has been even more difficult to find additional pieces to include in the book. However, with its exposure here, new items are now being found. Page 130 shows all the colors we have located except for green and black. We have seen very little of the lilac, represented by a dinner plate and high sherbet in the photo, although an entire set was marketed a few years ago. There are even fewer pieces of amber seen. Several pieces of black found include a candy, 6" bonbon, and a bud vase with a gold encrusted fairy. Newly pictured items in pink are the ice bucket, diamond shaped divided candy, an octagonal plate, and a blown candy or powder jar. The pattern is found only on the lid of the covered items; so, do not fret too much about condition of the bottom. Other bottoms will turn up as pieces without etchings. Cups and saucers are the items missing from most collections of this Central Glass Works pattern. Only crystal and pink cup and saucers have been seen thus far, with crystal leading the way.

The gold-decorated bud vase shown is dramatic against its dark amethyst background. We have now found this gold design on a black bud vase. Does anyone have a gold decorated piece other than a bud vase?

Even stemware has become more difficult to find, with the blue and lilac stems displaying some royal prices. Note that there are three styles of stemware. The beaded stems seem to come in solid colors of crystal, pink, or green. The "wafer" stem is found all pink, green stem with crystal top, and crystal stem with blue top. All lilac stems are solid lilac, but the bowls are shaped differently than other colors. These are the same mould line as "Balda" shown on page 15.

If you have knowledge of additional pieces, please share!

	*All Colors			*All Colors
Bonbon, 6", two handled	65.00		Stem, 3¼", sherbet	35.00
Bowl, 4¼", ftd., fruit	60.00		Stem, 4⅜", sherbet, beaded stem	40.00
Bowl, 10", console	100.00		Stem, 5⅛", cocktail, beaded stem	40.00
Bowl, 13", console	125.00		Stem, 5⅜", high, sherbet, beaded stem	45.00
Candlestick, pr.	150.00		Stem, 5⅞", high sherbet, straight stem	65.00
Candy, blown, pattern on top	550.00		Stem, 5⅞", wine	55.00
Candy w/lid, diamond shaped, 4 ftd.	495.00		Stem, 7¼", 10 oz., water	75.00
Comport, 6½" tall, 5" wide	75.00		Stem, 8¼", water	75.00
Comport, 6½" tall, 6" wide	85.00		Sugar, ftd.	75.00
Creamer, ftd.	75.00		Tumbler, oyster cocktail	40.00
Cup	150.00		Tumbler, 2⅛", whiskey	90.00
Decanter, w/stopper	350.00		Tumbler, 10 oz., flat water	40.00
Ice bucket, 4¾" x7½", 2 hdld.	600.00		Tumbler, 4⅜", ftd. juice	40.00
Mayonnaise	75.00		Tumbler, 5⅜", ftd., 10 oz., water	40.00
Mayonnaise liner	20.00		Tumbler, 5¾", ftd., water	40.00
Oil bottle	295.00		Tumbler, 5⅞", ftd., 12 oz., tea	65.00
Pitcher	495.00		Vase, 8", drape optic	175.00
Plate, 6½", fruit bowl liner	15.00	**	Vase, 9⅞", straight w/flared top	350.00
Plate, 7¼", salad	25.00		Vase, 10", bud	200.00
Plate, 8½", luncheon	35.00		Vase, 10", ruffled top	595.00
Plate, 9¼", dinner	125.00			
Saucer	25.00		* Crystal 10% to 20% lower.	
Server, 9½", octagonal, center handle	100.00		Blue, lilac 25% to 30% higher.	
Server, 10⅜", round, center handle	85.00		** Gold decorated $300.00	
Server, 11", octagonal, flat, center handle	95.00			

MT. VERNON, Cambridge Glass Company, late 1920s – 1940s

Colors: amber, crystal, Carmen, Royal Blue, Heatherbloom, Emerald green (light and dark); rare in Violet

Large sets of Mt. Vernon can only be accumulated in amber or crystal. You could procure small luncheon sets in red, cobalt blue, or Heatherbloom; but only a few complementary pieces are available in those colors. However, prices for any of those colors will go for up to double the prices listed for amber and crystal. Many collectors are blending their crystal Mt. Vernon with a splash of color. That makes a more affordable investment in a set than buying only hard to find and expensive colored pieces.

	Amber Crystal
Ash tray, 3½", #63	8.00
Ash tray, 4", #68	12.00
Ash tray, 6" x 4½", oval, #71	12.00
Bonbon, 7", ftd., #10	12.50
Bottle, bitters, 2½ oz., #62	65.00
Bottle, 7 oz., sq., toilet, #18	75.00

	Amber Crystal
Bowl, finger, #23	10.00
Bowl, 4½", ivy ball or rose, ftd., #12	27.50
Bowl, 5¼", fruit, #6	10.00
Bowl, 6", cereal, #32	12.50
Bowl, 6", preserve, #76	12.00
Bowl, 6½", rose, #106	18.00

	Amber Crystal
Bowl, 8", pickle, #65	17.50
Bowl, 8½", 4 pt., 2 hdld., sweetmeat, #105	32.00
Bowl, 10", 2 hdld., #39	20.00
Bowl, 10½", deep, #43	30.00
Bowl, 10½", salad, #120	25.00
Bowl, 11", oval, 4 ftd., #136	27.50
Bowl, 11", oval, #135	25.00
Bowl, 11½", belled, #128	30.00
Bowl, 11½", shallow, #126	30.00
Bowl, 11½", shallow cupped, #61	30.00
Bowl, 12", flanged, rolled edge, #129	32.50
Bowl, 12", oblong, crimped, #118	32.50
Bowl, 12", rolled edge, crimped, #117	32.50
Bowl, 12½", flanged, rolled edge, #45	35.00
Bowl, 12½", flared, #121	35.00
Bowl, 12½", flared, #44	35.00
Bowl, 13", shallow, crimped, #116	35.00
Box, 3", w/cover, round, #16	30.00
Box, 4", w/cover, sq., #17	32.50
Box, 4½", w/cover, ftd., round, #15	37.50
Butter tub, w/cover, #73	65.00
Cake stand, 10½" ftd., #150	35.00
Candelabrum, 13½", #38	150.00
Candlestick, 4", #130	10.00
Candlestick, 5", 2-lite, #110	25.00
Candlestick, 8", #35	27.50
Candy, w/cover, 1 lb., ftd., #9	85.00
Celery, 10½", #79	15.00
Celery, 11", #98	17.50
Celery, 12", #79	20.00
Cigarette box, 6", w/cover, oval, #69	32.00
Cigarette holder, #66	15.00
Coaster, 3", plain, #60	5.00
Coaster, 3", ribbed, #70	5.00
Cocktail icer, 2 pc., #85	27.50
Cologne, 2½ oz., w/stopper, #1340	45.00
Comport, 4½", #33	12.00
Comport, 5½", 2 hdld., #77	15.00
Comport, 6", #34	15.00
Comport, 6½", #97	17.50
Comport, 6½", belled, #96	22.50
Comport, 7½" #11	25.00
Comport, 8", #81	25.00
Comport, 9", oval, 2 hdld., #100	35.00
Comport, 9½", #99	30.00
Creamer, ftd., #8	10.00
Creamer, indiv., #4	10.00
Creamer, #86	10.00
Cup, #7	6.50
Decanter, 11 oz., #47	60.00
Decanter, 40 oz., w/stopper, #52	85.00
Honey jar, w/cover (marmalade), #74	35.00
Ice bucket, w/tongs, #92	35.00
Lamp, 9" hurricane, #1607	85.00
Mayonnaise, divided, 2 spoons, #107	25.00
Mug, 14 oz., stein, #84	30.00
Mustard, w/cover, 2½ oz., #28	25.00

	Amber Crystal
Pickle, 6", 1 hdld., #78	12.00
Pitcher, 50 oz., #90	90.00
Pitcher, 66 oz., #13	95.00
Pitcher, 80 oz., ball, #95	105.00
Pitcher, 86 oz., #91	125.00
Plate, finger bowl liner, #23	4.00
Plate, 6", bread & butter, #4	3.00
Plate, 6⅜", bread & butter, #19	4.00
Plate, 8½", salad, #5	7.00
Plate, 10½", dinner, #40	35.00
Plate, 11½", hdld., #37	20.00
Relish, 6", 2 pt., 2 hdld., #106	12.00
Relish, 8", 2 pt., hdld., #101	17.50
Relish, 8", 3 pt., 3 hdld., #103	20.00
Relish, 11", 3 part, #200	25.00
Relish, 12", 2 part, #80	30.00
Relish, 12", 5 part, #104	30.00
Salt, indiv., #24	7.00
Salt, oval, 2 hdld., #102	12.00
Salt & pepper, pr., #28	22.50
Salt & pepper, pr., short, #88	20.00
Salt & pepper, tall, #89	25.00
Salt dip, #24	9.00
Sauce boat & ladle, tab hdld., #30-445	75.00
Saucer, #7	7.50
Stem, 3 oz., wine, #27	15.00
Stem, 3½ oz., cocktail, #26	9.00
Stem, 4 oz., oyster cocktail, #41	9.00
Stem, 4½ oz., claret, #25	13.50
Stem, 4½ oz., low sherbet, #42	7.50
Stem, 6½ oz., tall sherbet, #2	10.00
Stem, 10 oz., water, #1	15.00
Sugar, ftd., #8	10.00
Sugar, indiv., #4	12.00
Sugar, #86	10.00
Tray, for indiv., sugar & creamer, #4	10.00
Tumbler, 1 oz., ftd., cordial, #87	22.00
Tumbler, 2 oz., whiskey, #55	10.00
Tumbler, 3 oz., ftd., juice, #22	9.00
Tumbler, 5 oz., #56	12.00
Tumbler, 5 oz., ftd., #21	12.00
Tumbler, 7 oz., old-fashioned, #57	15.00
Tumbler, 10 oz., ftd., water, #3	15.00
Tumbler, 10 oz., table, #51	12.00
Tumbler, 10 oz., tall, #58	12.00
Tumbler, 12 oz., barrel shape, #13	15.00
Tumbler, 12 oz., ftd., tea, #20	17.00
Tumbler, 14 oz., barrel shape, #14	20.00
Tumbler, 14 oz., tall, #59	22.00
Urn, w/cover (same as candy), #9	85.00
Vase, 5", #42	15.00
Vase, 6", crimped, #119	20.00
Vase, 6", ftd., #50	25.00
Vase, 6½", squat, #107	27.50
Vase, 7", #58	30.00
Vase, 7", ftd., #54	35.00
Vase, 10", ftd., #46	60.00

NAUTICAL, Duncan & Miller Glass Company, late 1930s

Color: crystal, blue, blue and pink opalescent

Nautical's exposure in the last edition created quite a stir among long-time collectors who had been buying this pattern reasonably since few part-time dealers actually knew what it was. Nautical should be easily recognized, but numerous pieces slip through the cracks. It is hard to miss those items with anchors and rope; but some pieces do not have the anchor which means they can escape all but the observant eye.

I did get some comments about the decanter I mentioned as a pattern shot in the last book. Sorry about that. After that wonderful opalescent comport was found and photographed, we substituted it for the decanter and my writings failed to change to match. It happens when deadlines are trying to be met, but it's great to know that the book is read!

Blue, and particularly, the opalescent, is the most often sought color; but collectors are inclined to mix the blue with crystal in order to have more choices. Notice the difference in the decanter and covered jar that are pictured side by side in the bottom row on page 134. The jars on each end are listed as candy jars. I confused the decanter with a jar myself when I first saw it. The opalescent decanter is pictured between the cocktail shaker and the blue candy jar. It is taller and thinner.

That 7" comport with an anchor for the stem can be found with two different tops. The opalescent one has a pointed edge top while the other style has a plain edge top. The covered jars, decanter, and comport are the choice pieces to own as you can see by their prices.

There are similar pieces that are confused with Nautical. You can find a pair of bookends that have a leaning anchor across the base. You will often see this same shaped bookend with a horse head. Those anchor bookends can be found in blue or crystal. There are lamps made to look like a captain's wheel that will blend well with Nautical as long as you do not pay Nautical prices for them.

	*Blue	Crystal	Opalescent
Ash tray, 3"	20.00	8.00	
Ash tray, 6"	30.00	12.50	
Candy jar, w/lid	550.00	295.00	650.00
Cigarette holder	35.00	15.00	
Cigarette jar	60.00	25.00	
Cocktail shaker (fish design)	150.00	60.00	
Comport, 7"	295.00	110.00	595.00
Creamer	30.00	15.00	
Decanter	495.00	225.00	650.00
Ice bucket	125.00	55.00	
Marmalade	65.00	25.00	
Plate, 6½", 2 hdld., cake	25.00	12.00	
Plate, 8"	20.00	10.00	
Plate, 10"	60.00	25.00	
Relish, 12", 7 part	75.00	35.00	
Relish, 2-part, 2 hdld.	45.00	22.50	
Shakers, pr.		35.00	
Sugar	30.00	15.00	
Tumbler, 2 oz., bar	25.00	12.50	
Tumbler, 8 oz., whisky & soda	25.00	12.00	
Tumbler, 9 oz., water, ftd.	28.00	15.00	
Tumbler, cocktail	22.00	12.00	
Tumbler, ftd., orange juice	28.00	15.00	
Tumbler, high ball	30.00	18.00	

*Add 10% for satinized.

Colors: crystal; all other colors found made very late

Fostoria's **crystal** Navarre pattern has become the crown jewel etching made by that company! American is the most widely collected Fostoria crystal pattern; but it was made for about 70 years and several generations came to know it. Navarre was made for over 40 years; and the thin delicate stems still enhance modern day china patterns. Navarre was distributed nationally, but prices on the West Coast were always more expensive due to shipping costs. With the price of gasoline skyrocketing, transportation costs may soon factor into dealers' prices of merchandise once again.

Only older crystal pieces of Navarre are priced in this Elegant book. Colors of pink, blue, and red were all made in the 1970s and 1980s as were additional crystal pieces not originally made in the late 1930s and 1940s. These later pieces include carafes, roemer wines, continental champagnes, and brandies. You can find these later pieces in my *Collectible Glassware from the 40s, 50s & 60s....* Most of these pieces are signed "Fostoria" although some carried only a sticker. I am telling you this to make you aware of the colors made in Navarre. You will even find a few pieces of Navarre that are signed Lenox. These were made after Fostoria closed. Some collectors shy away from the Lenox pieces; but it does not seem to make much difference to a majority of Navarre devotees. A few Depression era glass shows have not allowed these pieces or colors to be sold since they were of so recent manufacture. However, most shows are changing these stricter rules to allow patterns to be included that began production earlier.

Note the footed shakers in the photo below. They came with both glass and metal lids. Glass tops were used in the early production years, but soon gave way to metal. Metal lids were the ones most often shipped as replacements when customers ordered new lids.

	Crystal		Crystal
Bell, dinner	60.00	Bowl, #2496, 10½", hdld., ftd.	85.00
Bowl, #2496, 4", square, hdld.	14.00	Bowl, #2470½, 10½", ftd.	65.00
Bowl, #2496, 4⅜", hdld.	14.00	Bowl, #2496, 12", flared	70.00
Bowl, #869, 4½", finger	75.00	Bowl, #2545, 12½", oval, "Flame"	60.00
Bowl, #2496, 4⅝", tri-cornered	22.00	Candlestick, #2496, 4"	25.00
Bowl, #2496, 5", hdld., ftd.	20.00	Candlestick, #2496, 4½", double	40.00
Bowl, #2496, 6", square, sweetmeat	25.00	Candlestick, #2472, 5", double	50.00
Bowl, #2496, 6¼", 3 ftd., nut	20.00	Candlestick, #2496, 5½"	40.00
Bowl, #2496, 7⅜", ftd., bonbon	27.50	Candlestick, #2496, 6", triple	60.00
Bowl, #2496, 10", oval, floating garden	55.00	Candlestick, #2545, 6¾", double, "Flame"	85.00

	Crystal
Candlestick, #2482, 6¾", triple	90.00
Candy, w/cover, #2496, 3 part	150.00
Celery, #2440, 9"	35.00
Celery, #2496, 11"	50.00
Comport, #2496, 3¼", cheese	35.00
Comport, #2400, 4½"	35.00
Comport, #2496, 4¾"	35.00
Cracker, #2496, 11", plate	50.00
Creamer, #2440, 4¼", ftd.	20.00
Creamer, #2496, individual	17.50
Cup, #2440	20.00
Ice bucket, #2496, 4⅜" high	130.00
Ice bucket, #2375, 6" high	150.00
Mayonnaise, #2375, 3 piece	75.00
Mayonnaise, #2496½", 3 piece	75.00
Pickle, #2496, 8"	27.50
Pickle, #2440, 8½"	30.00
Pitcher, #5000, 48 oz., ftd.	365.00
Plate, #2440, 6", bread/butter	11.00
Plate, #2440, 7½", salad	15.00
Plate, #2440, 8½", luncheon	24.00
Plate, #2440, 9½", dinner	50.00
Plate, #2496, 10", hdld., cake	60.00
Plate, #2440, 10½", oval cake	55.00
Plate, #2496, 14", torte	75.00
Plate, #2464, 16", torte	135.00
Relish, #2496, 6", 2 part, square	32.50
Relish, #2496, 10" x 7½", 3 part	50.00

	Crystal
Relish, #2496, 10", 4 part	55.00
Relish, #2419, 13¼", 5 part	95.00
Salt & pepper, #2364, 3¼", flat, pr.	75.00
Salt & pepper, #2375, 3½", ftd., pr.	110.00
Salad dressing bottle, #2083, 6½"	425.00
Sauce dish, #2496, div. mayo., 6½"	40.00
Sauce dish, #2496, 6½" x 5¼"	135.00
Sauce dish liner, #2496, 8", oval	30.00
Saucer, #2440	5.00
Stem, #6106, 1 oz., cordial, 3⅞"	55.00
Stem, #6106, 3¼ oz., wine, 5½"	35.00
Stem, #6106, 3½ oz., cocktail, 6"	25.00
Stem, #6106, 4 oz., oyster cocktail, 3⅝"	27.50
Stem, #6106, 4½ oz., claret, 6½"	42.50
Stem, #6106, 6 oz., low sherbet, 4⅜"	25.00
Stem, #6106, 6 oz., saucer champagne, 5⅝"	25.00
Stem, #6106, 10 oz., water, 7⅝"	32.00
Sugar, #2440, 3⅝", ftd.	18.00
Sugar, #2496, individual	16.00
Syrup, #2586, metal cut-off top, 5½"	425.00
Tid bit, #2496, 8¼", 3 ftd., turned up edge	22.00
Tray, #2496½", for ind. sugar/creamer	22.00
Tumbler, #6106, 5 oz., ftd., juice, 4⅝"	25.00
Tumbler, #6106, 10 oz., ftd., water, 5⅜"	25.00
Tumbler, #6106, 13 oz., ftd., tea, 5⅞"	35.00
Vase, #4108, 5"	110.00
Vase, #4121, 5"	110.00

Colors: crystal, frosted crystal, some cobalt with crystal stem and foot

Except for stems, the celery tray, and candlesticks, the production of New Era falls outside production dates of this book; so, be warned, New Era will be transferred into my *Collectible Glassware from the 40s, 50s, and 60s* book after this Elegant edition. The New Era double branched candelabrum with bobeches is probably the most acknowledged Heisey candle. Stemware abounds, but look for flat pieces of New Era that often go unrecognized as Heisey!

	Crystal
Ash tray or indiv. nut	50.00
Bottle, rye, w/stopper	155.00
Bowl, 11", floral	60.00
Candelabra, 2-lite, w/2 #4044 bobeche & prisms	140.00
Creamer	35.00
Cup	12.00
Cup, after dinner	70.00
Pilsner, 8 oz.	25.00
Pilsner, 12 oz.	30.00
Plate, 5½" x 4½", bread & butter	15.00
Plate, 9" x 7"	25.00
Plate, 10" x 8"	42.50
Relish, 13", 3 part	32.00
Saucer	5.00
Saucer, after dinner	10.00

	Crystal
Stem, 1 oz. cordial	45.00
Stem, 3 oz. wine	30.00
Stem, 3½ oz., high, cocktail	15.00
Stem, 3½ oz., oyster cocktail	16.00
Stem, 4 oz., claret	20.00
Stem, 6 oz., champagne	15.00
Stem, 10 oz., goblet	20.00
Stem, low, 6 oz., sherbet	15.00
Sugar	35.00
Tray, 13", celery	35.00
Tumbler, 5 oz., ftd., soda	15.00
Tumbler, 8 oz., ftd., soda	15.00
Tumbler, 12 oz., ftd., soda	15.00
Tumbler, 14 oz., ftd., soda	19.00
Tumbler, low, footed, 10 oz.	15.00

Colors: Amber, Rose, and Topaz

New Garland is a Fostoria pattern that is beginning to be noticed by collectors. Some new collectors have been attracted to its older, squared mould shape of Fostoria's #2419 Mayfair line. Pink appears to be the color of choice, but we are getting requests for yellow recently.

	Amber Topaz	Rose
Bonbon, 2 hdld.	15.00	20.00
Bottle, salad dressing	125.00	195.00
Bowl, 5", fruit	10.00	12.50
Bowl, 6", cereal	12.00	18.00
Bowl, 7", soup	22.00	30.00
Bowl, 7½"	25.00	40.00
Bowl, 10", baker	35.00	45.00
Bowl, 11", ftd.	50.00	70.00
Bowl, 12"	55.00	70.00
Candlestick, 2"	15.00	20.00
Candlestick, 3"	17.50	22.50
Candlestick, 9½"	30.00	40.00
Candy jar, cover, ½ lb.	50.00	75.00
Celery, 11"	22.00	30.00
Comport, 6"	20.00	28.00
Comport, tall	30.00	40.00
Cream soup	18.00	22.50
Creamer	12.50	15.00
Creamer, ftd.	15.00	17.50
Creamer, tea	17.50	20.00
Cup, after dinner	20.00	25.00
Cup, ftd.	14.00	17.50
Decanter	125.00	195.00
Finger bowl, #4121	12.00	15.00
Finger bowl, #6002, ftd.	15.00	18.00
Ice bucket	55.00	70.00
Ice dish	20.00	25.00
Jelly, 7"	18.00	22.50
Lemon dish, 2 hdld.	15.00	18.00
Mayonnaise, 2 hdld.	18.00	22.50
Mint, 5½"	12.50	16.00
Nut, individual	10.00	13.00
Oil, ftd.	135.00	195.00
Pickle, 8½"	16.00	20.00
Pitcher, ftd.	225.00	295.00
Plate, 6"	4.00	6.00
Plate, 7"	7.00	10.00
Plate, 8"	12.00	15.00
Plate, 9"	25.00	35.00
Plate, 10" cake, 2 hdld.	27.50	35.00
Platter, 12"	35.00	45.00
Platter, 15"	50.00	75.00
Relish, 4 part	20.00	27.50
Relish, 8½"	14.00	18.00
Sauce boat	50.00	75.00
Sauce boat liner	20.00	25.00
Saucer	3.00	4.00
Saucer, after dinner	8.00	10.00
Shaker, pr.	40.00	60.00

	Amber Topaz	Rose
Shaker, pr., ftd.	75.00	100.00
Stem, #4120, 2 oz., whiskey	20.00	28.00
Stem, #4120, 3½ oz., cocktail	20.00	24.00
Stem, #4120, 5 oz., low sherbet	14.00	16.00
Stem, #4120, 7 oz., low sherbet	15.00	18.00
Stem, #4120, high sherbet	18.00	20.00
Stem, #4120, water goblet	22.00	25.00
Stem, #6002, claret	25.00	32.50
Stem, #6002, cordial	30.00	37.50
Stem, #6002, goblet	22.00	25.00
Stem, #6002, high sherbet	18.00	20.00
Stem, #6002, low sherbet	14.00	16.00
Stem, #6002, oyster cocktail	16.00	20.00
Stem, #6002, wine	22.00	25.00
Sugar	12.50	15.00
Sugar, ftd.	15.00	17.50
Sugar, tea	17.50	20.00
Tumbler, #4120, 5 oz.	12.00	15.00
Tumbler, #4120, 10 oz.	14.00	17.50
Tumbler, #4120, 13 oz.	15.00	18.00
Tumbler, #4120, 16 oz.	20.00	24.00
Tumbler, #6002, ftd., 2 oz.	18.00	22.00
Tumbler, #6002, ftd., 5 oz.	12.00	15.00
Tumbler, #6002, ftd., 10 oz.	14.00	17.50
Tumbler, #6002, ftd., 13 oz.	15.00	18.00
Vase, 8"	45.00	60.00

Colors: Emerald green, Peach Blo; #3095 colored Peach-blo w/ribbed bowl, crystal stem & foot, optic

Cambridge's Number 520 and Number 704, which follows on the next page, are usually referred to as "one of those Cambridge etched patterns," but few people take the trouble to learn which one. There are some avid collectors of both of these lines, and maybe adding names, "Byzantine" and "Windows Border" may help define the patterns as did "Rosalie" for Number 731. Collectors like names. Since no factory name has been forthcoming, let's adopt one collector's idea who told me it reminded her of the elaborate designs seen in her travels. "It's very Byzantine," she said.

I see about equal amounts of Peach Blo (pink) and Emerald, but there seem to be more admirers of the green. That green butter dish would fetch a king's ransom in some other pattern. Perhaps someday it will in "Byzantine."

	Peach Blo / green			Peach Blo / green
Bouillon, 2 hdld. soup cup, #934	22.50		Plate, finger bowl liner, #3060	12.50
Bowl, 5¼" fruit, #928	22.50		Platter for gravy boat	35.00
Bowl, 6½" cereal or grapefruit, #466	32.50		Saucer, #933	7.00
Bowl, finger, #3060	25.00		Saucer, cupped, liner for bouillon	12.00
Butter w/cover	155.00		Stem, 2½ oz. cocktail, #3060	22.50
Candy box, #300	95.00		Stem, 2½ oz. wine, #3060	35.00
Comport, 7¼" h., #531	40.00		Stem, 6 oz. hi sherbet, #3060	22.50
Comport, jelly, #2900	35.00		Stem, 7 oz., sherbet, #3060	22.50
Comport, #3095 (twist stem)	40.00		Stem, 9 oz. water, #3060	30.00
Creamer, rim ft., #138	20.00		Stem, cocktail, #3095	22.50
Cup, #933	18.00		Stem, high sherbet, #3095	20.00
Gravy or sauce boat	75.00		Stem, low sherbet, #3095	18.00
Oil bottle, #193	135.00		Sugar, rim ft., #138	20.00
Oil bottle w/cut flattened stop, 6 oz., #197	150.00		Tumbler, 3 oz ftd., #3060	20.00
Plate, 6", sherbet	10.00		Tumbler, 5 oz. ftd., #3060	22.50
Plate, 8", luncheon	18.00		Tumbler, 10 oz. ftd., #3060	25.00
Plate, 9½" dinner, #810	60.00		Tumbler, 12 oz. low ft., #3095	30.00

Colors: amber, Bluebell, crystal, Emerald, Peach-blo

Number 704 has been referred to by a collector as "Windows Border" and that might stick better than Number 704 has over the years. The photograph of pink was furnished by Barbara Adt Namon. The photographer has since died, but he diligently tried to capture the beauty of this pattern for you.

"Windows Border" is often displayed in sets in malls with people passing it without knowing it to be one of Cambridge's more intriguing pattern designs. I am hoping this exposure will enhance its appeal to collectors and bring it the recognition it truly deserves. Look at it! It's a wonderful etch!

	All Colors		All Colors
Bottle, decanter, #0315	175.00	Cheese plate & cover, #3075	125.00
Bottle, decanter, #3075	195.00	Cigarette box, #430	50.00
Bowl, 5¼", fruit	16.00	Cigarette box, #616	50.00
Bowl, 6", cereal	25.00	Cologne, 1 oz., #198 or #199	125.00
Bowl, 8½" soup	30.00	Comport, 5", #3075	30.00
Bowl, 8¾", oval	33.00	Creamer, flat, #137	22.50
Bowl, 10½", #912 casserole and cover	125.00	Creamer, flat, #942	22.50
Bowl, 12", oval, #914	50.00	Creamer, flat, #943	22.50
Bowl, 12", oval w/cover, #915	125.00	Creamer, flat, #944	22.50
Bowl, 2 hdld. cream soup, #922	20.00	Cup, #933	15.00
Bowl, finger, #3060	35.00	Cup, demi, #925	35.00
Bowl, finger, #3075	35.00	Gravy boat, double and stand, #917	125.00
Butter and cover, #920	125.00	Ice bucket w/bail, short, #970	65.00
Candlestick, 2", #227½	20.00	Ice bucket w/bail, tall, #957	75.00
Candlestick, 3½", #628	25.00	Ice tub, straight up tab hdlds., #394	65.00
Candlestick, 7½", #439		Jug, nite set, #103, 38 oz. w/tumbler	195.00
Candlestick, 8½", #438		Jug, #107	150.00
Candlestick, 9½", #437		Jug, #124, 68 oz., w/lid	195.00
Candy box and cover, 5", #98, 3-part, flat	75.00	Jug, 62 oz. flat, #955	195.00
Candy box and cover, 5", #299, 3-ftd.	75.00	Jug, #3077 w/lid	295.00
Candy box and cover, 6", #300, 3-ftd.	85.00	Mayonnaise, 3 pc., #169	75.00
Celery, 11", #908	35.00	Mayonnaise, 3 pc., #533	65.00
Celery tray, 11", #652	45.00	Oil, 6 oz., #193	65.00
Cheese plate, #468	35.00	Oyster cocktail, 4½ oz. ftd., #3060	14.00

	All Colors
Pickle tray, 9", #907	30.00
Plate, 6"	6.00
Plate, 7"	8.00
Plate, 8"	15.00
Plate, 8½"	22.50
Plate, 9½" dinner	65.00
Plate, 10½" service	75.00
Plate, 13½"	65.00
Plate, cupped, liner for creme soup, #922	8.00
Plate, liner for finger bowl, #3060	8.00
Plate, liner for finger bowl, #3075	8.00
Platter, 12½" oval service, #901	75.00
Platter, 16", oval, #904	95.00
Puff & cover, 3" or 4", #578, blown	85.00
Puff & cover, 4", #582	55.00
Saucer, #933	5.00
Saucer, demi, #925	10.00
Stem, 1 oz. cordial, #3075	65.00
Stem, 2½ oz. cocktail (wide bowl), #3075	18.00
Stem, 2½ oz. wine (slender bowl), #3075	35.00
Stem, 4½ oz. claret, #3075	50.00
Stem, 5 oz. parfait, #3060	40.00
Stem, 5½ oz. cafe parfait, #3075	40.00
Stem, 6 oz. high sherbet, #3060	20.00
Stem, 9 oz., #3060	28.00
Stem, 9 oz., #3075	28.00

	All Colors
Stem, low sherbet, #3075	15.00
Stem, hi sherbet, #3075	20.00
Sugar, flat, #137	20.00
Sugar, flat, #942	20.00
Sugar, flat, #943	20.00
Sugar, flat, #944	20.00
Syrup, 9 oz. w/metal cover, #170	100.00
Syrup, tall jug, #814	125.00
Toast dish and cover, 9", #951	150.00
Tray, 10", center handle	45.00
Tumbler, 2 oz., flat, #3060	33.00
Tumbler, 2 oz. whiskey, #3075	35.00
Tumbler, 3 oz. ftd., #3075	27.50
Tumbler, 5 oz. ftd., #3075	20.00
Tumbler, 5 oz., #3075	20.00
Tumbler, 6 oz. ftd. fruit salad (sherbet)	15.00
Tumbler, 8 oz. ftd., #3075	20.00
Tumbler, 10 oz., #3075	22.50
Tumbler, 10 oz. flat, #3060	20.00
Tumbler, 10 oz. ftd., #3075	22.50
Tumbler, 12 oz., #3075	27.50
Tumbler, 12 oz. flat, #3060	25.00
Tumbler, 12 oz. ftd., #3060	28.00
Tumbler, 12 oz. ftd., #3075	30.00
Vase, 6½", ftd., #1005	100.00
Vase, 9½", ftd., #787	150.00

OCTAGON, Blank #1231 Ribbed, Blank #500, and Blank #1229, A.H. Heisey & Co.

Colors: crystal, Flamingo pink, Sahara yellow, Moongleam green, Hawthorne orchid, Marigold deep amber/yellow, and Dawn

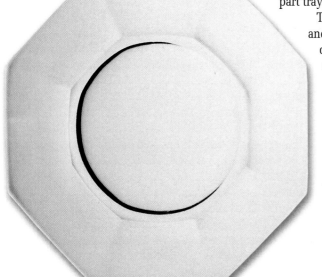

Octagon was regularly marked by Heisey's trademark **H** within a diamond, so it is one of those patterns that everyone can readily identify. Only a small number of collectors search for this plainer glassware. It is one of the uncomplicated Heisey patterns, but it does come in an array of colors! In the price list below, the only piece that vaults out at you is the very last listing of a 12", four-part tray. Octagon is reasonably priced and is often just waiting for a new home. Two Marigold pieces are pictured, the Octagon one shown on page 143 and a Twist piece on page 208. This is a seldom seen Heisey color; but be cautious when buying it because of the color is subject to peeling. If that should happen, it becomes uninviting to collectors!

	Crystal	Flamingo	Sahara	Moongleam	Hawthorne	Marigold
Basket, 5", #500	100.00	300.00	300.00	425.00	450.00	
Bonbon, 6", sides up, #1229	10.00	40.00	25.00	25.00	40.00	
Bowl, cream soup, 2 hdld.	10.00	20.00	25.00	30.00	40.00	
Bowl, 2 hdld, ind. nut bowl	10.00	17.50	25.00	20.00	60.00	65.00
Bowl, 5½", jelly, #1229	15.00	30.00	25.00	25.00	50.00	
Bowl, 6", mint, #1229	10.00	20.00	25.00	25.00	45.00	30.00
Bowl, 6", #500	14.00	20.00	22.00	25.00	35.00	
Bowl, 6½", grapefruit	10.00	20.00	22.00	25.00	35.00	
Bowl, 8", ftd., #1229 comport	15.00	25.00	35.00	45.00	55.00	
Bowl, 9", flat soup	10.00	15.00	20.00	27.50	30.00	
Bowl, 9", vegetable	15.00	32.00	25.00	30.00	50.00	
Candlestick, 3", 1-lite	15.00	30.00	30.00	40.00	50.00	
Cheese dish, 6", 2 hdld., #1229	7.00	15.00	10.00	15.00	15.00	
Creamer, #500	10.00	30.00	35.00	35.00	50.00	
Creamer, hotel	10.00	30.00	30.00	35.00	50.00	
Cup, after dinner	10.00	20.00	20.00	25.00	42.00	
Cup, #1231	5.00	15.00	20.00	20.00	35.00	
Dish, frozen dessert, #500	10.00	20.00	20.00	30.00	35.00	50.00
Ice tub, #500	30.00	70.00	75.00	80.00	115.00	150.00
Mayonnaise, 5½", ftd., #1229	10.00	25.00	30.00	35.00	55.00	
Nut, two hdld.	10.00	25.00	18.00	25.00	65.00	70.00
Plate, cream soup liner	3.00	5.00	7.00	9.00	12.00	
Plate, 6"	4.00	8.00	8.00	10.00	15.00	
Plate, 7", bread	5.00	10.00	10.00	15.00	20.00	
Plate, 8", luncheon	7.00	10.00	10.00	15.00	25.00	
Plate, 10", sand., #1229	15.00	20.00	25.00	30.00	80.00	

	Crystal	Flamingo	Sahara	Moongleam	Hawthorne	Marigold
Plate, 10", muffin, #1229, sides up	15.00	25.00	30.00	35.00	40.00	
Plate, 10½"	17.00	25.00	30.00	35.00	45.00	
Plate, 10½", ctr. hdld., sandwich	25.00	40.00	40.00	45.00	70.00	
Plate, 12", muffin, #1229, sides up	20.00	27.00	30.00	35.00	45.00	
Plate, 13", hors d'oeuvre, #1229	20.00	35.00	35.00	45.00	60.00	
Plate, 14"	22.00	25.00	30.00	35.00	50.00	
Platter, 12¾", oval	20.00	25.00	30.00	40.00	50.00	
Saucer, after dinner	5.00	8.00	10.00	10.00	12.00	
Saucer, #1231	5.00	8.00	10.00	10.00	12.00	
Sugar, #500	10.00	25.00	35.00	35.00	50.00	
Sugar, hotel	10.00	30.00	30.00	35.00	50.00	
Tray, 6", oblong, #500	8.00	15.00	15.00	15.00	30.00	
Tray, 9", celery	10.00	20.00	20.00	25.00	45.00	
Tray, 12", celery	10.00	25.00	25.00	30.00	50.00	
Tray, 12", 4 pt., #500 variety	60.00	120.00	140.00	160.00	250.00	*350.00

*Dawn

Blank #3380, A.H. Heisey & Co., 1930 – 1939

Colors: crystal, Flamingo pink, Sahara yellow, Moongleam green, Marigold deep amber/yellow

Due to the abundance of Sahara (yellow), Old Colony pricing will be based on Sahara as follows: crystal – Subtract 50%; Flamingo – Subtract 10%; Moongleam – add 10%; Marigold – add 20%. Space does not permit pricing each color separately.

	Sahara
Bouillon cup, 2 hdld., ftd.	25.00
Bowl, finger, #4075	15.00
Bowl, ftd., finger, #3390	25.00
Bowl, 4½", nappy	14.00
Bowl, 5", ftd., 2 hdld.	24.00
Bowl, 6", ftd., 2 hdld., jelly	30.00
Bowl, 6", dolphin ftd., mint	35.00
Bowl, 7", triplex, dish	35.00
Bowl, 7½", dolphin ftd., nappy	70.00
Bowl, 8", nappy	40.00
Bowl, 8½", ftd., floral, 2 hdld.	60.00
Bowl, 9", 3 hdld.	90.00
Bowl, 10", rnd., 2 hdld., salad	60.00
Bowl, 10", sq., salad, 2 hdld.	55.00
Bowl, 10", oval, dessert, 2 hdld.	50.00
Bowl, 10", oval, veg.	42.00
Bowl, 11", floral, dolphin ft.	80.00
Bowl, 13", ftd., flared	40.00
Bowl, 13", 2 pt., pickle & olive	24.00
Cigarette holder, #3390	44.00
Comport, 7", oval, ftd.	80.00
Comport, 7", ftd., #3368	70.00
Cream soup, 2 hdld.	22.00
Creamer, dolphin ft.	45.00
Creamer, indiv.	40.00
Cup, after dinner	40.00
Cup	32.00
Decanter, 1 pt.	325.00
Flagon, 12 oz., #3390	100.00
Grapefruit, 6"	30.00
Grapefruit, ftd., #3380	20.00
Ice tub, dolphin ft.	115.00
Mayonnaise, 5½", dolphin ft.	70.00

	Sahara
Oil, 4 oz., ftd.	105.00
Pitcher, 3 pt., #3390	230.00
Pitcher, 3 pt., dolphin ft.	240.00
Plate, bouillon	15.00
Plate, cream soup	12.00
Plate, 4½", rnd.	7.00
Plate, 6", rnd.	15.00
Plate, 6", sq.	15.00
Plate, 7", rnd.	20.00
Plate, 7", sq.	20.00
Plate, 8", rnd.	24.00
Plate, 8", sq.	24.00
Plate, 9", rnd.	23.00
Plate, 10½", rnd.	80.00
Plate, 10½", sq.	70.00
Plate, 12", rnd.	75.00
Plate, 12", 2 hdld., rnd., muffin	75.00
Plate, 12", 2 hdld., rnd., sand.	70.00
Plate, 13", 2 hdld., sq., sand.	50.00
Plate, 13", 2 hdld., sq., muffin	50.00
Platter, 14", oval	45.00
Salt & pepper, pr.	125.00
Saucer, sq.	10.00
Saucer, rnd.	10.00
Stem, #3380, 1 oz., cordial	135.00
Stem, #3380, 2½ oz., wine	35.00
Stem, #3380, 3 oz., cocktail	25.00
Stem, #3380, 4 oz., oyster/cocktail	20.00
Stem, #3380, 4 oz., claret	40.00
Stem, #3380, 5 oz., parfait	20.00
Stem, #3380, 6 oz., champagne	20.00
Stem, #3380, 6 oz., sherbet	20.00
Stem, #3380, 10 oz., short soda	20.00
Stem, #3380, 10 oz., tall soda	25.00
Stem, #3390, 1 oz., cordial	125.00
Stem, #3390, 2½ oz., wine	35.00
Stem, #3390, 3 oz., cocktail	20.00

	Sahara
Stem, #3390, 3 oz., oyster/cocktail	20.00
Stem, #3390, 4 oz., claret	30.00
Stem, #3390, 6 oz., champagne	25.00
Stem, #3390, 6 oz., sherbet	25.00
Stem, #3390, 11 oz., low water	25.00
Stem, #3390, 11 oz., tall water	27.00
Sugar, dolphin ft.	45.00
Sugar, indiv.	40.00
Tray, 10", celery	30.00
Tray, 12", ctr. hdld., sand.	75.00
Tray, 12", ctr. hdld., sq.	75.00
Tray, 13", celery	40.00
Tray, 13", 2 hdld., hors d'oeuvre	75.00

	Sahara
Tumbler, dolphin ft.	165.00
Tumbler, #3380, 1 oz., ftd., bar	45.00
Tumbler, #3380, 2 oz., ftd., bar	20.00
Tumbler, #3380, 5 oz., ftd., bar	16.00
Tumbler, #3380, 8 oz., ftd., soda	18.00
Tumbler, #3380, 10 oz., ftd., soda	20.00
Tumbler, #3380, 12 oz., ftd., tea	22.00
Tumbler, #3390, 2 oz., ftd.	24.00
Tumbler, #3390, 5 oz., ftd., juice	20.00
Tumbler, #3390, 8 oz., ftd., soda	25.00
Tumbler, #3390, 12 oz., ftd., tea	27.00
Vase, 9", ftd.	150.00

Colors: crystal, Flamingo pink, Sahara yellow, Moongleam green, cobalt, amber

As with its sister pattern Ipswich, Moongleam is the most desired Old Sandwich color. This time we are showing colors other than Moongleam. Sets can be scraped together in crystal, but other colored sets would be difficult and costly. Notice there are three sized creamers and one sugar.

Cobalt blue pieces of Old Sandwich are rare and expensive should you spot any.

	Crystal	Flamingo	Sahara	Moongleam	Cobalt
Ash tray, individual	9.00	60.00	35.00	60.00	45.00
Beer mug, 12 oz.	35.00	300.00	210.00	400.00	240.00
Beer mug, 14 oz.	45.00	325.00	225.00	425.00	250.00
* Beer mug, 18 oz.	60.00	400.00	270.00	475.00	380.00
Bottle, catsup, w/#3 stopper (like large cruet)	70.00	200.00	175.00	225.00	
Bowl, finger	12.00	50.00	60.00	60.00	
Bowl, ftd., popcorn, cupped	80.00	110.00	110.00	135.00	
Bowl, 11", rnd., ftd., floral	50.00	85.00	65.00	100.00	
Bowl, 12", oval, ftd., floral	50.00	80.00	70.00	80.00	
Candlestick, 6"	60.00	120.00	110.00	150.00	325.00
Cigarette holder	50.00	65.00	60.00	65.00	
Comport, 6"	40.00	95.00	90.00	100.00	
Creamer, oval	25.00	75.00	85.00	50.00	
Creamer, 12 oz.	32.00	165.00	170.00	175.00	575.00
Creamer, 14 oz.	35.00	175.00	180.00	185.00	
Creamer, 18 oz.	40.00	185.00	190.00	195.00	
Cup	40.00	65.00	65.00	125.00	
Decanter, 1 pint, w/#98 stopper	75.00	185.00	200.00	225.00	425.00
Floral block, #22	15.00	25.00	30.00	35.00	
Oil bottle, 2½ oz., #85 stopper	65.00	140.00	140.00	140.00	
Parfait, 4½ oz.	15.00	50.00	50.00	60.00	

	Crystal	Flamingo	Sahara	Moongleam	Cobalt
Pilsner, 8 oz.	14.00	28.00	32.00	38.00	
Pilsner, 10 oz.	16.00	32.00	37.00	42.00	
Pitcher, ½ gallon, ice lip	100.00	175.00	165.00	185.00	
Pitcher, ½ gallon, reg.	100.00	175.00	165.00	185.00	
Plate, 6", sq., ground bottom	10.00	20.00	17.00	22.00	
Plate, 7", sq.	10.00	27.00	25.00	30.00	
Plate, 8", sq.	15.00	30.00	27.00	32.00	
Salt & pepper, pr.	40.00	65.00	75.00	85.00	
Saucer	10.00	15.00	15.00	25.00	
Stem, 2½ oz., wine	18.00	45.00	45.00	55.00	
Stem, 3 oz., cocktail	15.00	30.00	32.00	40.00	
Stem, 4 oz., claret	17.00	35.00	35.00	50.00	150.00
Stem, 4 oz., oyster cocktail	12.00	27.00	27.00	32.00	
Stem, 4 oz., sherbet	7.00	17.00	17.00	20.00	
Stem, 5 oz., saucer champagne	12.00	32.00	32.00	35.00	
Stem, 10 oz., low ft.	20.00	30.00	35.00	40.00	
Sugar, oval	25.00	75.00	55.00	60.00	
Sundae, 6 oz.	18.00	30.00	30.00	35.00	
Tumbler, 1½ oz., bar, ground bottom	20.00	130.00	120.00	135.00	100.00
Tumbler, 5 oz., juice	7.00	15.00	15.00	25.00	
Tumbler, 6½ oz., toddy	20.00	35.00	40.00	40.00	
Tumbler, 8 oz., ground bottom, cupped & straight rim	20.00	35.00	35.00	40.00	
Tumbler, 10 oz.	15.00	40.00	40.00	45.00	
Tumbler, 10 oz., low ft.	15.00	40.00	42.00	45.00	
Tumbler, 12 oz., ftd., iced tea	20.00	45.00	45.00	55.00	
Tumbler, 12 oz., iced tea	20.00	45.00	45.00	55.00	

*Amber; 300.00; Round creamer & sugar, $30.00 ea. piece (unusual). Whimsey Basket made from footed soda, $725.00.

Colors: crystal

Heisey's Orchid is being transferred to my *Collectible Glassware from the 40s, 50s, and 60s* book and will no longer be found in the Elegant book after this edition. I know this switching location in books will upset some collectors, but I am trying to chronologically set up glass patterns so that finding them will be easier. On the other hand, so many patterns considered to be Depression glass are really Elegant glassware patterns and deserve to be moved into this book.

Orchid is predominantly found etched on two Heisey mould blanks. Blank #1519, known as Waverly, is illustrated on page 149 as well as via the plate on the left on page 150. Blank #1509, or Queen Ann, is pictured on page 151 along with the plate on the right on page 150. These two patterns have their own listings in this book, but I hope these photos will help alleviate confusion.

Prices on a few pieces of stemware have been slowly dropping! Particularly, water goblets, high sherbets, and iced teas have softened due to an oversupply at present. Remember, I am noting what is going on now and not attempting to foretell what will happen.

	Crystal
Ash tray, 3"	30.00
Basket, 8½", Lariat	1,250.00
Bell, dinner, #5022 or #5025	135.00
Bottle, 8 oz., French dressings	195.00
Bowl, finger, #3309 or #5025	92.50
Bowl, 4½", nappy, Queen Ann	37.50
Bowl, 5½", ftd., mint, Queen Ann	37.50
Bowl, 6", jelly, 2 hdld, Queen Ann	37.50
Bowl, 6" oval, lemon, w/cover, Queen Ann	295.00
Bowl, 6", oval, lemon, w/cover, Waverly	895.00
Bowl, 6½", ftd., honey, cheese, Queen Ann	42.50
Bowl, 6½", ftd., jelly, Waverly	65.00
Bowl, 6½", 2 pt., oval, dressings, Waverly	50.00
Bowl, 7", lily, Queen Ann	125.00
Bowl, 7", salad	60.00
Bowl, 7", 3 pt., rnd., relish	55.00
Bowl, 7", ftd., honey, cheese, Waverly	55.00
Bowl, 7", ftd., jelly	45.00
Bowl, 7", ftd., oval, nut, Waverly	95.00
Bowl, 8", mint, ftd., Queen Ann	65.00
Bowl, 8", nappy, Queen Ann	70.00
Bowl, 8", 2 pt., oval, dressings, ladle	55.00
Bowl, 8", pt., rnd., relish	62.50
Bowl, 8½", flared, Queen Ann	67.50
Bowl, 8½", floral, 2 hdld., ftd., Queen Ann	65.00
Bowl, 9", 4 pt., rnd., relish	75.00
Bowl, 9", ftd., fruit or salad	135.00
Bowl, 9", gardenia, Queen Ann	65.00
Bowl, 9", salad, Waverly	175.00
Bowl, 9½", crimped, floral, Queen Ann	75.00
Bowl, 9½", epergne	525.00
Bowl, 10", crimped	72.50
Bowl, 10", deep salad	125.00
Bowl, 10", gardenia	75.00
Bowl, 10½", ftd., floral	115.00
Bowl, 11", shallow, rolled edge	70.00
Bowl, 11", 3 ftd., floral, seahorse ft.	150.00
Bowl, 11", 3 pt., oblong, relish	70.00
Bowl, 11", 4 ftd., oval	125.00
Bowl, 11", flared	135.00
Bowl, 11", floral	70.00

	Crystal
Bowl, 11", ftd., floral	115.00
Bowl, 12", crimped, floral, Waverly	85.00
Bowl, 13", floral	115.00
Bowl, 13", crimped, floral, Waverly	95.00
Bowl, 13", gardenia	70.00
Butter, w/cover, ¼ lb., Cabochon	335.00
Butter, w/cover, 6", Waverly	175.00
Candleholder, 6", deep epernette, Waverly	1,050.00
Candlestick, 1-lite, Mercury	45.00
Candlestick, 1-lite, Queen Ann, w/prisms	135.00
Candlestick, 2-lite, Flame	160.00
Candlestick, 5", 2-lite, Trident	55.00
Candlestick, 2-lite, Waverly	65.00
Candlestick, 3-lite, Cascade	85.00
Candlestick, 3-lite, Waverly	100.00
Candy box, w/cover, 6", low ft.	175.00
Candy, w/cover, 5", high ft., Waverly	250.00
Candy, w/cover, 6", bow knot finial	175.00
Cheese (comport) & cracker (11½") plate	135.00
Cheese & cracker, 14", plate	155.00
Chocolate, w/cover, 5", Waverly	225.00
Cigarette box, w/cover, 4", Puritan	140.00
Cigarette holder, #4035	85.00
Cigarette holder, w/cover	165.00
Cocktail icer, w/liner, Universal, #3304	250.00
Cocktail shaker, pt., #4225	275.00
Cocktail shaker, qt., #4036 or #4225	225.00
Comport, 5½", blown	95.00
Comport, 6", low ft., Waverly	55.00
Comport, 6½", low ft., Waverly	60.00
Comport, 7", ftd., oval	145.00
Creamer, individual	35.00
Creamer, ftd.	35.00
Cup, Waverly or Queen Ann	42.50
Decanter, oval, sherry, pt.	250.00
Decanter, pt., ftd., #4036	325.00
Decanter, pt., #4036½	250.00
Ice bucket, ftd., Queen Ann	295.00
Ice bucket, 2 hdld., Waverly	450.00
Marmalade, w/cover	235.00
Mayonnaise and liner, #1495, Fern	250.00

	Crystal
Mayonnaise, 5½", 1 hdl.	55.00
Mayonnaise, 5½", ftd.	55.00
Mayonnaise, 5½", 1 hdl., div.	50.00
Mayonnaise, 6½", 1 hdl.	65.00
Mayonnaise, 6½", 1 hdl., div.	65.00
Mustard, w/cover, Queen Ann	145.00
Oil, 3 oz., ftd.	185.00
Pitcher, 73 oz.	500.00
Pitcher, 64 oz., ice tankard	525.00
Plate, 6"	13.00
Plate, 7", mayonnaise	20.00
Plate, 7", salad	22.00
Plate, 8", salad, Waverly	24.00
Plate, 10½", dinner	165.00
Plate, 11", demi-torte	62.50
Plate, 11", sandwich	75.00
Plate, 12", ftd., salver, Waverly	265.00
Plate, 12", rnd sandwich, hdld.	70.00
Plate, 14", ftd., cake or salver	325.00
Plate, 14", torte, rolled edge	65.00
Plate, 14", torte, Waverly	90.00
Plate, 14", sandwich, Waverly	80.00
Plate, 15", sandwich, Waverly	75.00
Plate, 15½", Queen Ann	110.00
Salt & pepper, pr.	85.00
Salt & pepper, ftd., pr., Waverly	80.00
Saucer, Waverly or Queen Ann	12.50
Stem, #5022 or #5025, 1 oz., cordial	125.00

	Crystal
Stem, #5022 or #5025, 2 oz., sherry	125.00
Stem, #5022 or #5025, 3 oz., wine	80.00
Stem, #5022 or #5025, 4 oz., oyster cocktail	60.00
Stem, #5025, 4 oz., cocktail	40.00
Stem, #5022 or #5025, 4½ oz., claret	145.00
Stem, #5022 or #5025, 6 oz., saucer champagne	30.00
Stem, #5022 or #5025, 6 oz., sherbet	25.00
Stem, #5022 or #5025, 10 oz., low water goblet	37.50
Stem, #5022 or #5025, 10 oz., water goblet	42.50
Sugar, individual	35.00
Sugar, ftd.	35.00
Tray, indiv., creamer/sugar, Queen Ann	90.00
Tray, 12", celery	55.00
Tray, 13", celery	60.00
Tumbler, #5022 or #5025, 5 oz., fruit	55.00
Tumbler, #5022 or #5025, 12 oz., iced tea	65.00
Vase, 4", ftd., violet, Waverly	120.00
Vase, 6", crimped top	125.00
Vase, 7", ftd., fan	90.00
Vase, 7", ftd.	140.00
Vase, 7", crimped top, Lariat	120.00
Vase, 8", ftd., bud	225.00
Vase, 8", sq., ftd., bud	225.00
Vase, 10", sq., ftd., bud	295.00
Vase, 12"	395.00
Vase, 14"	695.00

Colors: amber, Blue, crystal, green, Rose

Fostoria's Pioneer is readily recognized for its use as the mould blank on which Seville and Vesper are etched. There are collectors of #2350 Pioneer who search for the less expensive unadorned glassware. Blue, as the color pictured here was called, can be bought at prices well below those of Vesper. The Blue butter dish pictured here could be bought for $125.00, but one etched Vesper would break the bank.

Gathering plainer glassware can make for easier displays in your settings as you do not have to worry about the pattern showing to its full advantage.

*Regal Blue 22.50, Burgundy 22.50,
Empire Green 22.50, Ruby 25.00
**Regal Blue 6.00, Burgundy 6.00,
Empire Green 6.00, Ruby 7.50

	crystal/amber green	Ebony	Rose Topaz	Azure Orchid	Blue
Ash tray, 3¾"	16.00	18.00	20.00	24.00	
Ash tray, lg., deep	18.00	18.00	22.00	25.00	
Bouillon, flat	12.00				14.00
Bouillon, ftd.	10.00				
Bowl, 5" fruit (shallow)	8.00				15.00
Bowl, 6" cereal	10.00				20.00
Bowl, 7" rnd. soup	15.00				25.00
Bowl, 8" nappy	20.00				25.00
Bowl, 8" oval pickle	17.50				22.50
Bowl, 9" nappy	17.50				25.00
Bowl, 9" oval baker	35.00				45.00
Bowl, 10" oval baker	40.00				50.00
Bowl, 10" salad	25.00				40.00
Bowl, creme soup, flat	15.00				27.50
Bowl, creme soup, ftd.	18.00				
Butter & cover	75.00				125.00
Celery, 11", oval narrow	20.00				24.00
Comport, 8"	27.50		30.00	35.00	
Creamer, flat	9.00				15.00
Creamer, ftd.	9.00	10.00	12.00		15.00
Ruby 17.50					
Cup, flat	12.00				15.00
*Cup, ftd.	10.00	12.50			15.00

	crystal/amber green	Ebony	Rose Topaz	Azure Orchid	Blue
Egg Cup	20.00		25.00		
Grapefruit liner (looks like straight crystal glass)	6.00				
Grapefruit, strt. side	25.00				33.00
Plate, 6"	5.00	8.00			
Plate, 7" salad	6.00	9.00			9.00
Plate, 8"	8.00	10.00			15.00
Plate, 9"	12.50	14.00			20.00
Plate, 10"	17.50	20.00			30.00
Plate, 12" chop	18.00				32.50
Plate, 15" service	22.50				35.00
Plate, bouillon liner	5.00				
Plate, creme soup	6.00				7.00
Plate, oval sauce boat	10.00				12.50
Platter, 10½"	22.50				30.00
Platter, 12"	15.00				32.50
Platter, 15"	27.50				35.00
Relish, rnd., 3 pt.	12.50		15.00	17.50	
Sauce boat, flat	22.50				35.00
** Saucer	3.00	4.00			5.00
Sugar cover	17.50				32.50
Sugar, flat	9.00				15.00
Sugar, ftd.	9.00	10.00	12.00		15.00
Ruby 17.50					

PLANTATION, Blank #1567, A.H. Heisey & Co.

Colors: crystal; rare in amber

Historically, Plantation had been selling rather fast, but the lack of new collectors has begun to slow that somewhat. Hard to find pieces and all candlesticks continue to rapidly exit the market, but the commonly seen items are residing in dealer's inventories for now.

Plantation is another Heisey pattern that is being transferred into *Collectible Glassware from the 40s, 50s, and 60s.*

	Crystal
Ash tray, 3½"	45.00
Bowl, 9 qt., Dr. Johnson, punch	625.00
Bowl, 5", nappy	30.00
Bowl, 5½", nappy	38.00
Bowl, 6½", 2 hdld., jelly	45.00
Bowl, 6½", flared, jelly	60.00
Bowl, 6½", ftd., honey, cupped	75.00
Bowl, 8", 4 pt., rnd., relish	70.00
Bowl, 8½", 2 pt., dressing	70.00
Bowl, 9", salad	170.00
Bowl, 9½", crimped, fruit or flower	85.00
Bowl, 9½", gardenia	85.00
Bowl, 11", 3 part, relish	60.00
Bowl, 11½", ftd., gardenia	140.00
Bowl, 12", crimped, fruit or flower	100.00
Bowl, 13", celery	70.00
Bowl, 13", 2 part, celery	60.00
Bowl, 13", 5 part, oval relish	90.00
Bowl, 13", gardenia	90.00
Butter, ¼ lb., oblong, w/cover	115.00
Butter, 5", rnd. (or cov. candy)	150.00
Candelabrum, w/two #1503 bobeche & 10 "A" prisms	180.00
Candle block, hurricane type w/globe	250.00
Candle block, 1-lite	115.00
Candle holder, 5", ftd., epergne	125.00
Candlestick, 1-lite	100.00
Candlestick, 2-lite	90.00
Candlestick, 3-lite	115.00

	Crystal
Candy box, w/cover, 7" length, flat bottom	180.00
Candy, w/cover, 5", tall, ftd.	200.00
Cheese, w/cover, 5", ftd.	90.00
Cigarette box, w/cover	180.00
Coaster, 4"	60.00
Comport, 5"	50.00
Comport, 5", w/cover, deep	100.00
Creamer, ftd.	40.00
Cup	40.00
Cup, punch	35.00
Marmalade, w/cover	190.00
Mayonnaise, 4½", rolled ft.	65.00
Mayonnaise, 5¼", w/liner	55.00
Oil bottle, 3 oz., w/#125 stopper	130.00
Pitcher, ½ gallon, ice lip, blown	450.00
Plate, coupe (rare)	425.00
Plate, 7", salad	25.00
Plate, 8", salad	35.00
Plate, 10½", demi-torte	70.00
Plate, 13", ftd., cake salver	200.00
Plate, 14", sandwich	120.00
Plate, 18", buffet	125.00
Plate, 18", punch bowl liner	130.00
Salt & pepper, pr.	70.00
Saucer	10.00
Stem, 1 oz., cordial	125.00
Stem, 3 oz., wine, blown	75.00
Stem, 3½ oz., cocktail, pressed	35.00
Stem, 4 oz., fruit/oyster cocktail	35.00
Stem, 4½ oz., claret, blown	65.00
Stem, 4½ oz., claret, pressed	65.00
Stem, 4½ oz., oyster cocktail, blown	40.00
Stem, 6½ oz., sherbet/saucer champagne, blown	40.00
Stem, 10 oz., pressed	50.00
Stem, 10 oz., blown	50.00
Sugar, ftd.	40.00
Syrup bottle, w/drip, cut top	140.00
Tray, 8½", condiment/sugar & creamer	90.00
Tumbler, 5 oz., ftd., juice, pressed	60.00
Tumbler, 5 oz., ftd., juice, blown	40.00
Tumbler, 8 oz., water, pressed	125.00
Tumbler, 10 oz., pressed	95.00
Tumbler, 12 oz., ftd., iced tea, pressed	90.00
Tumbler, 12 oz., ftd., iced tea, blown	75.00
Vase, 5", ftd., flared	90.00
Vase, 9", ftd., flared	140.00

Colors: crystal, Flamingo pink, Moongleam green

Most Pleat & Panel pieces carry the well-known **H** in a diamond mark. Stems are marked on the stem itself and not the foot; so look there if you are searching for a mark.

Notice the color variations in the pink pictured. Only inexpensively made Depression glass companies were supposed to have color deviations. Yes, even Heisey had difficulty maintaining color consistencies!

	Crystal	Flamingo	Moongleam
Bowl, 4", chow chow	6.00	11.00	14.00
Bowl, 4½", nappy	6.00	11.00	14.00
Bowl, 5", 2 hdld., bouillon	7.00	14.00	17.50
Bowl, 5", 2 hdld., jelly	9.00	14.00	17.50
Bowl, 5", lemon, w/cover	20.00	45.00	55.00
Bowl, 6½", grapefruit/cereal	5.00	14.00	17.50
Bowl, 8", nappy	10.00	32.50	40.00
Bowl, 9", oval, vegetable	12.50	35.00	40.00
Cheese & cracker set, 10½", tray, w/compote	25.00	75.00	80.00
Compotier, w/cover, 5", high ftd.	35.00	60.00	80.00
Creamer, hotel	10.00	25.00	30.00
Cup	7.00	15.00	17.50
Marmalade, 4¾"	10.00	30.00	35.00
Oil bottle, 3 oz., w/pressed stopper	30.00	75.00	110.00
Pitcher, 3 pint, ice lip	45.00	140.00	165.00
Pitcher, 3 pint	45.00	140.00	165.00

	Crystal	Flamingo	Moongleam
Plate, 6"	4.00	8.00	8.00
Plate, 6¾", bouillon underliner	4.00	8.00	8.00
Plate, 7", bread	4.00	8.00	10.00
Plate, 8", luncheon	5.00	12.50	15.00
Plate, 10¾", dinner	15.00	48.00	52.00
Plate, 14", sandwich	15.00	32.50	40.00
Platter, 12", oval	15.00	42.50	47.50
Saucer	3.00	5.00	5.00
Sherbet, 5 oz., footed	4.00	10.00	12.00
Stem, 5 oz., saucer champagne	5.00	14.00	18.00
Stem, 7½ oz., low foot	12.00	30.00	35.00
Stem, 8 oz.	15.00	35.00	40.00
Sugar w/lid, hotel	10.00	30.00	35.00
Tray, 10", compartmented spice	10.00	25.00	30.00
Tumbler, 8 oz., ground bottom	5.00	17.50	22.50
Tumbler, 12 oz., tea, ground bottom	7.00	25.00	30.00
Vase, 8"	30.00	80.00	100.00

Colors: crystal, yellow, Heatherbloom, green, amber, Carmen, and Crown Tuscan w/gold

Portia items not listed here may be found under Rose Point. Prices for the Portia items will run 40% to 50% less than the same item in Rose Point.

	Crystal
Basket, 2 hdld. (upturned sides)	25.00
Basket, 7", 1 hdld.	295.00
Bowl, 3", indiv. nut, 4 ftd.	60.00
Bowl, 3½", cranberry	40.00
Bowl, 3½" sq., cranberry	40.00
Bowl, 5¼", 2 hdld., bonbon	25.00
Bowl, 6", 2 pt., relish	22.00
Bowl, 6", ftd., 2 hdld., bonbon	25.00
Bowl, 6", grapefruit or oyster	35.00
Bowl, 6½", 3 pt., relish	30.00
Bowl, 7", 2 pt., relish	35.00
Bowl, 7", ftd., bonbon, tab hdld.	35.00
Bowl, 7", pickle or relish	30.00
Bowl, 9", 3 pt., celery & relish, tab hdld.	50.00
Bowl, 9½", ftd., pickle (like corn bowl)	35.00
Bowl, 10", flared, 4 ftd.	50.00
Bowl, 11", 2 pt., 2 hdld., "figure 8" relish	40.00
Bowl, 11", 2 hdld.	55.00
Bowl, 12", 3 pt., celery & relish, tab hdld.	60.00
Bowl, 12", 5 pt., celery & relish	60.00
Bowl, 12", flared, 4 ftd.	65.00
Bowl, 12", oval, 4 ftd., "ears" handles	65.00
Bowl, finger, w/liner #3124	45.00
Bowl, seafood (fruit cocktail w/liner)	75.00
Candlestick, 5"	30.00
Candlestick, 6", 2-lite, "fleur-de-lis"	45.00
Candlestick, 6", 3-lite	55.00
Candy box, w/cover, rnd.	100.00
Cigarette holder, urn shape	60.00

	Crystal
Cocktail icer, 2 pt.	75.00
Cocktail shaker, w/stopper	150.00
Cocktail shaker, 80 oz., hdld. ball w/chrome top	225.00
Cologne, 2 oz., hdld. ball w/stopper	135.00
Comport, 5½"	50.00
Comport, 5⅜", blown	65.00
Creamer, ftd.	20.00
Creamer, hdld. ball	40.00
Creamer, indiv.	20.00
Cup, ftd. sq.	25.00
Cup, rd.	20.00
Decanter, 29 oz. ftd., sherry, w/stopper	250.00
Hurricane lamp, candlestick base	175.00
Hurricane lamp, keyhole base, w/prisms	235.00
Ice bucket, w/chrome handle	95.00
Ivy ball, 5¼"	75.00
Mayonnaise, div. bowl, w/liner & 2 ladles	55.00
Mayonnaise, w/liner & ladle	50.00
Oil, 6 oz., loop hdld., w/stopper	110.00
Oil, 6 oz., hdld. ball, w/stopper	100.00
Pitcher, ball	275.00
Pitcher, Doulton	355.00
Plate, 6", 2 hdld.	15.00
Plate, 6½", bread/butter	7.50
Plate, 8", salad	15.00
Plate, 8", ftd., 2 hdld.	20.00
Plate, 8", ftd., bonbon, tab hdld.	20.00
Plate, 8½", sq.	15.00

	Crystal
Plate, 10½", dinner	75.00
Plate, 13", 4 ftd., torte	50.00
Plate, 13½", 2 hdld., cake	50.00
Plate, 14", torte	65.00
Puff box, 3½", ball shape, w/lid	195.00
Salt & pepper, pr., flat	30.00
Saucer, sq. or rnd.	5.00
Set: 3 pc. frappe (bowl, 2 plain inserts)	60.00
Stem, #3121, 1 oz., cordial	65.00
Stem, #3121, 1 oz., low ftd., brandy	65.00
Stem, #3121, 2½ oz., wine	40.00
Stem, #3121, 3 oz., cocktail	30.00
Stem, #3121, 4½ oz., claret	50.00
Stem, #3121, 4½ oz., oyster cocktail	20.00
Stem, #3121, 5 oz., parfait	43.00
Stem, #3121, 6 oz., low sherbet	20.00
Stem, #3121, 6 oz., tall sherbet	22.00
Stem, #3121, 10 oz., goblet	28.00
Stem, #3124, 3 oz., cocktail	20.00
Stem, #3124, 3 oz., wine	35.00
Stem, #3124, 4½ oz., claret	50.00
Stem, #3124, 7 oz., low sherbet	18.00
Stem, #3124, 7 oz., tall sherbet	20.00
Stem, #3124, 10 oz., goblet	28.00
Stem, #3126, 1 oz., cordial	65.00
Stem, #3126, 1 oz., low ft., brandy	65.00
Stem, #3126, 2½ oz., wine	40.00
Stem, #3126, 3 oz., cocktail	22.00
Stem, #3126, 4½ oz., claret	45.00
Stem, #3126, 4½ oz., low ft., oyster cocktail	18.00
Stem, #3126, 7 oz., low sherbet	18.00
Stem, #3126, 7 oz., tall sherbet	20.00
Stem, #3126, 9 oz., goblet	28.00
Stem, #3130, 1 oz., cordial	65.00
Stem, #3130, 2½ oz., wine	40.00

	Crystal
Stem, #3130, 3 oz., cocktail	20.00
Stem, #3130, 4½ oz., claret	45.00
Stem, #3130, 4½ oz., fruit/oyster cocktail	20.00
Stem, #3130, 7 oz., low sherbet	18.00
Stem, #3130, 7 oz., tall sherbet	20.00
Stem, #3130, 9 oz., goblet	28.00
Sugar, ftd., hdld. ball	40.00
Sugar, ftd.	20.00
Sugar, indiv.	20.00
Tray, 11", celery	40.00
Tumbler, #3121, 2½ oz., bar	40.00
Tumbler, #3121, 5 oz., ftd., juice	20.00
Tumbler, #3121, 10 oz., ftd., water	22.00
Tumbler, #3121, 12 oz., ftd., tea	30.00
Tumbler, #3124, 3 oz.	18.00
Tumbler, #3124, 5 oz., juice	20.00
Tumbler, #3124, 10 oz., water	22.00
Tumbler, #3124, 12 oz., tea	25.00
Tumbler, #3126, 2½ oz.	40.00
Tumbler, #3126, 5 oz., juice	20.00
Tumbler, #3126, 10 oz., water	18.00
Tumbler, #3126, 12 oz., tea	30.00
Tumbler, #3130, 5 oz., juice	25.00
Tumbler, #3130, 10 oz., water	18.00
Tumbler, #3130, 12 oz., tea	30.00
Tumbler, 12 oz., "roly-poly"	30.00
Vase, 5", globe	65.00
Vase, 6", ftd.	75.00
Vase, 8", ftd.	95.00
Vase, 9", keyhole ft.	85.00
Vase, 10", bud	65.00
Vase, 11", flower	75.00
Vase, 11", pedestal ft.	85.00
Vase, 12", keyhole ft.	110.00
Vase, 13", flower	135.00

Colors: crystal, Limelight green

This pattern was first called Whirlpool in the 1930s; but Heisey changed its name to Provincial for the 1952 reissue. Limelight colored Provincial was Heisey's attempt at remaking the earlier, popular Zircon color!

	Crystal	Limelight Green
Ash tray, 3" square	12.50	
Bonbon dish, 7", 2 hdld., upturned sides	12.00	45.00
Bowl, 5 quart, punch	120.00	
Bowl, individual, nut/jelly	20.00	40.00
Bowl, 4½", nappy	15.00	70.00
Bowl, 5", 2 hdld., nut/jelly	20.00	
Bowl, 5½", nappy	20.00	40.00
Bowl, 5½", round, hdld., nappy	20.00	
Bowl, 5½", tri-corner, hdld., nappy	20.00	55.00
Bowl, 10", 4 part, relish	40.00	195.00
Bowl, 12", floral	40.00	
Bowl, 13", gardenia	40.00	
Box, 5½", footed, candy, w/cover	85.00	550.00
Butter dish, w/cover	100.00	
Candle, 1-lite, block	35.00	
Candle, 2-lite	80.00	
Candle, 3-lite, #4233, 5", vase	95.00	
Cigarette box w/cover	60.00	
Cigarette lighter	30.00	
Coaster, 4"	15.00	
Creamer, footed	25.00	95.00
Creamer & sugar, w/tray, individual	80.00	
Cup, punch	10.00	

	Crystal	Limelight Green
Mayonnaise, 7" (plate, ladle, bowl)	40.00	150.00
Mustard	110.00	
Oil bottle, 4 oz., #1 stopper	45.00	
Oil & vinegar bottle (french dressing)	65.00	
Plate, 5", footed, cheese	20.00	
Plate, 7", 2 hdld., snack	25.00	
Plate, 7", bread	10.00	
Plate, 8", luncheon	15.00	50.00
Plate, 14", torte	45.00	
Plate, 18", buffet	70.00	175.00
Salt & pepper, pr.	40.00	
Stem, 3½ oz., oyster cocktail	18.00	
Stem, 3½ oz., wine	20.00	
Stem, 5 oz., sherbet/champagne	10.00	
Stem, 10 oz.	20.00	
Sugar, footed	25.00	95.00
Tray, 13", oval, celery	22.00	
Tumbler, 5 oz., footed, juice	14.00	60.00
Tumbler, 8 oz.	17.00	
Tumbler, 9 oz., footed	17.00	75.00
Tumbler, 12 oz., footed, iced tea	20.00	80.00
Tumbler, 13", flat, ice tea	20.00	
Vase, 3½", violet	30.00	95.00
Vase, 4", pansy	35.00	
Vase, 6", sweet pea	45.00	

Colors: crystal

When Empress (#1401) is made in crystal it is generally referred to as Queen Ann (c. 1938). Although this has been accepted by almost everyone, it is not entirely factual. According to Heisey experts there is a **slight** difference between Queen Ann and Empress. Queen Ann's mould blank was used for several of Heisey's etched patterns including Orchid, Heisey Rose, Minuet, etc. This plainer, unetched line has been easy to find and inexpensive in the past; however, the prices are now adjusting to demand particularly for the exceptional pieces.

	Crystal
Ash tray	30.00
Bonbon, 6"	12.00
Bowl, cream soup	18.00
Bowl, cream soup, w/sq. liner	25.00
Bowl, frappe, w/center	25.00
Bowl, nut, dolphin ftd., indiv.	20.00
Bowl, 4½", nappy	8.00
Bowl, 5", preserve, 2 hdld.	15.00
Bowl, 6", ftd., jelly, 2 hdld.	15.00
Bowl, 6", dolp. ftd., mint	20.00
Bowl, 6", grapefruit, sq. top, ground bottom	12.00
Bowl, 6½", oval, lemon, w/cover	45.00
Bowl, 7", 3 pt., relish, triplex	18.00
Bowl, 7", 3 pt., relish, ctr. hand.	25.00
Bowl, 7½", dolphin ftd., nappy	28.00
Bowl, 7½", dolphin ftd., nasturtium	35.00
Bowl, 8", nappy	25.00
Bowl, 8½", ftd., floral, 2 hdld	32.00
Bowl, 9", floral, rolled edge	25.00
Bowl, 9", floral, flared	32.00
Bowl, 10", 2 hdld., oval dessert	30.00
Bowl, 10", lion head, floral	250.00
Bowl, 10", oval, veg.	30.00
Bowl, 10", square, salad, 2 hdld.	35.00
Bowl, 10", triplex, relish	25.00
Bowl, 11", dolphin ftd., floral	38.00
Bowl, 13", pickle/olive, 2 pt.	20.00
Bowl, 15", dolphin ftd., punch	400.00
Candlestick, 3", 3 ftd	50.00
Candlestick, low, 4 ftd., w/2 hdld.	30.00
Candlestick, 6", dolphin ftd.	70.00
Candy, w/cover, 6", dolphin ftd.	50.00
Comport, 6", ftd.	25.00
Comport, 6", square	40.00
Comport, 7", oval	35.00
Compotier, 6", dolphin ftd.	70.00
Creamer, dolphin ftd.	30.00
Creamer, indiv.	20.00

	Crystal
Cup	15.00
Cup, after dinner	20.00
Cup, bouillon, 2 hdld.	20.00
Cup, 4 oz., custard or punch	12.00
Cup, #1401½, has rim as demi-cup	20.00
Grapefruit, w/square liner	20.00
Ice tub, w/metal handles	60.00
Jug, 3 pint, ftd.	100.00
Marmalade, w/cover, dolphin ftd.	60.00
Mayonnaise, 5½", ftd., w/ladle	30.00
Mustard, w/cover	60.00
Oil bottle, 4 oz.	40.00
Plate, bouillon liner	8.00
Plate, cream soup liner	8.00
Plate, 4½"	5.00

	Crystal
Plate, 6"	5.00
Plate, 6", square	5.00
Plate, 7"	8.00
Plate, 7", square	7.00
Plate, 8", square	10.00
Plate, 8"	9.00
Plate, 9"	12.00
Plate, 10½"	40.00
Plate, 10½", square	40.00
Plate, 12"	25.00
Plate, 12", muffin, sides upturned	35.00
Plate, 12", sandwich, 2 hdld.	30.00
Plate, 13", hors d'oeuvre, 2 hdld.	60.00
Plate, 13", square, 2 hdld.	35.00
Platter, 14"	30.00
Salt & pepper, pr.	50.00
Saucer, square	5.00
Saucer, after dinner	5.00
Saucer	5.00
Stem, 2½ oz., oyster cocktail	15.00

	Crystal
Stem, 4 oz., saucer champagne	20.00
Stem, 4 oz., sherbet	15.00
Stem, 9 oz., Empress stemware, unusual	40.00
Sugar, indiv.	20.00
Sugar, dolphin ftd., 3 hdld.	30.00
Tray, condiment & liner for indiv. sugar/creamer	20.00
Tray, 10", 3 pt., relish	20.00
Tray, 10", 7 pt., hors d'oeuvre	60.00
Tray, 10", celery	12.00
Tray, 12", ctr. hdld., sand.	30.00
Tray, 12", sq. ctr. hdld., sand.	32.50
Tray, 13", celery	20.00
Tray, 16", 4 pt., buffet relish	35.00
Tumbler, 8 oz., dolphin ftd., unusual	75.00
Tumbler, 8 oz., ground bottom	20.00
Tumbler, 12 oz., tea, ground bottom	20.00
Vase, 8", flared	55.00

Color: crystal bowl w/Anna Rose (Pink) stem and foot

Queen Louise is an elegant pattern that I wish I had bought every piece that I have seen over the years. It is absolutely gorgeous with that silk screen process that must have cost a fortune when originally sold. It still commands a goodly sum today, but may be under valued considering its scarcity.

Pictured below are all the different pieces I have been able to accumulate over the last six or seven years. The stem on the far left is a wine and next to that is the parfait. The bowl in the center is a footed finger bowl although shaped like some of the Depression era sherbets. On the right is a cocktail and a water goblet. I have since found a saucer champagne for the next time.

I can make a few personal observations from watching this pattern. All stems sell in the same price range with waters being found the most often. Champagnes and parfaits may be the most difficult stems to find. Plates are rare and the footed bowl is not seen very often. A dealer told me that a dinner plate was rumored to have been seen in England, but he'd have to see it to believe it.

	Crystal w/pink
Bowl, finger, ftd.	200.00
Plate, 6" finger bowl liner	125.00
Plate, salad	150.00
Stem, 2½ oz. wine	350.00
Stem, 3 oz. cocktail	350.00
Stem, 5½ oz. saucer champagne	350.00
Stem, 5½ oz. sherbet	300.00
Stem, 7 oz. parfait	395.00
Stem, 9 oz. water	385.00

Colors: crystal, Sahara, Zircon, rare

	Crystal
Ash tray, round.	14.00
Ash tray, square	10.00
Ash tray, 4", round	22.00
Ash tray, 6", square	35.00
Ash trays, bridge set (heart, diamond, spade, club)	65.00
Basket, bonbon, metal handle	25.00
Bottle, rock & rye, w/#104 stopper	240.00
Bottle, 4 oz., cologne	130.00
Bottle, 5 oz., bitters, w/tube	130.00
Bowl, indiv., nut	15.00
Bowl, oval, indiv., jelly	20.00
Bowl, indiv., nut, 2 part	20.00
Bowl, 4½", nappy, bell or cupped	20.00
Bowl, 4½", nappy, scalloped	20.00
Bowl, 5", lemon, w/cover	65.00
Bowl, 5", nappy, straight	18.00
Bowl, 5", nappy, square	25.00
Bowl, 6", 2 hdld., divided, jelly	40.00
Bowl, 6", 2 hdld., jelly	30.00
Bowl, 7", 2 part, oval, relish	30.00
Bowl, 8", centerpiece	55.00
Bowl, 8", nappy, square	55.00
Bowl, 9", nappy, square	65.00
Bowl, 9", salad	40.00
Bowl, 10", flared, fruit	45.00
Bowl, 10", floral	45.00
Bowl, 11", centerpiece	50.00
Bowl, 11", punch	200.00
Bowl, 11½", floral	50.00
Bowl, 12", oval, floral	55.00
Bowl, 12", flared, fruit	50.00
Bowl, 13", cone, floral	65.00
Bowl, 14", oblong, floral	70.00
Bowl, 14", oblong, swan hdld., floral	280.00
Box, 8", floral	70.00
Candle block, 3", #1469½	30.00
Candle vase, 6"	35.00
Candlestick, 2", 1-lite	35.00
Candlestick, 2-lite, bobeche & "A" prisms	80.00
Candlestick, 7", w/bobeche & "A" prisms	120.00
Cheese, 6", 2 hdld.	22.00
Cigarette box, w/cover, oval	90.00
Cigarette box, w/cover, 6"	35.00
Cigarette holder, oval, w/2 comp. ashtrays	70.00
Cigarette holder, round	18.00
Cigarette holder, square	18.00
Cigarette holder, w/cover	30.00
Coaster or cocktail rest	10.00
Cocktail shaker, 1 qt., w/#1 strainer & #86 stopper	300.00
Comport, 6", low ft., flared	25.00
Comport, 6", low ft., w/cover	40.00
Creamer	30.00
Creamer, indiv.	20.00
Cup	16.00
Cup, beverage	12.00
Cup, punch	10.00
Decanter, 1 pint, w/#95 stopper	210.00
Ice tub, 2 hdld.	100.00
Marmalade, w/cover (scarce)	90.00
Mayonnaise and under plate	55.00

	Crystal
Mustard, w/cover	80.00
Oil bottle, 3 oz., w/#103 stopper	50.00
Pitcher, ½ gallon, ball shape	380.00
Pitcher, ½ gallon, ice lip, ball shape	380.00
Plate, oval, hors d'oeuvres	500.00
Plate, 2 hdld., ice tub liner	50.00
Plate, 6", round	12.00
Plate, 6", square	24.00
Plate, 7", square	26.00
Plate, 8", round	20.00
Plate, 8", square	32.00
Plate, 13½", sandwich	45.00
Plate, 13½", ftd., torte	45.00
Plate, 14", salver	50.00
Plate, 20", punch bowl underplate	140.00
Puff box, 5", and cover	90.00
Salt & pepper, pr.	45.00
Salt dip, indiv.	13.00
Saucer	5.00
Soda, 12 oz., ftd., no knob in stem (rare)	50.00
Stem, cocktail, pressed	25.00
Stem, claret, pressed	50.00
Stem, oyster cocktail, pressed	35.00
Stem, sherbet, pressed	20.00
Stem, saucer champagne, pressed	30.00
Stem, wine, pressed	40.00
Stem, 1 oz., cordial, blown	160.00
Stem, 2 oz., sherry, blown	90.00
Stem, 2½ oz., wine, blown	80.00
Stem, 3½ oz., cocktail, blown	35.00
Stem, 4 oz., claret, blown	55.00
Stem, 4 oz., oyster cocktail, blown	30.00
Stem, 5 oz., saucer champagne, blown	25.00
Stem, 5 oz., sherbet, blown	20.00
Stem, 8 oz., luncheon, low stem	30.00
Stem, 8 oz., tall stem	40.00
Sugar	30.00
Sugar, indiv.	20.00
Tray, for indiv. sugar & creamer	20.00
Tray, 10½", oblong	40.00
Tray, 11", 3 part, relish	45.00
Tray, 12", celery & olive, divided	50.00
Tray, 12", celery	40.00
Tumbler, 2½ oz., bar, pressed	45.00
Tumbler, 5 oz., juice, blown	30.00
Tumbler, 5 oz., soda, ftd., pressed	30.00
Tumbler, 8 oz., #1469¾, pressed	35.00
Tumbler, 8 oz., old-fashioned, pressed	40.00
Tumbler, 8 oz., soda, blown	40.00
Tumbler, 10 oz., #1469½, pressed	45.00
Tumbler, 12 oz., ftd., soda, pressed	50.00
Tumbler, 12 oz., soda, #1469½, pressed	50.00
Tumbler, 13 oz., iced tea, blown	40.00
Vase, #1 indiv., cuspidor shape	40.00
Vase, #2 indiv., cupped top	45.00
Vase, #3 indiv., flared rim	30.00
Vase, #4 indiv., fan out top	55.00
Vase, #5 indiv., scalloped top	55.00
Vase, 3½"	25.00
Vase, 6" (also flared)	35.00
Vase, 8"	75.00
Vase, 8", triangular, #1469¾	110.00

Colors: crystal

Rogene is an early Fostoria pattern that has recently been discovered by some new collectors. There are a multitude of pieces that are reasonably priced by standards set by other Fostoria patterns. Gather some while you still can find it.

	Crystal		Crystal
Almond, ftd., #4095	8.00	Plate, 8"	15.00
Comport, 5" tall, #5078	30.00	Plate, 11"	25.00
Comport, 6", #5078	30.00	Plate, 11" w/cut star	27.50
Creamer, flat, #1851	22.50	Plate, finger bowl liner	7.50
Decanter, qt., cut neck, #300	85.00	Plate, mayonnaise liner, #766	12.50
Finger bowl, #766	20.00	Shaker, pr., glass (pearl) top, #2283	60.00
Jelly, #825	22.50	Stem, ¾ oz. cordial, #5082	40.00
Jelly & cover, #825	37.50	Stem, 2½ oz. wine, #5082	25.00
Jug 4, ftd., #4095	95.00	Stem, 3 oz. cocktail, #5082	18.00
Jug 7, #318	135.00	Stem, 4½ oz. claret, #5082	30.00
Jug 7, #2270	150.00	Stem, 5 oz. fruit, #5082	12.50
Jug 7, #4095	175.00	Stem, 5 oz. saucer champagne, #5082	17.50
Jug 7, covered, #2270	225.00	Stem, 6 oz. parfait, #5082	22.50
Marmalade & cover, #1968	30.00	Stem, 9 oz., #5082	22.50
Mayonnaise bowl, #766	25.00	Stem, grapefruit, #945½	27.50
Mayonnaise ladle	22.50	Stem, grapefruit liner, #945½	12.50
Mayonnaise set, 3 pc., #2138 (ftd. compote, ladle, liner)	60.00	Sugar, flat, #1851	22.50
Nappy, 5" ftd. (comport/sherbet), #5078	17.50	Tumbler, 2½ oz. whiskey, #887	15.00
Nappy, 6" ftd., #5078	25.00	Tumbler, 2½ oz., ftd., #4095	17.50
Nappy, 7" ftd., #5078	30.00	Tumbler, 5 oz. flat, #889	12.50
Night set, 2 pc. #1697, (carafe & tumbler)	95.00	Tumbler, 5 oz., ftd., #4095	12.50
Oil bottle w cut stop, 5 oz., #1495	55.00	Tumbler, 8 oz, flat,, #889	14.00
Oyster cocktail, ftd., #837	12.50	Tumbler, 10 oz., ftd., #4095	15.00
Plate, 5"	6.00	Tumbler, 12 oz., flat, hdld., #837	25.00
Plate, 6"	7.50	Tumbler, 13 oz. flat, #889	17.50
Plate, 6", #2283	7.00	Tumbler, 13 oz., ftd., #4095	20.00
Plate, 7" salad, #2283	10.00	Tumbler, flat, table, #4076	14.00
		Vase, 8½" rolled edge	95.00

Colors: Amber, Bluebell, Carmen, crystal, Emerald green, Heatherbloom, Peach-Blo, Topaz, Willow blue

Rosalie, Cambridge's #731 line, is a Cambridge pattern that can be had without procuring a second mortgage. It is not as readily found as some other patterns, but there are several colors to sample. Pink (Peach Blo) or Emerald (light green), crystal, and amber are available with some searching; other colors will probably involve luck. Perhaps a small set of Willow Blue is possible; but Carmen, Bluebell, or Heatherbloom are colors that are too infrequently seen to be gathered into sets. Those colors make great accessory pieces in blended sets, and many collectors are doing that! In this pattern, Emerald color is the light green rather than the darker Emerald color used in some other Cambridge wares.

Some items photographed would bring a fortune in other Cambridge patterns, but Rosalie collectors can pluck these difficult pieces for budget prices. The photo at the bottom of page 166 shows a pink wafer tray in front. A green, smaller version of this tray was for sugar cubes and is shown at the bottom of page 166. The marmalade jar, salad dressing bottle, and twin spouted gravy boats are highly collectible pieces in all patterns! These items are gathered by collectors other than Cambridge glass lovers. They are known as item collectors, those who buy sugar cube trays, gravy boats, or salad dressing bottles. Competition does not always come from inside one's collecting field and that rivalry is another booster of prices.

	Blue Pink Green	Amber
Bottle, French dressing	150.00	100.00
Bowl, bouillon, 2 hdld.	30.00	15.00
Bowl, cream soup	30.00	20.00
Bowl, finger, w/liner	70.00	55.00
Bowl, finger, ftd., w/liner	75.00	60.00
Bowl, 3½", cranberry	45.00	35.00
Bowl, 3⅝", w/cover, 3 pt.	65.00	50.00
Bowl, 5½", fruit	20.00	15.00
Bowl, 5½", 2 hdld., bonbon	25.00	15.00
Bowl, 6¼", 2 hdld., bonbon	25.00	18.00
Bowl, 7", basket, 2 hdld.	35.00	22.00
Bowl, 8½", soup	55.00	35.00
Bowl, 8½", 2 hdld.	55.00	35.00
Bowl, 8½", w/cover, 3 pt.	125.00	65.00
Bowl, 10"	65.00	40.00

	Blue Pink Green	Amber
Bowl, 10", 2 hdld.	65.00	40.00
Bowl, 11"	70.00	40.00
Bowl, 11", basket, 2 hdld.	75.00	45.00
Bowl, 11½"	85.00	55.00
Bowl, 12", decagon	125.00	85.00
Bowl, 13", console	100.00	
Bowl, 14", decagon	245.00	195.00
Bowl, 15", oval console	125.00	75.00
Bowl, 15", oval, flanged	125.00	75.00
Bowl, 15½", oval	135.00	85.00
Candlestick, 4", 2 styles	35.00	25.00
Candlestick, 5", keyhole	40.00	30.00
Candlestick, 6", 3-lite keyhole	75.00	45.00
Candy and cover, 6"	135.00	75.00
Celery, 11"	40.00	25.00

	Blue Pink Green	Amber			Blue Pink Green	Amber
Cheese & cracker, 11", plate	75.00	45.00		Platter, 15"	150.00	100.00
Comport, 5½", 2 hdld.	30.00	15.00		Relish, 9", 2 pt.	45.00	20.00
Comport, 5¾"	30.00	15.00		Relish, 11", 2 pt.	50.00	30.00
Comport, 6", ftd., almond	45.00	30.00		Salt dip, 1½", ftd.	65.00	40.00
Comport, 6½", low ft.	45.00	30.00		Saucer	5.00	4.00
Comport, 6½", high ft.	45.00	30.00		Stem, 1 oz., cordial, #3077	100.00	65.00
Comport, 6¾"	55.00	35.00		Stem, 3½ oz., cocktail, #3077	22.00	16.00
Creamer, ftd.	20.00	15.00		Stem, 6 oz., low sherbet, #3077	18.00	14.00
Creamer, ftd., tall, ewer	65.00	35.00		Stem, 6 oz., high sherbet, #3077	20.00	16.00
Cup	35.00	25.00		Stem, 9 oz., water goblet, #3077	28.00	22.00
Gravy, double, w/platter	175.00	100.00		Stem, 10 oz., goblet, #801	35.00	22.00
Ice bucket or pail	85.00	55.00		Sugar, ftd.	20.00	13.00
Icer, w/liner	65.00	50.00		Sugar shaker	325.00	225.00
Ice tub	85.00	65.00		Tray for sugar shaker/creamer	30.00	20.00
Marmalade	150.00	95.00		Tray, ctr. hdld., for sugar/creamer	20.00	14.00
Mayonnaise, ftd., w/liner	65.00	25.00		Tray, 11", ctr. hdld.	30.00	20.00
Nut, 2½", ftd.	65.00	50.00		Tumbler, 2½ oz., ftd., #3077	45.00	25.00
Pitcher, 62 oz., #955	295.00	195.00		Tumbler, 5 oz., ftd., #3077	35.00	20.00
Plate, 6¾", bread/butter	10.00	7.00		Tumbler, 8 oz., ftd., #3077	20.00	16.00
Plate, 7", 2 hdld.	16.00	10.00		Tumbler, 10 oz., ftd., #3077	30.00	20.00
Plate, 7½", salad	15.00	8.00		Tumbler, 12 oz., ftd., #3077	40.00	25.00
Plate, 8⅜"	20.00	10.00		Vase, 5½", ftd.	75.00	50.00
Plate, 9½", dinner	65.00	40.00		Vase, 6"	85.00	55.00
Plate, 11", 2 hdld.	40.00	25.00		Vase, 6½", ftd.	110.00	60.00
Platter, 12"	85.00	50.00		Wafer tray	120.00	85.00

Colors: crystal

Several Rose pieces are rarely seen. The oyster cocktail and clarets are missing from many collections; buy them when you can! The 6" epernettes on the triple candle in the center have turned out to be one of the rarest pieces in Rose. Low sherbets appear to be harder to find than high ones; and the tray for the individual sugar and creamer is harder to find than they are! Be aware that the 10½" dinner plate has a large center with a small border, while the 10½" service plate has a small center and large border. There is an enormous price difference! Fair warning! Heisey's Rose is another pattern that will be found only in the *Collectible Glassware from the 40s, 50s, and 60s* after this edition.

	Crystal
Ash tray, 3"	37.50
Bell, dinner, #5072	150.00
Bottle, 8 oz., French dressing, blown, #5031	235.00
Bowl, finger, #3309	110.00
Bowl, 5½", ftd., mint	37.50
Bowl, 5¾", ftd., mint, Cabochon	80.00
Bowl, 6", ftd., mint, Queen Ann	50.00
Bowl, 6", jelly, 2 hdld., ftd., Queen Ann	55.00
Bowl, 6", oval, lemon, w/cover, Waverly	435.00
Bowl, 6½", 2 pt., oval, dressing, Waverly	70.00
Bowl, 6½", ftd., honey/cheese, Waverly	60.00
Bowl, 6½", ftd., jelly, Waverly	45.00
Bowl, 6½", lemon, w/cover, Queen Ann	275.00
Bowl, 7", ftd., honey, Waverly	60.00
Bowl, 7", ftd., jelly, Waverly	45.00
Bowl, 7", lily, Queen Ann	125.00
Bowl, 7", relish, 3 pt., round, Waverly	67.50
Bowl, 7", salad, Waverly	60.00
Bowl, 7", salad dressings, Queen Ann	60.00
Bowl, 9", ftd., fruit or salad, Waverly	210.00
Bowl, 9", salad, Waverly	145.00
Bowl, 9", 4 pt., rnd, relish, Waverly	90.00
Bowl, 9½", crimped, floral, Waverly	75.00
Bowl, 10", gardenia, Waverly	75.00
Bowl, 10", crimped, floral, Waverly	75.00
Bowl, 11", 3 pt., relish, Waverly	77.50
Bowl, 11", 3 ftd., floral, Waverly	165.00
Bowl, 11", floral, Waverly	70.00
Bowl, 11", oval, 4 ftd., Waverly	150.00
Bowl, 12", crimped, floral, Waverly	70.00
Bowl, 13", crimped, floral, Waverly	110.00
Bowl, 13", floral, Waverly	100.00

	Crystal
Bowl, 13", gardenia, Waverly	80.00
Butter, w/cover, 6", Waverly	210.00
Butter, w/cover, ¼ lb., Cabochon	335.00
Candlestick, 1-lite, #112	45.00
Candlestick, 2-lite, Flame	100.00
Candlestick, 3-lite, #142, Cascade	85.00
Candlestick, 3-lite, Waverly	100.00
Candlestick, 5", 2-lite, #134, Trident	75.00
Candlestick, 6", epergnette, deep, Waverly	1,295.00
Candy, w/cover, 5", ftd., Waverly	195.00
Candy, w/cover, 6", low, bowknot cover	185.00
Candy, w/cover, 6¼", #1951, Cabochon	185.00
Celery tray, 12", Waverly	65.00
Celery tray, 13", Waverly	70.00
Cheese compote, 4½" & cracker (11" plate), Waverly	145.00
Cheese compote, 5½" & cracker (12" plate), Queen Ann	145.00
Chocolate, w/cover, 5", Waverly	210.00
Cigarette holder, #4035	125.00
Cocktail icer, w/liner, #3304, Universal	285.00
Cocktail shaker, #4225, Cobel	245.00
Comport, 6½", low ft., Waverly	65.00
Comport, 7", oval, ftd., Waverly	145.00
Creamer, ftd., Waverly	35.00
Creamer, indiv., Waverly	40.00
Cup, Waverly	55.00
Decanter, 1 pt., #4036½, #101 stopper	235.00
Hurricane lamp, w/12" globe, #5080	395.00
Hurricane lamp, w/12" globe, Plantation	595.00

	Crystal		Crystal
Ice bucket, dolphin ft., Queen Ann	375.00	Stem, #5072, 1 oz., cordial	150.00
Ice tub, 2 hdld., Waverly	475.00	Stem, #5072, 3 oz., wine	115.00
Mayonnaise, 5½", 2 hdld., Waverly	55.00	Stem, #5072, 3½ oz., oyster cocktail, ftd.	60.00
Mayonnaise, 5½", div., 1 hdld., Waverly	55.00	Stem, #5072, 4 oz., claret	145.00
Mayonnaise, 5½", ftd., Waverly	60.00	Stem, #5072, 4 oz., cocktail	45.00
Oil, 3 oz., ftd., Waverly	185.00	Stem, #5072, 6 oz., sherbet	30.00
Pitcher, 73 oz., #4164	595.00	Stem, #5072, 6 oz., saucer champagne	33.00
Plate, 7", salad, Waverly	20.00	Stem, #5072, 9 oz., water	42.00
Plate, 7", mayonnaise, Waverly	20.00	Sugar, indiv., Waverly	40.00
Plate, 8", salad, Waverly	30.00	Sugar, ftd., Waverly	35.00
Plate, 10½", dinner Waverly	195.00	Tumbler, #5072, 5 oz., ftd., juice	55.00
Plate, 10½", service, Waverly	75.00	Tumbler, #5072, 12 oz., ftd., tea	65.00
Plate, 11", sandwich, Waverly	60.00	Tray, indiv. creamer/sugar, Queen Ann	65.00
Plate, 11", demi-torte, Waverly	70.00	Vase, 3½", ftd., violet, Waverly	110.00
Plate, 12", ftd., salver, Waverly	275.00	Vase, 4", ftd., violet, Waverly	120.00
Plate, 14", torte, Waverly	90.00	Vase, 7", ftd., fan, Waverly	120.00
Plate, 14", sandwich, Waverly	110.00	Vase, 8", #4198	195.00
Plate, 14", ctr. hdld., sandwich, Waverly	215.00	Vase, 8", sq., ftd., urn	195.00
Plate, 15", ftd., cake, Waverly	335.00	Vase, 10", #4198	275.00
Salt & pepper, ftd., pr., Waverly	65.00	Vase, 10", sq., ftd., urn	295.00
Saucer, Waverly	10.00	Vase, 12", sq., ftd., urn	335.00

Colors: crystal; some crystal with gold

Without a doubt, Rose Point is the most known pattern in Cambridge. There were so many mould lines used to make the pattern that individual collectors can choose what they prefer. Consequently, not all are always looking for the same pieces! Variety is a good thing! Pages 170 and 171 show a Pose Point brochure with a listing where pieces are identified by number and that should help you distinguish pieces. There are limitations to how much catalog information we can do and still show you the actual glass.

An uncertainty confronting new collectors is identifying different blanks on which Rose Point is found. On the top of the brochure is line #3900 and the bottom shows #3400 and #3500. These are the major mould lines upon which Rose Point was etched. The bottom of 171 pictures the #3500 stem and tumblers. Be sure to note the shape differences in the parfait and the footed, 5 ounce juice. They are often confused and there is quite a price difference. You might not mind buying juices for parfait prices, but vice versa?

	Crystal
Ash tray, stack set on metal pole, #1715	255.00
Ash tray, 2½", sq., #721	35.00
Ash tray, 3¼", #3500/124	35.00
Ash tray, 3¼", sq., #3500/129	55.00
Ash tray, 3½", #3500/125	35.00
Ash tray, 4", #3500/126	40.00
Ash tray, 4", oval, #3500/130	90.00
Ash tray, 4¼", #3500/127	45.00
Ash tray, 4½", #3500/128	50.00
Ash tray, 4½", oval, #3500/131	65.00
Basket, 3", favor, #3500/79	395.00
Basket, 5", 1 hdld., #3500/51	295.00
Basket, 6", 1 hdld., #3500/52	350.00
Basket, 6", 2 hdld., #3400/1182	40.00
Basket, 6", sq., ftd., 2 hdld, #3500/55	45.00
Basket, 7", 1 hdld., #119	495.00
Basket, 7", wide, #3500/56	60.00
Basket, sugar, w/handle and tongs, #3500/13	325.00
Bell, dinner, #3121	150.00
Bowl, 3", 4 ftd., nut, #3400/71	75.00
Bowl, 3½", bonbon, cupped, deep, #3400/204	85.00
Bowl, 3½", cranberry, #3400/70	95.00
Bowl, 5", hdld., #3500/49	45.00
Bowl, 5", fruit, #3500/10	85.00
Bowl, 5", fruit, blown, #1534	85.00
Bowl, 5¼", fruit, #3400/56	85.00
Bowl, 5½", nappy, #3400/56	75.00
Bowl, 5½", 2 hdld., bonbon, #3400/1179	40.00
Bowl, 5½", 2 hdld., bonbon, #3400/1180	40.00
Bowl, 6", bonbon, crimped, #3400/203	95.00
Bowl, 6", bonbon, cupped, shallow, #3400/205	80.00
Bowl, 6", cereal, #3400/53	110.00
Bowl, 6", cereal, #3400/10	110.00
Bowl, 6", cereal, #3500/11	110.00
Bowl, 6", hdld., #3500/50	47.50
Bowl, 6", 2 hdld., #1402/89	45.00

	Crystal
Bowl, 6", 2 hdld., ftd., bonbon, #3500/54	37.50
Bowl, 6", 4 ftd., fancy rim, #3400/136	165.00
Bowl, 6½", bonbon, crimped, #3400/202	85.00
Bowl, 7", bonbon, crimped, shallow, #3400/201	125.00
Bowl, 7", tab hdld., ftd., bonbon, #3900/130	38.00
Bowl, 8", ram's head, squared, #3500/27	395.00
Bowl, 8½", rimmed soup, #361	295.00
Bowl, 8½", 3 part, #221	225.00
Bowl, 9", 4 ftd., #3400/135	225.00
Bowl, 9", ram's head, #3500/25	395.00
Bowl, 9½", pickle like corn, #477	55.00
Bowl, 9½", ftd., w/hdl., #3500/115	150.00
Bowl, 9½", 2 hdld., #3400/34	85.00
Bowl, 9½", 2 part, blown, #225	495.00
Bowl, 2 hdld., #3400/1185	70.00
Bowl, 10", 2 hdld., #3500/28	77.50
Bowl, 10", 4 tab ftd., flared, #3900/54	70.00
Bowl, 10½", crimp edge, #1351	85.00
Bowl, 10½", flared, #3400/168	67.50
Bowl, 10½", 3 part, #222	375.00
Bowl, 10½", 3 part, #1401/122	375.00
Bowl, 11", ftd., #3500/16	115.00
Bowl, 11", ftd., fancy edge, #3500/19	145.00
Bowl, 11", 4 ftd., oval, #3500/109	325.00
Bowl, 11", 4 ftd., shallow, fancy edge, #3400/48	110.00
Bowl, 11", fruit, #3400/1188	105.00
Bowl, 11", low foot, #3400/3	175.00
Bowl, 11", tab hdld., #3900/34	77.50
Bowl, 11½", ftd., w/tab hdl., #3900/28	80.00
Bowl, 12", crimped, pan Pristine, #136	350.00
Bowl, 10", salad Pristine, #427	175.00
Bowl, 12", 4 ftd., oval, #3400/1240	135.00
Bowl, 12", 4 ftd., oval, w/"ears" hdl., #3900/65	90.00
Bowl, 12", 4 ftd., fancy rim oblong, #3400/160	90.00
Bowl, 12", 4 ftd., flared, #3400/4	75.00
Bowl, 12", 4 tab ftd., flared, #3900/62	77.50
Bowl, 12", ftd., #3500/17	130.00
Bowl, 12", ftd., oblong, #3500/118	175.00
Bowl, 12", ftd., oval w/hdld., #3500/21	225.00
Bowl, 12½", flared, rolled edge, #3400/2	175.00
Bowl, 12½", 4 ftd., #993	90.00
Bowl, 13", #1398	135.00

LIST OF ROSE POINT ITEMS

3500	10 oz. Goblet
3500	7 oz. Tall Sherbet
3500	7 oz. Low Sherbet
3500	3 oz. Cocktail
3500	2½ oz. Wine
3500	4½ oz. Claret
3500	4½ oz. Oyster Cocktail
3500	1 oz. Cordial
3500	5 oz Cafe Parfait
3500	12 oz. Ftd. Ice Tea
3500	10 oz. Ftd. Tumbler
3500	5 oz. Ftd. Tumbler
477	9½ in. Pickle
3400/1180	5¼ in. 2 Hdl. Bonbon
3400/1181	6 in. 2 Hdl. Plate
3400/90	6 in. 2 part Relish
3500/15	Ind. Sugar & Cream
3500/54	6 in. 2 Hdl. Ftd. Bonbon
3500/55	6 in. 2 Hdl. Ftd. Basket
3500/69	6½ in. 3 part Relish
3500/161	8 in. 2 Hdl. Ftd. Plate
3400/91	8 in. 3 part Relish
3500/57	8 in. 3 part Candy Box & Cover
3500/101	5⅜ in. Tall Comport
3900/17	Cup & Saucer
3900/19	2 pc. Mayonnaise Set
3900/20	6½ in. Bread & Butter Plate
3900/22	8 in. Salad Plate
3900/24	10½ in. Dinner Plate
3900/26	12 in. 4 Ftd. Plate
3900/28	11½ in. Ftd. Bowl
3900/33	13 in. 4 Ftd. Torte Plate, R. E.
3900/34	11 in. 2 Handled Bowl
3900/35	13½ in. 2 Handled Cake Plate
3900/40	Ind. Sugar & Cream
3900/41	Sugar & Cream
3900/54	10 in. 4 Ftd. Bowl, flared
3900/62	12 in. 4 Ftd. Bowl, flared
3900/65	12 in. 4 Ftd. Oval Bowl
3900/67	5 in. Candlestick
3900/72	6 in. 2 lite Candlestick
3900/74	6 in. 3 lite Candlestick
3900/100	6 oz. Oil, g. s.
3900/111	4 pc. Mayonnaise Set
3900/115	13 oz. Tumbler
3900/120	12 in. 5 part Celery & Relish
3900/123	7 in. Relish or Pickle
3900/124	7 in. 2 part Relish
3900/125	9 in. 3 part Celery & Relish
3900/126	12 in. 3 part Celery & Relish
3900/129	3 pc. Mayonnaise Set
3900/130	7 in. 2 handled Ftd. Bonbon
3900/131	8 in. 2 handled Ftd. Bonbon Plate
3900/136	5½ in. Comport
3900/165	Candy Box & Cover
3900/166	14 in. Plate, r. e.
3900/671	Ice Bucket
3900/671	Ice Bucket with chrome Handle
	Chrome Ice Tongs (long)
3900/1177	Salt & Pepper Shaker (doz. pr.)
274	10 in. Bud Flower Holder
278	11 in. Ftd. Flower Holder
279	13 in. Ftd. Flower Holder
968	2 pc. Cocktail Icer
1237	9 in. Ftd. Flower Holder
1238	12 in. Ftd. Flower Holder
1299	11 in. Ftd. Flower Holder
1309	5 in. Glode Flower Holder
1603	Hurricane Lamp (Etch. Chimney only)
1617	Hurricane Lamp (Etch. Chimney only)
6004	6 in. Ftd. Flower Holder
6004	8 in. Ftd. Flower Holder
P. 101	Cocktail Shaker (Patent—D133,198)

3900/17
3900/19
3900/115
3900/20
3900/22
3900/67
3900/28
3900/24
3900/34
3900/26
3900/40
3900/41

3900/131
3900/165
1309
3900/129
3900/166
1617
1237
6004-6
6004-8
3900/125
1603
3900/136
3900/671
P. 101
274
1299
1238
278
279

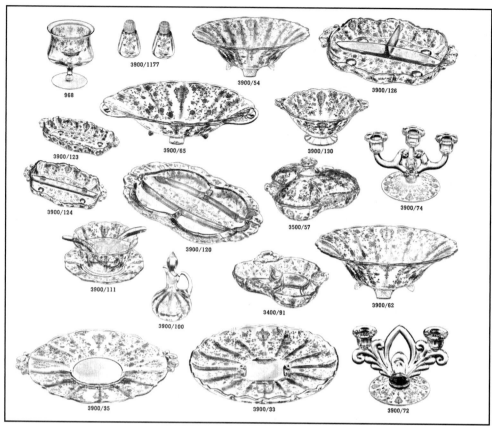

968
3900/1177
3900/54
3900/126
3900/65
3900/123
3900/130
3900/124
3900/74
3900/57
3900/111
3900/120
3900/100
3400/91
3900/62
3900/35
3900/33
3900/72

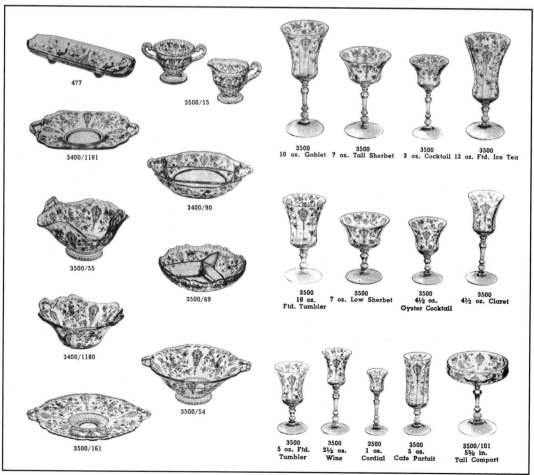

477

3500/15

3400/1181

3400/90

3500/55

3500/69

3400/1180

3500/54

3500/161

| 3500 10 oz. Goblet | 3500 7 oz. Tall Sherbet | 3500 3 oz. Cocktail | 3500 12 oz. Ftd. Ice Tea |

| 3500 10 oz. Ftd. Tumbler | 3500 7 oz. Low Sherbet | 3500 4½ oz. Oyster Cocktail | 3500 4½ oz. Claret |

| 3500 5 oz. Ftd. Tumbler | 3500 2½ oz. Wine | 3500 1 oz. Cordial | 3500 5 oz. Cafe Parfait | 3500/101 5⅜ in. Tall Comport |

ROSE POINT

	Crystal
Bowl, 13", 4 ftd., narrow, crimped, #3400/47	125.00
Bowl, 13", flared, #3400/1	85.00
Bowl, 14", 4 ftd., crimp edge, oblong, #1247	165.00
Bowl, 18", crimped, pan Pristine, #136	695.00
Bowl, cream soup, w/liner, #3400	175.00
Bowl, cream soup, w/liner, #3500/2	185.00
Bowl, finger, w/liner, #3106	110.00
Bowl, finger, w/liner, #3121	110.00
Butter, w/cover, round, #506	195.00
Butter, w/cover, 5", #3400/52	185.00
Butter dish, ¼ lb., #3900/52	395.00
Candelabrum, 2-lite w/bobeches & prisms, #1268	195.00
Candelabrum, 2-lite, #3500/94	120.00
Candelabrum, 3-lite, #1338	75.00
Candelabrum, 5½", 3-lite w/#19 bobeche & #1 prisms, #1545	175.00
Candelabrum, 6½", 2-lite, w/bobeches & prisms Martha, #496	195.00
Candle, torchere, cup ft., #3500/90	225.00
Candle, torchere, flat ft., #3500/88	195.00
Candlestick Pristine, #500	145.00
Candlestick, sq. base & lites, #1700/501	195.00
Candlestick, 2½", #3500/108	35.00
Candlestick, 3½", #628	40.00
Candlestick, 4", #627	60.00
Candlestick, 4", ram's head, #3500/74	125.00
Candlestick, 5", 1-lite keyhole, #3400/646	45.00
Candlestick, 5", inverts to comport, #3900/68	95.00
Candlestick, 5½", 2-lite Martha, #495	95.00
Candlestick, 6", #3500/31	95.00
Candlestick, 6", 2-lite keyhole, #3400/647	45.00
Candlestick, 6", 2-lite, #3900/72	50.00
Candlestick, 6", 3-lite, #3900/74	65.00
Candlestick, 6", 3-lite keyhole, #3400/638	65.00
Candlestick, 6", 3-tiered lite, #1338	85.00
Candlestick, 6½", Calla Lily, #499	110.00

	Crystal
Candlestick, 7", #3121	100.00
Candlestick, 7½", w/prism Martha, #497	145.00
Candy box, w/cover, 5", apple shape, #316	1,100.00
Candy box, w/cover, 5⅜", #1066 stem	165.00
Candy box, w/cover, 5⅜", tall stem, #3121/3	175.00
Candy box, w/cover, 5⅜", short stem, #3121/4	175.00
Candy box, w/cover, blown, 5⅜", #3500/103	195.00
Candy box, w/cover, 6", ram's head, #3500/78	295.00
Candy box, w/rose finial, 6", 3 ftd., #300	325.00
Candy box, w/cover, 7", #3400/9	165.00
Candy box, w/cover, 7", round, 3 pt., #103	175.00
Candy box, w/cover, 8", 3 pt., #3500/57	110.00
Candy box, w/cover, rnd., #3900/165	135.00
Celery, 12", #3400/652	55.00
Celery, 12", #3500/652	65.00
Celery, 12", 5 pt., #3400/67	85.00
Celery, 14", 4 pt., 2 hdld., #3500/97	175.00
Celery & relish, 9", 3 pt., #3900/125	65.00
Celery & relish, 12", 3 pt., #3900/126	75.00
Celery & relish, 12", 5 pt., #3900/120	75.00
Cheese 5" comport & cracker 13" plate, #3900/135	145.00
Cheese 5½" comport & cracker 11½" plate, #3400/6	145.00
Cheese 6" comport & cracker 12" plate, #3500/162	165.00
Cheese dish, w/cover, 5", #980	595.00
Cigarette box, w/cover, #615	150.00
Cigarette box, w/cover, #747	175.00
Cigarette holder, oval, w/ash tray ft., #1066	195.00
Cigarette holder, round, w/ash tray ft., #1337	175.00
Coaster, 3½", #1628	60.00
Cocktail icer, 2 pc., #3600	80.00
Cocktail shaker, metal top, #3400/157	195.00
Cocktail shaker, metal top, #3400/175	175.00
Cocktail shaker, 12 oz., metal top, #97	375.00
Cocktail shaker, 32 oz., w/glass stopper, #101	250.00
Cocktail shaker, 46 oz., metal top, #98	200.00
Cocktail shaker, 48 oz., glass stopper, #102	200.00
Comport, 5", #3900/135	50.00
Comport, 5", 4 ftd., #3400/74	75.00
Comport, 5½", scalloped edge, #3900/136	85.00
Comport, 5⅜", blown, #3500/101	75.00
Comport, 5⅜", blown, #3121 stem	75.00
Comport, 5⅜", blown, #1066 stem	75.00
Comport, 6", #3500/36	150.00
Comport, 6", #3500/111	160.00
Comport, 6", 4 ftd., #3400/13	50.00
Comport, 7", 2 hdld., #3500/37	135.00
Comport, 7", keyhole, #3400/29	145.00
Comport, 7", keyhole, low, #3400/28	95.00
Creamer, #3400/68	25.00
Creamer, #3500/14	27.00
Creamer, flat, #137	150.00
Creamer, flat, #944	165.00
Creamer, ftd., #3400/16	100.00
Creamer, ftd., #3900/41	25.00
Creamer, indiv., #3500/15 pie crust edge	25.00

	Crystal
Creamer, indiv., #3900/40 scalloped edge	20.00
Cup, 3 styles, #3400/54, #3500/1, #3900/17	32.50
Cup, 5 oz., punch, #488	37.50
Cup, after dinner, #3400/69	300.00
Decanter, 12 oz., ball, w/stopper, #3400/119	325.00
Decanter, 14 oz., ftd., #1320	450.00
Decanter, 26 oz., sq., #1380	495.00
Decanter, 28 oz., tall, #1372	795.00
Decanter, 28 oz., w/stopper, #1321	395.00
Decanter, 32 oz., ball, w/stopper, #3400/92	495.00
Dressing bottle, flat, #1263	375.00
Dressing bottle, ftd., #1261	350.00
Epergne candle w/vases, #3900/75	275.00
Grapefruit, w/liner, #187	125.00
Hat, 5", #1704	495.00
Hat, 6", #1703	495.00
Hat, 8", #1702	595.00
Hat, 9", #1701	795.00
Honey dish, w/cover, #3500/139	350.00
Hot plate or trivet	125.00
Hurricane lamp, w/prisms, #1613	375.00
Hurricane lamp, candlestick base, #1617	275.00
Hurricane lamp, keyhole base, w/prisms, #1603	275.00
Hurricane lamp, 8", etched chimney, #1601	295.00
Hurricane lamp, 10", etched chimney & base, #1604	335.00
Ice bucket, #1402/52	225.00
Ice bucket, w/chrome hand., #3900/671	175.00

	Crystal
Ice pail, #1705	250.00
Ice pail, #3400/851	175.00
Ice tub Pristine, #671	250.00
Icer, cocktail, #968 or, #18	80.00
Marmalade, 8 oz., #147	195.00
Marmalade, w/cover, 7 oz., ftd., #157	210.00
Mayonnaise sherbet type w/ladle, #19	75.00
Mayonnaise, div., w/liner & 2 ladles, #3900/111	95.00
Mayonnaise, 3 pc., #3400/11	75.00
Mayonnaise, 3 pc., #3900/129	75.00
Mayonnaise, w/liner & ladle, #3500/59	75.00
Mustard, 3 oz., #151	175.00
Mustard, 4½ oz., ftd., #1329	350.00
Oil, 2 oz., ball, w/stopper, #3400/96	110.00
Oil, 6 oz., ball, w/stopper, #3400/99	155.00
Oil, 6 oz., hdld., #3400/193	125.00
Oil, 6 oz., loop hdld., w/stopper, #3900/100	155.00
Oil, 6 oz., w/stopper, ftd., hdld., #3400/161	250.00
Pickle, 9", #3400/59	70.00
Pickle or relish, 7", #3900/123	40.00
Pitcher, 20 oz., #3900/117	325.00
Pitcher, 20 oz. w/ice lip, #70	325.00
Pitcher, 32 oz., #3900/118	350.00
Pitcher, 32 oz. martini slender, w/metal insert, #3900/114	495.00
Pitcher, 60 oz., martini, #1408	1,995.00
Pitcher, 76 oz., #3900/115	295.00
Pitcher, 76 oz., ice lip, #3400/100	215.00

	Crystal
Pitcher, 76 oz., ice lip, #3400/152	295.00
Pitcher, 80 oz., ball, #3400/38	250.00
Pitcher, 80 oz., ball, #3900/116	250.00
Pitcher, 80 oz., Doulton, #3400/141	365.00
Pitcher, nite set, 2 pc., w/tumbler insert top, #103	850.00
Plate, 6", bread/butter, #3400/60	15.00
Plate, 6", bread/butter, #3500/3	16.00
Plate, 6", 2 hdld., #3400/1181	22.00
Plate, 6⅛", canape, #693	195.00
Plate, 6½", bread/butter, #3900/20	16.00
Plate, 7½", #3500/4	20.00
Plate, 7½", salad, #3400/176	20.00
Plate, 8", salad, #3900/22	22.00
Plate, 8", 2 hdld., ftd., #3500/161	45.00
Plate, 8", tab hdld., ftd., bonbon, #3900/131	42.00
Plate, 8½", breakfast, #3400/62	25.00
Plate, 8½", salad, #3500/5	25.00
Plate, 9½", crescent salad, #485	295.00
Plate, 9½", luncheon, #3400/63	42.00
Plate, 10½", dinner, #3400/64	165.00
Plate, 10½", dinner, #3900/24	165.00
Plate, 11", 2 hdld., #3400/35	65.00
Plate, 12", 4 ftd., service, #3900/26	75.00
Plate, 12", ftd., #3500/39	92.00
Plate, 12½", 2 hdld., #3400/1186	75.00
Plate, 13", rolled edge, ftd., #3900/33	75.00
Plate, 13", 4 ftd., torte, #3500/110	130.00
Plate, 13", ftd., cake Martha, #170	250.00
Plate, 13", torte, #3500/38	185.00
Plate, 13½", #242	150.00
Plate, 13½", rolled edge, #1397	75.00
Plate, 13½", tab hdld., cake, #3900/35	75.00
Plate, 14", rolled edge, #3900/166	80.00
Plate, 14", service, #3900/167	80.00
Plate, 14", torte, #3400/65	155.00
Plate, 18", punch bowl liner Martha, #129	595.00
Punch bowl, 15", Martha, #478	3,750.00
Punch set, 15-pc. Martha	4,850.00
Relish, 5½", 2 pt., #3500/68	27.00
Relish, 5½", 2 pt., hdld., #3500/60	33.00
Relish, 6", 2 pt., #3400/90	35.00
Relish, 6", 2 pt., 1 hdl., #3400/1093	95.00
Relish, 6½", 3 pt., #3500/69	35.00
Relish, 6½", 3 pt., hdld., #3500/61	37.50
Relish, 7", 2 pt., #3900/124	37.50
Relish, 7½", 3 pt., center hdld., #3500/71	150.00
Relish, 7½", 4 pt., #3500/70	45.00
Relish, 7½", 4 pt., 2 hdld., #3500/62	58.00
Relish, 8", 3 pt., 3 hdld., #3400/91	40.00
Relish, 10", 2 hdld., #3500/85	75.00
Relish, 10", 3 pt., 2 hdld., #3500/86	58.00
Relish, 10", 3 pt., 4 ftd., 2 hdld., #3500/64	60.00
Relish, 10", 4 pt., 4 ftd., #3500/65	65.00
Relish, 10", 4 pt., 2 hdld., #3500/87	62.00
Relish, 11", 2 pt., 2 hdld., #3400/89	85.00
Relish, 11", 3 pt., #3400/200	60.00
Relish, 12", 5 pt., #3400/67	85.00

	Crystal
Relish, 12", 5 pt. Pristine, #419	275.00
Relish, 12", 6 pc., #3500/67	285.00
Relish, 14", w/cover, 4 pt., 2 hdld., #3500/142	995.00
Relish, 15", 4 pt., hdld., #3500/113	225.00
Salt & pepper, egg shape, pr., #1468	95.00
Salt & pepper, individual, rnd., glass base, pr., #1470	95.00
Salt & pepper, individual, w/chrome tops, pr., #360	75.00
Salt & pepper, lg., rnd., glass base, pr., #1471	90.00
Salt & pepper, w/chrome tops, pr., #395	185.00
Salt & pepper, w/chrome tops, pr., #3400/37	185.00
Salt & pepper, w/chrome tops, pr., ftd. #3400/77	60.00
Salt & pepper w/chrome tops, pr., flat, #3900/1177	50.00
Sandwich tray, 11", center handled, #3400/10	145.00
Saucer, after dinner, #3400/69	65.00
Saucer, 3 styles, #3400, #3500, #3900	7.00
Stem, #3104, 3½ oz., cocktail	295.00
Stem, #3106, ¾ oz., brandy	135.00
Stem, #3106, 1 oz., cordial	135.00
Stem, #3106, 1 oz., pousse cafe	145.00
Stem, #3106, 2 oz., sherry	55.00
Stem, #3106, 2½ oz., wine	55.00
Stem, #3106, 3 oz., cocktail	40.00
Stem, #3106, 4½ oz., claret	60.00
Stem, #3106, 5 oz., oyster cocktail	35.00
Stem, #3106, 7 oz., high sherbet	33.00
Stem, #3106, 7 oz., low sherbet	26.00
Stem, #3106, 10 oz., water goblet	40.00
Stem, #3121, 1 oz., brandy	135.00
Stem, #3121, 1 oz., cordial	75.00
Stem, #3121, 3 oz., cocktail	32.50
Stem, #3121, 3½ oz., wine	60.00
Stem, #3121, 4½ oz., claret	100.00
Stem, #3121, 4½ oz., low oyster cocktail	37.50
Stem, #3121, 5 oz., low ft. parfait	110.00
Stem, #3121, 6 oz., low sherbet	22.00

	Crystal
Stem, #3121, 6 oz., tall sherbet	24.00
Stem, #3121, 10 oz., water	42.00
Stem, #3500, 1 oz., cordial	73.00
Stem, #3500, 2½ oz., wine	65.00
Stem, #3500, 3 oz., cocktail	35.00
Stem, #3500, 4½ oz., claret	90.00
Stem, #3500, 4½ oz., low oyster cocktail	37.50
Stem, #3500, 5 oz., low ft. parfait	125.00
Stem, #3500, 7 oz., low ft. sherbet	22.00
Stem, #3500, 7 oz., tall sherbet	28.00
Stem, #3500, 10 oz. water	42.00
Stem, #7801, 4 oz. cocktail, plain stem	45.00
Stem, #7966, 1 oz., cordial, plain ft.	140.00
Stem, #7966, 2 oz., sherry, plain ft.	110.00
Sugar, #3400/68	22.00
Sugar, #3500/14	22.00
Sugar, flat, #137	150.00
Sugar, flat, #944	165.00
Sugar, ftd., #3400/16	100.00
Sugar, ftd., #3900/41	22.00
Sugar, indiv., #3500/15, pie crust edge	24.00
Sugar, indiv., #3900/40, scalloped edge	22.00
Syrup, w/drip stop top, #1670	425.00
Tray, 6", 2 hdld., sq., #3500/91	195.00
Tray, 12", 2 hdld., oval, service, #3500/99	255.00
Tray, 12", rnd., #3500/67	195.00
Tray, 13", 2 hdld., rnd., #3500/72	195.00
Tray, sugar/creamer, #3900/37	25.00
Tumbler, #498, 2 oz., straight side	125.00
Tumbler, #498, 5 oz., straight side	50.00
Tumbler, #498, 8 oz., straight side	50.00
Tumbler, #498, 10 oz., straight side	50.00
Tumbler, #498, 12 oz., straight side	65.00
Tumbler, #3000, 3½ oz., cone, ftd.	120.00
Tumbler, #3000, 5 oz., cone, ftd.	135.00
Tumbler, #3106, 3 oz., ftd.	40.00
Tumbler, #3106, 5 oz., ftd.	35.00
Tumbler, #3106, 9 oz., ftd.	35.00
Tumbler, #3106, 12 oz., ftd.	45.00
Tumbler, #3121, 2½ oz., ftd.	75.00
Tumbler, #3121, 5 oz., low ft., juice	37.50
Tumbler, #3121, 10 oz., low ft., water	32.00
Tumbler, #3121, 12 oz., low ft., ice tea	40.00
Tumbler, #3400/1341, 1 oz., cordial	110.00
Tumbler, #3400/92, 2½ oz.	125.00
Tumbler, #3400/38, 5 oz.	110.00
Tumbler, #3400/38, 12 oz.	60.00
Tumbler, #3900/115, 13 oz.	50.00
Tumbler, #3500, 2½ oz., ftd.	75.00
Tumbler, #3500, 5 oz., low ft., juice	45.00
Tumbler, #3500, 10 oz., low ft., water	35.00
Tumbler, #3500, 13 oz., low ftd.	45.00
Tumbler, #3500, 12 oz., tall ft., ice tea	45.00
Tumbler, #7801, 5 oz., ftd.	55.00
Tumbler, #7801, 12 oz., ftd., ice tea	85.00
Tumbler, #3900/117, 5 oz.	50.00
Tumbler, #3400/115, 13 oz.	55.00
Urn, 10", w/cover, #3500/41	695.00

	Crystal
Urn, 12", w/cover, #3500/42	795.00
Vase, 5", #1309	120.00
Vase, 5", globe, #3400/102	85.00
Vase, 5", ftd., #6004	65.00
Vase, 6", high ftd., flower, #6004	75.00
Vase, 6", #572	175.00
Vase, 6½", globe, #3400/103	95.00
Vase, 7", ivy, ftd., ball, #1066	295.00
Vase, 8", #1430	250.00
Vase, 8", flat, flared, #797	155.00
Vase, 8", ftd., #3500/44	135.00
Vase, 8", high ftd., flower, #6004	85.00
Vase, 9", ftd., keyhole, #1237	110.00
Vase, 9", ftd., #1620	145.00
Vase, 9½" ftd., keyhole, #1233	95.00
Vase, 10", ball bottom, #400	225.00
Vase, 10", bud, #1528	90.00
Vase, 10", cornucopia, #3900/575	235.00
Vase, 10", flat, #1242	175.00
Vase, 10", ftd., #1301	85.00
Vase, 10", ftd., #6004	85.00
Vase, 10", ftd., #3500/45	195.00
Vase, 10", slender, #274	65.00
Vase, 11", ftd., flower, #278	155.00
Vase, 11", ped. ftd., flower, #1299	175.00
Vase, 12", ftd., #6004	110.00
Vase, 12", ftd., keyhole, #1234	110.00
Vase, 12", ftd., keyhole, #1238	125.00
Vase, 13", ftd., flower, #279	225.00

Colors: amber, Ebony, Blue, green

Fostoria's Royal is sometimes mistakenly identified as Vesper since both etchings are similar, both are found on the #2350 blank and both were manufactured in the same colors! Royal does not attract as many collectors as Vesper, possibly due to a limited allotment of Royal. New collectors should find Royal priced more to their liking since there is less demand to inflate the prices.

Unusual and hard to find pieces of Royal are both styles of pitchers, covered cheese and butter dishes, cologne bottle, and sugar lid. Sufficient amber or green can be found to acquire a set; but only a minuscule number of pieces can be found in Blue or black. Fostoria's blue color found with Royal etching was called "Blue" as opposed to the "Azure" blue which is a lighter color found etched June, Kashmir, or Versailles. Personally, I prefer this Royal pattern Blue. I only look for pieces not previously photographed.

Published material indicates production of Royal continued until 1934 although the January 1, 1933, Fostoria catalog no longer listed Royal as being for sale. I have changed my cutoff date of production to 1932. If you can find a May 1928 copy of *House and Garden*, there is a fascinating Fostoria Royal advertisement displayed!

	*Amber Green			*Amber Green
Ash tray, #2350, 3½"	22.50		Ice bucket, #2378	65.00
Bowl, #2350, bouillon, flat	15.00		Mayonnaise, #2315	25.00
Bowl, #2350½, bouillon, ftd.	16.00		Pickle, 8", #2350	20.00
Bowl, #2350, cream soup, flat	16.00		Pitcher, #1236	395.00
Bowl, #2350½, cream soup, ftd.	18.00		Pitcher, #5000, 48 oz.	295.00
Bowl, #869, 4½", finger	20.00		Plate, 8½", deep soup/underplate	37.50
Bowl, #2350, 5½", fruit	15.00		Plate, #2350, 6", bread/butter	3.00
Bowl, #2350, 6½", cereal	25.00		Plate, #2350, 7½", salad	4.00
Bowl, #2267, 7", ftd.	35.00		Plate, #2350, 8½", luncheon	8.00
Bowl, #2350, 7¾", soup	30.00		Plate, #2321, 8¾, Maj Jongg (canape)	37.50
Bowl, #2350, 8", nappy	30.00		Plate, #2350, 9½", small dinner	13.00
Bowl, #2350, 9", nappy	32.00		Plate, #2350, 10½", dinner	30.00
Bowl, #2350, 9", oval, baker	45.00		Plate, #2350, 13", chop	30.00
Bowl, #2324, 10", ftd.	45.00		Plate, #2350, 15", chop	50.00
Bowl, #2350, 10", salad	35.00		Platter, #2350, 10½"	30.00
Bowl, #2350, 10½", oval, baker	55.00		Platter, #2350, 12"	45.00
Bowl, #2315, 10½", ftd.	45.00		Platter, #2350, 15½"	135.00
Bowl, #2329, 11", console	22.00		Salt and pepper, #5100, pr.	60.00
Bowl, #2297, 12", deep	22.00		Sauce boat, w/liner	150.00
Bowl, #2329, 13", console	30.00		Saucer, #2350/#2350½	3.00
Bowl, #2324, 13", ftd.	50.00		Saucer, #2350, demi	8.00
Bowl, #2371, 13", oval, w/flower frog	150.00		Server, #2287, 11", center hdld.	25.00
Butter, w/cover, #2350	295.00		Stem, #869, ¾ oz., cordial	70.00
Candlestick, #2324, 4"	22.00		Stem, #869, 2¾ oz., wine	32.50
Candlestick, #2324, 9"	75.00		Stem, #869, 3 oz., cocktail	22.50
Candy, w/cover, #2331, 3 part	85.00		Stem, #869, 5½ oz., oyster cocktail	20.00
Candy, w/cover, ftd., ½ lb.	195.00		Stem, #869, 5½ oz., parfait	32.50
Celery, #2350, 11"	25.00		Stem, #869, 6 oz., low sherbet	15.00
Cheese, w/cover/plate, #2276 (plate 11")	150.00		Stem, #869, 6 oz., high sherbet	18.00
Cologne, #2322, tall	100.00		Stem, #869, 9 oz., water	23.00
Cologne, #2323, short	90.00		Sugar, flat, w/lid	165.00
Cologne/powder jar combination	275.00		Sugar, #2315, ftd., fat	18.00
Comport, #1861½, 6", jelly	25.00		Sugar, #2350½, ftd.	15.00
Comport, #2327, 7"	28.00		Sugar lid, #2350½	125.00
Comport, #2358, 8" wide	30.00		Tumbler, #869, 5 oz., flat	22.50
Creamer, flat	18.00		Tumbler, #859, 9 oz., flat	25.00
Creamer, #2315½, ftd., fat	18.00		Tumbler, #859, 12 oz., flat	30.00
Creamer, #2350½, ftd.	15.00		Tumbler, #5000, 2½ oz., ftd.	35.00
Cup, #2350, flat	12.00		Tumbler, #5000, 5 oz., ftd.	15.00
Cup, #2350½, ftd.	13.00		Tumbler, #5000, 9 oz., ftd.	18.00
Cup, #2350, demi	25.00		Tumbler, #5000, 12 oz., ftd.	27.50
Egg cup, #2350	27.50		Vase, #2324, urn, ftd.	100.00
Grapefruit, w/insert	90.00		Vase, #2292, flared	125.00

*Add up to 50% more for blue or black.

Colors: Smokey Topaz, Jungle Green, French Crystal, Silver Gray, Lilac, Sunshine, Jade; some milk glass, Apple Green, black, French Opalescent

Ruba Rombic is one of those patterns that collectors either love or despise. There appear to be no in between feelings! Some dislike the shape and others dislike the colors. However, there are collectors who feel this is the most wonderful pattern in the book.

The predominate color shown here is Smokey Topaz, priced below with the Jungle Green. Smokey Topaz will be the color you are most likely to find.

The cased color column below includes three colors. They are Lilac (lavender), Sunshine (yellow), and Jade (green). French crystal is a white, applied color except that the raised edges are crystal with no white coloring at all. Silver is sometimes referred to as Gray Silver.

Prices for a few pieces of Ruba Rombic have toppled in some instances. A couple of collections have been broken up and supplied the market for now. Once a piece of glass reaches four digit prices, there is a limited number of collectors willing to pay that price. Once five digit prices are realized, there is only a handful. You can get a fairly good used car in that range. Ruba Rombic has always sold in a specialized market that eluded most dealers who did not have an outlet where they could sell it. The Internet will change that!

In the past, Ruba Rombic was sporadically exhibited at Depression glass shows; but upper echelon Art Deco collectors and museums started displaying Ruba Rombic, and prices ascended beyond the checkbook of the average collector.

	Smokey Topaz Jungle Green	Cased Colors	French Opal French Crystal Silver
Ash tray, 3½"	600.00	750.00	850.00
Bonbon, flat, 3 part	250.00	350.00	400.00
Bottle, decanter, 9"	1,800.00	2,200.00	2,500.00
Bottle, perfume, 4¾"	1,200.00	1,500.00	1,800.00
Bottle, toilet, 7½"	1,200.00	1,500.00	1,800.00
Bowl, 3", almond	225.00	250.00	300.00
Bowl, 8", cupped	950.00	1,200.00	1,300.00
Bowl, 9", flared	950.00	1,200.00	1,300.00
Bowl, 12", oval	1,500.00	1,800.00	1,800.00
Bowl, bouillon	175.00	250.00	275.00
Bowl, finger	95.00	125.00	140.00
Box, cigarette, 3½" x 4¼"	850.00	1,250.00	1,500.00
Box, powder, 5", round	850.00	1,250.00	1,500.00
Candlestick, 2½" high, pr.	500.00	650.00	750.00
Celery, 10", 3 part	850.00	950.00	1,000.00
Comport, 7", wide	850.00	950.00	1,000.00
Creamer	200.00	250.00	300.00
Light, ceiling fixture, 10"		1,500.00	1,500.00
Light, ceiling fixture, 16"		2,500.00	2,500.00
Light, table light		1,200.00	1,200.00

	Smokey Topaz Jungle Green	Cased Colors	French Opal French Crystal Silver
Light, wall sconce		1,500.00	1,500.00
Pitcher, 8¼"	2,500.00	3,000.00	4,000.00
Plate, 7"	75.00	100.00	150.00
Plate, 8"	75.00	100.00	150.00
Plate, 10"	250.00	275.00	300.00
Plate, 15"	1,200.00	1,400.00	1,400.00
Relish, 2 part	350.00	450.00	500.00
Sugar	200.00	250.00	300.00
Sundae	100.00	135.00	150.00
Tray for decanter set	2,000.00	2,250.00	2,500.00
Tumbler, 2 oz., flat, 2¾"	100.00	125.00	150.00
Tumbler, 3 oz., ftd	125.00	150.00	175.00
Tumbler, 9 oz., flat	125.00	175.00	200.00
Tumbler, 10 oz., ftd.	175.00	300.00	350.00
Tumbler, 12 oz., flat	175.00	300.00	350.00
Tumbler, 15 oz., ftd., 7"	350.00	450.00	500.00
Vase, 6"	850.00	1,000.00	1,500.00
Vase, 9½"	1,500.00	2,500.00	3,000.00
Vase, 16"	10,000.00	12,000.00	12,000.00

Colors: crystal, amber, pink, green, red, cobalt blue

Lancaster Colony continues to produce some Sandwich pieces in their lines today. The bright blue, green, or amberina color combinations are made by Indiana from Duncan moulds and were sold by Montgomery Ward in the early 1970s. I just saw a Sunset (amberina) cake stand priced for $150.00, labeled Duncan, at an antique fair over the weekend. The cobalt blue and true red pieces pictured here seem to excite a few Duncan collectors! Tiffin also made a few Sandwich pieces in milk glass out of Duncan moulds.

I have eliminated the factory catalog pages of Sandwich from this book. If those interest you, an older book will have to be found in the secondary market.

A profusion of Sandwich stemware makes it as inexpensive to use as nearly all currently made stemware. If you enjoy this design, now would be a good time to start picking it up while you can still afford the gasoline to search for it.

	Crystal
Ash tray, 2½" x 3¾", rect.	10.00
Ash tray, 2¾", sq.	8.00
Basket, 6½", w/loop hdl.	135.00
Basket, 10", crimped, w/loop hdl.	195.00
Basket, 10", oval, w/loop hdl.	195.00
Basket, 11½", w/loop hdl.	250.00
Bonbon, 5", heart shape, w/ring hdl.	15.00
Bonbon, 5½", heart shape, hdld.	15.00
Bonbon, 6", heart shape, w/ring hdl.	20.00
Bonbon, 7½", ftd., w/cover	50.00
Bowl, 2½", salted almond	11.00
Bowl, 3½", nut	10.00
Bowl, 4", finger	12.50
Bowl, 5½", hdld.	15.00
Bowl, 5½", ftd., grapefruit, w/rim liner	17.50
Bowl, 5½", ftd., grapefruit, w/fruit cup liner	17.50
Bowl, 5", 2 pt., nappy	12.00
Bowl, 5", ftd., crimped ivy	40.00
Bowl, 5", fruit	10.00
Bowl, 5", nappy, w/ring hdl.	12.00
Bowl, 6", 2 pt., nappy	15.00
Bowl, 6", fruit salad	12.00
Bowl, 6", grapefruit, rimmed edge	17.50
Bowl, 6", nappy, w/ring hdl.	18.00

	Crystal
Bowl, 10", salad, deep	75.00
Bowl, 10", 3 pt., fruit	85.00
Bowl, 10", lily, vertical edge	52.50
Bowl, 11", cupped nut	55.00
Bowl, 11½", crimped flower	57.50
Bowl, 11½", gardenia	45.00
Bowl, 11½", ftd., crimped fruit	65.00
Bowl, 12", fruit, flared edge	45.00
Bowl, 12", shallow salad	40.00
Bowl, 12", oblong console	40.00
Bowl, 12", epergne, w/ctr. hole	100.00
Butter, w/cover, ¼ lb.	40.00
Cake stand, 11½", ftd., rolled edge	100.00
Cake stand, 12", ftd., rolled edge, plain pedestal	80.00
Cake stand, 13", ftd., plain pedestal	80.00
Candelabra, 10", 1-lite, w/bobeche & prisms	85.00
Candelabra, 10", 3-lite, w/bobeche & prisms	225.00
Candelabra, 16", 3-lite, w/bobeche & prisms	275.00
Candlestick, 4", 1-lite	15.00
Candlestick, 4", 1-lite, w/bobeche & stub. prisms	35.00
Candlestick, 5", 3-lite	50.00
Candlestick, 5", 3-lite, w/bobeche & stub. prisms	135.00
Candlestick, 5", 2-lite, w/bobeche & stub. prisms	110.00
Candlestick, 5", 2-lite	32.00
Candy, 6" square	395.00
Candy box, w/cover, 5", flat	40.00
Candy jar, w/cover, 8½", ftd.	55.00
Cheese, w/cover (cover 4¾", plate 8")	125.00
Cheese/cracker (3" compote, 13" plate)	55.00
Cigarette box, w/cover, 3½"	22.00
Cigarette holder, 3", ftd.	27.50
Coaster, 5"	12.00
Comport, 2¼"	15.00
Comport, 3¼", low ft., crimped candy	20.00

	Crystal
Comport, 3¼", low ft., flared candy	17.50
Comport, 4¼", ftd.	20.00
Comport, 5", low ft.	20.00
Comport, 5½", ftd., low crimped	25.00
Comport, 6", low ft., flared	22.50
Condiment set (2 cruets, 3¾" salt & pepper, 4 pt. tray)	125.00
Creamer, 4", 7 oz., ftd.	9.00
Cup, 6 oz., tea	10.00
Epergne, 9", garden	150.00
Epergne, 12", 3 pt., fruit or flower	275.00
Jelly, 3", indiv.	7.00
Mayonnaise set, 3 pc.: ladle, 5" bowl, 7" plate	32.00
Oil bottle, 5¾"	35.00
Pan, 6¾" x 10½", oblong, camelia	65.00
Pitcher, 13 oz., metal top	65.00
Pitcher, w/ice lip, 8", 64 oz.	135.00
Plate, 3", indiv. jelly	6.00
Plate, 6", bread/butter	6.00
Plate, 6½", finger bowl liner	8.00
Plate, 7", dessert	7.50
Plate, 8", mayonnaise liner, w/ring	8.00
Plate, 8", salad	10.00
Plate, 9½", dinner	40.00
Plate, 11½", hdld., service	40.00
Plate, 12", torte	45.00
Plate, 12", ice cream, rolled edge	60.00
Plate, 12", deviled egg	70.00
Plate, 13", salad dressing, w/ring	50.00
Plate, 13", service	50.00
Plate, 13", service, rolled edge	55.00
Plate, 13", cracker, w/ring	35.00
Plate, 16", lazy susan, w/turntable	115.00
Plate, 16", hostess	120.00
Relish, 5½", 2 pt., rnd., ring hdl.	16.00
Relish, 6", 2 pt., rnd., ring hdl.	17.00
Relish, 7", 2 pt., oval	20.00
Relish, 10", 4 pt., hdld.	25.00
Relish, 10", 3 pt., oblong	27.50
Relish, 10½", 3 pt., oblong	27.50
Relish, 12", 3 pt.	40.00
Salad dressing set: (2 ladles, 5" ftd. mayonnaise, 13" plate w/ring)	90.00

	Crystal
Salad dressing set: (2 ladles, 6" ftd. div. bowl, 8" plate w/ring)	75.00
Salt & pepper, 2½", w/glass tops, pr.	18.00
Salt & pepper, 2½", w/metal tops, pr.	18.00
Salt & pepper, 3¾", w/metal top (on 6" tray), 3 pc.	30.00
Saucer, 6", w/ring	4.00
Stem, 2½", 6 oz., ftd., fruit cup/jello	11.00
Stem, 2¾", 5 oz., ftd., oyster cocktail	15.00
Stem, 3½", 5 oz., sundae (flared rim)	12.00
Stem, 4¼", 3 oz., cocktail	15.00
Stem, 4¼", 5 oz., ice cream	12.50
Stem, 4¼", 3 oz., wine	20.00
Stem, 5¼", 4 oz., ftd., parfait	32.00
Stem, 5¼", 5 oz., champagne	20.00
Stem, 6", 9 oz., goblet	18.50
Sugar, 3¼", ftd., 9 oz.	8.00
Sugar, 5 oz.	7.50
Sugar (cheese) shaker, 13 oz., metal top	75.00
Tray, oval (for sugar/creamer)	10.00
Tray, 6" mint, rolled edge, w/ring hdl.	17.50
Tray, 7", oval, pickle	15.00
Tray, 7", mint, rolled edge, w/ring hdl.	22.00
Tray, 8", oval	18.00
Tray, 8", for oil/vinegar	20.00
Tray, 10", oval, celery	18.00
Tray, 12", fruit epergne	52.00
Tray, 12", ice cream, rolled edge	55.00
Tumbler, 3¾", 5 oz., ftd., juice	12.00
Tumbler, 4¾", 9 oz., ftd., water	14.00
Tumbler, 5¼", 13 oz., flat, iced tea	20.00
Tumbler, 5¼", 12 oz., ftd., iced tea	17.50
Urn, w/cover, 12", ftd.	175.00
Vase, 3", ftd., crimped	20.00
Vase, 3", ftd., flared rim	15.00
Vase, 4", hat shape	22.00
Vase, 4½", flat base, crimped	25.00
Vase, 5", ftd., flared rim	22.50
Vase, 5", ftd., crimped	45.00
Vase, 5", ftd., fan	45.00
Vase, 7½", epergne, threaded base	65.00
Vase, 10", ftd.	75.00

Colors: crystal, Zircon or Limelight green, Dawn

Limelight and Zircon are the same color. Zircon was originally made in 1937. In 1955, it was made again by Heisey, but called Limelight. Zircon prices are rising slower than in the past, but the keyword is rising. I have watched a Zircon Saturn comport, like the one pictured on the bottom row on page 184, sit in an antique mall for over four years. It would seem that a reduction in price might be a smart move in order to sell it. Crystal Saturn prices are remaining steady.

	Crystal	Zircon Limelight
Ash tray	10.00	150.00
Bitters bottle, w/short tube, blown	75.00	
Bowl, baked apple	25.00	100.00
Bowl, finger	15.00	65.00
Bowl, rose, lg.	40.00	
Bowl, 4½", nappy	15.00	
Bowl, 5", nappy	15.00	90.00
Bowl, 5", whipped cream	15.00	150.00
Bowl, 7", pickle	35.00	
Bowl, 9", 3 part, relish	20.00	
Bowl, 10", celery	15.00	
Bowl, 11", salad	40.00	140.00
Bowl, 12", fruit, flared rim	35.00	100.00
Bowl, 13", floral, rolled edge	37.00	
Bowl, 13", floral	37.00	
Candelabrum, w/"e" ball drops, 2-lite	175.00	500.00
Candle block, 2-lite	95.00	350.00
Candlestick, 3", ftd., 1-lite	30.00	500.00
Comport, 7"	50.00	550.00
Creamer	25.00	180.00
Cup	10.00	160.00
Hostess Set, 8 pc. (low bowl w/ftd. ctr. bowl, 3 toothpick holders & clips)	65.00	300.00
Marmalade, w/cover	45.00	500.00
Mayonnaise	8.00	80.00
Mustard, w/cover and paddle	60.00	350.00*

*Zircon $800.00 at recent **auction**

	Crystal	Zircon Limelight
Oil bottle, 3 oz.	55.00	650.00
Pitcher, 70 oz., w/ice lip, blown	65.00	500.00
Pitcher, juice	40.00	450.00
Plate, 6"	5.00	35.00
Plate, 7", bread	5.00	45.00
Plate, 8", luncheon	10.00	55.00
Plate, 13", torte	25.00	
Plate, 15", torte	30.00	
Salt & pepper, pr.	45.00	550.00
Saucer	5.00	40.00
Stem, 3 oz., cocktail	15.00	75.00
Stem, 4 oz., fruit cocktail or oyster cocktail, no ball in stem, ftd.	10.00	75.00
Stem, 4½ oz., sherbet	8.00	70.00
Stem, 5 oz., parfait	10.00	110.00
Stem, 6 oz., saucer champagne	10.00	95.00
Stem, 10 oz.	20.00	100.00
Sugar	25.00	180.00
Sugar shaker (pourer)	80.00	
Sugar, w/cover, no handles	25.00	
Tray, tidbit, 2 sides turned as fan	25.00	110.00
Tumbler, 5 oz., juice	8.00	80.00
Tumbler, 7 oz., old-fashioned	10.00	
Tumbler, 8 oz., old-fashioned	10.00	
Tumbler, 9 oz., luncheon	15.00	
Tumbler, 10 oz.	20.00	80.00
Tumbler, 12 oz., soda	20.00	85.00
Vase, violet	35.00	160.00
Vase, 8½", flared	55.00	225.00
Vase, 8½", straight	55.00	225.00
Vase, 10½"		260.00

Colors: amber, green

Seville might be the most overlooked Fostoria pattern in this book. For some reason it has never caught on with collectors in either green or amber. Take a good look at this. It is attractive, seventy plus years old, and Fostoria made — and they are no longer in business!

Seville would be an inexpensive Elegant pattern to collect despite there not being huge displays at shows or large advertisements listing it. Green would be easier to acquire than amber as you may note by the lack of amber in my photos. The butter dish, pitcher, grapefruit and liner, and sugar lid are all troublesome to find, but oh, so gratifying when you do run across them! They are costly items, but not as dear as those same pieces in other Fostoria patterns such as June or Versailles.

To distinguish between the bouillon and the cream soup with liners, the bouillon is shown in the right corner of the top picture and the cream soup is in the center. Collectors are telling me that bowls are becoming harder to find in this pattern; you might pick them up when you get the chance.

	Amber	Green
Ash tray, #2350, 4"	17.50	22.50
Bowl, #2350, fruit, 5½"	10.00	12.00
Bowl, #2350, cereal, 6½"	18.00	22.00
Bowl, #2350, soup, 7¾"	20.00	27.50
Bowl, #2315, low foot, 7"	18.00	22.00
Bowl, #2350, vegetable	22.00	27.50
Bowl, #2350, nappy, 9"	30.00	37.50
Bowl, #2350, oval, baker, 9"	25.00	30.00
Bowl, #2315, flared, 10½", ftd.	25.00	30.00
Bowl, #2350, oval, baker, 10½"	35.00	40.00
Bowl, 10", ftd.	35.00	42.50
Bowl, #2350, salad, 10"	30.00	35.00
Bowl, #2329, rolled edge, console, 11"	27.50	40.00
Bowl, #2297, deep, flared, 12"	30.00	32.50
Bowl, #2371, oval, console, 13"	35.00	40.00
Bowl, #2329, rolled edge, console, 13"	32.00	40.00
Bowl, #2350, bouillon, flat	13.50	16.00
Bowl, #2350½, bouillon, ftd.	14.00	16.00
Bowl, #2350, cream soup, flat	14.50	17.50
Bowl, #2350½, cream soup, ftd.	15.50	17.50
Bowl, #869/2283, finger, w/6" liner	22.00	30.00
Butter, w/cover, #2350, round	195.00	250.00
Candlestick, #2324, 2"	18.00	22.00
Candlestick, #2324, 4"	16.00	22.00
Candlestick, #2324, 9"	45.00	50.00
Candy jar, w/cover, #2250, ½ lb., ftd.	95.00	120.00
Candy jar, w/cover, #2331, 3 pt., flat	65.00	85.00
Celery, #2350, 11"	15.00	17.50
Cheese and cracker, #2368 (11" plate)	40.00	45.00
Comport, #2327, 7½", (twisted stem)	20.00	25.00
Comport, #2350, 8"	27.50	35.00
Creamer, #2315½, flat, ftd.	13.50	15.00

	Amber	Green
Creamer, #2350½, ftd.	12.50	13.50
Cup, #2350, after dinner	25.00	30.00
Cup, #2350, flat	10.00	12.50
Cup, #2350½, ftd.	10.00	12.50
Egg cup, #2350	30.00	35.00
Grapefruit, #945½, blown	45.00	50.00
Grapefruit, #945½, liner, blown	35.00	40.00
Grapefruit, #2315, molded	25.00	32.00
Ice bucket, #2378	55.00	65.00
Pickle, #2350, 8"	13.50	15.00
Pitcher, #5084, ftd.	250.00	295.00
Plate, #2350, bread and butter, 6"	3.50	4.00
Plate, #2350, salad, 7½"	5.00	5.50
Plate, #2350, luncheon, 8½"	6.00	6.50
Plate, #2321, Maj Jongg (canape), 8¾"	35.00	40.00
Plate, #2350, sm. dinner, 9½"	12.00	13.50
Plate, #2350, dinner, 10½"	35.00	45.00
Plate, #2350, chop, 13¾"	30.00	35.00
Plate, #2350, round, 15"	45.00	50.00
Plate, #2350, cream soup liner	5.00	6.00
Platter, #2350, 10½"	30.00	35.00
Platter, #2350, 12"	40.00	50.00
Platter, #2350, 15"	75.00	95.00
Salt and pepper shaker, #5100, pr.	60.00	65.00
Sauce boat liner, #2350	25.00	30.00
Sauce boat, #2350	55.00	75.00
Saucer, #2350	3.00	3.00
Saucer, after dinner, #2350	5.00	5.00
Stem, #870, cocktail	15.00	16.00
Stem, #870, cordial	65.00	70.00
Stem, #870, high sherbet	18.00	18.00
Stem, #870, low sherbet	14.00	15.00
Stem, #870, oyster cocktail	16.50	17.50
Stem, #870, parfait	30.00	35.00
Stem, #870, water	22.00	24.00
Stem, #870, wine	25.00	28.00
Sugar cover, #2350½	80.00	110.00
Sugar, fat, ftd., #2315	13.50	14.50
Sugar, ftd., #2350½	12.50	13.50
Tray, 11", center handled, #2287	27.50	30.00
Tumbler, #5084, ftd., 2 oz.	35.00	40.00
Tumbler, #5084, ftd., 5 oz.	13.50	15.00
Tumbler, #5084, ftd., 9 oz.	15.00	16.50
Tumbler, #5084, ftd., 12 oz.	18.00	20.00
Urn, small, #2324	75.00	100.00
Vase, #2292, 8"	60.00	75.00

"SPIRAL FLUTES," Duncan & Miller Glass Company, introduced 1924

Colors: amber, green, pink, crystal

"Spiral Flutes" is a Duncan & Miller pattern that has been readily identified by collectors. Many Duncan & Miller patterns have suffered from lack of exposure due to limited books on that company. "Spiral Flutes" reminds many collectors of Depression glass rather than an Elegant pattern. Some pieces are sporadically found, specifically the 6¾" flanged bowls, 7 oz. footed tumblers, and 7½" plates; after that, there is little found easily. Green can be gathered more quickly than any other color. Amber and crystal sets may be rounded up, but few collectors are presently attempting them! I have seen few two-tone (amber/crystal) pieces like the comport in front of the picture. If you spot others, let me know.

	Amber Green Pink
Bowl, 2", almond	13.00
Bowl, 3¾", bouillon	15.00
Bowl, 4⅜", finger	7.00
Bowl, 4¾", ftd., cream soup	15.00
Bowl, 4" w., mayonnaise	17.50
Bowl, 5", nappy	6.00
Bowl, 6½", cereal, sm. flange	32.50
Bowl, 6¾", grapefruit	7.50
Bowl, 6", handled nappy	22.00
Bowl, 6", handled nappy, w/cover	85.00
Bowl, 7", nappy	15.00
Bowl, 7½", flanged (baked apple)	22.50
Bowl, 8", nappy	17.50
Bowl, 8½", flanged (oyster plate)	22.50
Bowl, 9", nappy	27.50
Bowl, 10", oval, veg., two styles	45.00
Bowl, 10½", lily pond	40.00
Bowl, 11¾" w. x 3¾" t., console, flared	30.00
Bowl, 11", nappy	30.00
Bowl, 12", cupped console	30.00

	Amber Green Pink
Candle, 3½"	20.00
Candle, 7½"	55.00
Candle, 9½"	85.00
Candle, 11½"	125.00
Celery, 10¾" x 4¾"	17.50
* Chocolate jar, w/cover	295.00
Cigarette holder, 4"	35.00
Comport, 4⅜"	15.00
Comport, 6⅝"	17.50
Comport, 9", low ft., flared	55.00
Console stand, 1½" h. x 4⅝" w.	12.00
Creamer, oval	8.00
Cup	9.00
Cup, demi	25.00
* Fernery, 10" x 5½", 4 ftd., flower box	395.00
Grapefruit, ftd.	20.00
Ice tub, handled	60.00
Lamp, 10½", countess	295.00
Mug, 6½", 9 oz., handled	28.00
Mug, 7", 9 oz., handled	36.00
Oil, w/stopper, 6 oz.	195.00
Pickle, 8⅝"	12.00
Pitcher, ½ gal.	175.00
Plate, 6", pie	3.00
Plate, 7½", salad	4.00
Plate, 8⅜", luncheon	4.00
Plate, 10⅜", dinner	22.50
Plate, 13⅝", torte	27.50
Plate, w/star, 6" (fingerbowl item)	6.00
Platter, 11"	35.00
Platter, 13"	50.00

*Crystal, $135.00

	Amber Green Pink
Relish, 10" x 7⅜", oval, 3 pc. (2 inserts)	100.00
Saucer	3.00
Saucer, demi	5.00
Seafood sauce cup, 3" w. x 2½" h.	25.00
Stem, 3¾", 3½ oz., wine	17.50
Stem, 3¾", 5 oz., low sherbet	8.00
Stem, 4¾", 6 oz., tall sherbet	12.00
Stem, 5⅝", 4½ oz., parfait	17.50
Stem, 6¼", 7 oz., water	17.50
Sugar, oval	8.00
Sweetmeat, w/cover, 7½"	115.00

	Amber Green Pink
Tumbler, 3⅜", ftd., 2½ oz., cocktail (no stem)	7.00
Tumbler, 4¼", 8 oz., flat	30.00
Tumbler, 4⅜", ftd., 5½ oz., juice (no stem)	14.00
Tumbler, 4¾", 7 oz., flat, soda	35.00
Tumbler, 5⅛", ftd., 7 oz., water (1 knob)	8.00
Tumbler, 5⅛", ftd., 9 oz., water (no stem)	20.00
Tumbler, 5½", 11 oz., ginger ale	70.00
Vase, 6½"	20.00
Vase, 8½"	30.00
Vase, 10½"	40.00

Colors: crystal, some blown stemware in Zircon

Heisey's Stanhope is an additional pattern kept active by Deco collectors! As with New Era, there continues to be competition for this! Notice that prices have ballooned except for stemware!

"T" knobs, in the price listings, are insert handles (black or red, round, wooden knobs) which are like wooden dowel rods that act as horizontal handles. The insert handles are whimsical to some; but others think them magnificent! Selling Stanhope pieces with missing inserts is a difficult job at best. Even collectors who despise them will seldom buy with the colored knobs missing. I had a devil of a time selling that rare candy in the photo below since it was missing the insert.

Some people mistake the salad bowl shown at the bottom of page 190 for a punch bowl; it would not hold much punch!

	Crystal
Ash tray, indiv.	25.00
Bottle, oil, 3 oz. w or w/o rd. knob	325.00
Bowl, 6" mint, 2 hdld., w or w/o rd. knobs	35.00
Bowl, 6" mint, 2 pt., 2 hdld., w or w/o rd. knobs	35.00
Bowl, 11", salad	90.00
Bowl, finger, #4080 (blown, plain)	10.00
Bowl, floral, 11", 2 hdld., w or w/o "T" knobs	80.00
Candelabra, 2-lite, w bobeche & prisms	180.00
Candy box & lid, rnd., w or w/o rd. knob	180.00
Cigarette box & lid, w or w/o rd. knob	65.00
Creamer, 2 hdld., w or w/o rd. knobs	45.00
Cup, w or w/o rd. knob.	25.00
Ice tub, 2 hdld., w or w/o "T" knobs	70.00
Jelly, 6", 1 hdld., w or w/o rd. knobs	25.00
Jelly, 6", 3 pt., 1 hdld., w or w/o rd. knobs	25.00
Nappy, 4½", 1 hdld., w or w/o rd. knob	25.00
Nut, indiv., 1 hdld., w or w/o rd. knob	40.00
Plate, 7"	20.00

	Crystal
Plate, 12" torte, 2 hdld., w or w/o "T" knobs	35.00
Plate, 15" torte, rnd. or salad liner	45.00
Relish, 11" triplex buffet, 2 hdld., w or w/o "T" knobs	35.00
Relish, 12", 4 pt., 2 hdld., w or w/o "T" knobs	55.00
Relish, 12", 5 pt., 2 hdld., w or w/o "T" knobs	55.00
Salt & pepper, #60 top	100.00
Saucer	10.00
Stem, 1 oz., cordial, #4083 (blown)	70.00
Stem, 2½ oz., pressed wine	35.00
Stem, 2½ oz., wine, #4083	25.00
Stem, 3½ oz., cocktail, #4083	20.00
Stem, 3½ oz., pressed cocktail	25.00
Stem, 4 oz., claret, #4083	25.00
Stem, 4 oz., oyster cocktail, #4083	10.00
Stem, 5½ oz., pressed saucer champagne	20.00
Stem, 5½ oz., saucer champagne, #4083	15.00
Stem, 9 oz., pressed goblet	45.00
Stem, 10 oz., goblet, #4083	22.50
Stem, 12 oz., pressed soda	45.00
Sugar, 2 hdld., w or w/o rd. knobs	45.00
Tray, 12" celery, 2 hdld., w or w/o "T" knobs	55.00
Tumbler, 5 oz., soda, #4083	20.00
Tumbler, 8 oz., soda, #4083	22.50
Tumbler, 12 oz., soda, #4083	25.00
Vase, 7", ball	100.00
Vase, 9", 2 hdld., w or w/o "T" knobs	85.00

Colors: crystal, red, blue, green, yellow

There are extra listings for Fostoria's Sun Ray included since several readers have been kind enough to send them! Pricing is still arduous due to the disparity of prices I have seen. I only price crystal; but be aware of pieces found in red, blue, green, and yellow. I rarely see Sun Ray in colors; so, I doubt that you could buy a set in color. A few colored pieces among your crystal would probably add to its charm.

I need to point out the fourth item in Row 4. It is not Sun Ray although it may be difficult to determine from the angle it is pictured. This shows that there are similar patterns that could blend with Sun Ray or drive you to distraction if you are a purist. The cream soup is tab handled (first item in Row 4). By putting a lid on the cream soup (last item Row 5), it becomes an onion soup according to Fostoria's catalogs. The condiment tray with cruets and mustards in Row 5 is shaped like a cloverleaf similar to the one in American. It is seemingly more unusual than the American one, but not as many collectors are seeking it!

Notice the two tumblers on the left in Row 1. One has frosted panels and the other is clear. Pieces with frosted panels were given a separate designation of Glacier by Fostoria. Some Sun Ray enthusiasts are willing to mix the two, but most gather one or the other. Both patterns sell in the same price range.

	Crystal		Crystal
Almond, ftd., ind.	12.00	Pitcher, 64 oz., ice lip	215.00
Ash tray, ind., 2510½	8.00	Plate, 6"	8.00
Ash tray, square	10.00	Plate, 7½"	8.00
Bonbon, hdld.	16.00	Plate, 8½"	12.00
Bonbon. 3 toed	17.50	Plate, 9½"	28.00
Bowl, 5", fruit	8.00	Plate, 11", torte	35.00
Bowl, 9½", flared	30.00	Plate, 12", sandwich	35.00
Bowl, 12", salad	35.00	Plate, 15", torte	65.00
Bowl, 13", rolled edge	40.00	Plate, 16"	70.00
Bowl, custard, 2¼", high	12.00	Relish, 2 part	16.00
Bowl, hdld.	35.00	Relish, 3 part	20.00
Butter, w/lid, ¼ lb.	25.00	Relish, 4 part	22.00
Candelabra, 2-lite	45.00	Salt dip	10.00
Candlestick, 3"	18.00	Saucer	3.00
Candlestick, 5½"	25.00	Shaker, 4", pr.	45.00
Candlestick, duo	60.00	Shaker, individual, 2¼", #2510½	15.00
Candy jar, w/cover	45.00	Stem, 3½", 5½ oz., sherbet, low	12.00
Celery, hdld.	25.00	Stem, 3¼", 3½ oz., fruit cocktail	12.00
Cigarette and cover	22.00	Stem, 3", 4 oz., cocktail, ftd.	12.00
Cigarette box, oblong	25.00	Stem, 4⅞", 4½ oz., claret	25.00
Coaster, 4"	6.00	Stem, 5¾", 9 oz., goblet	16.00
Comport	25.00	Sugar, ftd.	12.00
Cream soup	25.00	Sugar, individual	12.00
Cream soup liner	8.00	Sweetmeat, hdld., divided	30.00
Cream, ftd.	12.00	Tray, 6½", ind sug/cream	10.00
Cream, individual	12.00	Tray, 10½", oblong	30.00
Cup	12.00	Tray, 10", square	35.00
Decanter, w/stopper, 18 oz.	45.00	Tray, condiment, 8½"	40.00
Decanter, w/stopper, oblong, 26 oz.	70.00	Tray, oval hdld.	25.00
Ice bucket, no handle	45.00	Tumbler, 2¼", 2 oz., whiskey, #2510½	12.00
Ice bucket, w/handle	50.00	Tumbler, 3½", 5 oz., juice, #2510½	12.50
Jelly	16.00	Tumbler, 3½", 6 oz., old fashion, #2510½	14.00
Jelly, w/cover	45.00	Tumbler, 4⅛", 9 oz., table, #2510½	13.00
Mayonnaise, w/liner, ladle	35.00	Tumbler, 4¾", 9 oz., ftd. table	14.00
Mustard, w/cover, spoon	45.00	Tumbler, 4⅝", 5 oz., ftd. juice	15.00
Nappy, hdld., flared	13.00	Tumbler, 5¼", 13 oz., ftd. tea	18.00
Nappy, hdld., reg.	12.00	Tumbler, 5⅛", 13 oz., tea, #2510½	22.00
Nappy, hdld., square	14.00	Vase, 3½", rose bowl	22.00
Nappy, hdld., tri-corner	15.00	Vase, 5", rose bowl	30.00
Oil bottle, w/stopper, 3 oz.	32.00	Vase, 6", crimped	37.50
Onion soup, w/cover	40.00	Vase, 7"	50.00
Pickle, hdld.	22.00	Vase, 9", sq. ftd.	55.00
Pitcher, 16 oz., cereal	40.00	Vase, sweet pea	65.00
Pitcher, 64 oz.	65.00		

Colors: pink, green, blue, crystal

Sunrise Medallion (Morgantown's etching #758) at one time had been dubbed "Dancing Girl" by collectors. Familiar names are hard to vanquish; however, more new collectors are embracing the Sunrise Medallion name.

One major problem for researchers is that catalog measurements were frequently recorded in ounces, not heights. Most measurements for height in this book come from physically measuring the item, Those twisted stem items (#7642½) are slightly taller than their plain stem (#7630) counterparts. Measurements listed here are mainly from the #7630 line that I find more often than the twisted one. Twisted blue and crystal champagnes and waters are the only #7642½ stems I have found. If you have others, I would appreciate having measurements.

Blue is the favorite color of collectors, but that is true in almost all patterns. Pink and crystal turn up occasionally and are not as expensive. Green seems to be rare with only a few pieces turning up. I have only owned a green sugar and 10" vase, and I have seen a picture of the creamer; but it was not for sale.

Two different styled oyster cocktails, which look more like a bar tumbler to me, are pictured in the foreground of the lower photo. These measure 2⁷⁄₁₆" to 2⁹⁄₁₆" tall. I had six and they varied from a little over to a little under four ounces.

The cordials regularly turn up in crystal, but only a few blue ones have been seen. I have never seen a twisted stem cordial.

	Crystal	Blue	Pink Green
Bowl, finger, ftd.		85.00	
Creamer		325.00	275.00
Cup	40.00	100.00	80.00
Parfait, 5 oz.	55.00	110.00	80.00
Pitcher		595.00	
Plate, 5⅞", sherbet	6.00	12.50	10.00
Plate, 7½", salad	10.00	25.00	20.00
Plate, 8⅜"	12.50	30.00	22.50
Saucer	15.00	22.50	17.50
Sherbet, cone	20.00		
Stem, 1½ oz., cordial	110.00	375.00	225.00
Stem, 2½ oz., wine	45.00	85.00	55.00
Stem, 6¼", 7 oz., champagne (twist stem, 6¾")	25.00	40.00	30.00
Stem, 6⅛", cocktail	30.00	55.00	40.00
Stem, 7¾", 9 oz., water (twist stem, 8¼")	35.00	65.00	45.00
Sugar		300.00	250.00
Tumbler, 2½", 4 oz, ftd.	25.00	150.00	
Tumbler, 3½", 4 oz., ftd.			35.00
Tumbler, 4¼", 5 oz., ftd.	45.00	50.00	35.00
Tumbler, 4¼", flat	20.00		
Tumbler, 4¾", 9 oz., ftd.	20.00	55.00	40.00
Tumbler, 5½", 11 oz., ftd.	35.00	85.00	65.00
Tumbler, 5½", flat	25.00		
Vase, 6" tall, 5" wide			395.00
Vase, 10", slender, bud	65.00	400.00	295.00
Vase, 10", bulbous bottom			350.00

Colors: amber, Carmen, crystal, Forest Green, Royal Blue

Tally Ho is a rather large Cambridge pattern that has been represented in this book by Imperial Hunt Scene and a few additional etched patterns including Rose Point, Elaine, and Valencia. For purposes of identification, the heavy pressed one-color stems are listed as goblets in the listing below and the tall crystal stems with colored bowls are listed as stems.

Ice buckets seem to be plentiful in all colors or I seem to run into them quite often as evidenced by the photo. Crystal punch bowl sets can be found with cups and ladles with colored handles as well as all crystal.

	amber crystal	Carmen Royal	Forest Green
Ash tray, 4"	12.50	22.50	18.00
Ash tray, 4" w/ctr. hdld.	17.50	27.50	25.00
Ash well, 2 pc. ctr. hdld.	20.00	35.00	30.00
Bowl, 4½" ftd. fruit/sherbet	12.50	22.50	20.00
Bowl, 5", frappe cocktail 10 side rim	17.50	27.50	25.00
Bowl, 6" ftd. iced fruit, 10 side rim	25.00	40.00	35.00
Bowl, 6" iced fruit, 10 side rim	25.00	40.00	35.00
Bowl, 6", 2 hdld.	17.50	27.50	25.00
Bowl, 6", 2 hdld. nappy	17.50	27.50	25.00
Bowl, 6½" grapefruit, flat rim	20.00	35.00	30.00
Bowl, 6½", 2 hdld.	20.00	35.00	30.00
Bowl, 7" fruit, 10 side rim	20.00	35.00	30.00
Bowl, 8"	25.00	40.00	35.00
Bowl, 8½", 3 comp.	45.00	70.00	65.00
Bowl, 9"	45.00	70.00	65.00
Bowl, 9" pan	45.00	70.00	65.00

	amber crystal	Carmen Royal	Forest Green
Bowl, 10" pan	55.00	80.00	75.00
Bowl, 10½", belled	55.00	80.00	75.00
Bowl, 10½", 2 comp. salad	55.00	90.00	75.00
Bowl, 10½", 2 hdld.	55.00	90.00	75.00
Bowl, 10½", 3 comp.	55.00	90.00	75.00
Bowl, 10½", low ft.	65.00	105.00	85.00
Bowl, 11", flat, flared	55.00	80.00	75.00
Bowl, 12" oval celery	25.00	40.00	35.00
Bowl, 12" pan	65.00	100.00	85.00
Bowl, 12½" flat rim	65.00	110.00	95.00
Bowl, 12½", belled	60.00	85.00	75.00
Bowl, 13" ftd. punch	195.00	350.00	250.00
Bowl, 13½" salad bowl, flared	55.00	80.00	75.00
Bowl, 17" pan	125.00	195.00	175.00
Bowl, 2 comp. 2 ladle salad dressing, flared	40.00	100.00	65.00
Bowl, 2 comp. 2 ladle, salad dressing, rnd.	40.00	100.00	65.00

	amber crystal	Carmen Royal	Forest Green		amber crystal	Carmen Royal	Forest Green
Bowl, 2 ladle, spouted salad dressing	40.00	100.00	65.00	Plate, 7", 2 hdld.	20.00	30.00	25.00
Bowl, finger	17.50	27.50	25.00	Plate, 7½" salad	12.50	20.00	17.50
Bowl, sauce boat	25.00	40.00	35.00	Plate, 8" salad	15.00	20.00	18.00
Candelabrum, 6½" w/bobeche & prism	80.00	145.00	125.00	Plate, 9½" lunch	45.00	65.00	45.00
Candlestick, 5"	25.00	40.00	35.00	Plate, 10½" dinner	45.00		
Candlestick, 6"	30.00	45.00	40.00	Plate, 11½" 2 hdld. sandwich	55.00	95.00	75.00
Candlestick, 6½"	40.00	55.00	50.00	Plate, 13½" raised edge	65.00	105.00	85.00
Cheese & cracker, 11½", 2 hdld	85.00	135.00	115.00	Plate, 14" chop	65.00	105.00	85.00
Cheese & cracker, 13½"	95.00	145.00	125.00	Plate, 14" w/4" seat in center	65.00	105.00	85.00
Cheese & cracker, 17½"	120.00	165.00	125.00	Plate, 17½" Sunday Nite Supper	65.00	100.00	85.00
Cheese & cracker, 18"	120.00	175.00	165.00	Plate, 17½"	85.00	125.00	115.00
Coaster, 4"	12.50	22.50	18.00	Plate, 18" w/4" seat in center	65.00	125.00	115.00
Cocktail shaker, 50 oz. ftd., chrome top	95.00	195.00	135.00	Plate, 18", buffet lunch	65.00	125.00	115.00
Cocktail shaker, hdld., ftd., chrome top	95.00	225.00	135.00	Plate, 18", ftd. week end supper	65.00	100.00	85.00
Comport, tall frappe cocktail, 10 side rim	45.00	70.00	65.00	Plate, finger bowl	10.00	15.00	12.50
Comport, 4½" tall	17.50	27.50	25.00	Plate, salad dressing liner	12.50	20.00	17.50
Comport, 6" tall ft., flat mint	40.00	55.00	50.00	Plate, sauce boat liner	12.50	20.00	17.50
Comport, 6½" tall ft., raised edge	40.00	55.00	50.00	Relish, 6", 2 comp. 2 hdld.	25.00	35.00	30.00
Comport, 7", low ft.	40.00	55.00	50.00	Relish, 8", 2 hdld., 3 comp.	40.00	55.00	50.00
Comport, 8", low ft.	45.00	70.00	65.00	Relish, 10", 4 comp.	45.00	75.00	65.00
Comport, 9", low ft. raised edge	55.00	80.00	75.00	Saucer	5.00	12.50	10.00
Comport, low ft. mint	17.50	27.50	25.00	Shaker, w/glass top	25.00	50.00	35.00
Cookie Jar w/lid, chrome hdld. (ice pail w/lid)	85.00	160.00	135.00	Stem, 1 oz. "T" stem cordial	65.00	120.00	95.00
Creamer, ftd.	12.50	27.50	20.00	Stem, 2½ oz., high stem wine	40.00	65.00	50.00
Cup, 2½ oz. hdld. whiskey	12.50	27.50	20.00	Stem, 3 oz. ftd. tumbler	12.50	20.00	17.50
Cup, ftd.	10.00	20.00	17.50	Stem, 3 oz., high stem cocktail	17.50	32.50	27.50
Cup, punch, flat	10.00	20.00	17.50	Stem, 4 oz. low stem cocktail	15.00	25.00	20.00
Cup, punch, ftd.	12.50	20.00	15.00	Stem, 4½ oz. low sherbet	12.50	20.00	17.50
Decanter, 34 oz.	85.00	165.00	145.00	Stem, 4½ oz., high stem claret			
Decanter, 34 oz. hdld.	95.00	195.00	155.00	Stem, 5 oz. ftd. tumbler	12.50	20.00	17.50
Goblet, brandy inhaler	40.00	65.00	50.00	Stem, 5 oz. low stem juice	15.00	25.00	20.00
Goblet, claret	35.00	45.00	40.00	Stem, 6 oz. high stem juice			
Goblet, cocktail	14.00	24.00	16.00	Stem, 6½ oz. low stem sherbet	15.00	25.00	20.00
Goblet, cordial	40.00	65.00	50.00	Stem, 7½ oz. high sherb.	20.00	50.00	30.00
Goblet, goblet	20.00	35.00	30.00	Stem, 10 oz., high stem	35.00	75.00	50.00
Goblet, low ft. brandy inhaler	40.00	65.00	50.00	Stem, 10 oz., low stem lunch	40.00	65.00	50.00
Goblet, low sherbet	12.50	20.00	17.50	Stem, 12 oz., ftd. tumbler	17.50	32.50	27.50
Goblet, oyster cocktail	17.50	32.50	27.50	Stem, 14 oz., high stem	40.00	65.00	50.00
Goblet, tall sherbet	15.00	25.00	20.00	Stem, 16 oz., ftd. tumbler	40.00	65.00	50.00
Goblet, wine	25.00	50.00 – 55.00	40.00	Stem, 18 oz., tall stem	35.00	70.00	60.00
Ice pail, chrome hdld.	65.00	120.00	95.00	Sugar, ftd.	12.50	27.50	20.00
Jug, 74 oz. tankard, flat bottom	125.00	225.00	195.00	Top Hat, 10"	150.00	295.00	225.00
Jug, 88 oz., rnd. bottom	145.00	295.00	235.00	Tumbler, 2½ oz.	17.50	32.50	27.50
Mug, 12 oz. hdld. stein	25.00	40.00	35.00	Tumbler, 5 oz.	12.50	20.00	17.50
Mug, 14 oz. hdld. stein, rnd. bottom	30.00	50.00	35.00	Tumbler, 7 oz. old fashioned	15.00	25.00	20.00
Mug, 6 oz. punch	12.50	25.00	15.00	Tumbler, 10 oz., short	15.00	25.00	20.00
Plate, 6" bread & butter	10.00	15.00	12.50	Tumbler, 10 oz., tall	17.50	32.50	27.50
				Tumbler, 14 oz. rnd. bottom	17.50	32.50	27.50
				Tumbler, 15 oz.	20.00	35.00	30.00
				Vase, 12" ftd.	95.00	195.00	155.00

Colors: crystal

As with Duncan's Sandwich, Tear Drop stemware is obtainable and priced economically enough that you could use it today without buying today's expensive stems! Tear Drop was heavily used by those who owned it; so, mint condition dinner plates and additional serving pieces are not easily located. This is an excellent starting point for those looking for an easily found and reasonably priced Elegant pattern.

Colored pieces pictured may have been produced at Tiffin from Duncan moulds. Reprints of original Duncan catalogs showing stemware and tumblers can be found in earlier editions of this book.

	Crystal
Ash tray, 3", indiv.	6.00
Ash tray, 5"	8.00
Bonbon, 6", 4 hdld.	12.00
Bottle, w/stopper, 12", bar	155.00
Bowl, 4¼", finger	7.00
Bowl, 5", fruit nappy	6.00
Bowl, 5", 2 hdld., nappy	8.00
Bowl, 6", dessert, nappy	6.00
Bowl, 6", fruit, nappy	6.00
Bowl, 7", fruit, nappy	7.00
Bowl, 7", 2 hdld., nappy	10.00
Bowl, 8" x 12", oval, flower	50.00
Bowl, 9", salad	27.50
Bowl, 9", 2 hdld., nappy	22.50
Bowl, 10", crimped console, 2 hdld.	30.00
Bowl, 10", flared, fruit	27.50
Bowl, 11½", crimped, flower	32.50
Bowl, 11½", flared, flower	30.00
Bowl, 12", salad	40.00
Bowl, 12", crimped, low foot	40.00
Bowl, 12", ftd., flower	50.00
Bowl, 12", sq., 4 hdld.	45.00
Bowl, 13", gardenia	35.00
Bowl, 15½", 2½ gal., punch	110.00
Butter, w/cover, ¼ lb., 2 hdld.	22.00
Cake salver, 13", ftd.	50.00
Canape set (6" plate w/ring, 4 oz., ftd., cocktail)	30.00
Candlestick, 4"	9.00
Candlestick, 7", 2-lite, ball loop ctr.	28.00
Candlestick, 7", lg. ball ctr. w/bobeches, prisms	110.00
Candy basket, 5½" x 7½", 2 hdld., oval	85.00
Candy box, w/cover, 7", 2 pt., 2 hdld.	65.00
Candy box, w/cover, 8", 3 pt., 3 hdld.	70.00
Candy dish, 7½", heart shape	25.00
Celery, 11", 2 hdld.	15.00
Celery, 11", 2 pt., 2 hdld.	18.00
Celery, 12", 3 pt.	20.00
Cheese & cracker (3½" comport, 11" 2 hdld. plate)	45.00

	Crystal
Coaster/ashtray, 3", rolled edge	7.00
Comport, 4¾", ftd.	12.00
Comport, 6", low foot., hdld.	15.00
Condiment set, 5 pc. (salt/pepper, 2 3 oz. cruets, 9", 2 hdld. tray)	125.00
Creamer, 3 oz.	5.00
Creamer, 6 oz.	6.00
Creamer, 8 oz.	8.00
Cup, 2½ oz., demi	10.00
Cup, 6 oz., tea	6.00
Flower basket, 12", loop hdl.	135.00
Ice bucket, 5½"	70.00
Marmalade, w/cover, 4"	35.00
Mayonnaise, 4½" (2 hdld. bowl, ladle, 6" plate)	40.00
Mayonnaise set, 3 pc. (4½" bowl, ladle, 8" hdld. plate)	40.00
Mustard jar, w/cover, 4¼"	35.00
Nut dish, 6", 2 pt.	11.00
Oil bottle, 3 oz.	20.00
Olive dish, 4¼", 2 hdld., oval	15.00
Olive dish, 6", 2 pt.	15.00
Pickle dish, 6"	15.00
Pitcher, 5", 16 oz., milk	55.00
Pitcher, 8½", 64 oz., w/ice lip	120.00
Plate, 6", bread/butter	4.00
Plate, 6", canape	10.00
Plate, 7", 2 hdld., lemon	12.50
Plate, 7½", salad	5.00
Plate, 8½", luncheon	7.00
Plate, 10½", dinner	40.00
Plate, 11", 2 hdld.	27.50
Plate, 13", 4 hdld.	25.00
Plate, 13", salad liner, rolled edge	27.50
Plate, 13", torte, rolled edge	30.00
Plate, 14", torte	35.00
Plate, 14", torte, rolled edge	35.00
Plate, 16", torte, rolled edge	37.50
Plate, 18", lazy susan	90.00
Plate, 18", punch liner, rolled edge	60.00

	Crystal		Crystal
Relish, 7", 2 pt., 2 hdld.	15.00	Sugar, 8 oz.	8.00
Relish, 7½", 2 pt., heart shape	20.00	Sweetmeat, 5½", star shape, 2 hdld.	35.00
Relish, 9", 3 pt., 3 hdld.	30.00	Sweetmeat, 6½", ctr. hdld.	35.00
Relish, 11", 3 pt., 2 hdld.	30.00	Sweetmeat, 7", star shape, 2 hdld.	40.00
Relish, 12", 3 pt.	27.50	Tray, 5½", ctr. hdld. (for mustard jar)	11.00
Relish, 12", 5 pt., rnd.	30.00	Tray, 6", 2 hdld. (for salt/pepper)	10.00
Relish, 12", 6 pt., rnd.	30.00	Tray, 7¾", ctr. hdld. (for cruets)	12.50
Relish, 12", sq., 4 pt., 4 hdld.	27.50	Tray, 8", 2 hdld. (for oil/vinegar)	12.50
Salad set, 6" (compote, 11", hdld. plate)	37.50	Tray, 8", 2 hdld. (for sugar/creamer)	7.50
Salad set, 9" (2 pt. bowl, 13" rolled edge plate)	75.00	Tray, 10", 2 hdld (for sugar/creamer)	8.00
		Tumbler, 2¼", 2 oz., flat, whiskey	18.00
Salt & pepper, 5"	25.00	Tumbler, 2¼", 2 oz., ftd., whiskey	14.00
Saucer, 4½", demi	3.00	Tumbler, 3", 3 oz., ftd., whiskey	14.00
Saucer, 6"	1.50	Tumbler, 3¼", 3½ oz., flat, juice	6.00
Stem, 2½", 5 oz., ftd., sherbet	5.00	Tumbler, 3¼", 7 oz., flat, old-fashioned	12.00
Stem, 2¾", 3½ oz., ftd., oyster cocktail	7.50	Tumbler, 3½", 5 oz., flat, juice	6.00
Stem, 3½", 5 oz., sherbet	6.00	Tumbler, 4", 4½ oz., ftd., juice	8.00
Stem, 4", 1 oz., cordial	32.00	Tumbler, 4¼", 9 oz., flat	8.00
Stem, 4½", 1¾ oz., sherry	32.00	Tumbler, 4½", 8 oz., flat, split	8.00
Stem, 4½", 3½ oz., cocktail	15.00	Tumbler, 4½", 9 oz., ftd.	8.00
Stem, 4¾", 3 oz., wine	18.00	Tumbler, 4¾", 10 oz., flat, hi-ball	11.00
Stem, 5", 5 oz., champagne	10.00	Tumbler, 5", 8 oz., ftd., party	9.00
Stem, 5½", 4 oz., claret	20.00	Tumbler, 5¼", 12 oz., flat, iced tea	15.00
Stem, 5¾", 9 oz.	10.00	Tumbler, 5¾", 14 oz., flat, hi-ball	17.50
Stem, 6¼", 8 oz., ale	15.00	Tumbler, 6", 14 oz., iced tea	17.50
Stem, 7", 9 oz.	14.00	Urn, w/cover, 9", ftd.	135.00
Sugar, 3 oz.	5.00	Vase, 9", ftd., fan	30.00
Sugar, 6 oz.	6.00	Vase, 9", ftd., round	37.50

Washington. Pa. 1-1-43

THE DUNCAN & MILLER GLASS CO.

TERRACE, No. 111, Duncan & Miller Glass Company, 1937

Color: crystal, amber, cobalt, red

Terrace is another Duncan pattern that has been ignored over the years by collectors due to limited distribution and lack of information. I have bought at least 90% of the items pictured within fifty miles of Washington, Pennsylvania, where it was produced. From what collectors have told me, I doubt if much of this pattern was ever sold west of the Mississippi. The majority of Terrace collectors seek red and cobalt blue. Little amber is available and those wanting crystal usually look for First Love or some other etching rather than Terrace itself. Finding enough colored Terrace to photograph has been difficult; I have labored to accumulate what you see.

Note the crystal bowls with cobalt bases. Learn to recognize that base pattern so you do not pass one of these. I am sure food was seen better in that crystal top than in blue or red.

Item	Crystal Amber	Cobalt Red
Ash tray, 3½", sq.	17.50	30.00
Ash tray, 4¾", sq.	22.00	95.00
Bowl, 4¼", finger, #5111½	35.00	40.00
Bowl, 6¾" x 4¼", ftd., flared rim	30.00	
Bowl, 8" sq. x 2½", hdld.	55.00	
Bowl, 9" x 4½", ftd.	42.00	
Bowl, 9½" x 2½", hdld.	45.00	
Bowl, 10" x 3¾", ftd., flared rim	55.00	
* Bowl, 10¼" x 4¾", ftd.	75.00	145.00
Bowl, 11" x 3¼", flared rim	32.50	
Butter or cheese, 7" sq. x 1¼"	120.00	
Candle, 3", 1-lite	25.00	70.00
Candle, 4", low	25.00	
Candlesticks, 1-lite, bobeche & prisms	175.00	
Candlesticks, 2-lite, 7" x 9¼", bobeche & prisms	225.00	
Candy urn, w/lid	135.00	425.00
Cheese stand, 3" x 5¼"	25.00	40.00
Cocktail shaker, metal lid	85.00	195.00
Comport, w/lid, 8¾" x 5½"	150.00	425.00
Comport, 3½" x 4¾" w	30.00	80.00
Creamer, 3", 10 oz.	18.00	45.00
Cup	15.00	40.00
Cup, demi	20.00	
Mayonnaise, 5½" x 2½", ftd., hdld., #111	35.00	
Mayonnaise, 5½" x 3½", crimped,	32.00	
Mayonnaise, 5¾" x 3", w/dish hdld. tray	35.00	75.00
Mayonnaise, w/7" tray, hdld	35.00	
Nappy, 5½" x 2", div., hdld.	18.00	
Nappy, 6" x 1¾", hdld.	22.00	35.00
Pitcher	325.00	995.00
Plate, 6"	12.00	25.00
Plate, 6", hdld., lemon	14.00	30.00
Plate, 6", sq.	14.00	30.00
Plate, 7"	17.50	35.00
Plate, 7½"	18.00	35.00
Plate, 7½", sq.	19.00	38.00
Plate, 8½"	20.00	25.00
Plate, 9", sq.	35.00	75.00
Plate, 11"	47.50	90.00

Item	Crystal Amber	Cobalt Red
Plate, 11", hdld.	40.00	
Plate, 11", hdld., cracker w/ring	40.00	110.00
Plate, 11", hdld., sandwich	40.00	
Plate, 12", torte, rolled edge	40.00	
Plate, 13", cake, ftd.	75.00	210.00
* Plate, 13", torte, flat edge	50.00	
Plate, 13", torte, rolled edge	57.50	
Plate, 13¼", torte	57.50	195.00
Relish, 6" x 1¾", hdld., 2 pt.	20.00	50.00
Relish, 9", 4 pt.	35.00	100.00
Relish, 10½" x 1½", hdld., 5 pt.	75.00	
Relish, 12", 4 pt., hdld.	40.00	
Relish, 12", 5 pt., hdld.	50.00	
Relish, 12", 5 pt., w/lid	165.00	295.00
Salad dressing bowl, 2 pt., 5½" x 4¼"	45.00	95.00
Saucer, sq	6.00	12.00
Saucer, demi	5.00	
Stem, 3¾", 1 oz., cordial, #5111½	42.50	
Stem, 3¾", 4½ oz., oyster cocktail, #5111½	22.50	
Stem, 4", 5 oz., ice cream, #5111½	14.00	
Stem, 4½", 3½ oz., cocktail, #5111½	22.50	
Stem, 5", 5 oz., saucer champagne, #5111½	18.00	50.00
Stem, 5¼", 3 oz., wine, #5111½	32.50	
Stem, 5¼", 5 oz., ftd. juice, #5111½	24.00	
Stem, 5¾", 10 oz., low luncheon goblet, #5111½	17.50	
Stem, 6", 4½ oz., claret, #5111½	45.00	
Stem, 6½", 12 oz., ftd. ice tea, #5111½	35.00	
Stem, 6¾", 10 oz., tall water goblet, #5111½	24.00	
Stem, 6¾", 14 oz., ftd. ice tea, #5111½	35.00	
Stem, cordial	17.50	
Sugar, 3", 10 oz.	15.00	45.00
Sugar lid	12.50	60.00
Tumbler	17.50	40.00
Tray, 8" x 2", hdld., celery	17.50	
Urn, 4½" x 4½"	27.50	
Urn, 10½" x 4½"	150.00	450.00
Vase, 10, ftd.	115.00	

*Colored foot

200

Colors: crystal and crystal w/pale burgundy, champagne (yellow) & green-blue lustre stain; more intense ruby color replaced pale burgundy later; black turtles in 1952

Westmoreland's Thousand Eye is probably that company's most recognized pattern and had one of the longest production runs of any pattern save English Hobnail. It was introduced in 1934 and discontinued, except for turtles, in 1956. The turtle cigarette box has been reproduced. Those decorated turtles pictured are an earlier production. Evidently these were one of the favorite retail pieces as there are so many seen today. Fairy lamps, both footed and flat versions, were a late 1970s production.

Many Thousand Eye pieces are reminiscent of earlier pattern glass items. This seems to be one of the patterns that collectors really love or cannot abide. Stemware abounds and like some of the Duncan patterns, you could buy these older pieces and use them less expensively than many of today's those in department stores. Thousand Eye is durable, but it was used rather extensively. You need to check plates and other flat pieces for scratches and wear. Mint condition flatware is harder to find than any of the stems or tumblers. That footed comport in the front (next page) is a mayonnaise. The heavy crimped piece on the left in the back would make a great paperweight, but I think it was meant to be a vase.

	Crystal		Crystal
Ash tray (sm. turtle)	8.00	Bowl, 7½" hld.	22.50
Basket, 8" hld. oval	45.00	Bowl, 10", 2 hdl.	35.00
Bowl, 4½" nappy	8.00	Bowl, 11" belled	35.00
Bowl, 5½" nappy	12.00	Bowl, 11", crimped, oblong	45.00

	Crystal
Bowl, 11", triangular	45.00
Bowl, 11, round	40.00
Bowl, 12", 2 hdl. flared	45.00
Candelabra, 2 light	40.00
Cigarette box & cover (lg. turtle)	30.00
Comport, 5" high ft.	22.50
Creamer, high ft.	12.50
Creamer, low rim	10.00
Cup, ftd. bead hdld.	8.00
Fairy lamp, flat.	45.00
Fairy lamp, ftd.	50.00
Jug, ½ gal.	95.00
Mayonnaise, ftd. w ladle	30.00
Plate, 6"	5.00
Plate, 7"	7.50
Plate, 8½"	10.00
Plate, 10" service	22.50
Plate, 16"	35.00
Plate, 18"	55.00
Relish, 10" rnd.	30.00
Saucer	3.00
Shaker, ftd.	15.00

	Crystal
Stem, 1 oz. cordial	15.00
Stem, 2 oz. wine	12.00
Stem, 3 oz. sherry	12.50
Stem, 3½ oz. cocktail	10.00
Stem, 5 oz. claret	12.50
Stem, 8 oz.	10.00
Stem, high ft. sherbet	8.50
Stem, low ft. sherbet	7.50
Stem, parfait, ftd.	12.50
Sugar, high ft.	12.50
Sugar, low rim	10.00
Tumbler, 1½ oz. whiskey	10.00
Tumbler, 5 oz. flat ginger ale	8.00
Tumbler, 5 oz. ftd.	8.00
Tumbler, 6 oz. old fashioned	10.00
Tumbler, 7 oz. ftd.	9.00
Tumbler, 8 oz. flat.	9.00
Tumbler, 9 oz. ftd.	10.00
Tumbler, 12 oz. ftd. tea	12.50
Vase, crimped bowl	25.00
Vase, flair rim	25.00

Colors: azure, green

"Tinkerbell" is the only name I have heard this pattern called. Around twenty years ago, there were eight champagnes and eight water goblets sitting an a flea market in Louisville, KY. I looked at them once a month for several months, but did not know what they were. Finally, Cathy went to that market with me; and when she saw them, she strongly suggested that I buy them. They were $400 with no discounts. I did not know who made them and figured that $25 was more than enough for a pattern I did not recognize especially with champagnes. We called them "Tinkerbell" for lack of a better name after I was coerced into buying them. That stem is known as #7631 Jewel stem line.

It took about ten years to finally find out who made them. I talked to Jerry Gallagher at the Heisey show and told him about some "Tinkerbell" etched stems we had found. He said they sounded like Morgantown to him and "Tinkerbell" was what he was calling them, also. We took half of them to Heisey the next year and they sold like hot cakes. The next year we took a couple of each and they sold a little slower. We kept one of each in case I ever added the pattern to my book; so here they are. I have seen more stems than anything else, but I have only seen them in blue. I was never able to find a cordial for my collection, but that is only one of many that escaped me.

The green vase was found in an antique mall near Columbus, OH. It is the only piece of green "Tinkerbell" I have seen. A four piece water bottle set is one of the most interesting pieces in this pattern. Hopefully, I can show it to you in the future.

	azure green
Bowl, finger, ftd	75.00
Night or medicine set bottle, 4 pc. (med. btle w/stop, night glass, w/water bottle)	500.00
Plate, finger bowl liner	35.00
Stem, 1½ oz. cordial	145.00
Stem, 2½ oz. wine	120.00

	azure green
Stem, 3½ oz cocktail	95.00
Stem, 5½ oz. saucer champagne	95.00
Stem, 5½ oz. sherbet	85.00
Stem, 9 oz. goblet	125.00
Vase, 10" plain top, ftd. #36 Uranus	300.00
Vase, 10", ruffled top, ftd., #36 Uranus	350.00

Colors: Rose pink, Topaz yellow; some green

Rose Trojan sells very fast as the supply of this color is smaller than the demand. At the present time, yellow is selling quite well, but Topaz has always been more prevalent in the market. A few years ago there was a surplus of topaz being offered for sale due to the dispersal of some large collections. Collectors are once again having trouble finding accessory pieces at prices they are willing to pay.

Trojan stemware is available except for cordials and clarets in either color. Clarets are nearly unattainable in most Fostoria patterns. If you need them, you had better buy them whenever you find them! The claret has the same shape as the wine, but holds 4 ounces as opposed to the 3 ounces of the wine. Yes, wine glasses in those days held 2 to 3½ ounces of liquid. This confuses today's collector who is used to wine goblets holding 8 ounces or more. In those days, that capacity was for **water**. The top row on page 206 shows the low and high sherbet together. The high sherbet is 6" tall, as is the claret. Do not mistake this as a claret.

Additionally in that photo, the two-handled plate in the top row served as a cake plate, and as the cracker plate for cheese compote pictured in the bottom row. The photographer needed additional height in that row which was accomplished with that plate.

Soup and cereal bowl prices have increased more than all other Trojan pieces in the last two years. If you find either one, be pleased and pull out the checkbook or credit card. There are limited chances to obtain these.

If you order or ship via ads, you need to know the following Fostoria facts: liners for cream soups and mayonnaise liners are the same piece; two-handled cake plates come with and without an indent in the center. The indented version also serves as a plate for one of two styles of cheese comports as discussed above; bonbon, lemon dish, sweetmeat, and whipped cream bowls all come with loop or bow handles; and sugars come with a straight or ruffled edge. Strangely enough, it is the ruffled top sugar that takes a lid.

	Rose	Topaz
Ash tray, #2350, lg.	50.00	40.00
Ash tray, #2350, sm.	30.00	25.00
Bottle, salad dressing, #2983	595.00	395.00
Bowl, baker, #2375, 9"		65.00
Bowl, bonbon, #2375		22.00
Bowl, bouillon, #2375, ftd.		18.00
Bowl, cream soup, #2375, ftd.	35.00	30.00
Bowl, finger, #869/2283,		
w/6¼" liner	55.00	50.00
Bowl, lemon, #2375	24.00	20.00
Bowl, #2394, 3 ftd., 4½", mint.	25.00	22.00
Bowl, #2375, fruit, 5"	25.00	22.00
Bowl, #2354, 3 ftd., 6"	50.00	45.00
Bowl, cereal, #2375, 6½"	60.00	45.00
Bowl, soup, #2375, 7"	125.00	110.00
Bowl, lg. dessert, #2375, 2 hdld	85.00	75.00
Bowl, #2395, 10"	115.00	80.00
Bowl, #2395, scroll, 10"	85.00	75.00
Bowl, combination #2415,		
w/candleholder handles	250.00	195.00
Bowl, #2375, centerpiece, flared		
optic, 12"	70.00	65.00
Bowl, #2394, centerpiece, ftd., 12"	75.00	70.00
Bowl, #2375, centerpiece,		
mushroom, 12"	75.00	65.00
Candlestick, #2394, 2"	25.00	24.00
Candlestick, #2375, flared, 3"	30.00	25.00
Candlestick, #2395½, scroll, 5"	75.00	65.00

	Rose	Topaz
Candy, w/cover, #2394, ¼ lb.	295.00	260.00
Candy, w/cover, #2394, ½ lb.	225.00	200.00
Celery, #2375, 11½"	42.00	35.00
Cheese & cracker, set, #2375, #2368	85.00	75.00
Comport, #5299 or #2400, 6"	65.00	50.00
Comport, #2375, 7"	65.00	50.00
Creamer, #2375, ftd.	22.50	20.00
Creamer, tea, #2375½	60.00	50.00
Cup, after dinner, #2375	50.00	40.00
Cup, #2375½, ftd.	20.00	18.00
Decanter, #2439, 9"	1,250.00	995.00
Goblet, claret, #5099, 4 oz., 6"	135.00	85.00
Goblet, cocktail, #5099, 3 oz., 5¼"	35.00	32.00
Goblet, cordial, #5099, ¾ oz., 4"	110.00	75.00
Goblet, water, #5299, 10 oz., 8¼"	40.00	33.00
Goblet, wine, #5099, 3 oz., 5½"	60.00	45.00
Grapefruit, #5282½	60.00	50.00
Grapefruit liner, #945½	50.00	40.00
Ice bucket, #2375	75.00	65.00
Ice dish, #2451, #2455	45.00	35.00
Ice dish liner (tomato, crab, fruit),		
#2451	20.00	10.00
Mayonnaise ladle	30.00	30.00
Mayonnaise, w/liner, #2375	60.00	50.00
Oil, ftd., #2375	395.00	295.00
Oyster, cocktail, #5099, ftd.	30.00	27.50
Parfait, #5099	70.00	50.00
Pitcher, #5000	395.00	335.00

	Rose	Topaz
Plate, #2375, canape	30.00	20.00
Plate, #2375, bread/butter, 6"	8.00	7.00
Plate, #2375, salad, 7½"	12.00	10.00
Plate, 2375, cream soup or mayo liner, 7½"	15.00	12.00
Plate, #2375, luncheon, 8¾"	22.00	20.00
Plate, #2375, sm., dinner, 9½"	32.00	28.00
Plate, #2375, cake, handled, 10"	65.00	32.50
Plate, #2375, grill, rare, 10¼"	100.00	90.00
Plate, #2375, dinner, 10¼"	85.00	70.00
Plate, #2375, chop, 13"	75.00	65.00
Plate, #2375, round, 14"	75.00	65.00
Platter, #2375, 12"	70.00	60.00
Platter, #2375, 15"	150.00	120.00
Relish, #2375, 8½"		40.00
Relish, #2350, 3 pt., rnd., 8¾"	55.00	50.00
Sauce boat, #2375	150.00	105.00
Sauce plate, #2375	50.00	45.00
Saucer, #2375, after dinner	10.00	10.00
Saucer, #2375	8.00	6.00

	Rose	Topaz
Shaker, #2375, pr., ftd.	110.00	90.00
Sherbet, #5099, high, 6"	30.00	25.00
Sherbet, #5099, low, 4¼"	22.00	18.00
Sugar, #2375½, ftd.	22.50	20.00
Sugar cover, #2375½	150.00	125.00
Sugar pail, #2378	225.00	165.00
Sugar, tea, #2375½	55.00	45.00
Sweetmeat, #2375	25.00	22.00
Tray, 11", ctr. hdld, #2375	40.00	35.00
Tray, #2429, service & lemon insert		265.00
Tumbler, #5099, ftd., 2½ oz.	60.00	45.00
Tumbler, #5099, ftd., 5 oz., 4½"	35.00	30.00
Tumbler, #5099, ftd., 9 oz., 5¼"	25.00	20.00
Tumbler, #5099, ftd., 12 oz., 6"	45.00	35.00
Vase, #2417, 8"	175.00	120.00
Vase, #4105, 8"	275.00	200.00
Vase, #2369, 9"		250.00
Whipped cream bowl, #2375	23.00	20.00
Whipped cream pail, #2378	150.00	125.00

Colors: crystal, Flamingo pink, Moongleam green, Marigold amber/yellow; Sahara yellow; some Alexandrite (rare)

For the first time I have a little space to discuss Twist due to a change in layout for this book. There have been some major price increases especially in Flamingo tumblers recently. Few collectors have searched for crystal, but there is a growing number of new collectors being attracted to this Deco looking pattern. That amber/yellow color on page 208 is called Marigold. Be aware that it is difficult to find in mint condition because it has a tendency to chip or peel. Items that are beginning to deteriorate will continue to do so. If you have a choice in owning a piece of this rarely seen color that has some problems, pass it by unless it is very inexpensive. Nothing can be done to restore it and there have been many who have tried.

Oil bottles, large bowls, and the three-footed utility plates have seen upward price adjustments. The individual sugar and creamer have both disappeared into collections; grab one if you get a chance. The Moongleam cocktail shaker is missing from most collections. Cocktail shakers in other colors have never been found. Alexandrite is rare in Twist, but there is not enough demand to push those prices higher than they already are.

Most Twist pieces are marked with the **H** in diamond. Stemmed pieces are usually marked on the stem itself.

	Crystal	Flamingo	Moongleam	Marigold	Alexandrite	Sahara
Baker, 9", oval	25.00	35.00	45.00	60.00		
Bonbon, individual	15.00	35.00	40.00	40.00		
Bonbon, 6", 2 hdld.	10.00	20.00	25.00	30.00		
Bottle, French dressing	50.00	90.00	110.00	135.00		
Bowl, cream soup/bouillon	15.00	25.00	32.00	50.00		
Bowl, ftd., almond/indiv. sugar	35.00	45.00	55.00	75.00		
Bowl, indiv. nut	10.00	25.00	40.00	45.00		
Bowl, 4", nappy	10.00	30.00	35.00	40.00		
Bowl, 6", 2 hdld.	7.00	20.00	20.00	25.00		
Bowl, 6", 2 hdld., jelly	10.00	20.00	28.00	30.00		
Bowl, 6", 2 hdld., mint	7.00	20.00	35.00	30.00		20.00
Bowl, 8", low ftd.		80.00	80.00	85.00		
Bowl, 8", nappy, ground bottom	20.00	50.00	55.00	60.00		
Bowl, 8", nasturtium, rnd.	45.00	70.00	90.00	80.00	450.00	80.00
Bowl, 8", nasturtium, oval	45.00	70.00	90.00	80.00		
Bowl, 9", floral	25.00	40.00	50.00	65.00		
Bowl, 9", floral, rolled edge	30.00	40.00	45.00	65.00		
Bowl, 12", floral, oval, 4 ft.	45.00	100.00	110.00	90.00	550.00	85.00
Bowl, 12", floral, rnd., 4 ft.	30.00	40.00	50.00	65.00		
Candlestick, 2", 1-lite		40.00	50.00	85.00		
Cheese dish, 6", 2 hdld.	10.00	20.00	25.00	30.00		
Claret, 4 oz.	15.00	30.00	40.00	50.00		
Cocktail shaker, metal top			400.00			
Comport, 7", tall	40.00	90.00	120.00	150.00		
Creamer, hotel, oval	25.00	40.00	45.00	50.00		
Creamer, individual (unusual)	30.00	50.00	60.00	65.00		
Creamer, zigzag handles, ftd.	20.00	40.00	50.00	70.00		
Cup, zigzag handles	10.00	25.00	32.00	35.00		
Grapefruit, ftd.	15.00	25.00	35.00	60.00		
Ice tub	50.00	125.00	110.00	125.00		125.00
Ice bucket					425.00	
Pitcher, 3 pint	95.00	175.00	230.00			
Mayonnaise	35.00	65.00	80.00	80.00		
Mayonnaise, #1252½	20.00	35.00	45.00	50.00		
Mustard, w/cover, spoon	40.00	90.00	100.00	100.00		
Oil bottle, 2½ oz., w/#78 stopper	50.00	140.00	150.00	175.00		
Oil bottle, 4 oz., w/#78 stopper	50.00	110.00	120.00	120.00		90.00
Plate, cream soup liner	5.00	7.00	10.00	15.00		
Plate, 8", Kraft cheese	20.00	40.00	60.00	50.00		

	Crystal	Flamingo	Moongleam	Marigold	Alexandrite	Sahara
Plate, 8", ground bottom	7.00	14.00	20.00	30.00		20.00
Plate, 10", utility, 3 ft.	40.00	70.00	70.00			
Plate, 12", 2 hdld., sandwich	30.00	60.00	90.00	80.00		
Plate, 12", muffin, 2 hdld., turned sides	40.00	80.00	90.00	80.00		
Plate, 13", 3 part, relish	10.00	17.00	22.00	35.00		
Platter, 12"	15.00	50.00	60.00	75.00		
Salt & pepper, ftd.	100.00	140.00	160.00	200.00		140.00
Saucer	3.00	5.00	7.00	10.00		
Stem, 2½ oz., wine, 2 block stem	30.00	50.00	50.00	60.00		
Stem, 3 oz., oyster cocktail, ftd.	10.00	30.00	40.00	50.00		
Stem, 3 oz., cocktail, 2 block stem	10.00	30.00	45.00	50.00		
Stem, 5 oz., saucer champagne, 2 block stem		10.00	35.00	25.00	30.00	
Stem, 5 oz., sherbet, 2 block stem	10.00	18.00	40.00	28.00		
Stem, 9 oz., luncheon (1 block in stem) *	40.00	60.00	70.00	70.00		
Sugar, ftd.	20.00	30.00	37.50	60.00		
Sugar, hotel, oval	25.00	45.00	50.00	50.00		
Sugar, individual (unusual)	30.00	50.00	60.00	65.00		
Sugar, w/cover, zigzag handles	25.00	40.00	60.00	80.00		
Tray, 7", pickle, ground bottom	7.00	35.00	35.00	45.00		
Tray, 10", celery	30.00	50.00	50.00	40.00		40.00
Tray, 13", celery	25.00	50.00	60.00	50.00		
Tumbler, 5 oz., soda, flat bottom	10.00	25.00	32.00	36.00		
Tumbler, 6 oz., ftd., soda	10.00	25.00	32.00	36.00		
Tumbler, 8 oz., flat, ground bottom	15.00	45.00	70.00	40.00		
Tumbler, 8 oz., soda, straight & flared	12.00	35.00	40.00	40.00		
Tumbler, 9 oz., ftd. soda	20.00	45.00	50.00	60.00		
Tumbler, 12 oz., iced tea, flat bottom	20.00	50.00	60.00	70.00		
Tumbler, 12 oz., ftd. iced tea	20.00	45.00	50.00	60.00		

*also made 2 block stem, 9 oz.

Colors: crystal, pink

Valencia is repeatedly mistaken with another similar Cambridge pattern, Minerva. Notice in the photo of Valencia that the lines in the pattern are perpendicular to each other (think of a volleyball net). On Minerva, the lines in the pattern meet on a diagonal forming diamonds instead of squares. I have explained that in every book, but have continually been amazed at the number of dealers who have handed me a piece and asked which one is it. Valencia had a limited distribution; dealers are not as familiar with it as many other Cambridge patterns.

Valencia has many pieces that would fetch astronomical sums in other Cambridge patterns which have thousands of collectors searching for them. With Valencia, there are so few collectors that rare pieces often are underpriced. Collectors often exclaim, "Why isn't that Rose Point?" Most pieces shown are ardently desired in Rose Point, but are only just being noticed in Valencia. Valencia items are, without a doubt, rarer than the enormously popular Rose Point. Rarity is only secondary in collecting, however; demand is the driving force!

Some of the more exceptional pieces pictured include the square, covered honey dish (Row 3, #1), the Doulton pitcher, and that metal-handled piece in the top row. That handled item was called a sugar basket by Cambridge. This is similar to Fostoria's sugar pail, but closer in size to Fostoria's whipped cream pail. Different terminology used by glass companies in those days sometimes confuses collectors today.

	Crystal		Crystal
Ash tray, #3500/124, 3¼", round	12.00	Relish, #1402/91, 8", 3 comp.	40.00
Ash tray, #3500/126, 4", round	16.00	Relish, #3500/64, 10", 3 comp.	40.00
Ash tray, #3500/128, 4½", round	20.00	Relish, #3500/65, 10", 4 comp.	45.00
Basket, #3500/55, 6", 2 hdld., ftd.	30.00	Relish, #3500/67, 12", 6 pc.	195.00
Bowl, #3500/49, 5", hdld.	18.00	Relish, #3500/112, 15", 3 pt., 2 hdld.	90.00
Bowl, #3500/37, 6", cereal	25.00	Relish, #3500/13, 15", 4 pt., 2 hdld.	90.00
Bowl, #1402/89, 6", 2 hdld.	18.00	Salt and pepper, #3400/18	65.00
Bowl, #1402/88, 6", 2 hdld., div.	20.00	Saucer, #3500/1	3.00
Bowl, #3500/115, 9½", 2 hdld., ftd.	38.00	Stem, #1402, cordial	70.00
Bowl, #1402/82, 10"	40.00	Stem, #1402, wine	40.00
Bowl, #1402/88, 11"	45.00	Stem, #1402, cocktail	25.00
Bowl, #1402/95, salad dressing, div.	45.00	Stem, #1402, claret	50.00
Bowl, #1402/100, finger, w/liner	40.00	Stem, #1402, oyster cocktail	20.00
Bowl, #3500, ftd., finger	35.00	Stem, #1402, low sherbet	16.00
Candy dish, w/cover, #3500/103	135.00	Stem, #1402, tall sherbet	20.00
Celery, #1402/94, 12"	32.00	Stem, #1402, goblet	28.00
Cigarette holder, #1066, ftd.	55.00	Stem, #3500, cordial	70.00
Comport, #3500/36, 6"	30.00	Stem, #3500, wine, 2½ oz.	40.00
Comport, #3500/37, 7"	45.00	Stem, #3500, cocktail, 3 oz.	22.00
Creamer, #3500/14	17.00	Stem, #3500, claret, 4½ oz.	50.00
Creamer, #3500/15, individual	20.00	Stem, #3500, oyster cocktail, 4½ oz.	20.00
Cup, #3500/1	20.00	Stem, #3500, low sherbet, 7 oz.	16.00
Decanter, #3400/92, 32 oz., ball	225.00	Stem, #3500, tall sherbet, 7 oz.	18.00
Decanter, #3400/119, 12 oz., ball	150.00	Stem, #3500, goblet, long bowl	28.00
Honey dish, w/cover, #3500/139	150.00	Stem, #3500, goblet, short bowl	28.00
Ice pail, #1402/52	85.00	Sugar, #3500/14	15.00
Mayonnaise, #3500/59, 3 pc.	45.00	Sugar, #3500/15, individual	20.00
Nut, #3400/71, 3", 4 ftd.	65.00	Sugar basket, #3500/13	135.00
Perfume, #3400/97, 2 oz., perfume	175.00	Tumbler, #3400/92, 2½ oz.	25.00
Plate, #3500/167, 7½", salad	12.00	Tumbler, #3400/100, 13 oz.	25.00
Plate, #3500/5, 8½", breakfast	14.00	Tumbler, #3400/115, 14 oz.	27.00
Plate, #1402, 11½", sandwich, hdld.	35.00	Tumbler, #3500, 2½ oz., ftd.	25.00
Plate, #3500/39, 12", ftd.	40.00	Tumbler, #3500, 3 oz., ftd.	18.00
Plate, #3500/67, 12"	40.00	Tumbler, #3500, 5 oz., ftd.	17.00
Plate, #3500/38, 13", torte	50.00	Tumbler, #3500, 10 oz., ftd.	20.00
Pitcher, 80oz., Doulton, #3400/141	395.00	Tumbler, #3500, 12 oz., ftd.	25.00
Relish, #3500/68, 5½", 2 comp.	25.00	Tumbler, #3500, 13 oz., ftd.	25.00
Relish, #3500/69, 6½", 3 comp.	30.00	Tumbler, #3500, 16 oz., ftd.	30.00

Colors: blue, yellow, pink, green

Fostoria line numbers, which can also be applied to June and Fairfax listings, are cataloged for each piece of Versailles. All colors of Versailles are in demand. Blue Versailles no longer stands at the top of the class since both pink and green have attracted hordes of new collectors. I used to avoid buying green Versailles as it was difficult to sell. That is no longer true; I am having trouble keeping it if I am lucky enough to find any to display. That 7" soup bowl shown behind the finger bowl in the top photo is the nemesis of most collectors. All Fostoria soup and cereal bowls are quietly disappearing from the market. There is a liner for the finger bowl, missing from my photograph. In front is the hard to find canapé set that has an indent for the 2½ ounce footed bar tumbler.

Be sure to see page 82 for Fostoria stemware identification. Confusion reigns because stem heights are so similar. Here, shapes and capacities are more important. Clarets and cordials are the most exhilarating stems to find especially at the right price.

	Pink Green	Blue	Yellow
Ash tray, #2350	30.00	50.00	30.00
Bottle, #2083, salad dressing, crystal glass top	495.00	895.00	450.00
Bottle, #2375, salad dressing, w/ sterling top or colored top	495.00	895.00	450.00
Bowl, #2375, baker, 9"	75.00	135.00	75.00
Bowl, #2375, bonbon	25.00	30.00	25.00
Bowl, #2375, bouillon, ftd.	25.00	40.00	25.00
Bowl, #2375, cream soup, ftd.	28.00	42.00	28.00
Bowl, #869/2283, finger, w/6" liner	50.00	85.00	50.00
Bowl, lemon	25.00	22.00	30.00
Bowl, 4½", mint, 3 ftd.	33.00	45.00	27.50
Bowl, #2375, fruit, 5"	30.00	45.00	30.00
Bowl, #2394, 3 ftd., 6"			40.00
Bowl, #2375, cereal, 6½"	55.00	85.00	45.00
Bowl, #2375, soup, 7"	80.00	150.00	75.00
Bowl, #2375, lg., dessert, 2 hdld.	65.00	135.00	60.00
Bowl, #2375, baker, 10"	65.00	135.00	60.00
Bowl, #2395, centerpiece, scroll, 10"	65.00	95.00	60.00
Bowl, #2375, centerpiece, flared top, 12"	50.00	85.00	50.00
Bowl, #2394, ftd., 12"	55.00	85.00	60.00
Bowl, #2375½, oval, centerpiece 13"	65.00	135.00	
Candlestick, #2394, 2"	28.00	40.00	30.00
Candlestick, #2395, 3"	25.00	55.00	30.00
Candlestick, #2395½, scroll, 5"	65.00	65.00	35.00
Candy, w/cover, #2331, 3 pt.	185.00	285.00	
Candy, w/cover, #2394, ¼ lb.			225.00
Candy, w/cover, #2394, ½ lb.			135.00
Celery, #2375, 11½"	75.00	125.00	75.00
Cheese & cracker, #2375 or #2368, set	85.00	125.00	85.00
Comport, #5098, 3"	35.00	50.00	30.00
Comport, #5099/2400, 6"	75.00	95.00	75.00
Comport, #2375, 7½"	50.00	95.00	
Comport, #2400, 8"	75.00	140.00	
Creamer, #2375½, ftd.	20.00	25.00	20.00
Creamer, #2375½, tea	45.00	75.00	45.00
Cup, #2375, after dinner	50.00	100.00	40.00
Cup, #2375½, ftd.	20.00	21.00	19.00
Decanter, #2439, 9"	1,200.00	2,000.00	750.00
Goblet, cordial, #5098 or #5099, ¾ oz., 4"	125.00	150.00	110.00
Goblet, #5098 or #5099, claret, 4 oz., 6"	110.00	165.00	100.00
Goblet, cocktail, #5098 or #5099, 3 oz., 5¼"	35.00	45.00	33.00
Goblet, water, #5098 or #5099, 10 oz., 8¼"	40.00	50.00	40.00
Goblet, wine, #5098 or #5099, 3 oz., 5½"	75.00	110.00	65.00
Grapefruit, #5082½	75.00	125.00	75.00

	Pink Green	Blue	Yellow
Grapefruit liner, #945½	75.00	125.00	75.00
Ice bucket, #2375	65.00	110.00	80.00
Ice dish, #2451	35.00	60.00	35.00
Ice dish liner (tomato, crab, fruit), #2451	20.00	20.00	10.00
Mayonnaise, w/liner, #2375	60.00	75.00	60.00
Mayonnaise ladle	30.00	40.00	30.00
Oil, #2375, ftd.	395.00	595.00	350.00
Oyster cocktail, #5098 or #5099	30.00	40.00	28.00
Parfait, #5098 or #5099	60.00	95.00	55.00
Pitcher, #5000	395.00	595.00	395.00
Plate, #2375, bread/butter, 6"	9.00	12.00	8.00
Plate, #2375, canape, 6"	25.00	40.00	32.00
Plate, #2375, salad, 7½"	13.00	18.00	13.00
Plate, #2375, cream soup or mayo liner, 7½"	13.00	20.00	13.00
Plate, #2375, luncheon, 8¾"	15.00	25.00	15.00
Plate, #2375, sm., dinner, 9½"	35.00	50.00	35.00
Plate, #2375, cake, 2 hdld., 10"	40.00	55.00	40.00
Plate, #2375, dinner, 10¼"	100.00	110.00	75.00
Plate, #2375, chop, 13"	55.00	90.00	50.00
Platter, #2375, 12"	85.00	135.00	85.00
Platter, #2375, 15"	125.00	195.00	125.00
Relish, #2375, 8½"	33.00		38.00
Sauce boat, #2375	150.00	195.00	125.00
Sauce boat plate, #2375	25.00	55.00	25.00
Saucer, #2375, after dinner	10.00	25.00	10.00
Saucer, #2375	4.00	6.00	5.00
Shaker, #2375, pr., ftd.	110.00	165.00	110.00
Sherbet, #5098/5099, high, 6"	30.00	35.00	30.00
Sherbet, #5098/5099, low, 4¼"	25.00	30.00	25.00
Sugar, #2375½, ftd.	20.00	25.00	20.00
Sugar cover, #2375½	140.00	200.00	125.00
Sugar pail, #2378	175.00	250.00	165.00
Sugar, #2375½, tea	45.00	75.00	45.00
Sweetmeat, #2375	20.00	25.00	20.00
Tray, #2375, ctr. hdld., 11"	35.00	50.00	35.00
Tray, service & lemon	325.00	450.00	250.00
Tumbler, flat, old-fashioned (pink only)	100.00		
Tumbler, flat, tea (pink only)	110.00		
Tumbler, #5098 or #5099, 2½ oz., ftd.	75.00	100.00	65.00
Tumbler, #5098 or #5099, 5 oz., ftd., 4½"	25.00	40.00	25.00
Tumbler, #5098 or #5099, 9 oz., ftd., 5¼"	30.00	45.00	30.00
Tumbler, #5098 or #5099, 12 oz., ftd., 6"	40.00	65.00	40.00
Vase, #2417, 8"			195.00
Vase, #4100, 8"	195.00	295.00	
Vase, #2385, fan, ftd., 8½"	195.00	295.00	
Whipped cream bowl, #2375	25.00	30.00	25.00
Whipped cream pail, #2378	195.00	225.00	175.00

Note: See page 82 for stem identification.

Colors: amber, green; some Blue

Blue and green Vesper pictures have been sketchy in my earlier books. I have tried to cure that on page 217! There is little blue Vesper to be found on the market at a price collectors are willing to pay! The Fostoria name for the blue color in Vesper is Blue. Hardly original, I agree; but that does distinguish it from the lighter blue dubbed Azure by Fostoria. Hard to find, attractive, colored glassware often is priced out of the reach of the average collector. Blue Vesper has not reached that point yet, but it is rapidly rising in price. Green Vesper is more easily found than Blue, but has not charmed many collectors. That lack of appeal makes for more reasonable prices than for Blue or amber. Amber is the most commonly found color; and therefore; the most easily gathered by collectors.

Amber Vesper is not as collected as some other Fostoria colors; but as you can see here, amber has a multitude of pieces! Many are easily found; others will take some patience and searching. There are many pieces of amber Vesper that perplex their admirers. In the top photo on page 215 are shown several of these rarely seen pieces including both styles of candy dishes, a pitcher, and the Maj Jongg (8¾" canapé) plate. It is the high sherbet that fits the ring on that plate. Not pictured, but also difficult to acquire are the vanity set (combination perfume and powder jar), moulded and blown grapefruits, egg cup, and the butter dish. All of these have been pictured in earlier editions; but finding them, today, has been a problem for me, also.

Vesper comes on stem line #5093 and tumbler line #5100. The shapes are slightly different from those Fostoria etches found on the Fairfax blank (page 82). Cordials, clarets, and parfaits are the most difficult stems to acquire while the footed, 12 ounce iced tea and 2 ounce footed bar are the tumblers most adept at hiding.

Etched amber Fostoria patterns might possibly be the "sleepers" in the glass collecting field. I have seen gorgeous table settings made with amber glass with the appropriate accoutrements.

	Green	Amber	Blue
Ash tray, #2350, 4"	25.00	30.00	
Bowl, #2350, bouillon, ftd.	20.00	22.00	35.00
Bowl, #2350, cream soup, flat	25.00	30.00	
Bowl, #2350, cream soup, ftd.	22.00	25.00	35.00
Bowl, #2350, fruit, 5½"	12.00	18.00	30.00
Bowl, #2350, cereal, sq. or rnd., 6½"	30.00	35.00	50.00
Bowl, #2267, low, ftd., 7"	25.00	30.00	
Bowl, #2350, soup, shallow, 7¾"	30.00	45.00	55.00
Bowl, soup, deep, 8¼"		45.00	
Bowl, 8⅞"	32.00	40.00	
Bowl, #2350, baker, oval, 9"	65.00	75.00	100.00
Bowl, #2350, rd.	45.00	55.00	
Bowl, #2350, baker, oval, 10½"	75.00	90.00	135.00
Bowl, #2375, flared bowl, 10½"	50.00	55.00	
Bowl, #2350, ped., ftd., 10½"	55.00	65.00	
Bowl, #2329, console, rolled edge, 11"	37.50	40.00	
Bowl, #2375, 3 ftd., 12½"	50.00	55.00	125.00
Bowl, #2371, oval, 13"	55.00	60.00	
Bowl, #2329, rolled edge, 13"	50.00	55.00	
Bowl, #2329, rolled edge, 14"	55.00	60.00	
Butter dish, #2350	395.00	850.00	
Candlestick, #2324, 2"	22.00	28.00	
Candlestick, #2394, 3"	23.00	25.00	
Candlestick, #2324, 4"	24.00	25.00	50.00
Candlestick, #2394, 9"	85.00	100.00	100.00
Candy jar, w/cover, #2331, 3 pt.	115.00	125.00	250.00
Candy jar, w/cover, #2250, ftd., ½ lb.	295.00	250.00	
Celery, #2350	25.00	28.00	45.00
Cheese, #2368, ftd.	22.00	25.00	
Comport, 6"	26.00	30.00	50.00
Comport, #2327 (twisted stem), 7½"	35.00	40.00	75.00
Comport, 8"	55.00	60.00	85.00
Creamer, #2350½, ftd.	16.00	22.00	

	Green	Amber	Blue
Creamer, #2315½, fat, ftd.	20.00	25.00	35.00
Creamer, #2350½, flat		25.00	
Cup, #2350	15.00	16.00	40.00
Cup, #2350, after dinner	42.00	42.00	85.00
Cup, #2350½, ftd.	15.00	16.00	35.00
Egg cup, #2350		45.00	
Finger bowl and liner, #869/2283, 6"	32.00	35.00	65.00
Grapefruit, #5082½, blown	55.00	60.00	90.00
Grapefruit liner, #945½, blown	50.00	50.00	55.00
Grapefruit, #2315, molded	55.00	60.00	
Ice bucket, #2378	65.00	75.00	225.00
Oyster cocktail, #5100	25.00	30.00	40.00
Pickle, #2350	26.00	30.00	50.00
Pitcher, #5100, ftd.	335.00	395.00	595.00
Plate, #2350, bread/butter, 6"	7.00	8.00	12.00
Plate, #2350, salad, 7½"	10.00	12.00	18.00
Plate, #2350, luncheon, 8½"	14.00	18.00	25.00
Plate, #2321, Maj Jongg (canape), 8¾"		55.00	
Plate, #2350, sm., dinner, 9½"	25.00	30.00	40.00
Plate, dinner, 10½"	45.00	82.00	
Plate, #2287, ctr. hand., 11"	30.00	35.00	65.00
Plate, chop, 13¾"	40.00	45.00	85.00
Plate, #2350, server, 14"	55.00	65.00	110.00
Plate, w/indent for cheese, 11"	25.00	30.00	
Platter, #2350, 10½"	45.00	50.00	
Platter, #2350, 12"	65.00	75.00	125.00
Platter, #2350, 15",	100.00	110.00	195.00
Salt & pepper, #5100, pr.	75.00	90.00	
Sauce boat, w/liner, #2350	150.00	165.00	
Saucer, #2350, after dinner	12.00	12.00	25.00
Saucer, #2350	4.00	5.00	8.00
Stem, #5093, high sherbet	18.00	20.00	35.00
Stem, #5093, water goblet	28.00	32.00	55.00
Stem, #5093, low sherbet	16.00	18.00	30.00
Stem, #5093, parfait	40.00	45.00	70.00
Stem, #5093, cordial, ¾ oz.	70.00	75.00	150.00
Stem, #5093, wine, 2¾ oz.	37.50	40.00	65.00
Stem, #5093, cocktail, 3 oz.	28.00	30.00	50.00
Sugar, #2350½, flat		22.00	
Sugar, #2315, fat ftd.	18.00	20.00	32.00
Sugar, #2350½, ftd.	14.00	16.00	
Sugar, lid	200.00	195.00	
Tumbler, #5100, ftd., 2 oz.	35.00	45.00	70.00
Tumbler, #5100, ftd., 5 oz.	18.00	22.00	45.00
Tumbler, #5100, ftd., 9 oz.	18.00	22.00	50.00
Tumbler, #5100, ftd., 12 oz.	30.00	40.00	65.00
Urn, #2324, small	100.00	110.00	
Urn, large	115.00	135.00	
Vase, #2292, 8"	100.00	110.00	195.00
Vanity set, combination cologne/ powder & stopper	250.00	295.00	395.00

Note: See stemware identification on page 82.

Colors: crystal, Sahara, Cobalt, rare in pale Zircon

Victorian has appeared on the market more in the last few years than I have ever seen it. Pieces that were fairly priced sold quickly. Those items that were priced high because it was Heisey did not sell even when there were some rarely found pieces in the sets. One dealer had a set of 85 pieces displayed that did not find a new owner. She asked me why, so I tried to explain what I see happening in the markets. Sets are more difficult to sell than individual pieces because of cost and the make up of the set. Collectors rarely buy sets of anything. Few collectors are willing to buy a set containing pieces they already have just to get a piece or two that they want. Besides, most collectors do not have the finances to buy a set all at once; then, too, the fun of the quest is gone! A display of any set will attract more collectors than only having a few pieces offered. Similarly, offering those pieces individually and giving several people the chance to buy is the way to go rather than pricing the whole as a set, thereby eliminating most of your market except for other dealers who will expect a wholesale price.

Heisey Victorian was only made in the colors listed. If you find pink, green, or amber Victorian in your travels, then you have Imperial's legacy to this pattern made in 1964 and 1965. These colors are usually marked with the H in diamond trademark; they were made from Heisey moulds after the company was no longer in business. I just saw 33 pieces of amber offered rather reasonably last weekend. A sign proclaimed rare Heisey amber and only $4.00 each. Rare and $4.00 do not seem to belong in the same sentence. Amber Victorian is striking, but know that it is Imperial and not Heisey.

Imperial also made about ten pieces in crystal, but they cannot be separated from the original Heisey. They are not as strictly spurned by Heisey collectors as are the colored Imperial Victorian pieces! I rather believe that point of view may be erroneous thinking, particularly since Imperial is no longer in business. In the grand scheme of things, those colored wares may be more coveted by future collectors.

	Crystal
Bottle, 3 oz., oil	65.00
Bottle, 27 oz., rye	180.00
Bottle, French dressing	80.00
Bowl, 10½", floral	50.00
Bowl, finger	25.00
Bowl, punch	250.00
Bowl, rose	90.00
Bowl, triplex, w/flared or cupped rim	125.00
Butter dish, ¼ lb.	70.00
Candlestick, 2-lite	110.00
Cigarette box, 4"	80.00
Cigarette box, 6"	100.00
Cigarette holder & ash tray, ind.	30.00
Comport, 5"	60.00
Comport, 6", 3 ball stem	140.00
Compote, cheese (for center sandwich)	40.00
Creamer	30.00
Cup, punch, 5 oz.	10.00
Decanter and stopper, 32 oz.	70.00
Jug, 54 oz.	350.00
Nappy, 8"	40.00
Plate, 6", liner for finger bowl	10.00
Plate, 7"	20.00
Plate, 8"	35.00
Plate, 12", cracker	75.00
Plate, 13", sandwich	90.00

	Crystal
Plate, 21", buffet or punch bowl liner	200.00
Relish, 11", 3 pt.	50.00
Salt & pepper	65.00
Stem, 2½ oz., wine	30.00
Stem, 3 oz., claret	28.00
Stem, 5 oz., oyster cocktail	20.00
Stem, 5 oz., saucer champagne	20.00
Stem, 5 oz., sherbet	18.00
Stem, 9 oz., goblet (one ball)	26.00
Stem, 9 oz., high goblet (two ball)	30.00
Sugar	30.00
Tray, 12", celery	40.00
Tray, condiment (s/p & mustard)	150.00
Tumbler, 2 oz., bar	40.00
Tumbler, 5 oz., soda (straight or curved edge)	25.00
Tumbler, 8 oz., old fashioned	35.00
Tumbler, 10 oz., w/rim foot	40.00
Tumbler, 12 oz., ftd. soda	30.00
Tumbler, 12 oz., soda (straight or curved edge)	28.00
Vase, 4"	50.00
Vase, 5½"	60.00
Vase, 6", ftd.	100.00
Vase, 9", ftd., w/flared rim	140.00

Colors: crystal; rare in amber

This Heisey mould blank is better known for the Orchid and Rose etchings appearing on it than for itself, though it's a wonderful, graceful blank!

	Crystal
Bowl, 6", oval, lemon, w/cover	45.00
Bowl, 6½", 2 hdld., ice	60.00
Bowl, 7", 3 part, relish, oblong	30.00
Bowl, 7", salad	20.00
Bowl, 9", 4 part, relish, round	25.00
Bowl, 9", fruit	30.00
Bowl, 9", vegetable	35.00
Bowl, 10", crimped edge	25.00
Bowl, 10", gardenia	20.00
Bowl, 11", seahorse foot, floral	70.00
Bowl, 12", crimped edge	35.00
Bowl, 13", gardenia	30.00
Box, 5", chocolate, w/cover	80.00
Box, 5" tall, ftd., w/cover, seahorse hdl.	90.00
Box, 6", candy, w/bow tie knob	45.00
Box, trinket, lion cover (rare)	600.00
Butter dish, w/cover, 6", square	65.00
Candleholder, 1-lite, block (rare)	100.00
Candleholder, 2-lite	40.00
Candleholder, 2-lite, "flame" center	65.00
Candleholder, 3-lite	70.00
Candle epergnette, 5"	15.00
Candle epergnette, 6", deep	20.00
Candle epergnette, 6½"	15.00
Cheese dish, 5½", ftd.	20.00
Cigarette holder	60.00
Comport, 6", low ftd.	20.00
Comport, 6½", jelly	35.00
Comport, 7", low ftd., oval	50.00
Creamer, ftd.	25.00
Creamer & sugar, individual, w/tray	50.00
Cruet, 3 oz., w/#122 stopper	75.00
Cup	14.00
Honey dish, 6½", ftd.	50.00
Mayonnaise, w/liner & ladle, 5½"	50.00
Plate, 7", salad	9.00
Plate, 8", luncheon	10.00
Plate, 10½", dinner	50.00
Plate, 11", sandwich	20.00
Plate, 13½", ftd., cake salver	70.00
Plate, 14", center handle, sandwich	65.00
Plate, 14", sandwich	35.00
Salt & pepper, pr.	60.00
Saucer	4.00
Stem, #5019, 1 oz., cordial	60.00
Stem, #5019, 3 oz., wine, blown	20.00
Stem, #5019, 3½ oz., cocktail	15.00
Stem, #5019, 5½ oz., sherbet/champagne	9.00
Stem, #5019, 10 oz., blown	20.00
Sugar, ftd.	25.00
Tray, 12", celery	20.00
Tumbler, #5019, 5 oz., ftd., juice, blown	20.00
Tumbler, #5019, 13 oz., ftd., tea, blown	22.00
Vase, 3½", violet	60.00
Vase, 7", ftd.	35.00
Vase, 7", ftd., fan shape	45.00

WILDFLOWER, Cambridge Glass Company, 1940s – 1950s

Colors: crystal, Ebony w/gold, Emerald green, Gold Krystol

Wildflower can be found etched on numerous Cambridge blanks. I have attempted to price a representative segment of the pattern, but (as with other Cambridge patterns shown in this book) there seems to be a never-ending list! You can reason that, like Rose Point, almost any Cambridge blank may have been used to etch this pattern. I have given you the basics. Price gold encrusted, crystal items up to 25% higher. Price colored items about 50% higher except for Ebony, gold encrusted which bring double or triple the prices listed. Most collectors are searching for crystal because that can be found. Wildflower may not be as popular as Rose Point, but it is rapidly attaining the status of second in the collectibility race among Cambridge patterns.

	Crystal
Basket, #3400/1182, 2 hdld., ftd., 6"	30.00
Bowl, #3400/1180, bonbon, 2 hdld., 5¼"	20.00
Bowl, bonbon, 2 hdld., ftd., 6"	17.50
Bowl, #3400/90, 2 pt., relish, 6"	17.50
Bowl, 3 pt., relish, 6½"	25.00
Bowl, #3900/123, relish, 7"	20.00
Bowl, #3900/130, bonbon, 2 hdld., 7"	22.00
Bowl, #3900/124, 2 pt., relish, 7"	25.00
Bowl, #3400/91, 3 pt., relish, 3 hdld., 8"	25.00
Bowl, #3900/125, 3 pt., celery & relish, 9"	25.00
Bowl, #477, pickle (corn), ftd., 9½"	25.00
Bowl, #3900/54, 4 ft., flared, 10"	37.50
Bowl, #3900/34, 2 hdld., 11"	45.00
Bowl, #3900/28, w/tab hand., ftd., 11½"	47.50
Bowl, #3900/126, 3 pt., celery & relish, 12"	40.00
Bowl, #3400/4, 4 ft., flared, 12"	40.00
Bowl, #3400/1240, 4 ft., oval, "ears" hand., 12"	45.00
Bowl, 5 pt., celery & relish, 12"	40.00
Butter dish, #3900/52, ¼ lb.	185.00
Butter dish, #3400/52, 5"	135.00
Candlestick, #3400/638, 3-lite, ea.	35.00
Candlestick, #3400/646, 5"	27.50
Candlestick, #3400/647, 2-lite, "fleur-de-lis," 6"	32.50
Candy box, w/cover, #3900/165	75.00
Candy box, w/cover, #3900/165, rnd.	75.00
Cocktail icer, #968, 2 pc.	65.00
Cocktail shaker, #3400/175	95.00
Comport, #3900/136, 5½"	35.00
Comport, #3121, blown, 5⅜"	45.00
Creamer, #3900/41	15.00
Creamer, #3900/40, individual	20.00
Cup, #3900/17 or #3400/54	17.50
Hat, #1704, 5"	195.00
Hat, #1703, 6"	250.00
Hurricane lamp, #1617, candlestick base	160.00
Hurricane lamp, #1603, keyhole base & prisms	225.00
Ice bucket, w/chrome hand, #3900/671	70.00
Oil, w/stopper, #3900/100, 6 oz.	85.00
Pitcher, ball, #3400/38, 80 oz.	165.00
Pitcher, #3900/115, 76 oz.	175.00
Pitcher, Doulton, #3400/141	325.00
Plate, crescent salad	175.00

	Crystal
Plate, #3900/20, bread/butter, 6½"	7.50
Plate, #3900/130, bonbon, 2 hdld., 7"	17.50
Plate, #3400/176, 7½"	10.00
Plate, #3900/161, 2 hdld., ftd., 8"	22.50
Plate, #3900/22, salad, 8"	17.50
Plate, #3400/62, 8½"	15.00
Plate, #3900/24, dinner, 10½"	67.50
Plate, #3900/26, service, 4 ftd., 12"	40.00
Plate, #3900/35, cake, 2 hdld., 13½"	45.00
Plate, #3900/167, torte, 14"	45.00
Plate, #3900/65, torte, 14"	45.00
Salt & pepper, #3400/77, pr.	50.00
Salt & pepper, #3900/1177	37.50
Saucer, #3900/17 or #3400/54	3.50
Set: 2 pc. Mayonnaise, #3900/19 (ftd. sherbet w/ladle)	32.50
Set: 3 pc. Mayonnaise, #3900/129 (bowl, liner, ladle)	40.00
Set: 4 pc. Mayonnaise #3900/111 (div. bowl, liner, 2 ladles)	45.00
Stem, #3121, cordial, 1 oz.	57.50
Stem, #3121, cocktail, 3 oz.	22.50
Stem, #3121, wine, 3½ oz.	35.00
Stem, #3121, claret, 4½ oz.	45.00
Stem, #3121, 4½ oz., low oyster cocktail	18.00
Stem, #3121, 5 oz., low parfait	37.50
Stem, #3121, 6 oz., low sherbet	22.00
Stem, #3121, 6 oz., tall sherbet	25.00
Stem, #3121, 10 oz., water	35.00
Sugar, 3900/41	14.00
Sugar, indiv., 3900/40	20.00
Tray, creamer & sugar, 3900/37	15.00
Tumbler, #3121, 5 oz., juice	18.00
Tumbler, #3121, 10 oz., water	22.00
Tumbler, #3121, 12 oz., tea	27.00
Tumbler, #3900/115, 13 oz.	32.00
Vase, #3400/102, globe, 5"	40.00
Vase, #6004, flower, ftd., 6"	40.00
Vase, #6004, flower, ftd., 8"	60.00
Vase, #1237, keyhole ft., 9"	100.00
Vase, #1528, bud, 10"	40.00
Vase, #278, flower, ftd., 11"	95.00
Vase, #1299, ped. ft., 11"	75.00
Vase, #1238, keyhole ft., 12"	110.00
Vase, #279, ftd., flower, 13"	125.00

Note: See pages 228 – 229 for stem identification.

Colors: crystal, Flamingo pink, Sahara yellow, Moongleam green, Hawthorne orchid/pink, Marigold deep, amber/yellow; some cobalt, and Alexandrite

Hawthorne Yeoman is pictured on page 225. That color is the most sought in this pattern. Etched designs on Yeoman blank #1184 will bring 10% to 25% more than the prices listed below. Empress etch is the most commonly found pattern on Yeoman blanks and the most collectible. Yeoman has some very desirable pieces for item collectors such as cologne bottles, oil bottles, and sugar shakers. Most Yeoman pieces are marked with the familiar H in a diamond. One of the primary reasons this pattern is so collectible is due to the colors in which it was made!

	Crystal	Flamingo	Sahara	Moongleam	Hawthorne	Marigold
Ash tray, 4", hdld. (bow tie)	10.00	20.00	22.00	25.00	30.00	35.00
Bowl, 2 hdld., cream soup	12.00	20.00	25.00	30.00	35.00	40.00
Bowl, finger	5.00	11.00	17.00	20.00	27.50	30.00
Bowl, ftd., banana split	7.00	23.00	30.00	35.00	40.00	45.00
Bowl, ftd., 2 hdld., bouillon	10.00	20.00	25.00	30.00	35.00	40.00
Bowl, 4½", nappy	4.00	7.50	10.00	12.50	15.00	17.00
Bowl, 5", low, ftd., jelly	12.00	20.00	25.00	27.00	30.00	40.00
Bowl, 5", oval, lemon and cover	30.00	60.00	65.00	75.00	90.00	90.00
Bowl, 5", rnd., lemon and cover	30.00	60.00	65.00	75.00	90.00	90.00
Bowl, 5", rnd., lemon, w/cover	15.00	20.00	25.00	30.00	40.00	50.00
Bowl, 6", oval, preserve	7.00	12.00	17.00	22.00	27.00	30.00
Bowl, 6", vegetable	5.00	10.00	14.00	16.00	20.00	24.00
Bowl, 6½", hdld., bonbon	5.00	10.00	14.00	16.00	20.00	24.00
Bowl, 8", rect., pickle/olive	12.00	15.00	20.00	25.00	30.00	35.00
Bowl, 8½", berry, 2 hdld.	14.00	22.00	25.00	30.00	35.00	50.00
Bowl, 9", 2 hdld., veg., w/cover	35.00	60.00	60.00	70.00	95.00	175.00
Bowl, 9", oval, fruit	20.00	25.00	35.00	45.00	55.00	55.00
Bowl, 9", baker	20.00	25.00	35.00	45.00	55.00	55.00
Bowl, 12", low, floral	15.00	25.00	35.00	45.00	60.00	55.00
Candle Vase, single, w/short prisms & inserts	90.00			150.00		
Cigarette box (ashtray)	25.00	60.00	65.00	70.00	80.00	100.00
Cologne bottle, w/stopper	100.00	160.00	160.00	160.00	170.00	180.00
Comport, 5", high ftd., shallow	15.00	25.00	37.00	45.00	55.00	70.00
Comport, 6", low ftd., deep	20.00	30.00	34.00	40.00	42.00	48.00
Creamer	10.00	25.00	20.00	22.00	50.00	28.00
Cruet, 2 oz., oil	20.00	70.00	80.00	85.00	90.00	85.00
Cruet, 4 oz., oil	30.00	70.00	80.00	85.00		
Cup	5.00	20.00	20.00	25.00	50.00	
Cup, after dinner	20.00	40.00	40.00	45.00	50.00	60.00
Egg cup	20.00	35.00	40.00	45.00	60.00	60.00
Grapefruit, ftd.	10.00	17.00	24.00	31.00	38.00	45.00
Gravy (or dressing) boat, w/underliner	13.00	25.00	30.00	45.00	50.00	45.00
Marmalade jar, w/cover	25.00	35.00	40.00	45.00	55.00	65.00
Parfait, 5 oz.	10.00	15.00	20.00	25.00	30.00	35.00
Pitcher, quart	70.00	130.00	130.00	140.00	160.00	180.00
Plate, 2 hdld., cheese	5.00	10.00	13.00	15.00	17.00	25.00
Plate, cream soup underliner	5.00	7.00	9.00	12.00	14.00	16.00
Plate, finger bowl underliner	3.00	5.00	7.00	9.00	11.00	13.00
Plate, 4½", coaster	3.00	5.00	10.00	12.00		
Plate, 6"	3.00	6.00	8.00	10.00	13.00	15.00
Plate, 6", bouillon underliner	3.00	6.00	8.00	10.00	13.00	15.00

	Crystal	Flamingo	Sahara	Moongleam	Hawthorne	Marigold
Plate, 6½", grapefruit bowl	7.00	12.00	15.00	19.00	27.00	32.00
Plate, 7"	5.00	8.00	10.00	14.00	17.00	22.00
Plate, 8", oyster cocktail	9.00					
Plate, 8", soup	9.00					
Plate, 9", oyster cocktail	10.00					
Plate, 10½"	20.00	50.00		50.00	60.00	
Plate, 10½", ctr. hand., oval, div.	15.00	26.00		32.00		
Plate, 11", 4 pt., relish	20.00	27.00		32.00		
Plate, 14"	20.00					
Platter, 12", oval	10.00	17.00	19.00	26.00	33.00	
Salt, ind. tub (cobalt: $30.00)	10.00	20.00		30.00		
Salver, 10", low ftd.	15.00	50.00		70.00		
Salver, 12", low ftd.	10.00	50.00		70.00		
Saucer	3.00	5.00	7.00	7.00	10.00	10.00
Saucer, after dinner	3.00	5.00	7.00	8.00	10.00	10.00
Stem, 2¾ oz., ftd., oyster cocktail	4.00	8.00	10.00	12.00	14.00	
Stem, 3 oz., cocktail	10.00	12.00	17.00	20.00		
Stem, 3½ oz., sherbet	5.00	8.00	11.00	12.00		
Stem, 4 oz., fruit cocktail	3.00	10.00	10.00	12.00		
Stem, 4½ oz., sherbet	3.00	10.00	10.00	12.00		
Stem, 5 oz., soda	9.00	8.00	30.00	20.00		
Stem, 5 oz., sherbet	5.00	5.00	7.00	9.00		
Stem, 6 oz., champagne	6.00	16.00	18.00	22.00		
Stem, 8 oz.	5.00	12.00	18.00	20.00		
Stem, 10 oz., goblet	10.00	15.00	45.00	25.00		
Sugar, w/cover	15.00	45.00	45.00	50.00	70.00	40.00
Sugar shaker, ftd.	50.00	95.00		110.00		
Syrup, 7 oz., saucer ftd.	30.00	75.00				
Tray, 7" x 10", rect.	26.00	30.00	40.00	35.00		
Tray, 9", celery	10.00	14.00	16.00	15.00		
Tray, 11", ctr. hand., 3 pt.	15.00	35.00	40.00			
Tray, 12", oblong	16.00	60.00	65.00			
Tray, 13", 3 pt., relish	20.00	27.00	32.00			
Tray, 13", celery	20.00	27.00	32.00			
Tray, 13", hors d'oeuvre, w/cov. ctr.	32.00	42.00	52.00	75.00		
Tray insert, 3½" x 4½"	4.00	6.00	7.00	8.00		
Tumbler, 2½ oz., whiskey	3.00	20.00	25.00	40.00		
Tumbler, 4½ oz., soda	4.00	6.00	10.00	15.00		
Tumbler, 8 oz.	4.00	15.00	20.00	20.00		
Tumbler, 10 oz., cupped rim	4.00	15.00	20.00	22.50		
Tumbler, 10 oz., straight side	5.00	15.00	20.00	22.50		
Tumbler, 12 oz., tea	5.00	20.00	25.00	30.00		
Tumbler cover (unusual)	35.00					

Diane
1066
11 oz. Goblet

Tally Ho
1402
Brandy Inhaler (Tall)

Appleblossom
3025
10 oz. Goblet

Gloria
3035
3 oz. Cocktail

Cleo
3077
6 oz. Tall Sherbet

Elaine
3104
1 oz. Cordial

Diane
3106
9 oz. Goblet Tall Bowl

Cleo
3115
3½ oz. Cocktail

Gloria
3120
6 oz. Tall Sherbet

Wildflower
3121
10 oz. Goblet

Diane
3122
9 oz. Goblet

Portia
3124
3 oz. Wine

Portia
3126
11 oz. Tall Sherbet

Apple Blossom
3130
6 oz. Tall Sherbet

Gloria
3135
6 oz. Tall Sherbet

Apple Blossom
3400
11 oz. Lunch Goblet

Elaine
3500
10 oz. Goblet

Chantilly
3600
2½ oz. Wine

Chantilly
3775
4½ oz. Claret

Chantilly
3625
4½ oz. Claret

Chantilly
3779
1 oz. Cordial

Row 1:

Ball vase, 9" (4045)	800.00
Ball vase, 6" (4045)	525.00
Ball vase, 4" (4045)	440.00

Row 2:

Tumbler, 2½ oz., bar, Glenford (3481)	200.00
Tumbler, 5 oz., ftd., soda, Creole (3381)	100.00
Tumbler, 8½ oz., ftd., soda, Creole (3381)	110.00
Tumbler, 12 oz., ftd., soda, Creole (3381)	120.00

Row 3:

Candlesticks, Trident, pr. (134)	780.00
Plate, Yeoman (1184)	40.00

Row 4:

Vase, Cathedral (1413)	825.00
Plate, Colonial Star (1150)	325.00
Stem, 2½ oz., wine, Creole (3381)	170.00
Stem, 11 oz., water goblet, Creole (3381)	190.00

Row 1:

Iced Tea, footed, 12 oz., Old Williamsburg (341)	400.00
Tumbler, 2½ oz., wine, Gascony (3397)	190.00
Tumbler, 11 oz., low footed goblet, Gascony (3397)	400.00
Decanter, Gascony (3397)	740.00
Tumbler, 14 oz., footed soda, New Era (4044)	175.00
Stem, 10 oz., goblet, New Era (4044)	200.00

Row 2:

Plate, Cactus (1432)	250.00
Candleholder, single, Old Sandwich (1404)	325.00
Beer mug, Old Sandwich (1404)	380.00
Cream pitcher, Old Sandwich (1404)	575.00

Row 3:

Stem, water, Plymouth (3409)	600.00
Floral bowl, Empress (1401)	400.00
Ash tray, Empress (1401)	300.00
Candy, w/cover, Empress (1401)	450.00

Row 4:

Tumbler, Arch (1417)	100.00
Vase, favor (4230)	225.00
Vase, favor (4229)	225.00
Vase, favor (4228)	225.00
Vase, ivy ball (4224)	250.00
Salt & pepper (25) pr	255.00
Ash tray, individual, Old Sandwich (1404)	60.00
Tub, salt, Revere (1183)	100.00

Row 5:

Vase, 6", ball (4045)	360.00
Vase, 2", ball (4045)	475.00
Vase, 9", ball (4045)	700.00
Vase, 12", ball (4045)	2,500.00

Row 1:

Cocktail shaker, Cobel (4225)	450.00
Vase, 9", Tulip (1420)	500.00
Candleholder, 2-lite, Crocus (140)	400.00
Candy, w/cover, tall, Aristocrat (1430)	1,000.00

Row 2:

Tumbler, 12 oz., soda, ftd., Carcassonne (3390)	70.00
Stem, 11 oz., tall stem, Carcassonne (3390)	100.00
Tumbler, 8 oz., soda, ftd., Carcassonne (3390)	65.00
Stem, 6 oz., saucer champagne, Carcassonne (3390)	55.00
Tumbler, 2½ oz., wine, ftd., Carcassonne (3390)	110.00
Tumbler, 1 oz., cordial, Carcassonne (3390)	150.00

Row 3:

Candleholder, 2-lite, Thumbprint and Panel (1433)	150.00
Bowl, 12", floral, Thumbprint and Panel (1433)	275.00
Cigarette holder, Carcassonne (3390)	110.00

Row 4:

Vase, 9", Warwick (1428)	330.00
Vase, 7", Warwick (1428)	250.00
Bowl, 11", floral, Warwick (1428)	400.00

Row 1:

Tumbler, 5¼", 13 oz., iced tea, Coleport (1487)	50.00
Tumbler, 4", water, Coleport (1487)	40.00
Sherbet, 20th Century (1415)	40.00
Oil, 3 oz., Saturn (1485)	350.00
Plate, 10", dinner, Town & Country (1637)	175.00
Cocktail shaker, Roundelay (6009)	3,000.00
Ash tray, 6", square, Prism Square (1593)	125.00

Row 2:

Bowl, 13", handled fruit, Fern (1495)	220.00
Bowl, 6¾", jelly, Leaf (1565)	50.00
Tray, 12", 4-part relish, Octagon (500)	350.00
Salt & pepper, Saturn (1485)	340.00

Page 234, Row 1:

Sugar, Cabochon (1951)	65.00
Butter dish, ¼ lb., Cabochon (1951)	180.00
Creamer, Cabochon (1951)	65.00

Row 2:

Relish, 3 part, Cabochon (1951)	75.00
Candy and cover, 6¼", Cabochon (1951)	280.00

Row 3:

Bowl, 12½", Town & Country (1637)	140.00
Bowl, 5", Town & Country (1637)	55.00
Bowl, 8", Town & Country (1637)	75.00

Row 4:

Plate, 10", Dinner, Town & Country (1637)	175.00
Tumbler, 5¼", 13 oz., iced tea, Town & Country	50.00
Tumbler, 4⅜", 9 oz., Town & Country (1637)	35.00
Plate, 8⅝", luncheon, Town & Country (1637)	75.00

Tumbler, 5 oz., ftd. soda,	
Kohinoor (4085)	$550.00+ ea.

Notice the soda to the right has a blue top and foot with a crystal stem while the bottom left one has a blue top and crystal stem and foot. The bottom right soda is all blue.

Row 1:

Stem, 5 oz., champagne, Duquesne blank (3389)	165.00
Stem, 5 oz., parfait, Duquesne blank (3389)	170.00
Stem, water, 9 oz., Duquesne blank (3389)	220.00
Tumbler, juice, ftd., 5 oz., Duquesne blank (3389)	140.00

Row 2:

Vase, favor (4229)	600.00
Vase, favor (4232)	600.00
Plate, 8", square, Empress (1401)	150.00
Tumbler, 12 oz., ftd. soda, Spanish (3404)	360.00
Stem, 10 oz., water goblet, Spanish (3404)	430.00

Row 3:

Tumbler, 3 oz., cocktail, Gascony (3397)	180.00
Tumbler, 14 oz., ftd. soda, Gascony (3397)	160.00
Tumbler, 12 oz., ftd. soda, Gascony (3397)	150.00
Goblet, 11 oz., low ftd. Gascony (3397)	270.00
Tumbler, 10 oz., ftd. soda, Gascony (3397)	160.00

Row 4:

Vase, ivy (4224)	225.00
Candleholder, Trident (134)	800.00
Tumbler, 14 oz., ftd. soda, Gascony (3397)	160.00
Fruit cocktail or finger side bowl, 6 oz., Gascony (3397)	225.00

Cup, Empress blank (1401)	800.00
Saucer, Empress blank (1401)	200.00
Sugar, Empress blank (1401)	650.00
Creamer, Empress blank (1401)	650.00

There are two colors of Tiffin's Twilight. The older is represented by the first two Fontaine items in row 3 that do not change color in different light. Newer Twilight has the ability to look blue in artificial light and pink in natural light. It is sometimes confused with similar colors of other companies, namely Heisey's Alexandrite, Cambridge's Heatherbloom, and Fostoria's Wisteria. All the preceding colors are enjoying a surge in collecting popularity. Tiffin's Twilight is just beginning to be noticed as all other companies' supplies are being exhausted by collecting pressure. The Empress line, introduced in 1959, was a cased, bi-colored ware. It's a favorite of collectors, today.

Row 1:

#1 Flower bowl, 9½" (#9153)	95.00
#2 Flower arranger, 5½" (#9115)	135.00
#3 Empress Modern candleholder 7"(#6556)	100.00
#4 Candle Garden (#9153)	125.00
w/insert	160.00

Row 2:

#1 Violet bowl, 5551	75.00
#2 Flower basket, Empress Modern, 13" (#6553)	150.00
#3 Flower arranger, Empress Modern, (#6552)	165.00

Row 3:

#1 Fontaine #8869 cup and saucer	125.00
#2 Fontaine #15033 water goblet	95.00
#3 Modern cigar ashtray #1	150.00
#4 Canterbury #115 creamer	40.00

Row 4:

#1 Centerpiece bowl, 8" #17430	125.00
#2 Rose bowl, #17430 optic, applied ft.	165.00
#3 Rose bowl, #9 vase, 5", crimped	75.00
#4 Sweet pea vase, #17430 optic, applied ft.	135.00

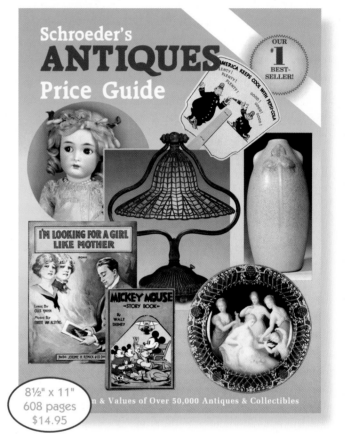